JEFFERSON COLLEGE

3 6021 00016

P9-DGG-669

" Vot is dot?" the headshrinker asked.

" Vot is vot?" I asked, mimicing him.

" Dot," he said, pointing to the ghost figure. " Vot is dot?"

" Oh, <u>that</u>. That's a spook."

" Spook? Vot is spook?"

" <u>That's</u> a spook. It's a beauty, too."

" You mean is a ghost?"

" No. I mean is a spook."

" Explain. Vot is spook?"

NO LONGER
PROPERTY OF
JEFFERSON
COLLEGE
LIBRARY

an Americ... ...u were
...s and
there are ...ts,
but I dig ...e,
and that ...o
ghost coul... ...t not
up."

put his pi... ...then
to himsel... ...umbling
returned ... ...thought
was a gh...

Ukranian ...

70-1365

HV9468
.S65      Smith, Edgar
A3        Brief against death.

NO LONGER
PROPERTY OF
JEFFERSON
COLLEGE
LIBRARY

JUNIOR COLLEGE DISTRICT OF
JEFFERSON COUNTY, MISSOURI
LIBRARY

595/

70-1365

*Brief Against Death*

JUNIOR COLLEGE DISTRICT OF
JEFFERSON COUNTY, MISSOURI
LIBRARY

NO LONGER
PROPERTY OF
JEFFERSON
COLLEGE
LIBRARY

# Brief Against Death

## BY EDGAR SMITH

*With an Introduction by*
### WILLIAM F. BUCKLEY, JR.

NEW YORK  *Alfred · A · Knopf*  1968

THIS IS A BORZOI BOOK

PUBLISHED BY ALFRED A. KNOPF, INC.

First Edition Copyright © 1968 by Edgar Smith

All rights reserved under International and Pan-American Copy-right Conventions.
Published in the United States by Alfred A. Knopf, Inc., New York,
and simultaneously in Canada by Random House of Canada
Limited, Toronto.
Distributed by Random House, Inc., New York.

Library of Congress Catalog Card Number: 68–30940

Copyright © 1965, 1968 by William F. Buckley, Jr.

Manufactured in the United States of America

*To my mother*

# FRIEND IN THE DEATH HOUSE
## *by William F. Buckley, Jr.*

**IT IS VERY DIFFICULT, IN NEW**
Jersey, to arrange to see a prisoner in the Death House.
The visiting regulations were clearly designed in an age when
neither legal hanky-pank, nor a deep social ambivalence concerning capital punishment, nor a Supreme Court that sometimes seems more tortured by punishment than by crime, could
separately or in combination work to keep a man in the Death
House almost endlessly. A few months used to be routine; and
then the prisoner was executed, or, under special circumstances,
the Governor would reprieve the sentence. Meanwhile, there
were to be very few amenities, and practically none at all of a
social character. One member of your immediate family may
visit you once a month, and you can write home five times every
month. The correspondence, in and out, is checked by prison
monitors, who are supposed to look out for any signs that you
are preparing a jailbreak, but who, inevitably, by their faceless
presence on every page, inhibit a prisoner, as also a naturally
reserved correspondent. The monitor, whose stool is set up
alongside your own, is also there to listen to every word spoken
to or by the prisoner.

Several years ago I wrote to a prisoner at the Death House,
having seen a newspaper clipping which described, among
other things, his reading habits, to ask if he would care to
receive *National Review,* a journal I edit. The clipping from a
New Jersey newspaper reported on a day in the life of Edgar
Smith, #34837 D.H., as he is officially designated, then twenty-
seven years old. The article mentioned that he used to read

viii / *Friend in the Death House*

*National Review* but no longer saw it because the chaplain whose copy he used to borrow had been transferred. My letter was returned by the prison authorities, with a form note to the effect that I was not an authorized correspondent of the prisoner. One needs, then, to dig around a bit. I did so, and in due course the prisoner and I exchanged, under a temporary dispensation, one or two letters. "I hope all these problems," he wrote me, "will soon be solved and that the temporary difficulties will not reduce your interest in my case." The temporary difficulties had to do with an attempt by a colleague, Donald Coxe, to visit Smith—we had decided to prepare an article on his extraordinary case. But the application to visit the prisoner was ruled out of the question even for Coxe, who is a lawyer. Judge Arthur O'Dea of Bergen County—who presided at the trial and sentenced Smith to death (he had no alternative: the jury did not recommend mercy), appears to have done his duty vigorously during the subsequent years, in galloping off to every corner of the legal battleground just in time to shoot down Edgar Smith's latest, most unexpected, most ingenious legal flyer—said No: in unambiguous terms. He will not permit, he was quoted as saying, the Edgar Smith case to become another Caryl Chessman case. Besides—the judge didn't say this, but I infer from his behavior that he profoundly believes it—Edgar Smith is, as the jury found, guilty as sin, and the time has come to stop humoring him in the courts of law, and get on with the sentence demanded by law.

But after two and one half years, Judge O'Dea relented. He is, one judges, a very good lawyer (and, undoubtedly, a very good man); and he felt he had to authorize one (1) visit when, in 1965, I undertook to think through the problem of financing Smith's final fight to save his life. It was Smith, not I, who detected, in this new role of mine, safe passage around the dragon's lair. In February of that year he wrote to tell me that the United States Supreme Court had denied his most recent petition for a retrial. And then, as is characteristic when he has bad news to report—which has been exactly as often as any court of law has ruled on one of his myriad appeals (a total

of fourteen times in the period I have been in touch with him)
—he follows up the gloomy news with a dash of optimism or,
less frequently, of good news. "Well, I'm not a total failure.
Judge O'Dea has granted the request for the Court order
allowing visitation. The dungeons have been thrown open for
your inspection."

I drove around the squat red-stone prison, which casts its
gloom over the entire center of Trenton, looking for the tiny
doorway through which visitors are unwelcome, and thought
about the problem of the immediately preceding few days.
Smith, for the first time in my experience, was furious. Judge
O'Dea's permission to visit Smith had been actively opposed
by the prison's warden and, one gathers, by a New Jersey
newspaperman resentful that another journalist was being permitted, though to be sure not in his professional capacity, into
the forbidden area. Two days earlier, Smith had written me
that the anti-visit forces had made their move.

> You won't have any trouble getting in to see me—the Order
> assures that, but the visit would probably be a waste of your
> time. Rather than follow the accepted procedure of appealing
> the Order, someone came up with the bureaucrat's typical back-
> door approach; they obtained a letter-opinion from a Deputy
> Attorney General, giving the Order an interpretation which vir-
> tually nullifies its effect. This interpretation is that the Order
> bans any discussion of my case—past, present, and future.

In other words, although I was to be permitted to see him, I
was not to be permitted to discuss any of the reasons why I was
visiting him at a penitentiary, instead of at the home where his
mother brought him up, in Ramsey, New Jersey, or at the trailer
camp where he lived with his wife and baby in next-door
Mahwah at the time the murder was committed. "Bill, I'll tell
you right now that Smith has just about had it." I was truly
alarmed, after long experience with his preternatural serenity.

> I don't think we should give in and allow the Order to be cir-
> cumvented. You can come down next Friday if you wish, but

my opinion is that we should go back to Court. This Deputy Attorney General doesn't have a leg to stand on; I think his interpretation should be appealed. Please, let me know what you think. I'm too burned up right now to write any more.

I wired him that I would arrive as scheduled.

I was taken in to see Mr. Edmonds, the assistant to Warden Yeager, who was in conference. Mr. Edmonds asked me whether I knew of the restrictions the Attorney General had imposed on my visit, and I said I did. Would I wait just a few moments, to meet Warden Yeager, before going in to see Smith? I would, with pleasure; and attempted to make some appropriate conversation. When was the last execution? A long time ago, in January 1963. When was the first? At the turn of the century. How many men had died on that chair? One hundred sixty. How many men were currently in the Death House? Fourteen. Capacity? Eighteen. Where had Bruno Hauptmann, the killer of Lindbergh's baby, stayed? In the cell now occupied by Smith.

Warden Yeager was ready, and I met him and his staff, and we exchanged pleasantries. A big man, tough, duty-minded, but nonetheless friendly. It remained for me to be frisked, and an official took me to a private room and asked me to empty my pockets of anything with metal in it. I did so perfunctorily and he began to move a metal-detecting type instrument down from my head. It reached my chest and let out an angry and sustained beep. He shut it off and asked me to examine my breast pocket. Out came a Scripto pencil, with the little offending aluminum catch. The search went on. Twice more the Frisker (pat. pending, I noticed) caught me in flagrante, but finally it reached my shoes, and finding there not a file nor even a razor, I was moved on and introduced to Captain Malkin, who was to be my companion. We moved to a great partition, and a turnkey opened a door. We stepped into a circular, silo-like structure, from which two corridors went out, where the regular prisoners were quartered. It is completely enclosed, and high above it, surrounded by bulletproof glass, is the central communications center of the prison. From there an official will confirm, or deny, an escort's instructions to the turnkeys, who communicate with the center by walkie-talkie. The central command had to be consulted before we were let out of the silo, at the opposite end from which we had entered it, out onto the open compound, to walk a hundred fifty yards to the small, isolated, windowless fort-within-a-fort, where the condemned go before stepping conveniently into the far end of the same building, to sit down in the electric chair.

Again, radio control confirmed Captain Malkin's instructions to open the door, and it creaked open, admitting a ray of daylight for the briefest moment, visible to the first three or four of the double-decker cells. Naked light bulbs hung overhead, and three television sets blared in the corridor, one for three prisoners, programs by majority vote, stations tuned in by the guards. I was led to the very end of the corridor, to within a few feet of the electric chair, from which I was separated by a metal door. On my right was Edgar H. Smith, Jr., who long since has broken the New Jersey record for the longest stay in the death cell—it was then over eight years since he had seen daylight. I couldn't see him well, because in addition to the steel bars, they roll a steel screen that fits snugly over the entire front of the cell. I found myself wondering why it was necessary to exercise the Frisker on me. It was all I could do to see Smith. I could not have passed him a needle, even assuming Captain Malkin had nodded. I could, however, see clearly the dimensions of his cell, eight feet long, eight feet wide, nine feet high. Every Friday he steps out into the corridor and takes a shower under a naked spigot; once a month, he steps out into the corridor for a haircut. I commiserated with him once.

"I appreciate your thoughts about my lack of exercise. It isn't all that bad. I walk a lot, like the pussycats in the zoo."

He spoke for an hour—careful, though not overly so, not to touch on "the case," which it was Captain Malkin's duty to see that we didn't. We spoke about future appeals. He explained to me in some detail what his present legal situation was and how he hoped, ultimately, to force the courts to grant him a retrial. I found myself, for the hundredth time, marveling at the discipline of his thought. His voice betrayed a background of football lockers and poolrooms and beer taverns, faintly coarse, utterly inconsistent with his writing style, which is Victorian to the point of prudery. (*"Damn!"* he wrote on hearing my wife had broken her leg a few weeks earlier. *"What bad luck!"*) He had never finished high school, going instead into the Marines, where he served as a paratrooper and was discharged before his tour of duty was over because of a slight deafness in one ear. He was seven when his mother and father were divorced, and was brought up by his devoted mother and his stepfather. His mother sent him, as a day student, to a Catholic boarding school nearby, which Smith left after two years because the school committed the unpardonable sin of abolishing football, to which, above all other things, Smith was committed. He went to a public school but left before his senior year to join the Marines.

On getting out of the service he drifted from job to job, a leading member of the fresh set, taking and leaving jobs every few weeks or months. When he married, he bought a trailer. And when he ran out of money, he sold the trailer's wheels— even though they, as part of the trailer, were derivatively mortgaged. Mr. A. D. Nicol, a private investigator from Hackensack who was retained by Smith's mother until her savings were exhausted (he worked thereafter, and continues to work today, free of charge, tirelessly running down leads), could only come up with three people, of the hundreds he interviewed, who thought that Smith, notwithstanding his diffuse impulsiveness, could be capable of an act of violence. Two of the three—a taxi driver and a station attendant—didn't know him well. The third, Don Hommell, was the man Smith swears he left the girl with on the evening of March 4, 1957, a few minutes before nine at night, twelve hours before she was discovered, sixty feet away, just beyond the profile of the sandpit, her brains splattered about by a fourteen-pound boulder.

I was listening to an almost forbiddingly technical analy-

sis of his legal situation, and it was a full half hour before I got
the gist of it. Smith has become if not a finished lawyer—that
takes experience—an extraordinarily resourceful and ingenious
one, whose most recent appeal was described by Judge O'Dea
as having been drafted with the "consummate skill of a seasoned practitioner." For eighteen months Smith had been conducting his own legal defense, filing briefs forty and fifty pages
long, which had been typed by a fellow prisoner, and submitted to the Courts in *forma pauperis*. He had exhausted the
philanthropic reserves of a lawyer who had taken his case, unsuccessfully, to the U.S. Supreme Court, and for a while had
submitted to a different lawyer designated by the New Jersey
court. After a few months with him, Smith, dissatisfied, fired
him—only to have him refuse to withdraw, leaving Smith in a
most unusual state of virtual speechlessness. [The lawyer]

> has flatly refused to retire from my case. He said he would go
> ahead and argue the appeal on May 18. I will press him to with-
> draw and make certain he does. Can you imagine a lawyer
> saying he would not be dismissed? It all adds up to the aroma I
> detected when he was appointed.

My monitor was getting restless, and I got up to go. We
said good-bye, and I started down the corridor, when suddenly
my escort drew aside to talk to a guard, leaving me directly
opposite the elderly prisoner whose cell is adjacent to Smith's.
"Hello, Mr. Buckley," he said (the prisoners know the names
of other prisoners' visitors). "Hello," I said, not quite knowing
how to take the conversation from there. "Whom did *you* kill?"
seemed inappropriate. But so was any talk about the weather,
the weather being as far removed from the notice of men living
in solitary confinement, without windows, as the fluctuations
of the stock market. We smiled nervously at each other; Captain Malkin rejoined me. I bade good-bye to Smith's neighbor
and walked out. As we went back across the compound toward
the fortified silo, Captain Malkin explained that most of the
prisoners in the death cell are quickly abandoned even by their

own families. "Edgar's wife used to come regularly for a couple of years. Then she went off, married someone else. She doesn't even write him any more. But his mother never misses." I said good-bye to the Warden. "Smith seems quite confident he'll leave here one of these days," I observed chattily. "Well, that's a safe prediction," he chuckled. "He'll leave here one way or another."

I do wish [Smith wrote] our visit could have been longer, and free of restrictions. Perhaps someday we will be able to sit down and have a long talk, without worrying about any regulations. How about adopting me? You could then be on my regular family visiting list! That would go over big with Judge O'Dea!

After the events described in the first part of this extraordinary book, Smith settled down at the Death House to initiate a series of appeals, all of which have been unsuccessful—except those that asked for a stay of execution pending the adjudication of the incumbent appeal. The first appeals concentrated on discrepancies uncovered in the evidence given at the trial. Gradually, Smith turned to matters of law rather than fact. So much so as to dismay some of his friends, a diminishing band, who would have preferred, somehow, to see him devote his long weeks and years in the death cell to constructing a compelling case against the killer—whoever he was. (Early in our correspondence I raised the question. "You say in your letter," he replied, "that I am convinced of my innocence and, under the circumstances, I must have 'a strong case against somebody?' You end this statement with a question mark. I am not sure of your meaning. As for my innocence, it is not a matter of 'convincing' myself, I know!!") But Smith turned cool; cool especially on the matter of putting his finger on the killer.

And, within a very short period, he was left with very few friends. His mother emptied her purse in his behalf, and could no longer pay legal or investigative bills. A. D. Nicol, the private eye, was paid $100 a week during the eleven weeks preceding the trial. Convinced of Smith's innocence, he never stopped working for him. Nicol is a middle-aged Scotsman, a prodigious worker, addicted to meticulous detail, who drove four thousand miles merely to interview people who had known Smith. He took the job, as did Smith's trial attorney, believing Smith to be guilty, but believing also that he was entitled to representation. Within a very short period, they both believed him innocent. Nicol is a diffident man, noncombative in his views. Even so, after the conviction, in a conversation with the prosecutor, he listened to Mr. Calissi say: "I would stake my own life that Edgar Smith is guilty."

"I would like to say, with all due respect," Nicol said, "that I would stake mine that he wasn't guilty."

Smith's letters are obstinately optimistic concerning his ultimate vindication—at least legally (he never talks about getting his hands on The Killer; or at least not to me). His imperturbability, a word he has come to dislike, I found out after twice using it, is sometimes understandable, sometimes less so. July 26, 1963: "It is my sad task," he began a letter in a style so often arch, "to advise you of the denial of my appeal. The denial came on 24 July [1963] via a 2–1 vote." But quickly the note of optimism. "However, for the first time, a Judge saw things my way."

And then the rejection by the Supreme Court (February 20).

> From what I hear from Washington, Justice Douglas voted to give me a full hearing. Four votes are needed. Apparently Justice Douglas was the only one to see things my way. Bless his liberal heart!

And on the twenty-fifth of March, when a colleague of mine expressed concern over an execution date fixed for the twenty-seventh of April: "Don't worry about that April 27 date, a stay is more or less a formality." And changing the subject quickly to more serious matters:

Do me a favor, will you? Call me something besides Mr. Smith; no one else does except Mr. Buckley. Maybe there's some psychological significance, but I feel uncomfortable when people call me Mr. Smith. I prefer anything else, Ed, Smitty, even Edgar. To what might be called the in-group, I answer most often to Igor.

On July 7:

I have just learned that the State Supreme Court has rejected my appeal. Again, I am surprised! [Smithese for "I am not surprised."] Perhaps by the time you return from celebrating Barry Goldwater's victory in San Francisco, I will be able to give you a positive statement as to my future plans.

On July 13, his buoyancy was visibly diminished, though finally it surfaced.

I have received the New Jersey Supreme Court opinion on my last appeal; it is even more abrupt than I had expected it to be. I was surprised by the Court's reliance on inference and supposition—all in the State's favor. I have, in the past, been willing to accept the various Court decisions with a reasonable degree of equanimity; this time I find I am rather unhappy. However, what is done is done.

For a year, he believed that the Supreme Court's decision in *Mapp v. Ohio,* which defined the rules of search and seizure in such a way as to flatly illegalize the means by which the State of New Jersey had got evidence from Smith, would be his deliverance. The question was whether the Supreme Court would rule that its decision in *Mapp* should apply retroactively, i.e., that prisoners whose plight was traceable to a violation of these rules should be given a retrial. Smith was jubilantly confident that the Supreme Court would so rule in the spring of 1965—and confident that the New Jersey prosecutor was ignorant that the Supreme Court had accepted two test cases which would require it to come to a decision on the matter.

Nothing doing. June 9:

I would suppose you [have] read that the Supreme Court has held Mapp to be non-retroactive. They really surprised everyone this time. It makes my problem somewhat more difficult, but I've managed to survive worse setbacks.

His optimism sometimes has stemmed from his confidence in his own superior knowledge if not of the law, at least of legal tactics. To his dumb amazement, on one occasion the State missed its deadline for filing a brief in opposition to his own. The rules on the matter are very strict—if no brief in opposition is filed, a Court is entitled to take the position that the petitioner's point is unopposed, in which case it is, as a rule, automatically conceded. An entire month went by.

The State filed, without explanation, a reply brief on January 21, one month late. I filed a Motion the same day, calling for rejection of the reply [on the grounds of its lateness]. Actually, it might be better in the long run if the reply is accepted. My humble opinion is that the reply is the worst brief I have ever seen.

The Supreme Court, once again, turned him down. February 3: "Throw me a parachute," he wrote me to Switzerland. "—I've been shot down by the Warren Escadrille. The decision came Monday, the 1st." And then, like a composer facing an immense organ console, meditating the harmonic combination best suited for the next desired effect: "It may take a few weeks to determine which way, legally speaking, I will go next."

By March 1 he had decided on his strategy, which he communicated shortly after writing that he had secured a Court order authorizing me to visit him.

After a month or so of hard work, mostly trying to decipher Earl Warren's [opinions], I'm beginning to see a ray of hope. All I have to do now is to convince one of the lower courts that

the Supreme Court means precisely what it says; if I can do that
—no mean task—I may wind up visiting you.

On March 17, 1965, almost as if to interrupt Edgar Smith
in mid-thought, Judge O'Dea set an execution date—April 28.
Smith appealed to the New Jersey Supreme Court to stay the
execution, pending his appeal. The New Jersey Courts delayed. At the last minute, Associate Justice Brennan of the U.S.
Supreme Court ordered the stay of execution (which Smith sent
me, marked "No need to return"). This time he had been
visibly shaken.
April 18:

My predicted schedule is a fait accompli. Mr. Justice Brennan
ordered the stay of execution on Good Friday, which is in itself
singularly appropriate. I will now sit back and bide my time
until the end of the [Supreme Court's] term, the 21st of June.
Then, with all the Court's decisions at hand [the Supreme
Court makes some of its most important decisions at the end of
its term and was due to rule then on the applicability of *Mapp*],
I will be able to file my petition on latest authority. That petition will be acted upon the first Monday in October. If the
Court then declines to take jurisdiction, off I go to the District
Court. All of which means you can keep aboard your boat,
head for Nassau and the Out Islands, and forget about Young
Smith for the next six months.

He did not, contrary to his habit, sustain the levity:

Bill, you know as well as anyone that I've never been one to
grouse about the manner in which my case has been handled
in the courts, but today I'm peeved. Back in 1958, my lawyers
tried for two days to get a stay [of execution] from one of the
State Courts, but couldn't even get the time of day. Finally, with
twenty-four hours to go, they managed to find a Federal Judge
to issue a stay and take jurisdiction away from the State Courts.
Within an hour, the State Supreme Court and the Attorney-
General both issued stays, claiming prior jurisdiction. The
Federal Judge released the case to the State, after he had fin-

ished chewing out the Attorney-General for, as the Judge put it, "playing games." Well, 1965 was nearly a repeat performance.

After filing in the State Court for a stay, I wrote the Chief Justice three letters, explaining the exigency of my situation and requesting a speedy decision. I waited eleven days for a decision usually made in one day, and then heard a story to the effect that the Court was going to sit on the application until the last possible moment, then deny it. So being prudent where my skin is involved, I wrote to the Court and the Attorney-General, telling them I'd wait three more days before asking the Federal Court to again take jurisdiction. *Mirabile dictu,* I received a decision the following day.

Frankly, my friend, things were a bit close for a while; I had the suspicion I was batting a sticky wicket. You can bet your best ski boots that the State isn't going to throw any parties for Justice Brennan this month.

'Tis time I ceased bending your ear. Will keep you posted, always and endlessly (one hopes).

Edgar's mother gave me a picture less composed: "At the time I arrived for my visit [with Edgar] he did not know about the stay. It was my pleasure to tell him. He did not believe it was true until it came on the noon news."

In the fall of 1965, funds were collected to re-retain Mr. Stephen Lichtenstein, who had shepherded Smith's case through the courts earlier as a charity case. Smith's admiration of Lichtenstein's talents is boundless, and Lichtenstein slaved over a brief of commanding cogency which in due course went before the Court of Appeals. There it sat, for months and months and months, and optimism began to creep in. Surely the formulation had finally been contrived that would focus on the injustices of the proceedings? And then, in January of this year, the ruling: negative, by a vote of 2–1, the dissenting judge expressing himself as vigorously on Smith's side as Lichtenstein himself, that "the majority was wrong, in error, in both fact and law." Smith's reaction was less measured:

I mean, Bill, like just once, you know, just one time, it would be nice, if only like for a change, just a small change, you know, like nothing too drastic—wouldn't want to shake the judicial foundations, would we?—we could get one goddamned Federal Court—even a state court would do in a pinch—to say: "Smith, this appeal stinks." But no! Five years and I still can't get a court even to consider it. Strange game! The courts go on giving me stays, one after another, yet no one, not just me, I mean like no one, including the courts giving me the stays, yet knows if my appeal has merit. Like what kind of daffy system is that? I'm beginning to suspect that Barry's old campaign "strategists" are now operating the courts. This time it took eight months to decide *not* to consider the appeal, and previously Judge Lane a year to reach the same decision. God help me if they ever get down to the issues! I may win an appeal decided by a Federal Judge appointed by President John-John Kennedy.

Smith doesn't write only about his legal problems. In prison he has read as widely as his prior commitment to the law will permit him. He has taken correspondence courses from several universities, in several fields, and is also an avid television viewer. (" 'Tis time for me to settle back for another evening of TV. Tonight is educational TV night, I watch the one and only *Beverly Hillbillies*. Late at night, eleven to one, I watch Johnny Carson.") He spotted Dwight Macdonald one night, describing himself as a "conservative anarchist."

> Our "conservative anarchist" is a real enigma. Perhaps some Sunday afternoon the Hayden Planetarium could devote a special show to attempting to depict the various seasonal positions of the stars in the liberal galaxy. . . .

His political conservatism is not altogether orthodox. "P.S. [he wrote, a few days after the New Hampshire primary] Would you disown me if you found out I had contributed $ to McCarthy?"

He takes a modest pride in his scholarly achievements. December 8, 1963:

> I thought you might care to know that I have taken and passed
> the first of two tests given by Mensa.[1] They advertise in the

[1] The organization of top I.Q.-ers.

classified section of NR. I am also carrying a ninety-eight per-
cent average in the Accounting and Economics courses I am
taking from Penn State University. I will complete the first
semester in about three weeks.

And on another occasion (August 20, 1964):

Thought you would be interested in my college grades to date.
They are: Accounting 1 and 2, six semester hours, final grade B;
Business Organization, three hours, final grade B; European
History (Renaissance to Waterloo), four hours, final grade A;
Advanced Rhetoric (incomplete), three hours, A average. By
the way, for my final exam in Rhetoric, I wrote an essay about
BG [Goldwater] and the press.

And on January 5, 1965, acknowledging a book I sent him at
Christmastime:

. . . I guess I'm something of a nut on World War II. Once I
get going with all the maps and things I withdraw from the
world for days at a time. By the way, did you know that Kosygin
was one of the planners of the industrial move to the East in
1941?

And sometimes, in his letters, just acute high-spiritedness.

P.S. [July 22, 1964] I see *National Review* is now listing its
Zip Code number. A sign of moderation? [September 16]:
Yesterday I received *National Review*. Who had the bright idea
for that section printed on blue paper? I almost went blind
trying to read it. (Don't I have a lot of nerve for one who is
receiving a free subscription?)

I replied: "The blue paper was a catastrophe. The printer
simply substituted his shade of blue for the blue we had designated. We are flatly refusing to pay them for the supplement, so
I may end up in jail myself. You would, of course, write to
me?" And a reply:

My opinion is that you'll have to pay for the blue paper. Being in interstate commerce, you cannot discriminate on the basis of color—including the various shades of blue. If you go to jail, I'll write—provided you maintain a modicum of imperturbability.

I thanked him, last December, for sending my wife the Museum of Modern Art's annual calendar. December 18:

Glad you liked the calendar. I would have liked to have done more, but circumstances made it impossible. Perhaps I'll remember you in my will, and leave you my collection of *National Geographic* maps.

I thought I saw a wayward trace of bitter-sadness here, and tried to move fast to cope with it, and lead it back to where it normally slumbered. "Thank you for promising to remember me in your will," I replied. "Since I am ten years older than you and engage in activities far more perilous than yours, with perhaps a single exception, I should think it highly unlikely that I shall reap any such harvest. But I thank you for the thought." He did not acknowledge the letter, but several months later alluded to it.

Good Lord! [he began, with his conventional tushery]. How did you get shanghaied into that election business? [I had declared my candidacy for Mayor of New York.] Did you ever stop to think that through some strange twist of fate you might be unlucky enough to win? It isn't likely, but the possibility is frightening. At least you have the editors of the *Times* pulling for you to come out safely in the end. As for myself, I'm almost afraid to send you a contribution—it might help. Oh well, if nothing else, I can now agree with you when you say you have as many problems as I do. [June 25, 1965.]

Smith never asked for help in raising the funds to retain a lawyer. Our single discussion of his needs centered on the purely mechanical problem of replacing an inadequate and slow prison typist with a professional legal stenographer accustomed to the proper typographical façade; and to the irksome problem of supplying the dozens and dozens of copies that need to be furnished when complicated appeals are filed. I have never known a less importunate man, for whom the least favor is taken as a charitable act of great magnitude. "It is very kind of you people," he wrote a short time later, "to take such an interest in my situation." Much later, when I undertook to get his appeals typed and duplicated:

I know you are going to suggest that you will have the work done for me. Please, humor me; I am just conservative enough to insist on paying my own way for as long as I can.

I replied that I would purchase the literary right to the letters he had sent me in return for the cost of duplicating his appeals. His next letter joked about the suggested deal. I persevered. He replied:

No, I didn't refuse you the "litprop" in my letters. All I did was deny that any existed, and I still deny it. You'll never realize how happy I am knowing that you have to read my letters, not I. That isn't an opening into which you are expected to insert a compliment. I'm being perfectly candid when I say I haven't been able to figure out what in hell there is about Smith that keeps you interested.

What indeed? It has not occurred to him that one can develop a friendship for a man in a Death House; or that a condemned man's friendship can be gratefully accepted. Probably it has not occurred to him because probably he suspects that any such friendships are emotionally condescending, that they are based on pity, or morbidity. I suspect that that is the reason why his natural dignity has always prevented him from emotional self-revelation.

One time, I riled him. He did not recover until the end of a long paragraph. I had written him that God was apparently In in the subways, to judge from graffiti I had come upon that morning. "God is Dead—Nietzsche," someone had written in chalk. Under which had been scrawled in block letters, "NIETZSCHE IS DEAD—GOD." I then made a second comment, coming apparently too close on the heels of the first, about his imperturbability.

> I had not intended to write again so soon [he began glacially], but I am, quite frankly, somewhat disturbed by your very apparent misapprehensions as to my state of mind. Your references to my serenity, imperturbability, etc., impute [sic] that I am some Buddha-like anachronism, fast approaching Nirvana. Tell me—does the fact that I am in the Death House mean to you that I should be perpetually atop a soapbox, shouting my protestations to a cold, cruel, unhearing world? The fact is that what you mistake for serenity, or an air of detachment, is nothing more or less than the realization on my part of the fact that my situation is not going to be improved by breast-beating and lamentations, however loud or sustained—it can only be changed by and in a court of law. Perhaps my letters should be appropriately tear-stained when they arrive at your office, giving them a more pathetically desperate quality. Again, if it would do me any good, I would cry you a river—à la Julie London.

Then, rapidly, the pulse slowed; and Queen Victoria remounted her throne.

> I trust you will not misinterpret the tone of this letter. I was not especially unhappy that you failed to understand my feelings, but I did think it was worth clearing up.
>
> P.S. What ever were you doing in a New York subway? You're right, you do live more dangerously than I do—much more.

And now an incredible telephone call from an editor at Alfred A. Knopf. They have received a manuscript from one Edgar Smith, at the Death House in Trenton, New Jersey. He has read the manuscript, and the book is scheduled for publication. I was astounded. I asked Smith why he hadn't advised me he was writing a book. "Didn't want to get you into any trouble," he said. "You have enough to worry about."

Nothing, I judge, to compare with the worry the jurors are likely to feel on reading this book by the man they condemned.

This is the story of a man's fight for his life. Documentation has been reduced to a bare minimum, to avoid the trying and distracting proliferation of footnotes and textual breaks pin-pointing sources that would give the book the forbidding appearance of a legal textbook. But for those readers wishing to know in a general way how to judge the authenticity of the dialogue, the following may be helpful:

1/ All dialogue between attorneys, the judge, and the witnesses, found within the portion of my book dealing with my trial, is quoted directly from the official printed transcript of the trial.

2/ All dialogue between myself, my attorneys, the police, and other persons, except where otherwise noted, is reconstructed from my memory of the original conversations, supplemented in some instances by the memories of the other persons involved.

3/ All dialogue that took place other than in my presence is reconstructed from three major sources: a) the trial testimony of the persons involved; b) newspaper and magazine accounts of the case; and c) statements made either to me or to my attorneys by one or more of the persons involved.

4/ Descriptions of events that took place not in my presence were reconstructed for the most part from the sources mentioned above, with heavy reliance on the trial record.

Obviously, after so many years have passed since the actual events described, no one's memory could be letter-perfect as to every detail. I am confident, however, that nothing of substance has been misrepresented. Memories have been culled, photographs studied, documents checked and cross-checked, and, where all else failed, investigators have re-examined the original scenes. The result is, I believe, as accurate a reconstruction of the case as can be rendered at this late date. For any minor discrepancies that will inevitably have crept into a work of this nature, I assume full responsibility.

E. S.

*Brief Against Death*

*Maps of Western Ramsey and the Township of Mahwah (Fardale Section) and of the murder scene will be found on pages 11 and 68, respectively.*

**''I LOOKED AROUND AND I SEEN WHERE HER** *brains were scattered for seven or eight feet along the bank. Then I looked down over the bank and there her body was in a jackknifed position.*

*"One arm was sticking up. Her head was face down and there was a hole in the back of her head where all the brains was knocked out completely. She had no hair left on her head.*

*"I discovered that she had her sweater pulled over her shoulders. She had her dungarees on, and one stocking was all the way off, and the other was part way off."*

With these words, spoken in a hushed courtroom, Anthony Zielinski described how, shortly after nine o'clock on the morning of March 5, 1957, he had climbed onto a windswept dirt mound in a Mahwah, New Jersey, sandpit and found the mutilated, blood-drenched body of his fifteen-year-old daughter, Victoria, who had been missing since eight-forty the previous evening.

The search for the girl had not been a long one, and within three months of the discovery of her half-nude body I had been arrested, tried, convicted of first-degree murder by a jury that had deliberated for less than two hours, and sentenced to die in the electric chair.

It had been an indescribably horrible crime—the savagery of the attack can be gauged from the fact that what the victim's father had thought was the back of the girl's head with the hair missing was in fact the remains of her face—and the public and the press screamed for vengeance. As a result, following my

3

arrest and conviction, the police were showered with praise for their efficiency and for the dispatch with which they had "solved" the murder; the jury, which included an acquaintance and former co-worker of the victim's father, was congratulated for its diligence, attention to duty, and arrival at a popular verdict; and the trial judge, who had found it necessary to call recesses when some of the more lurid testimony and evidence had distressed him, was applauded for his decorous handling of the proceedings.

I must confess that through my own fears, ignorance, and mistrust of the police, I had done much to contribute to my own conviction. When first taken into custody for questioning, I had lied, partially out of fear, partially out of misplaced loyalty toward friends. It had not taken the police long, however, to see through my lies, to discover that I had been with the girl, at the murder scene, shortly before her death; and as I continued to lie and deny all knowledge of the events preceding the crime, the officers were more and more justified in thinking they had found the murderer. Thus, when at last I did begin to tell the truth, only weeks before my trial, it was too late; the police were convinced they had solved the crime, and the prosecutor was irrevocably committed to putting me on trial for my life. Nor was the public, aroused to fever pitch by the pretrial publicity—one headline read *"WHY DID HE KILL?"* —disposed to accepting any thesis but that Edgar Smith murdered Vickie Zielinski.

I do not expect that this book, or any number of books, will conclusively establish my innocence, or that it will answer every question. Indeed, the book may give rise to more questions than it settles. What I do believe, however, is that any person who approaches my story with an open mind will come away from it asking himself: "Did this man *really* do it?"

More than eleven years have passed since the trial, and I remain under sentence of death. Among those who have closely followed my ordeal from the beginning, or who have taken the time to study it in recent years—and even among those who once might have volunteered to tighten the straps and pull the switch—doubts have arisen.

Were the police, in response to the public outcry, expedient rather than efficient? Did they act with too much dispatch?

Did the jury in its brief deliberations give the evidence and testimony of a two-week trial the scrutiny it deserved?

Was the judge, himself the father of a fifteen-year-old girl, the detached, impartial arbiter he should have been?

Did Justice triumph?

Is Edgar Smith guilty?

# CHAPTER ONE

VICTORIA ZIELINSKI WAS A VERY PRETTY
girl. Five foot two, one hundred and twenty pounds, with
brown eyes and dark-brown, shoulder-length hair, she was an
exceptionally well-developed fifteen-year-old, with a figure that
belied her age—a fact she knew, was proud of, and made no
effort to conceal. To the contrary, her favorite clothes were
tight, form-revealing sweaters and blue jeans.

Born in the coal-mining region of northeastern Pennsylvania on September 6, 1941, the second child of Mary and
Anthony Zielinski, Vickie—as she was known to her friends—
moved with her family to Ramsey, New Jersey, in 1950. She
lived with her parents, two sisters, and a brother in a white
wood-frame house on the western edge of town, four hundred
feet from the Ramsey-Mahwah township boundary line.

Ramsey, and the adjoining towns of Allendale, Mahwah,
Upper Saddle River, and Wyckoff, are situated in the extreme
northeast corner of New Jersey, just south and east of the
Ramapo Mountains, among the open fields, woodlands, and
low rolling hills of the Ramapo Valley. They are exceedingly
quiet, predominantly white, middle-class communities of sin-
gle-family private dwellings. They are the sort of towns in
which one can walk the tree-shaded streets for hours late at
night without ever meeting another person, except perhaps a
neighbor walking his dog. Serious crimes are rare, murder
practically unheard of—a murder per year would be regarded
as a major crime wave.

From these towns, about eighteen miles northwest of New

York City, and astride the main line of the Erie Railroad, thousands of commuters each weekday morning and evening make the long trip to and from their offices in the city. During the day they are inhabited mostly by women.

Ramsey—the population in 1957 was approximately 8,000, having doubled since the official 1950 census—was a particularly dull town for young people, utterly devoid of even elementary recreational facilities. The town's tiny, dingy movie theater had been closed for years, and the unsanitary community swimming pool was eventually closed by the Board of Health. As a result, most of the young people went "upstate," the local euphemism for going to the dozens of taverns just over the New York State border, three miles to the north, where the minimum drinking age was, and still is, eighteen. Teen-agers were always more than welcome here, where on any given night they were also likely to find the majority of their friends. Along Route 59, otherwise known as "Beer Alley," it was a rarity to find anything but New Jersey license plates on the automobiles packed into the tavern parking lots.

Actually, New York's minimum drinking age was a myth. Only the most naïve, unbefriended teen-ager could fail to find at least one place where no questions were asked, or where an obviously erased and retyped birth certificate was unacceptable. Girls, however young they might seem, were seldom asked their age, since the presence of young girls in an establishment was the surest guarantee that the boys would come too; as it still is, of course.

I met Vickie Zielinski for the first time about a year before her death, and in the following months both my wife and I came to know her quite well. We would often see her walking to or from town—the main shopping district and the high school were a mile and a half from her home—and on these occasions we would always stop and offer her a ride.

Vickie was a precocious girl who spoke freely of her

problems. She was a bright, studious girl who looked forward to attending college, but also a confused, physically mature woman-child, fascinated by the relative sophistication—or what she regarded as such—of the older men she had been secretly dating, though apprehensive of the emotions they were able to arouse in her.

These secret dates—mostly with men I knew, fellows in their early or mid-twenties—usually were arranged with the connivance of her older sister. The girls would leave home together for some ostensibly innocent purpose, go their separate ways on dates, then meet later in the evening at some prearranged time and place and return home together—often to be cross-examined by their father.

Anthony Zielinski apparently was a father who laid down excessively harsh rules of conduct for his daughters, and who, according to Vickie, resorted to brutal physical punishment for any infractions of his rules. He usually referred to Vickie, his favorite daughter, as "my little girl," she told me, and he seemed to be jealous of the boys her age who took her on the infrequent dates she was permitted. After these dates, she explained, her father often would demand a detailed report on everything her date had said and done. Her father's passion for protecting his "little girl" went so far, she said, and the newspapers reported after her death[1] that he taught her judo and wrestling, to enable her to protect her honor. "He thinks every guy in town is trying to get in my pants," she told my wife and me one afternoon. "He always wants to demonstrate what guys will try to do to me, pawing all over me. He makes me sick to my stomach." When my wife asked if she had told her mother, Vickie replied: "Mom is just as scared of him as we are."

Vickie was so afraid of her father, I learned soon after meeting her, that whenever anyone offered her a ride home, even if it were the middle of the day and other girls were in the car with her, she would insist that she be dropped off far

---

[1] *Herald-News*, Passaic, N.J., March 6, 1957, p. 1.

enough from her home so that "my old man won't see me getting out of a car."

I remember particularly an incident which took place one afternoon a few weeks before her death, while I was driving her home from a high-school basketball game at which we had met. I had stopped for cigarettes at one of the stores on the main street of town. When I returned to the car, Vickie was down on the floor, crouched beneath the dashboard. My first thought was that she was playing some sort of game, but she quickly explained that she was hiding from her father, who was walking down the other side of the street. This seemed terribly ludicrous to me, and to tease her, I offered to call her father over to the car, introduce myself, and invite him to ride home with us. My suggestion terrified her. When her father had gone, she made me promise never to make jokes like *that* again. "It's not a bit funny," she said. "He'd kill us both if he ever caught me in the car with you."

On Monday evening, March 4, 1957, the temperature outdoors was in the low 30's, and the ground was still covered in places with patches of dirty snow remaining from the season's last storm as Vickie prepared to walk the seven tenths of a mile from her own home to the home of her friend and classmate, sixteen-year-old Barbara Nixon. Earlier in the day, the girls, both in their second year at Ramsey High School, had agreed to work together that night on their homework, and to study for a forthcoming bookkeeping examination.

Wyckoff Avenue, where both the Zielinski and Nixon homes were situated, was an especially lonely road, and along the section Vickie had to walk to reach her friend's home— located across the boundary line in the Township of Mahwah —there were no sidewalks and but a few widely separated streetlights. The seven houses along the route were set far back off the road, and between them loomed dark, forbidding stands of woods, the ground beneath a tangled mass of underbrush growing almost to the road's edge. The trees, their barren branches swaying in the early evening breeze, cast eerie, mobile shadows across the black pavement.

Vickie cherished every opportunity to get out of her unhappy—some say "unsavory"—home, but she did not look forward to walking alone. Twice in the preceding month, while returning from the Nixons' late at night, strangers in automobiles had stopped and invited her to "go for a little ride." She decided, therefore, to ask her blond thirteen-year-old sister, Myrna, to accompany her.

Myrna was in the kitchen, helping her mother with the supper dishes, when Vickie entered and asked: "Hey, Myrna, how about walking down to Barbara's with me? I don't feel like walking by myself."

"I can't, not tonight. After I get these dishes dried and put away, I have a mess of homework to do."

"That's okay. I'm only going to Barbara's for an hour. I'll help you with the dishes, and when we get back I'll help you with your homework."

Mrs. Zielinski, whom Vickie had told of the strangers offering her rides, suggested that Myrna walk at least halfway with her sister. "I'll feel better about it if you do," she added.

"Well, okay, Mom. If you want me to, I'll walk part of the way with her, but I really do have to get back and do my homework."

It was agreed that Myrna would walk halfway with her sister, then return home; at eight-thirty, Vickie was to begin walking home from the Nixons'. Myrna, leaving home at the same time, would then meet her halfway.

It was exactly 7:30 p.m. when the sisters set out on their last walk together. As usual, Vickie was wearing figure-hugging blue jeans; a sweater—a coral-red cardigan, one of her favorites; and a blue-and-gold jacket. In her hands, she carried a large brown leather pocketbook—the type girls call a saddlebag; a red-bound textbook—*20th Century Accounting and Bookkeeping;* and a manila file folder, across the face of which

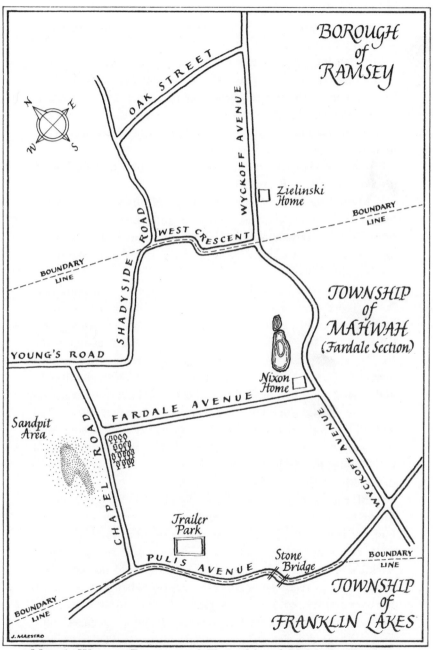

Map 1. Western Ramsey and Township of Mahwah (Fardale Section).

had been written in ink: "I love you more and more every day —Tommy Collins."

When the girls reached the halfway point, Myrna, equally glad to be out of the house, offered to continue walking with her sister until the Nixon home was in sight. "I'll walk down around the last bend in the road with you," she told Vickie. "Maybe the old man will be in bed by the time I get back. He's in one of his bitchy moods tonight."

"I know. He almost bit my head off when I asked him if it was okay to go to Barbara's."

Myrna accompanied her sister to within a few hundred feet of the Nixon residence before turning back. Once, while retracing her steps homeward, she looked back and caught a brief glimpse of Vickie walking under a streetlight. She never saw her sister again.

Vickie arrived at her girl friend's home at 7:45 p.m., and the girls went at once to Barbara's second-floor bedroom. At 8:40 p.m., having spent more time trading girlish gossip and listening to the radio than doing homework assignments, Vickie, already ten minutes late, suddenly remembered about meeting Myrna. Quickly gathering her coat and schoolbooks and saying good-bye to Barbara, she hurried off. Barbara, who had gone to the door with her, recalled later that Vickie had walked down the driveway, turned left on Wyckoff Avenue, and had walked off into the darkness. At that same moment, Myrna was leaving the Zielinski home. By some strange, fatal coincidence, Myrna too was ten minutes late.

Myrna arrived at the Nixon home at 8:50 p.m., having failed to encounter her sister on the way. Certain that Vickie had not yet left the Nixons', she was angry that she had had to walk the long, dark road alone, though she did not share Vickie's fears; and she resolved that there would not be a next time. One can readily imagine her surprise when Laura Nixon, Barbara's sister, told her: "Vickie left ten minutes ago. She said she was ten minutes late and had to hurry to meet you."

"Where did she go? We couldn't have walked past each other."

"Maybe she got a ride with someone," Laura suggested.

"She wouldn't have done that, I don't think. I'd better get home and tell my mother."

Mrs. Zielinski was in the kitchen doing the family wash when Myrna rushed in with the news. It was 9:10 p.m. Mr. Zielinski, a laborer employed by the Borough of Ramsey, had gone to bed.

"Oh, don't worry," the mother said when she had heard the girl's tale. "She probably met George and Mary and is with them."

Eighteen-year-old Mary was the Zielinski's oldest child, who at the time was out on a date with her steady boy friend, George Self, a soldier stationed at a Nike missile base in the foothills of the Ramapo Mountains, four miles west of Ramsey.

"But when I was walking to Barbara's, not one car passed in either direction," Myrna protested. "And on the way back, the only one I saw was Donald Hommell. Besides, Vickie wouldn't go with Mary when she knew I was coming to meet her."

"Where did you see Hommell?" the mother asked. She knew that Hommell, twenty years old, had been one of those secretly dating Vickie, and she lived with the fear that Mr. Zielinski would learn of it.

"He passed me just down the street when I was coming home. He must have been doing sixty around the bend by Crescent Avenue, but he looked like he was alone."

"Well, perhaps she is with Mary. They would have gone in the other direction to take George back to the missile base, so they wouldn't have passed you. Let's wait until Mary gets home."

Myrna, unconvinced, wanted to awaken her father, but Mrs. Zielinski opposed this, probably hoping that Vickie's absence could be concealed from her father. Whatever her reasons for failing to act promptly, had Mr. Zielinski and the police been notified as soon as Myrna had returned home alone, and had they acted, Vickie might be alive today. But Mrs. Zielinski waited for three and a half hours, crucial hours, during which her daughter's fate was sealed.

Mary and George returned from their date at 10:45 p.m. and learned for the first time of Vickie's disappearance. They had left the house together early that evening, unaware of Vickie's plan to visit Barbara Nixon. Mrs. Zielinski was in the kitchen when she heard the front door slam.

"Mother, it's us," Mary called out.

Looking through the kitchen door leading to the living room, and seeing only her oldest daughter and her boy friend, the mother felt the first twinges of fear. "Isn't Vickie with you?" she asked hesitantly.

"No, why should she be with us? Isn't she home?"

The mother, now plainly worried, explained the arrangement Myrna and Vickie had made to meet halfway on the road from the Nixons'. "Myrna walked all the way to the Nixons' and Vickie wasn't there. Laura Nixon said Vickie had left ten minutes before Myrna got there," she concluded.

"Have you told Daddy?"

"No, I thought she might be with you. I didn't want to wake your father—you know how upset he gets. I guess I'll have to tell him now."

George Self, who until then had not taken part in the conversation, suggested that he and Mary could drive into town. Perhaps Vickie would be there, or someone might know where she had gone.

"All right, George, but if you don't find her, I'll have to wake her father. I shouldn't have waited this long."

George and Mary left at once, and for more than an hour drove through Ramsey and the surrounding towns, stopping at all the places where they knew the local teen-agers congregated. Vickie was not in any of them, nor had anyone seen her that night. They returned home at 12:30 a.m. and immediately awakened Mr. Zielinski. As he blinked the sleep from his eyes, Mary gave him the frightening news: "Daddy, Vickie is missing."

Mr. Zielinski dressed quickly, and as he did so his wife filled in the details of Vickie's disappearance and Mary's fruitless search. He was angry that his wife had waited so long to awaken him, but his first concern was "to find my little girl."

Leaving George Self to wait with Mrs. Zielinski, Mary and her father set out to search for Vickie. Their first stop was Robbie's Corral, a luncheonette on the town's main street. The owner was just turning out the lights when they arrived. He did not know Vickie, he said. "All of these kids look alike —same clothes, same haircuts, and they all play the same records on the jukebox. You can't tell one from another. Describe one and you've described them all. They should put numbers on their backs like football players."

Mary and her father returned to their automobile and were about to drive off to search elsewhere when Mary, who was driving, noticed the Ramsey police car coming toward them. By flashing her automobile's headlights on and off, she was able to signal the driver of the police car to stop.

Two officers were in the police car, and they listened patiently while Mr. Zielinski related the details of his daughter's failure to return home from Barbara Nixon's. They asked him to describe the clothing she had been wearing when she left home at seven-thirty.

"She was wearing a pair of blue zip-front jeans, a red cardigan sweater—you know, the kind that buttons down the front; white socks; black loafers; a dark-blue snap-front jacket, yellow snaps, with gold stripes down the sleeves, and a gold Ramsey High School emblem on the back. She had a brown leather pocketbook, and was carrying some schoolbooks. She also had on her white-gold wristwatch, and had a silver heart on a chain around her neck. She always wore that."

Mary and her father returned to their home at 1 a.m., immediately after reporting Vickie's disappearance to the police officers. Twice more during the next hour—at 1:10 a.m., with his wife, and again at 1:45 a.m., alone—Mr. Zielinski searched for his daughter. These searches were, however, perfunctory in nature, consisting merely of driving along the route Vickie was to have walked. After the third and final trip, the father returned home "to wait for daybreak." The time: 2 a.m. When questioned regarding his failure to continue to search, Mr. Zielinski replied: "It was too dark to look around, but I stayed up all night."

Mr. Zielinski made no further effort to contact the police until 7:50 a.m., Tuesday, six hours after he had suspended his search because of darkness; and there is no indication in the records of the case, or in the father's subsequent testimony, that he thought of notifying the New Jersey State Police, who maintained a troop barracks and headquarters on the main street of Ramsey.

For their part, the Ramsey police succeeded only in establishing beyond a reasonable doubt their own ineptitude. When one studies the official reports of the various law-enforcement agencies involved in this case, one is led inescapably to the conclusion that the police officers who received Mr. Zielinski's report did not take it seriously, though their reasons for brushing the report aside are not equally clear. Perhaps, as seems likely, the officers were aware of Vickie's dates with some of the young men from Ramsey known to them, and not wishing to cause unnecessary trouble for their friends, they made a subjective judgment as to the criticality of the situation—*the* cardinal sin for a police officer.

In any case, it is certain that the officers failed to take action to supplement or widen the search for the girl; that they failed to notify their superiors of the Zielinski report; that although they were fully aware that the Nixon home, where Vickie had been last seen, was in Mahwah Township, the records show they failed to notify the Mahwah Police Department of the girl's disappearance—standard police procedure when another jurisdiction is involved; and finally, not once during the entire night did they so much as telephone the Zielinskis to learn whether the girl had returned home. Mr. Zielinski's report seems to have fallen into the file-and-forget-it category. It was far from an exemplary police performance.

If in 1957 one had driven south on Wyckoff Avenue from the Zielinskis' to the Nixons'—whose home was situated on the northwest corner of the intersection of Wyckoff Avenue and Fardale Road—turned right on Fardale and driven straight ahead for one mile, he would have found that Fardale Avenue came to a dead end at Chapel Road. Directly ahead, however, across Chapel Road, he would have noticed a narrow dirt driveway, approximately seventy-five feet in length, leading to a flat, sandy area above an infrequently used sandpit, which could be seen off to the left of the driveway.

To the right, running in a semicircle around the flat, sandy area, one would have seen a low mound of earth, six or seven feet in height, slightly flattened at the top, beyond which stretched a weed-covered field.

It was there, where the field began at the base of the dirt mound, that the search for Victoria Zielinski ended.

Mr. and Mrs. Zielinski resumed the search for their daughter at 7:40 a.m. Knowing that Vickie would not have stayed away from home all night of her own free will drove the fear deeper into their hearts. They dreaded the thought of what they might find in the light of day, but neither could sit home any longer waiting for news of their child, news which had not come throughout the long, sleepless night. Their first stop was the Ramsey Police Headquarters, where at 7:50 a.m. they delivered a photograph of Vickie to the officer on duty.

The police station, located directly opposite the high school, was deserted except for the officer on desk duty; and elsewhere on the main street, the town seemed normally quiet as the first few shopkeepers began preparing for business as usual, unaware that within two hours their town would be the focus of attention and the gathering place for hundreds of police officers, newspaper reporters and photographers, radio and television reporters, and the morbidly curious who, almost as if they had lain festering beneath the pavement waiting for the moment, are more often than not among the very first to appear at the scenes of tragedies. The shopkeepers were to have a busy day.

As the Zielinskis were returning to their car, the first few school buses began rolling into the high-school parking lot. Mr. Zielinski frowned as he watched them drive out of sight behind the school building, and he wondered to himself whether the police really cared about finding his daughter. Why didn't they—someone, anyone—do something? But still the thought seems not to have occurred to him to drive one block farther up the main street and request assistance from the state police. Instead, he drove to the Nixon house.

Mr. and Mrs. Nixon were having breakfast when the Zielinskis arrived. They were shocked when they heard that Vickie, Barbara's very best friend, had not returned from her visit to their home the night before, but they could offer no information. Nor, apparently, did they offer their assistance; and so, as the Nixons returned to their breakfast, the anxious parents drove off to resume their lonely search.

The Zielinskis had been driving aimlessly over the back roads of Ramsey and Mahwah for nearly an hour when they came finally to the intersection of Fardale Avenue and Chapel Road. It was 9 a.m., exactly twelve hours and twenty minutes after Barbara Nixon had watched her friend walk down the driveway and disappear into the darkness.

As they turned left from Chapel Road onto Fardale Avenue, to complete a circle back to the Nixon home, Mr. Zielinski spotted a black loafer lying on the edge of the roadway. It was Vickie's. Twenty feet farther up the road, according to Mr. Zielinski's estimate, they found her kerchief. It was blood-stained.

"There's something happened to my daughter," Mr. Zielinski said to his wife. "You'd better go and call the police."

As the mother rushed on foot to a nearby house to telephone the police, her husband began searching a small stand of woods directly across the road from where he had found the shoe and kerchief. Finding nothing in the woods, he walked down Fardale Avenue, across Chapel Road, and up the dirt road leading to the flat area above the sandpit, and there he found a pair of red gloves which he did not immediately recognize. He did not continue the search. His wife, who had returned from telephoning the police, called him back to the car where she was waiting. Together, they remained by their car until the police arrived.

The first police officer to arrive upon the scene was Captain Edmund Wickham, of the Mahwah Township police, a man with twenty years' police experience. He had been on routine patrol in a radio car when Mrs. Zielinski's call for help was relayed to him from his headquarters at 9:12 a.m. She had called the Mahwah police because the sandpit area is in what is known as the Fardale Section of Mahwah.

Mahwah, with a 1957 population of approximately 1,900, was the largest municipality in Bergen County in terms of area —twenty-six square miles. Nevertheless, Captain Wickham, who had been patrolling the northern section of the township, arrived at the sandpit, in the extreme southern section, at 9:20, just eight minutes after Mrs. Zielinski's telephone call had been received.

The investigation report filed by Captain Wickham reveals that he had not known prior to meeting the Zielinskis at the sandpit that Vickie was missing, and this in turn establishes that the Ramsey police had not advised the Mahwah police of the girl's disappearance within the latter's jurisdiction. Captain Wickham's report states:

> I proceeded to Fardale Avenue and Chapel Road and met Mr. and Mrs. Zielinski. *They told me of their missing daughter,* who was last seen at approximately 8:45 p.m., March 4th, 1957, when she left her girl friend's home. The girl friend was Barbara Nixon of Wyckoff Ave., Mahwah, N.J.[2] [Italics added.]

Advising the tearful mother to remain with the car, Captain Wickham went with Mr. Zielinski to the flat area above

[2] Police Department Investigation Report No. 9180, Township of Mahwah, N.J., March 11, 1957, p. 1.

the sandpit. This, the officer said, was the "most likely" place to begin to search for the girl. In light of the fact that a) the flat area was approximately three hundred feet from where the shoe and kerchief had been found, and b) Mr. Zielinski had not recognized the red gloves as belonging to his daughter, the officer's statement that the sandpit was the most likely place to begin the search makes little sense.

The investigation report describes what followed:

> After notifying the Ramsey Police by radio . . . we walked in a dirt driveway at the end of Fardale Avenue, on the west side of Chapel Road. The road is right at the intersection where the west end of Fardale Avenue ends or runs into Chapel Road, which general direction is north and south.
>
> About 150 feet from the dirt roadway, I saw a pair of red wool gloves with leather palms which were lying on the ground. Anthony Zielinski stated his daughter had a pair just like them. The gloves were identified by Mrs. Zielinski. . . .
>
> *Near where the gloves were found, I saw tire marks from a vehicle which indicated to me the driver had driven to the area [and] backed around heading out toward Chapel Road. I walked around those tire marks. . . .*
>
> Zielinski called to me [and] said that he had found his daughter's locket and chain. Then excitedly he called that he had found his daughter's body. I . . . saw a body of a girl in a semi-crouched position, with the body facing downward. Mr. and Mrs. Zielinski identified the body as their missing daughter, Victoria. . . . I walked back to the rear of the area [and] felt the arm of the girl. The arm was stiff [and] cold with rigor mortis apparently set in. The left part of the skull had a large hole in it.[3] [Italics added.]

Mr. Zielinski's descriptions of the physical scene and condition of the body were essentially similar, with one significant exception. He later described having found footprints on the top of the dirt mound less than six feet from Vickie's body.

"There is a flat area at the end of the dirt road," he said, "and there was a mound up on the righthand side; it went up

[3] Ibid., pp. 1–2.

for about six or seven feet. Then it had a little flat surface on top, and in some places it widens out. So when I got up on top I discovered the footmarks."

Following their discovery of the body, Captain Wickham ordered Mr. Zielinski to wait in the car with his wife, who had come to the sandpit to stare horror-stricken at her child's battered corpse, when the father had called out: "Mother, dear, come here, I found her." I have never been able to understand his *wanting* the mother to see such a gruesome sight.

While the Zielinskis waited in their car, consoling each other, and wondering how they would tell their other children that Vickie was dead, Captain Wickham radioed his headquarters to report the crime to his chief. Within minutes, radio and telephone alerts had gone out to the Bergen County Prosecutor's Office, the Bergen County Medical Examiner, the state and county police, and the Ramsey police.

The search had ended, and the police finally were beginning to act; but for Victoria Zielinski, it was too late.

# CHAPTER TWO

IN THE STATE OF NEW JERSEY, THE INVES-
tigation of a major crime is the exclusive function and
responsibility of the prosecutor of the county within which the
crime has been committed. Each of New Jersey's twenty-one
county prosecutors—the term is synonymous with district attorney—is appointed by the governor, with the advice and consent
of the state senate. Their term of office is five years, and there is
no limitation on the number of terms to which they may be
reappointed.

To enable the county prosecutors to carry out their dual
function of investigation and prosecution, the law provides
that each shall have a staff of investigative and legal assistants
whose number shall be regulated according to the population
of the county.

Bergen County, directly across the Hudson River from
New York City, had a 1957 population of approximately
750,800—today the population is approaching 1,000,000—and
for the purpose of apportioning the prosecutor's staff, is designated a "first-class county."

The statutes authorize the following staff personnel for
prosecutors of first-class counties: fifteen assistant prosecutors,
one of whom shall be designated first assistant prosecutor;
twelve legal assistants; and eighteen investigators. Each of these
staff members is appointed by the prosecutor, and serves at his
"pleasure and discretion."

Additionally, the prosecutor of a first-class county is
authorized to appoint, as vacancies occur, twenty-four county

detectives, who shall be given civil service rating after appointment.

As even the most innocent reader may observe, this system of appointments has built into it the inherent capacity to make the county prosecutor's office, the state's primary law enforcement agency, a focal point for political maneuvering. It is axiomatic that any change in political control in the governor's mansion brings with it changes in the prosecutor's office. It is no coincidence that New Jersey, having had successive Democratic governors, does not have a single Republican prosecutor.

It is at the staff level, however, that the most drastic changes follow shifts in political power, since only the county detectives do not automatically lose their jobs when the prosecutor loses his. The result is, of course, that only the county detectives are likely to remain on the job long enough to acquire the *sine qua non* of quality law enforcement—experience.

The telephone call from the Mahwah police was received in the Bergen County Prosecutor's Office, located in the county courthouse, in Hackensack, ten miles south of Mahwah, at 9:46 a.m. By 10:35 a.m. James Stewart, chief of county detectives, had arrived at the scene of the crime with two of his assistants— Detectives Gordon Graber and Russell Ridgeway. Chief Harry Voss of Ramsey, Chief Charles Smith of Mahwah, Captain Alvin Doremus of Ramsey, and several patrolmen from both towns already were on the scene. Chief Smith, who later was to prove especially fond of publicity, was standing with Captain Wickham on Fardale Avenue, while the others milled about the area searching for clues. Some of the first sightseers to arrive were being permitted to roam about at will, and it seemed as if the only constructive idea among the officers was to send Mr. and Mrs. Zielinski home.

Chief Stewart, a veteran of many murder investigations, at once sensed the dilemma of the local officers and took command of the situation, directing the patrolmen to cordon off the area and set up roadblocks, ordering Detectives Graber and Ridgeway to take and record measurements of the scene before anything was disturbed, and ordering that a police photographer be summoned by radio. At the same time the request for a photographer was being relayed to the Bergen County Police—the local departments had neither photographers nor cameras—a second request was sent out for a technician to take plaster impressions of tire marks found on the dirt road leading into the sandpit, and of a set of footprints found on the flat area between the end of the dirt road and the mound of earth over which Vickie's body had been found. The footprints found atop the mound by Mr. Zielinski were ignored, though these were the nearest to the body and most likely belonged to the murderer.

As these matters were being attended to, other members of the prosecutor's staff, many of whom had been contacted at their homes, began arriving at the scene. Vahe Garabedian, an investigator, was one of the first to arrive. He was assigned to assist in taking measurements. Other officers were sent to interview the Zielinski family, to obtain a list of Vickie's friends and acquaintances.

William Nixon, Barbara's oldest brother, was the first person on the list obtained from the Zielinski family, if only because Vickie had been visiting the Nixon home prior to her disappearance. Brought to the Mahwah Police Headquarters in the town's combination municipal building–firehouse, Nixon was interrogated by Fred Galda, the first assistant prosecutor, a brusque, red-faced, red-haired, bull-in-the-china-shop-style prosecutor and politician. He was the Democratic mayor of Paramus, New Jersey, and later would be an unsuccessful candidate for the state senate.

It required less than ten minutes of questioning to determine that William Nixon had not known of the murder until brought into custody, and he was released, no longer a suspect.

Meanwhile, back at the sandpit, Chief Stewart was becoming increasingly worried. The press and the curiosity seekers had begun arriving at the scene almost as quickly as the police. Within an hour the chief had as many officers controlling the crowd as he had working on the investigation, and the body had not yet been removed. Deciding against waiting any longer for the arrival of the police photographer, Chief Stewart asked Ronald Ambler, a young photographer recently employed by the *Bergen Evening Record,* the only local newspaper of significance with countywide circulation, to take color photographs of the body for future use as evidence. Somehow, perhaps in return for his services—the question has never been explored officially—Ambler managed to provide his newspaper with a photograph of the half-naked corpse in all its gory details, which the *Record* promptly splashed across the front page of its next edition[1]—a particularly disgusting example of journalistic bad taste. But good taste, and indeed accuracy, were not to be given much consideration in the news media's handling of this story.

As Ronald Ambler was taking the last of the color photographs, Lieutenant Arthur Abrams of the Bergen County Police was completing the delicate task of preparing plaster casts of tire marks found on the dirt driveway—tire marks whose existence the prosecution was later to ignore. No casts were made of the footprints Mr. Zielinski had found atop the dirt mound, less than six feet from Vickie's body. Nor were casts made of three distinct tire tracks found on the shoulder of Fardale Avenue, inches away from Vickie's black loafer.

The photographer and the officer completed their work by 11:45 a.m., and Howard Sneider, a local mortician, who had been standing by for more than an hour, finally was permitted to remove the body to the Van Emburgh Funeral Chapel in Ramsey, where an autopsy would be performed. Chief Stewart, no longer as concerned with controlling the reporters, photographers, and spectators, turned to other matters, assigning several officers to the task of interviewing the families living along Fardale Avenue—there were no houses on Chapel Road.

The officers assigned to that task became more puzzled

[1] *Bergen Evening Record,* March 6, 1957, p. 1.

with each interview they conducted. Not a single person recalled having seen or heard anything unusual—no loud voices or noises, no screams, and no sound of automobiles stopping or starting; yet this area, far removed from any main road, normally was so quiet at night that the sound of an automobile could be heard a half mile away.

The Kromka family, in front of whose home Vickie's shoe and kerchief had been found, and where the police also had found bloodstains and a few strands of what appeared to be the girl's hair, had been up late the night before; but they, too, had heard nothing unusual. It was this information the detectives found most perplexing. The Kromka home was less than two hundred feet from the sandpit entrance, but their dog, tethered in the yard all night, had been silent. Could such a murder as this, one that had left clothing, blood, and brains scattered over a wide area, have been committed so silently that the Kromka's watchdog had not been aroused? Didn't the girl struggle or scream? Several of the detectives toyed with the theory that the crime had been committed elsewhere, and that the sandpit was merely the dumping ground for the body; but the blood and brains scattered about seemed to militate against that theory.

The questioning of the persons on the list provided by the Zielinski family was not going well. All had been questioned and their stories checked—boys Vickie had dated, boys she had known casually, friends of her sisters, friends of Barbara Nixon, anyone and everyone with whom she might have accepted a ride—with two significant exceptions: the police had not been given my name, or the name of Donald Hommell.

It was strange that my name was not on the list. Myrna and Mary, and especially the latter, whom I knew quite well, both were aware that I often had driven Vickie home from school. And I am quite certain that Mrs. Zielinski knew it also. But the absence of Hommell's name from the list of friends and acquaintances was even more inexplicable.

Certainly the police were not totally inept. One of their first questions to Myrna must have been whether on her walk to and from the Nixon home she had seen anyone that her sister might have known. Why then did she fail to report having seen Hommell speeding by at sixty miles an hour? She later admitted that her sister had known him, although denying under oath that Vickie and Hommell had ever dated. Perhaps, just perhaps, she was ignorant of something that was common knowledge around town. Hommell, himself, freely admitted at my trial that he had dated Vickie "approximately ten times." My own opinion, for what it is worth, is that Myrna, at the time the police were compiling the list of Vickie's friends, had not yet accepted the enormity of her sister's death, and was attempting to conceal the fact that her sister had accepted rides and dates with older fellows.

All possible leads seemed to have been exhausted by mid-afternoon. The police were stymied. Then someone—Captain Wickham?—remembered that a Mahwah man living in a trailer park a mile from the sandpit, the same trailer park in which I lived, recently had been loitering about a grammar school on Fardale Avenue and had attempted to lure young girls into his automobile. Now here was the sort of suspect who brought a gleam to a policeman's eye—the proverbial "dirty old man." Perhaps, they reasoned—police officers tend to reason in straight lines—he had graduated from little girls to big girls, had found he was unable to handle it, and in his frustration had become violent. A nice theory, but one any competent psychologist would debunk.

The police officers questioned the man for more than an hour, searched his trailer home, examined his automobile, and came up with nothing. He had an airtight alibi for the entire night.

Another suspect turned up when one of the residents of Fardale Avenue mentioned that a neighborhood boy had spent some time in a mental institution. More questions, more probing around in home and auto, and again nothing. The police were right back where they had started—they had a body.

One of the county detectives, Captain Carl DeMarco, told

me a few days later: "This was one of the most frustrating cases I've ever worked on. Everywhere we turned we ran into a stone wall. It got to where I had my doubts about the girl's father. From the way it looked, he was the only guy in Bergen County who wasn't home in bed all night."

Another detective voiced somewhat the same complaint. "The old man was a tough guy to figure. Here I am trying to get the names of the kid's friends, and the old man keeps mentioning something about 'insurance.' Then when we're riding around town, and I'm checking times and distances, it don't match up with the time the old man was out during the night."

All that could be done at the scene of the crime had been done by late afternoon, and the detectives moved their base of operations to police headquarters in Mahwah. The body was in the funeral chapel, autopsy completed. The sandpit area had been scoured for some clue to what had happened there the night before. The evidence from the scene—clothing, strands of hair, some large bloodstained stones, the plaster casts —all had been packed in cardboard boxes, along with the clothing removed from the body by the autopsy surgeon, and Chief Stewart had directed Detective Walter Spahr to deliver the evidence to the Edel Laboratories, a commercial facility in Newark, Essex County, New Jersey. The prosecutor had decided not to use the readily available New Jersey State Police laboratory.

The prospects were for a long, tedious investigation. The break came at 7:30 p.m.

As the police were scouring the scene of the crime one last time for anything that might have been overlooked, three miles away in downtown Ramsey, Joseph Gilroy, my closest friend, was sitting on the desk in the office of Tony's Amoco Station, listening as some of his friends—William Anderson, Tommy Doyle, and Eddie Horton—discussed the murder. Much of the talk centered about the failure of the police to question any of the fellows who had been dating Vickie, chief among them Donald Hommell. "Donnie better have some good answers ready," one of the fellows remarked.

Gilroy, who seemed always to be hungry, decided at 5:15 p.m. to go home for supper. He had not known Vickie, except as someone he had heard the other fellows talking about, so the conversation was not one to keep him from eating. Ten minutes after leaving the gas station, however, he returned.

As Gilroy had gotten out of his car at home, he noticed a dime-sized spot of what appeared to be blood on the front seat cover. Upon closer examination, he also found on the front floor mat, on the passenger's side, a spot about twelve inches in diameter, which appeared to be oil.

The fellows were still sitting in Tony's gas station when Gilroy returned. Also present was the owner of the station, Tony Saveriano.

"Hey, Tony," Joe called out as he entered, "how about taking a look at my car? Something funny is going on. Smitty had the car last night around the time of the murder, and now there is blood on the seat."

William Anderson, Tommy Doyle, and Tony each examined the spot on the seat cover, and although the spot was quite small, and of a somewhat brownish color, each agreed that it appeared to be blood.

"You don't think Smitty had anything to do with it, do you?" Anderson asked.

"I don't know," Gilroy told him, "but it's awfully funny. Smitty told me last night he had gotten sick and thrown away the pants he was wearing. Then today he had an old pair of shoes he was going to have fixed. One minute he had them, the next he didn't, and I don't think he went to the shoemaker. I can't believe he could be involved, but I don't know."

"You'd better go to the cops," Tony advised. "If Smitty was mixed up in it with your car, you'd be up the creek if you didn't report it."

Tommy Doyle stood by silently, but Anderson agreed with Tony.

It was a tough decision for Gilroy. If he failed to tell the police, he might be accused of concealing evidence. If he did report it, and was wrong, the fellows around town might regard him as a "fink" for the police. So, reasoning that the car would not evaporate, he decided to return home, have supper, and think things over.

John Cozma, one of the Ramsey patrolmen, was standing in front of the town's only bank, across the street from the gas station, when Gilroy walked over to report the blood in his car. The officer knew all the fellows from around town—he and I had double-dated with a couple of local girls, one of whom he later married—and he had no difficulty following Joe's story about Smitty and the blood in the car.

"Listen, Joe," the officer told him, "you put your car behind Tony's place, and lock it up. Where's Smitty now?"

"I don't know. Home, I guess."

"Okay, go lock the car and wait for me. I'll get the police car and take you up to Mahwah. The prosecutor's people are up there and you can tell them your story."

Mahwah Police Headquarters, on the second floor of the Municipal Building, up a narrow, rickety flight of stairs from the firehouse below, consisted of a single office at the rear of the municipal courtroom and council chamber. The only furniture in the office was a battered wooden desk and chair set against the right-hand wall, beneath a multicolored map of the township; a row of four filing cabinets standing in a corner in the back of the room; and a couple of wooden office chairs next to the filing cabinets. Giving the place some semblance of officiality, a wooden fence with a swinging gate stood between the door and the desk, dividing the room in two. Directly across from the desk, two large windows looked out over a supermarket-size parking lot that appeared to be terribly out of place next to the dingy building. It was the sort of thing that made one wonder if the mayor's brother-in-law was in the asphalt-paving business.

It had been a tough, frustrating day for the investigators. Fred Galda, the first assistant prosecutor, who had been directing the investigation, slumped morosely in the chair behind the desk and stared across the room, silently contemplating his own reflection in the windows. Captain Wickham, now wearing civilian clothes, sat on the desk, absent-mindedly toying with a pack of matches. Off in the corner, Detectives Sinatra and Garabedian leaned against the filing cabinets, quietly discussing the soon-to-open baseball season. Other detectives, including Captain Carl DeMarco, Gordon Graber, and Russell Ridgeway, lounged about the courtroom outside, now and then engaging in brief conversations with two newspaper reporters. The other reporters, sensing that the investigation had come to a standstill, had returned to their newspaper offices to work on stories for the next editions. The chiefs—Stewart, Voss, and Smith—had gone to dinner in a nearby diner. Everyone, from the prosecutor on down, had run out of ideas. Every possible lead had been checked, rechecked, and checked again. There seemed to be nothing for them to do but sit, wait, and hope for a break.

Such was the scene when Joe Gilroy arrived to tell the story that would start me on my way to the Death House.

He was expected. The Ramsey police had radioed ahead that they were bringing in a man who might be able to provide the first solid lead in the Zielinski case, and upon his arrival, Gilroy was ushered into the office where Galda waited to question him.

"All right now, son," Galda said, "what's this about finding blood on your car?"

"It's on the seat cover, not the car. You see, Eddie Smith had the car, and when he didn't have the shoes, and I found the blood and remembered—"

"Hold on," Galda interrupted, "who is Eddie Smith?"

"Eddie's a friend of mine. He borrowed my car last night and now it has blood on it, and Eddie had this pair of shoes and—"

Again Galda interrupted: "Look, at this rate we'll be here all night. Grab that chair over there, sit down, and start right from the beginning. When did Eddie Smith borrow your car? By the way, where is your car now?"

"It's behind Tony Saveriano's house, in Ramsey. The Ramsey cops told me to leave it there. It's locked."

"What kind of car do you have?"

"A Mercury. A 1950 turquoise convertible."

Turning to Detective Gordon Graber, Galda said: "Gordon, you and Captain Wickham take this boy's keys and go check his car. And don't be all night about it."

As Gilroy pulled a chair over from near the filing cabinet, sat down in front of the desk, and lit a cigarette, Galda told him: "Now take your time and don't leave anything out. But first give this officer your keys."

Gilroy did as he was instructed, handing his keys to Captain Wickham. Then, waiting until Wickham and Graber had left the office, he began his story:

"Eddie Smith called me up at home about three-thirty in the afternoon, Monday, and asked me to pick him up at the Paramus Bowling Alleys. He was with Rocky—Charles Rockefeller—who works there.

"I got there about four-thirty and we bowled some games, four or five—me, Rocky, and Eddie. About six-thirty we left there and went up to Ramsey, to Tony's Amoco. I went down to the drugstore, I walked down, to get some cough medicine. When I got back, Eddie asked if he could borrow the car. His car was in the shop, getting the transmission fixed, I think. He needed to get some kerosene. The heater in his house trailer wasn't working. Eddie has a new house trailer. He lives in Fardale, about a mile from the sandpit. I told him he could use the car, so he drove me and Rocky home and took the car. That was about seven o'clock. Eddie and me were supposed to go out later and have a couple of beers, but at ten or fifteen after nine Eddie called me up. I was watching *I Love Lucy*, so I remember the time. He said he had been sick and the heater wouldn't work. Would I drive him and his wife and baby to Ridgewood, to his mother-in-law's. I told him okay. He came up and got me about a quarter of ten. On the way back to get his wife and baby, Eddie told me he got sick and he threw up on his pants, and that he had to throw them away. We got to his trailer and—"

Galda interrupted: "Did he tell you where he threw his pants?"

"No, he didn't say."

"Okay, Joe, what happened then?"

"Well, we got to Eddie's trailer and picked up his wife and baby. We went to Ridgewood. I dropped Eddie and his wife and baby at his mother-in-law's place. I figure it must have been about ten o'clock. It's only five or six miles to Ridgewood. I went back to Ramsey, to Tony Saveriano's house, on the Franklin Turnpike. Tony owns the gas station. I stayed there watching television with Tony till about one-thirty, then I went home. The next day Eddie called me at home about twelve-thirty. He wanted me to pick him up in Ridgewood. First I went downtown to the gas station, and I met Donald Hommell, another friend. About two o'clock, Donnie said he would drive me to Ridgewood to pick up Smitty. Well, on the way down, Donnie said: 'Eddie had your car last night, didn't he? Maybe he had something to do with this.' He was talking about the murder. I said Eddie couldn't be involved, so Donnie said: 'Well, when we get to Ridgewood, I am going to tell him they know it is a Mercury.' "

Again Galda broke in to ask: "How did he know Eddie Smith had your car? Did you tell him?"

"I don't know, I don't think so."

Captain DeMarco, who had been standing to one side listening to Gilroy's story, asked: "At this point, on the afternoon after the murder, had you found any blood in the car?"

"No," Joe replied, "I was wondering about that myself."

"Okay, Joe, go on with the story. What happened when you got to Ridgewood?"

"Well, Eddie came out of the house. *He asked if that was Vickie that got killed.* Donnie told him it was, and that the cops were looking for a Mercury. Eddie got a startled look on his face. Then Eddie's wife came out with the baby and got in the car, and we went toward Ramsey. Eddie and his wife were in back, and one of them found a lipstick on the floor and gave it to Donnie. I don't know which one found it. They gave it to Donnie. Donnie said: 'Maybe it was Vickie's,' and threw it out the window.

"Well, we got to Eddie's trailer and they got out. We

waited for Eddie. He came back carrying an old pair of shoes. He got in the car, and going back to town Donnie wanted to drive past the murder, the sandpit. Well, we rode past and all of us waved to the Ramsey cops we knew. When we got downtown, we stopped over by Tony's Amoco. We were going to play basketball together. So after we got out of the car, I went with Donnie to McPeek's Department Store, where he was going to buy a pair of sneakers, and Eddie told us he was going to get a cup of coffee. He had the old pair of shoes with him. But when me and Donnie came out of the store where Donnie bought the sneakers, Eddie was coming from across the street, but without the shoes. I wondered what he did with them.

"Well, Donnie asked Eddie if he was coming to play basketball, but Eddie said: 'No, I have to get a haircut.' So Donnie and I went to play without him. Later on, above five o'clock, we came back to town. I saw Eddie sitting in Dave Villarosa's car. He's one of the guys from around town. That's the last I seen of Eddie. I hung around Tony's Amoco for a while, then I went home, and that's when I found the blood. The guys at Tony's told me to go to the police, so that's what I did."

"Who advised you to do that?" Galda asked.

"Tony, Tony Saveriano. He owns the station."

"And what did the other fellows say about the stains?"

"Nothing," Gilroy answered, stopping to light another cigarette. "They just looked."

"Have you told Hommell or Smith about finding the blood?"

"No. Hommell wasn't there. Eddie wasn't either."

Turning to Captain DeMarco, Galda asked: "What do you think, Carl?"

"I don't know," the detective replied. Then, looking at Gilroy, he asked: "Did Smith know the Zielinski girl?"

"I suppose so. I don't think he ever took her out."

"But Hommell did?"

"Yeah, a couple of times."

"Did you?"

"No."

"And how about Smith's pants. Did he say where he threw them?"

Thinking about that for a minute, Gilroy finally replied: "No, he didn't say. I was wondering, but I didn't ask him."

"Just two more questions, Joe. How did Hommell know Smith had your car? And how is it you didn't notice the blood from last night until tonight?"

"Well, maybe one of the guys told Hommell, I don't know. And the blood I can't explain."

"But you used the car after Smith brought it back last night, and again all day today, right?"

"Yeah, but I never noticed."

"And you got in and out of the car quite a few times today?"

"Yeah, but like I said, I never noticed the blood."

"Do you know where Hommell was last night?" Galda asked.

"I didn't see him, but coming up from Ridgewood today, he told us he saw Vickie's kid sister walking last night, and that he blew the horn to her."

"He told you that?"

"Yeah, in the car today, right after Eddie or his wife found the lipstick."

Gilroy's story had been almost too complete and detailed for the first assistant prosecutor to accept. He seemed to be pointing a finger at everyone but himself, and the prosecutor knew that criminals, smart ones, when they felt the police were getting close to them, often took the initiative by going to the police and, playing the role of a good citizen, shifting suspicion to someone else.

Gilroy was asked to wait outside in the courtroom for a few minutes, and Detective Sinatra was sent along to make certain that the boy did not wander away. Detective Graber and Captain Wickham had returned from checking the bloodstains.

"Okay, Gordon, what's the story?" Galda asked.

"We brought the floor mat back with us," the detective

replied, as he spread a dirty, black rubber mat on the desk. "It doesn't look like blood, more like oil or gasoline. The spot is round, like a can of gas might make, but it seems too oily for gas."

"Perhaps kerosene," suggested Captain DeMarco.

"Maybe," Graber went on, "but the spot on the seat cover damn sure is blood. Just a tiny drop, not a smear, but damn sure blood. Pretty well dried out, too. We didn't want to pull the seat covers out until we got a photographer to shoot them in the car."

"Carl, you fill Gordon in on Gilroy's story," Galda told Captain DeMarco. "Meanwhile, Captain Wickham, I'd like you to contact the Ramsey police. I want to know who Gilroy is; if he has a record; who Hommell and Smith are; if they have records; if the Zielinskis know any of these guys; if any of them dated the girl; if Gilroy has any personal reason to want to put the finger on Smith; and anything else they can tell you."

The answers came back within an hour, and for the first time since the investigation had begun, Galda felt that he was on to something.

Captain DeMarco agreed, but he cautioned the assistant prosecutor: "We'll have to play it by ear with Smith. That time-of-death factor will be a problem. Gilroy can alibi Smith for all of the time after nine-thirty, so we'll run right into the medical examiner's estimate that she died between ten and eleven, and maybe later."

"That's close enough for me," Galda replied. Then, calling Detectives Graber and Garabedian in from the courtroom, where they had been talking to Gilroy, he told them: "You guys go find Smith and bring him back. Ask Gilroy where he lives. No, better yet, take Gilroy along to show you."

As the detectives turned to leave, Captain DeMarco added wearily: "And bring back some coffee. It's going to be a long goddam night."

# CHAPTER THREE

**THE TEMPERATURE WAS TEN BELOW, AND A**
raging blizzard was roaring out of the northwest the night
I was born, at 2 a.m. on February 8, 1934, in Hasbrouck
Heights, an upper middle-class suburb of some 5,000 people,
ten miles west of New York City. My mother, my brother, six
years older than myself, and I continued to live there after
my parents were divorced in 1941. I was too young to know
the cause of their separation two years earlier, my first hint
of trouble coming when suddenly my father ceased to live
at home, and to this day my mother has not discussed the
matter with me—nor am I particularly interested in learning
the cause of the breakup. The last time I saw my father was
on a summer afternoon in 1952, when I stopped to say hello
and borrow some money while passing through Richmond,
Virginia, where he was living and working.

My father was what is known in the retail trade as a
window dresser, a designer and decorator of store-window
displays, and though it is only a vague memory to me, I do
recall his taking my brother and me to New York City each
Christmas to see his windows. I am told that he was one of the
best men in the business, working only for the finest stores in
the city.

I have stated that I do not care to know the cause of my
parents' divorce, and aside from the fact that I consider it to
be none of my business, there is another reason. My father
knows what has happened to me and where I am today—he
has known of my troubles from the very beginning—yet in the

eleven years since my arrest, I have not received so much as a single birthday or Christmas card from him: no wishes of good luck when I was going on trial; no word of commiseration when I was convicted and sentenced to death; no "keep up the spirits" message as my years of confinement dragged on; not even a note or a phone call to my mother to ask if he could help, when at one point I was only hours from the electric chair.

My mother, who went to work immediately after the separation—she still works for the same company—did all she could to hold the family together; but for two years during the war, when it was impossible to find someone to care for my brother and me while she worked, we were sent to live with relations in Jersey City—my brother with our maternal grandmother, myself with an aunt, one of my mother's sisters. Though living in separate homes, we saw each other practically every day, so it really was not too difficult for us. Moreover, with very few exceptions, all of our relations—aunts, uncles, and cousins—lived in Jersey City, so we were in fact much closer to the family than we might otherwise have been.

By 1944, with the problems created by the war beginning to ease, my brother and I had returned to Hasbrouck Heights to live with our mother. Hasbrouck Heights in those days would have served as an ideal model for Smalltown, U.S.A. A town of well-kept private homes and tree-shaded streets, many of which still had the old-fashioned slate sidewalks, it was a good town in which to grow up. In the winter, some of the streets were closed off and left snow-covered for the children and their sleds; and on summer evenings, the softball games between the police and fire departments, or the Elks and Lions, always drew big crowds. Once each year, a circus or carnival would come to town; and on the Fourth of July, the biggest holiday, there would be a parade in the afternoon, and fireworks and a block dance at night.

A mile from my home was Teterboro Airport, then a small private facility with a single asphalt runway, today the world's busiest airport devoted exclusively to servicing private and corporate aircraft. The airport became my playground and home away from home early in life. Practically every day after school, and every day when school was not in session, I was there poking my nose into everything. Airplanes were my first love, and I thought nothing of climbing into the cockpit of any airplane that suited my fancy, pretending I was flying to all sorts of strange and exotic places, or shooting down vast numbers of German planes while sitting at the controls of a Piper Cub or an Aeronca Champ.

My brash behavior with other people's airplanes soon earned me the nickname "The Pest," but it also brought me into contact with some well-known personalities. There is a special camaraderie among people who fly, and when my love for airplanes became obvious, the owners and mechanics showed a bit more tolerance toward me; but I am certain that they expected any day to see me trying to get one of the planes off the ground.

Arthur Godfrey, who grew up in Hasbrouck Heights, a boyhood chum of the man who is now my stepfather, quite often flew out of Teterboro. Godfrey was not yet the world-famous, highly paid performer he has become since; as I recall, he flew a small, blue, single-engine Navion, a far cry from his million-dollar, multi-engine jet of today, though he continues to use Teterboro with some regularity.[1]

The first time I met Arthur Godfrey was when he drove up in his car, roaring: "Hey, you, kid, get the hell away from my plane!"—my normal, first encounter with most owners of air-planes. But after seeing me around a few times, and learning that I had never gotten off the ground, he offered to take me for a ride if I would bring a note from home. I did not get the note, or the ride. At Teterboro I also met, and pestered, Clar-ence Chamberlain, the man Lindbergh beat across the Atlantic to Paris but who, two weeks later, flew to Eisleben in Germany, three hundred miles beyond Paris; Bill Odom, who in 1947 flew a converted twin-engine bomber around the world in record time and who, two years later, just before his death in a

[1] Readers might recall Godfrey's recent recording, *Teterboro Tower*.

plane crash, set another record flying a single-engine Bonanza nonstop from Honolulu to Teterboro; and Roy "Red" Ryder, the old-time flying-circus daredevil, later the great test pilot of the Bendix Aviation Corporation.

Another interesting man I met in those days, though not connected with the airport, was "Willie" Moretti, reputed to be, with Joe Adonis, one of the Mafia bosses of North Jersey. Bergen County in those days was one of the nation's major gambling centers. By the early 1950's, the laxity of the law-enforcement agencies and the stench of political corruption had become so obvious that the Attorney General of New Jersey was forced to step in and assume control of the Bergen County Prosecutor's Office. In short order, Moretti was assassinated, Adonis deported, and a few public officials turned out to pasture. Still, many people, including myself, believe the affair was nothing but an elaborate and well-publicized cover-up, to forestall a more searching probe by the then-functioning Senate Committee to Investigate Organized Crime in Interstate Commerce, led by Tennessee's Estes Kefauver.

Moretti lived around the corner from my grandmother, my father's mother, in a beautiful pink stucco, Spanish-style villa. Behind his home, in the middle of a block-wide garden and patio surrounded by a low wall, stood a fenced enclosure containing two of the most vicious dogs—chows, I believe, pitch-black—that ever lived. They acted as if they would have enjoyed eating alive everyone and everything that moved within five blocks of the house, and they probably would have if they had ever got loose.

Moretti looked like someone's grandfather or favorite uncle—both of which he was—and when he came or went in one of his two 1941 Lincoln Continentals, complete with bodyguards, he always found time to stop and say hello to the children who were at the house visiting his three daughters, with the youngest of whom, Angelina, I attended school. He had a remarkable memory and always greeted each of us by name.

Willie, though a racketeer in the eyes of the townspeople,

was regarded as something of a folk hero by the neighborhood children—a sort of knight in shining *black* armor. He was unusually generous to the town's Catholic church, which he did not often attend. Each year, at Christmas, the church would publish the names and donations of the major contributors. Willie's name invariably headed the list. After he was shot to death in a Bergen County restaurant in 1951, at the height of the gambling investigations—it happened at lunchtime, no one saw a thing, and the crime has never been solved—he was given the gaudiest funeral Hasbrouck Heights has ever seen.

I was attending a Catholic high school at the time, and I cut classes to attend the funeral. The next day, when I returned to school, the mother superior summoned me to her office and threatened to expel me if I did not have a good excuse for my absence the previous day.

"I went to a funeral," I told her.

"Oh. Who was it? Someone in your family?"

"No. I went to Willie Moretti's funeral."

The mother superior looked as though she were going to call a priest to exorcise Satan from my soul. She said that attending the funeral of "that dirty gangster" was the most sinful thing any student of hers had ever done. When I told her that he had been buried with the full rites of the Catholic Church, all she said was: "Oh." The subject of expulsion from school was dropped.

I also met, during the forties, Frank Sinatra. Those were the days when he was still "Frankie," idol of the bobby-soxers, appearing at New York's Paramount Theater, and at the Rustic Cabin, a night spot on the New Jersey side of the Hudson River. Sinatra lived a couple of blocks from our home, and was a familiar figure around town. Quite often, late in the afternoon, before leaving for work, he would take his daughter, Nancy, then about three years old, out for a short walk, with a gaggle of children always tagging along. We all knew, of course, that he was some sort of celebrity, and that for some reason the older girls adored him, but at that age—I was ten or eleven—we were not overly impressed.

Sinatra was rather shy and seemed more at ease with the children than with adults, perhaps because we accepted him as just another neighborhood father. He seemed already to resent anyone or anything threatening to intrude upon his private life, yet several times he did treat us when the Good Humor ice-cream truck came around, as it did every evening in good weather. Nancy, however, was a sprightly, bubbling little doll, always wanting to hold someone's hand while she walked along showing off her famous daddy.

I particularly recall a summer evening in 1945, when Sinatra arrived at the high-school athletic field, driving his powder-blue '41 Buick convertible, to sing the National Anthem to begin an outdoor Boy Scout meeting. As he was preparing to leave, he stopped to chat with those of us who had ignored the festivities to gather around and admire his automobile, which impressed us more than did his singing. He was going to Hollywood to make a movie, he told us, and when he was a big movie star, if any of the kids from Hasbrouck Heights ever needed help, we should let him know.

My mother remarried when I was fourteen, and in the summer of 1948, following my graduation from grammar school, our family moved to another small town a few miles north of Hasbrouck Heights. In September I entered the ninth grade of the local junior high school—the town did not have a senior high school—and in December of that year I had my first contact with the police, an incident the details of which are so indelibly fixed in my mind that after nineteen years I am able to recall what I had for dinner the night of the incident.

It was 7 p.m., during the first week of December, and I had just finished my homework and had sat down with the family to a spaghetti-and-meatball dinner when a policeman arrived and announced that a neighborhood girl, a couple of years younger than I, had accused me of attempting to molest her ten minutes earlier, several blocks from my home. I denied the accusation, of course, and the policeman, finding me before a partly eaten dinner, obviously doubted that I had been several blocks away ten minutes earlier. Nevertheless, the officer did ask me to come to the police station with my parents after finishing my dinner. We did as he requested, and when his superiors had heard my story, I was released. A report would be filed, I was told, but for all practical purposes the incident was closed—or so I thought until three days later, when I returned home from school for lunch and found a woman from the Bergen County Child Welfare Department sitting on our front porch.

The woman asked me to go with her to her office in Hackensack. "It's only going to take a few minutes," she told me. "We want to get your story about the incident with the young girl the other night. I'll drive you back to school in time for afternoon classes. You can have lunch in my office."

My parents were at work at the time, and the woman suggested that I not telephone and needlessly worry them, so taking her word that it was a mere formality, I went with her. One hour later, clad in oversized, torn pajamas, I was locked in a cell in the county juvenile home.

Upon our arrival at the juvenile home, where the woman told me her office was located, I was taken to the third floor and turned over to a man named Woods, whom I shall remember as long as I live: tall, thin, pinched face, wearing steel-rimmed glasses, apparently about fifty years old, he was the nastiest human being I have ever met; it took me five seconds to dislike him, five minutes to hate him—about par for the course, I learned later from the other boys in the home. He told me to sit in a chair in the corner of his office until he had time for me, and when I started to explain that I had to get back to school, he cut me off with: "Shut your goddam mouth and sit down." I had hardly done as ordered when another boy, about my own age, entered the office and threw a pair of threadbare, ragged pajamas on the floor.

"Take off your clothes and put them on," Woods ordered, kicking the pajamas over to where I was sitting.

"But I am supposed to get back to school. The woman who brought me here said so," I protested. I was certain he was making a mistake, perhaps thinking that I was some other boy, but he quickly cured me of that notion.

"Listen, kid, you ain't playing with little girls now. Do what you're told and keep your mouth shut. I won't tell you again."

Again I did as ordered, and after I had donned the pajamas, which had neither a drawstring nor buttons and had to be held up by hand, I was taken down a corridor and locked in a cell.

My cell was a small room, five or six feet wide, about eight feet long, furnished with a bed, but with not a chair, table, sink, nor a toilet. The door, two inches thick, was made of wood, with a small round peephole cut at eye height. There was no window. I remained in that cell for two weeks. When I had to go to the bathroom, it was necessary to shout through the peephole, and to keep shouting until someone got around to answering. No reading material was permitted; at no time during the two weeks was I permitted to wash or brush my teeth; no clean pajamas or bedsheets were issued; and no mail or visitation was permitted. The latter restriction proved to be the most onerous. For two weeks I had no contact with the outside world—my cell *was* my world—and lying there on the bed, the room seemingly getting smaller every minute, I was consumed by the fear that my family had not been told where I was. More than once I awakened from my sleep drenched in sweat, my body shaking uncontrollably.

As a juvenile, I was not considered to be a criminal, so I did not therefore have to suffer the "embarrassment" and "degradation" of going through adult criminal procedures: I was spared the discomfort of having to listen to explanations of my right to remain silent; did not have to worry about telling my story to a lawyer; and did not have to appear in open court to be formally charged with a specific offense or be set free; and did not have to concern myself with arranging for bail, since juveniles could not be set free on bail. The state, in its infinite wisdom and concern for my welfare, spared me all that by holding me incommunicado, in a solitary confinement cell. Only a fool would fail to see that the best way to protect a juvenile is to deny him all his rights as a citizen.

Near the end of my second week of solitary "protection," I was taken to Mr. Woods's office and told, not asked, to sit down and write a description of how I had molested the girl. When I refused and instead explained that I had been home with my family at the time the incident was supposed to have occurred, Woods told me I would be set free if I did as I was told, but that if I refused I would be sent to a reform school until I was twenty-one. Then, to drive home his warning, he brought in a Negro prisoner just back, he said, from reform school, and who thereupon gave me a long lecture about the horrors of that institution. It sounded terrifying, as it was meant to, and I *was* frightened, but I continued to refuse to give a confession. Woods fumed and shouted for a few more minutes, telling me I would be "sorry," then ordered me returned to my cell. Three or four more times in the next week this routine was repeated. At the end of the second week, however, my clothing was returned and I was moved into a dormitory; my family had retained a lawyer. The question to ponder is: if my family had not retained a lawyer to inquire about me, how many more weeks would I have spent in that cell?

I was taken before a juvenile court judge a week before Christmas. It was an informal proceeding in his office, and I was the only other person present. The judge, it soon became evident, was even more dubious than the local police had been. Investigation revealed that the girl had in the past accused other boys of the same offense, each time relating an essentially similar tale, which had always proved to be untrue. In my case, when asked what sort of clothing I had been wearing at the time of the alleged incident, she said she had forgotten. Clearly, the girl had lied, but the truth or falsity of juvenile charges often means very little; juvenile courts will almost invariably put the defendant on probation, even when the charges are disproved, perhaps following the where-there's-smoke-there-must-be-fire theory. The judge told me that he was putting me on what he termed "administrative probation," which he explained: I would not have to report to a probation officer, or account for my whereabouts and activities; and if I desired to enter military service when old enough, the record would be wiped clean. Meanwhile, I was to be released at once, to return to school. He was in effect dropping the charges, as the local police, already familiar with the girl's stories, had done the first night.[2] At this point in the proceeding, my mother and lawyer were brought in to hear the decision.

Lawyers, I have since learned, are as a rule never content unless they are talking—this might explain why so many of them enter politics—and mine was no exception. When the judge asked me if I would have any trouble facing my schoolmates after the accusation that had been leveled against me, my lawyer interrupted to suggest that I could attend Don Bosco Prep, a private school in Ramsey, New Jersey, about ten miles from my home, a school my brother had attended. The judge had not had any such idea in mind, but the lawyer's suggestion caught his fancy, and it was decided that I would attend Don Bosco for at least the remainder of that school year.

My lawyer's fears about my schoolmates were groundless. In the three days between the accusation and my arrest, everyone in school had heard about the incident—the girl had bragged about it—and the whole affair was treated as a joke. "The kid's a screwball," was the consensus about her. The following summer, an election was held among those participating in the town's recreation program, to elect an honorary town government—mayor and council—to serve for one day. I was elected police commissioner.

Don Bosco Prep was a small Catholic boarding school operated by the Salesian order of teaching priests and brothers,

---

[2] The following summer I gained access to the local police files. I found that they had recommended that no action be taken on the charges, and that neither they nor my school had been told in advance of the child welfare department's intention to arrest me.

with an enrollment of only eighty students and an excellent curriculum within an intense religious atmosphere. Classes were held five and a half days a week, and there were two hour-long study periods each evening, seven days a week. There was one unvarying course of study for all. If a student failed two subjects, he had to repeat the year. If he failed one subject, he was required to make it up during summer recess, or during the subsequent term. The first-year subjects were English, French, Latin, ancient and medieval history, algebra, general science, and religion.

The religious regimen was uncompromising. Each morning at seven o'clock, before breakfast, students were required to attend Mass in the school chapel. Again, at 4:30 p.m., everyone was required to attend Benediction and afternoon prayer services. On Sunday, in addition to the 7 a.m. Mass, all students attended a nine-o'clock solemn High Mass. Meals, classes, athletic events, and any other event at which the students gathered, were begun and concluded with prayers. In the spring, classes were suspended for a two-week religious retreat, during which complete silence was mandatory, except for a one-hour period at the end of the day. Virtually the entire two weeks were spent in chapel, struggling with Gregorian chants in Latin.

Many of my fellow classmates thrived in this religious atmosphere, and a considerable number went on to become priests. For a brief period of time, I, too, entertained the thought of entering the priesthood; but as time went by, the enforced religious devotions had a reverse effect upon me. First, I disliked having religion shoved down my throat, then I began to resent the religion itself.

I returned to Don Bosco for my sophomore year, with a course of studies consisting of English, Latin, French, modern European history, algebra and geometry, biology, and religion. Somehow, I managed to struggle through the year, and as in all of my school years, history continued to be my strongest subject.

June 27, 1950, found me on summer vacation, sitting in a girl friend's back yard, listening to the radio and trying to make up my mind about my future. I knew that if I continued at Don Bosco and graduated, I could take my pick of any college. But school had become a crushing bore, and my estrangement from Catholicism was nearly complete. My thoughts were interrupted by a radio bulletin: President Truman had ordered the troops into South Korea. The next morning at nine o'clock I was in the local Marine Corps recruiting station.

Being nearly six feet tall at sixteen, I had thought bluffing my way into the Marines would be easy, but the recruiting officer wasted no time in pouring cold water on that idea. "Sorry, boy, you'll either have to prove you are eighteen, or be seventeen and have the written approval of a parent or guardian." This was crushing—I would have to return to school in the fall.

My family moved again that summer, buying a home in Ramsey, two miles across town from the Don Bosco campus. In a case filled with coincidences, it is another that my family moved to Ramsey at exactly the same time that Victoria Zielinski and her family moved there. Our homes were less than a half mile apart.

When it became apparent to my family that I was determined not to go back into that religious hothouse, they reluctantly agreed that I could attend the local public high school. It was a lamentable mistake.

Ramsey High School, after two years of relentless study at Don Bosco, proved disappointing. The teachers were dull, uninspired, and uninspiring. Most were elderly and seemed only to be hanging on until they could collect their pensions. By the time my seventeenth birthday rolled around, I was fed up with school in general, and Ramsey High School in particular. I cut school that day, went to the military induction center in New York City, and took the physical and written examinations for the Marine Corps. When I returned home that night with the papers for my mother to sign, the answer was No, N–O, No. I quit school the next day, intending to loaf around until my eighteenth birthday.

So boring were the months after I had withdrawn from school that in September I enrolled in a small Catholic high school a few miles from Ramsey. I had thought I would be able to stick it out until I was old enough to enlist in the Marine Corps without parental approval, but by the time the football season had ended—football had temporarily replaced airplanes as the love of my life—school was a lost cause. I withdrew for the second time, and a short while thereafter borrowed fifty dollars from my mother and went to Florida for the winter. There I obtained a job as a mate on a fifty-three-foot charter fishing boat, operating out of Stuart during the early part of the season, and from the Pelican Yacht Club in Fort Pierce during the latter part. It was a great life: days spent out in the Gulf Stream chasing sailfish, dolphin, and king mackerel, and an occasional trip to Bimini or Nassau for a few days of fishing for marlin and tuna; nights spent at the dog track in Palm Beach, or at yacht-club parties and dances in Fort Pierce. And to top it all off, I lived rent-free aboard the boat, $125,000 worth of air-conditioned comfort. I could have stayed with the boat when it was moved north to South Carolina for the summer fishing season, but one week after my eighteenth birthday I returned to New Jersey and joined the Marines. (The juvenile authorities did expunge my probation record so that I could enlist, as the judge had told me they would do. However, the Marine Corps had already investigated and cleared the enlistment.)

My first duty assignment after boot camp was to the Marine Corps Air Station at Opa Locka, Florida, northwest of Miami. Airplanes had returned to my life, and every spare minute I had I was out on the flight line pestering pilots for a ride, anywhere, in anything. If it had wings and would get more than five feet off the ground, I wanted a ride in it.

One of the officers in my outfit was Captain Edward McMahon, a young reserve officer called to active duty because of the Korean War. Today, he is a lieutenant colonel in the

Marine Corps Reserve, but is better known to millions of television fans as Ed McMahon, Johnny Carson's announcer and sidekick on the *Tonight Show.*

The Marines were not quite certain what to do with me. I had scored exceptionally high marks on my written tests, and the preliminary indications were that I would be sent to an aviation ordnance school, a dreadful possibility to which I was not looking forward. I beat the assignment people to the punch, volunteering for parachute training at the Marine Corps Aviation and Technical School, at Quantico, Virginia. There, in twenty-six weeks, I was taught everything there was to know about parachutes, from their manufacture to their use. As part of this training, we were required to make a series of free-fall jumps from altitudes ranging up to a maximum of 2,500 feet, using parachutes we ourselves had prepared for the purpose. Never in military history have parachutes been inspected and packed more carefully than ours.

I had known prior to submitting my request for training that the school would require parachute jumps before graduation; indeed, the opportunity to make these jumps was the prime factor in my decision to apply. It was something I wanted to do. The Marines had disbanded the last of their paratroop units after the Second World War—they were the first to see the future of the helicopter as a troop carrier—which meant that I would be one of a very small group of Marines able to boast of having gone through jump school, as paratroop training is known. Moreover, mine was the last class which would go through a jump school operated by Marines for Marines—future classes were to be trained in the Navy school at Lakehurst, New Jersey. Finally, graduation would entitle me to wear the gold wings of a parachute rigger, the official designation for technicians.

Mentally, jump school was no great problem—the classroom work was easy—but the physical training was exhausting. Each morning before breakfast we went through a thirty-minute period of calisthenics, then ran three miles in close military formation. In the late afternoon, after classes, we performed another thirty minutes of exercises; ran five miles—by day's end we had run up and down practically every street on the base— then spent an hour working on the actual mechanics of jumping: how to leave the aircraft; how to land—practiced by jumping frontward, backward, and sideward from a fifteen- foot tower; and how to control the parachute during descent. Our instructors also developed an interesting technique for giving us a practical lesson in the hazard of landing in a strong wind: a propeller-driven fighter plane was parked, engine idling, at the edge of a weed-covered field adjoining an auxiliary runway. Then a student, parachute strapped on, lay down on the ground directly behind the plane. When the engine was revved up to full power, the student pulled the ripcord and the prop wash sent him for a ride, bouncing and skittering across the field. The idea was to pull the lines of the parachute in such a way that the canopy collapsed, ending the ride—easier said than done. Our instructors preferred to conduct this exercise immediately after a rainstorm, when the field was a sea of mud.

The majority of the forty men in my class arrived at the school in reasonably good physical condition, but none of us were quite prepared for those first few weeks of running. Nothing prevented a man from dropping out of formation when he could run no farther; nothing, that is, but his pride. No man wanted to be the first to quit, to admit that he was not as good a man as the others; so with dry mouths, burning eyes, leaden feet, and lungs feeling as though they were stuffed with needles, we huffed and puffed and sweated along, each man watching those around him for signs of weakness, each thinking to himself: I'll be goddamned if I'll be the first to quit. If these other bastards can keep going, so can I. And thus it went, mile after mile, day after day, until suddenly there came a day—for each man his own special day—when we had run our three miles, or five, and we were no longer huffing and puffing. When that day arrived, we knew we had got past the major obstacle on the road to graduation, and that actually jumping out of the plane would be little more than a formality.

Most people probably think it takes a great deal of a special brand of courage to go to the open door of an airplane, look down at a frozen, checkerboard landscape sliding by, and then step out. Not so; it is as easy as jumping into a cold swimming pool. For twenty-six weeks we worked toward our goal, knowing from the opening day of school the exact date, time, and place we would make our first jump. When the big moment finally arrived, and the light beside the door flashed from red to green, we were so eager to get out and get it over with that the Green Bay Packers could not have blocked us. I was the third man out the door—we had drawn positions from a hat; and from green light to the jolt of the chute popping open—it pops open with a sound like a cannon—the only things I remember are that the plane's engine made a godawful loud noise in the cold, thin air; and that the air blast from the propeller was as cold as a polar bear's nose. The temperature that day was seventeen degrees. I do not recall going out the door, or pulling my ripcord, but when I landed it was clenched tightly in my right hand. Tradition had it that anyone who lost his ripcord bought everyone else in the class a drink.

In addition to the parachute training, I was given a complete schooling in the maintenance and use of every piece of survival equipment carried aboard Marine Corps aircraft, from life rafts to radios, from oxygen systems to medical kits. Then I was shipped off to the El Toro Marine Corps Air Station, south of Santa Ana, California.

A strange place, California, like a zoo for people, into which they have brought a matched set of every sort of oddball the world has produced. But it was even more fun than my previous winter in Florida had been, and when after a few months the Marine Corps transferred me to Hawaii, I hated to leave. I had met a girl in California, a beautiful redhead, and had I not been transferred I would have married her. Romance, however, as I soon learned, is not something easily sustainable through the facilities of the United States Postal Service. The last I heard, from her mother, my lovely redhead had married another Marine and had gone off to live in Cleveland.

Using Hawaii as a jumping-off point, my new outfit, a Marine transport squadron flying the military version of the DC-4 and DC-6 aircraft, made regular flights throughout the Pacific and the Far East. The squadron was in fact divided into two sections: one section operated from an airfield eight miles west of Honolulu; the other section operated from Itami, Japan, on an air base the Japanese had used during the Second World War. While we were in Japan, our barracks were the same unpainted wooden buildings which had once housed kamikaze pilots, and the airfield control tower, a concrete blockhouse structure, still bore the pockmark scars of twenty-millimeter cannon fire. The airfield had been a prime target during the latter stages of the war.

The first thing I learned upon arriving in Hawaii was that I was a parachute technician in a squadron which had no parachutes. As a matter of policy, our aircraft did not carry parachutes, since all of our flights were over water. The theory was that in the event of trouble, it was better to have everyone stay with the plane during a forced landing on the water, a relatively safe procedure. To have from ten to fifty people parachute into the middle of the Pacific Ocean, where they would be scattered for miles, would only complicate matters. Moreover, the life rafts, each made to accommodate twenty men, were in the airplane, and they could not be parachuted with the people.

The result of the no-parachute policy was that there was not much for us parachute technicians to do, besides maintaining the other aircraft survival equipment, conducting training exercises at the base swimming pool for the flight crew members, and teaching them the use of the equipment. For a while I drove a staff car, chauffeuring the executive officer; and at other times I worked on the flight line, driving a tractor used to tow the aircraft, or driving a gasoline truck loaded with six thousand gallons of 145-octane aviation gas. Driving one of those monsters around a flight line, where there is always a propeller whirling or a jet engine spitting flames, is nearly as big a thrill as flying without a parachute.

My favorite job was working as a flight crew member, and it was in that capacity that I finally made it to Korea on June 19, 1953. From the afternoon in 1950, when I first heard the news of the American commitment to defend South Korea, it had taken me eight days short of three years to get from New Jersey to a tiny mountaintop airstrip known only as K-6, and all I had to show for my three-year ambition was two more ribbons for my chest—the Korean Service Medal, and the United Nations Service Ribbon—but therein lies a story.

About two or three months after my first trip to Korea, I was examining my service record folder in our headquarters in Hawaii, checking some minor point, when I noticed that my records listed me as authorized to wear a bronze battle star on the Korean Service Ribbon, signifying my participation in a major engagement with the enemy. That was news to me; I had neither seen an enemy—except possibly a Japanese taxi driver— nor known a battle had been in progress while I was in Korea. When I inquired at the records desk, the sergeant told me there had been no mistake. "You're entitled to it, Smitty, you're a hero, don't knock it." I did not pursue the matter, but I have always regretted having been in a battle in which to this day I do not know who fought whom, when, or where. It must have been a brief battle, however, since the war ended eight days after my arrival in Korea.

Our aircraft made regular daily flights between Japan and Korea, carrying military mail, supplies, replacement troops, and some seriously wounded men being brought to hospitals in Japan. Other places on our scheduled routes were: Johnston Island, Kwajalein, Guam, Okinawa, Formosa, Hong Kong, Midway Island, and Manila. During 1954, in the months prior to the fall of Dien Bien Phu, we flew into what is now North Vietnam, in logistical support of the French. The majority of our cargoes were ammunition and medical supplies picked up at the Sangley Point Naval Air Station in the Philippines. Some of the cargoes were dropped by parachute. These flights, however, were not something we advertised, since the United States was not "officially" involved; for the record we were there to support and supply the American diplomatic mission.

I was discharged from the Marine Corps in November 1954, having spent the last four months of service in military hospitals in Hawaii, California, Texas, and Pennsylvania, undergoing twice daily examinations for a hearing loss in my left ear. The condition was thought to have been engendered by a combination of high-altitude flying in unpressurized aircraft and exposure on the flight line to the high-pitched sounds of jet engines. Since my discharge, I have lost all hearing in that ear, for which I receive a small monthly compensation from the Veterans Administration.

I returned to my family's home in Ramsey after my release from service, but soon became bored and disillusioned with life as a civilian. Most of my friends from high-school days, who had gone into service when I did, had not yet been discharged, and those who had remained at home were married and settled down. Then, too, after nearly two years in the frantic, swinging cities of the Far East, Ramsey was boredom to the *n*th degree. The work that was available, compared to flying, seemed a waste of time, but with my parents nagging day and night—"Get a job." "Did you get a job yet?" "When are you going to get a job?" "Everyone else has a job." "Why don't you have a job?"—I could not very well loaf at home until I had found what I wanted to do. So, with a "job" apparently the acme of small-town respectability, I got jobs, lots of them. Within a year, I had been a sewing-machine salesman, drinking gallons of coffee with millions, it seemed, of bored housewives, but selling few machines; a truck driver; a high-school football coach; a now-and-then bartender; an "assistant" to one of the local bookies; and a machinist. It was a desultory life. At one point I gave some thought to writing a book, a novel based upon my experiences in service, but I gave up hope of doing that at home; writing a book, one of the most difficult yet satisfying of all labors, does not *look* like a job—"What does your son do?" "He is writing a book." "Oh, doesn't he have a job?"

I enjoyed most my brief stint as a football coach. Don Bosco Prep had abandoned the sport following the 1949 season, for financial reasons, but had decided to field a team again for the 1955 season—the school's enrollment had grown to nearly seven hundred. When I heard the news, I immediately volunteered to join the coaching staff, and my offer was accepted. I was given the task of coaching the freshman team, instilling in the boys some sense of the fundamentals of the game, and in addition I was responsible for coaching the varsity's defensive backfield. Few of the boys had ever played football on an organized basis, and it was a great challenge to attempt to teach them defensive theories in the short time I had to do so. We spent more time at a classroom blackboard than we did on the practice field, and those weeks were among the happiest of my life, until it was all spoiled by an unfortunate incident.

One afternoon after practice, a few weeks into the football season, I was summoned to the office of the director of athletics, a priest. He advised me that one of the boys on my freshman team had left his wristwatch on a table in the team's dressing room, and when he had returned the watch was gone. The priest asked if I knew anything about it—a rather disingenuous way of asking if I had stolen it. I told him I had never bothered to wear a watch, adding that if I ever decided to adopt the fashion I would buy one. It was clear from his look that he did not believe me, but he said no more about it.

The following afternoon, when I arrived for practice, I was again summoned to the athletic director's office; this time, however, the priest was all smiles, apologies, and handshakes. The boy's watch had been found. He had left it in his dormitory washroom, not on the table in the team's dressing room. "I'm terribly sorry," the priest told me. "It was foolish of me to have suspected you of such a thing."

"Yes, Father, it was foolish," I replied, "because now that this matter has been cleared up, you'll have to find your-

self a new football coach. I quit." And with that, I walked
out.


In the late summer of 1955, disenchanted with the way
my life was going, I took the federal civil service examination
of the Border Patrol of the United States Immigration and
Naturalization Service. The night after taking the examination,
I went with another fellow, a Ramsey police officer, to a party
in a nearby town. When I walked into the party, the first thing
I saw was a girl who knocked my eyeballs out.

Eighteen years old, five foot seven, with green-flecked gray
eyes, auburn hair tied back into a pony tail, and a *Playboy*
fold-out figure, she was as lovely as a kitten and as timid as
a bird. She was also, I decided right then and there, going to
be Mrs. Smith.

The Immigration and Naturalization Service requested
early in 1956 that I advise them if it was my intention to accept
an appointment. I had placed first on the competitive examination. It was just what I wanted, and I was ready to go; but
Patricia, the girl I was planning to marry, was dead-set against
it. The plans for our wedding had been made, and to accept
the appointment would have meant packing up and moving to
El Paso, Texas, the site of the service's training school. Patricia
did not object to advancing the wedding date—she had been
ready to elope the second week after we had met—but the idea
of living in Texas left her cold. "It is a nice place to visit,
but . . ." Reluctantly, I rejected the appointment.

I had a very good job as a machinist, earning a hundred
and sixty a week with overtime, and the first few months of
our marriage worked out reasonably well. We had been living
in a furnished apartment, but Patricia, who was well on her
way to becoming a mother, wanted a place of her own before
the baby was born. One night, a friend took us to look at a
house trailer on display at a small trailer park two miles from
my family's home in Ramsey.

I had always pictured house trailers as tiny uncomfortable things, suitable only for camping trips. To my surprise, our friend showed us a forty-five-foot trailer with two bedrooms, tile bath, fully equipped electric kitchen with birch cabinets, wall-to-wall carpeting, central hot-air heating, and wood paneling throughout. My wife decided she wanted it. We moved in a few weeks later.

Chief among the reasons Patricia wanted us to have a home of our own was the fact that our marriage had begun to run into trouble. She hoped that a new home and the birth of our child would bring about a change for the better. *I* was the trouble with the marriage: immature, unsettled, totally unprepared for the responsibilities involved, which I sought to evade, spending most of my time with my old cronies from my bachelor days. A young fellow by the name of Joseph Gilroy, two years younger than I, was my number-one crony.

Gilroy had been my best buddy before my marriage. Six foot tall, with curly blond hair, he had a good job and earned plenty of money, but judging from what I saw of him, he did not own a suit, a white shirt, or a tie. To the best of my knowledge, the only time Gilroy "dressed up" during the three years I knew him was when he served as an usher at my wedding. Whenever I saw him, and that was every day, he would be wearing an old flannel shirt and gray work pants. That was his uniform. Possibly related to this is the fact that not once in three years was he with a girl in my presence, nor did I ever hear of him having a date. He was extremely shy, and seemed perfectly content to spend his nights drinking beer with the boys. I did not give it a thought.

My wife was incredibly patient with me. She must have loved me greatly. Practically every night I would leave her at home while I went out drinking, bowling, or simply to sit in a local gas station, talking the night away. When I returned home, often in the early hours of the morning, sweet, sad-faced Patricia would be waiting, pretending she had not been too lonely. I realized only much too late what those nights must have been like for her; sitting home alone, wondering where

I had gone, who I was with, what I was doing, and imagining the worst. The heartache I must have caused her is the greatest regret of my life. She deserved better.

Our daughter, named Patricia Anne, after her mother, was born two days before Christmas, 1956. She was unusually pretty, and a great delight to me. Seventy-two days later I was in jail, charged with murder.

# CHAPTER FOUR

**I WAS AT MY MOTHER-IN-LAW'S HOME IN** Ridgewood, a town eight miles south of Ramsey, when the police came for me. I was in Ridgewood with my wife because she had insisted that we spend the night with her mother, saying she was afraid to remain overnight in our unlocked house trailer a mile from the murder scene. A few days earlier, she had gone out and closed the door behind her, leaving the keys on the kitchen table. I had managed to spring the lock without damaging the door, but it could not be relocked.

We had just got into bed at my mother-in-law's, shortly after eleven o'clock, when the doorbell rang and someone pounded on the door. It was Detective Gordon Graber.

"Are you Edgar Smith?" he asked when I had gone to the door.

"That's right. Who are you?"

"I'm Detective Gordon Graber of the Bergen County Prosecutor's Office. We'd like to ask you a few questions."

"About what?"

"The murder up in Mahwah. You knew the girl, didn't you?"

"Sure, I knew her. So ask."

"We'd like you to come up to the Mahwah Police Head-quarters."

By this time my wife had joined me at the door. She asked the detective why they wanted to question me. "It's just routine," he told her. "We are questioning all those who knew the girl." I went to get dressed, leaving Graber piously assuring my wife that it was "nothing, just routine, nothing at all for you to be alarmed about."

I dressed quickly, not even bothering to put on a jacket, and after telling my wife to return to bed, went with the detective to his car parked in front of the house. Finding Gilroy sitting in the front seat with another detective, I said: "Hi, Joe, what's happening?" Gilroy remained silent.

It was a quiet ride to Mahwah, so quiet that I almost fell asleep in the back seat. I should have. The next time I would get some sleep would be twenty-one hours later, in a cell in the Bergen County Jail.

Assistant Prosecutor Fred Galda was sitting behind the desk, looking up at me in his most stern, official manner. Bergen County Prosecutor Guy Calissi—thin, bald-headed, and looking as if he had a permanent case of indigestion—had arrived a few minutes earlier and was standing by the filing cabinets with Chief of Detectives Stewart and Captain De-Marco. Chiefs Smith of Mahwah and Voss of Ramsey stood by the windows, talking quietly with Captain Wickham. Several other officers, patrolmen from the two towns, all in civilian clothes, sat on the wooden fence. The first team was in the game.

The small room was crowded, and more than a bit stinking from the cigars Prosecutor Calissi and Captain DeMarco were alternately smoking and chewing. Gilroy was not present. He had been left outside, sitting in the courtroom with Detectives Sinatra and Garabedian.

Assistant Prosecutor Galda, without a single word to indicate that I had any right to remain silent, or to have the advice of an attorney, led off the questioning: "Before we begin, Mr. Smith, would you like to sit?"

"I'll stand."

"Fine, as you wish. We are all friends here. Now, as we understand it, you borrowed Joseph Gilroy's automobile Monday night, is that correct?"

"Correct."

"Why did you borrow the car?"

"Mine was having some transmission work done."

"No, I don't think you understand," Galda said. "We want to know why you took the car instead of asking Gilroy to take you wherever you wanted to go."

"Oh, that's no problem. Joe wanted to get home for supper. I had to get some kerosene or heating fuel. I didn't know just how long it would take because the heating unit in my house trailer wasn't working."

"Did you get kerosene?"

"No. Kerosene isn't easy to find these days, so I went up to Moore's Truck Stop, on the highway in Mahwah, and bought five gallons of number one diesel fuel. It's the same thing as heating fuel. I got a five-gallon can full, in a can I borrowed from Tony's Amoco."

"Describe the can, please."

"It was a round, Amoco hydraulic fluid can, about twelve to fourteen inches in diameter, about sixteen high."

"Then what did you do?"

"I went home and worked on the heater. I thought the tank was low, that's why I picked up the five gallons. The oil man was due the next day."

"Where do you live?" Captain DeMarco asked from the back of the room.

"Bogert's Trailer Ranch, on Pulis Avenue, over in Fardale. I have a new house trailer I bought last December," I replied, turning to look at the officer as I spoke.

Captain DeMarco was a small man—five-nine, one hundred and fifty pounds, with dark wavy hair, an olive complexion, and a round, flat face. A two-inch cigar stub jutted pugnaciously from beneath a thin black mustache. There was an indefinable something about the man which made him *look* like a detective, and one who knew his business.

"Is that the place down near the murder scene? About a mile away?" he asked.

"That's it."

"All right," Galda said. "Go ahead, what happened with the heater? Did you get it working?"

"No, the damn thing wouldn't start. It was cold in the trailer, so I told my wife I'd get some more fuel oil. If it didn't work after that, the hell with it, we'd go down to her mother's for the night. I had been sick on and off for a day or two. I was in no mood to play with the heater all night."

"You were sick? What was wrong with you?"

"I don't know. A virus or something."

"Fine. Did you go for more kerosene?"

"Yes. I tried the Fardale Esso station on Wyckoff Avenue. They didn't have any, but the woman who was there said I could get some at Secor's Sunoco—I hadn't known that—on the highway in Ramsey, right by Pellington's Milk Bar."

"What time did you get to—what place is that?"

"Secor's Sunoco. S-E-C-O-R-S. I got there about eight-twenty, maybe eight-thirty. After getting another five gallons of kerosene, I headed for home."

Prosecutor Calissi cut in: "What time was that?"

"Eight-thirty, eight-forty, probably about eight-forty or a few minutes later. I figure a few minutes later because I got home about five to nine."

"How do you know that?" Galda asked, picking up the questioning. "Are you certain?"

"Pretty close. I fiddled with the heater for ten minutes at the most. Then I gave up and decided to ask Gilroy to drive me, my wife, and baby to Ridgewood. I called Joe at nine-ten. I looked at the electric clock on the range in the kitchen."

At this point, Prosecutor Calissi walked over, sat on the corner of the desk and, looking up at me, asked: "What happened on the way home? Did you stop anywhere, or see anyone along the way?"

I thought about the prosecutor's question for a few seconds, trying to measure the situation. I knew just about what Gilroy could have told him, but I was bothered by what Hommell had told me earlier in the day: that the police knew from tire tracks found at the sandpit that a Mercury had been there. It seemed obvious to me that the police had matched the tracks to the tires on Gilroy's automobile, and had picked him up for questioning. I did not know then—nor would I until more than a month later—that he had gone to the police voluntarily to report the bloodstain in the automobile.

Another concern for me was the fact that I had told Gilroy that I had thrown my pants away after having been sick. I was certain that Joe had told the police about that.

I was in a most difficult position. I felt at the time, as a matter of loyalty and friendship, that I had to clear Gilroy by assuming responsibility for being the driver of his automobile when the tire tracks were made in the sandpit, while at the same time explaining my presence there, as well as my reason for discarding my pants; and, until I knew what Hommell had told the police, I could not, *for reasons which later will become apparent*, tell the truth.

I say that I *had* to do these things because I thought at the time that I had no other choice. What I did not know, for the simple reason that the police did not bother to tell me, was that I had the right, the *absolute* right, not to answer their questions. Had I known of that right, or the right to have the advice of an attorney, I would have shut my mouth then and there. But being unaware of my rights, and facing interrogation by a roomful of hostile police officers for the first time in my life, I did the most stupid thing I could have done: I lied.

"Well, on the way home I started to get sick," I told the prosecutor. "I had been sick for several days. I didn't want to mess up Gilroy's car, so when I got near St. Paul's Church on Wyckoff Avenue, I stopped real quick and threw up at the edge of a wooded area alongside the church."

Prosecutor Calissi did not say a word. He just sat there, swiveling his cigar around in his mouth, staring at me and waiting for me to continue. I lied again.

"I took the back route home after that—Young's Road, Chapel Road—just in case I got sick again. When I got to Chapel Road, near the sandpit, I began feeling sick again. I turned into the dirt road to the sandpit, went in one car length or so, and threw up again. Then I got back in the car and went home." That, I thought, would explain the tire tracks, at least for the time being.

The prosecutor frowned, mulling over my tale. Then, with a trace of a self-satisfied smile on his face, he said: "That's fine," and got up and returned to lean on the filing cabinets.

As the prosecutor walked back to his leaning post at the filing cabinet, Galda, who had sat by silently during our exchange, resumed the questioning: "What happened after you got home?"

"Well, the heater still wouldn't work, so I phoned Gilroy and asked him to drive me to Ridgewood. He agreed. I picked him up close to nine-thirty."

"What did you and Gilroy talk about after you picked him up?" Calissi asked, again walking over to sit on the desk.

Now I knew what Gilroy had told them, and that they did not know anything else. I decided to stick with that story and continue stalling. That was my second mistake.

"I told Joe that I had messed up my pants when I had gotten sick, and that I had thrown them away."

"Where did you throw them?"

"Just past the stone bridge on Pulis Avenue," I said, this time telling the truth.

"And what did you do with the shoes you were wearing that night?"

That surprised me. The shoes were the last thing on my mind. They were old and falling apart, but perhaps good enough for work if new soles and heels were put on them, so I had taken them to the shoemaker to be repaired.

"I threw them away. The shoemaker said they weren't worth repairing, that new soles and heels would tear loose around the edges because the undersoling was shot. I threw them in a garbage can."

"What shoemaker? And what garbage can?" Galda asked.

"The old guy in town. Nick something or other. Right in the middle of town. After going to the shoemaker, I went over to Robbie's Corral for a cup of coffee. Robbie has a side door that goes out to an alley, and behind his place is a string of garbage cans, his and those of the other stores. So I walked back after having coffee and dumped the shoes."

Captain DeMarco, silent since asking me where I lived, walked over and asked: "How did you get that scrape on the back of your index finger?"

"Oh, that. That's from an automobile tailpipe. It's nothing. I was putting on a new hanger, the thing the pipe hangs on, and the kid helping me shoved the pipe backward too soon. The end of the pipe, the mouth, scraped my finger. It's okay."

While DeMarco was examining my finger, Prosecutor Calissi was whispering to Galda. When he had finished, he turned to Captain DeMarco and said: "Take Smith outside and bring in Gilroy."

I was taken to the front of the courtroom and told to sit at one end of a long, narrow table. Gilroy, who had been sitting at the other end, was taken into the office. I lit a cigarette given me by one of the Ramsey patrolmen as I had left the office, and looked around. Only two other persons were in the room—a reporter from the *Bergen Evening Record,* who sat dozing in a chair, and Detective Sinatra, who stood in the doorway leading to the stairs. I had acquired a "bodyguard."

As I sat there in the courtroom, watching the smoke from my cigarette curl lazily to the ceiling, and listening to the hiss and rattle of the old, half-rusted radiator behind me, I tried to decide what I was going to do. The prosecutor knew that I had lied about being sick. It was clear, however, that he had not made up his mind about Gilroy. Perhaps the prosecutor thought I was lying to protect him. That seemed likely, but I knew that sooner or later they would look for the pants, and when they found them, there would be trouble.

Gilroy was questioned for approximately ten minutes, and when he was returned to the courtroom, Captain DeMarco approached me and said: "Smith, you're going to take a ride. We want you to show us where you threw your pants, and where you were sick. Do you mind?"

"Do I have a choice?" I asked, wondering why he did not mention the shoes.

"Nobody gets choices in murder cases."

It was a few minutes past midnight when we left the Mahwah Police Headquarters. Captain Wickham was in the front seat with Detective George O'Har of the prosecutor's office, who was driving. I was in the back seat with Detective Sinatra, who had become my bodyguard-shadow. As we drove along toward Ramsey, Sinatra and Wickham questioned me, asking the same questions I already had answered. By this time, for lack of any better idea, I had resolved to stick with the story I had told at the start.

The ride to St. Paul's Church, on Wyckoff Avenue—about midway between the center of town and the Zielinski home—took only a few minutes, ten at the most. When we arrived, all of us got out of the car. Captain Wickham, who was carrying a large, portable spotlight, asked me where I had thrown up.

"Over there," I said, pointing to a spot in a wooded area alongside the church. It looked as good as any other place.

Wickham switched on the light and began examining the ground in the area to which I had pointed. After five minutes he turned to me and said: "I don't see anything but dead leaves." I remained silent, and after one more sweep of the area with the light, he asked: "Are you sure this is the place?"

"Pretty sure. I didn't pay that much attention."

"Where was it you told the prosecutor you threw the pants?"

"Pulis Avenue, right near the stone bridge."

"Okay, let's take a look over there."

Pulis Avenue, a narrow, winding road, crosses Wyckoff Avenue about a quarter of a mile past the Nixon residence. We turned right onto Pulis Avenue, heading west, and as we did so Captain Wickham asked: "Where did you throw your pants?"

"Just this side of the bridge."

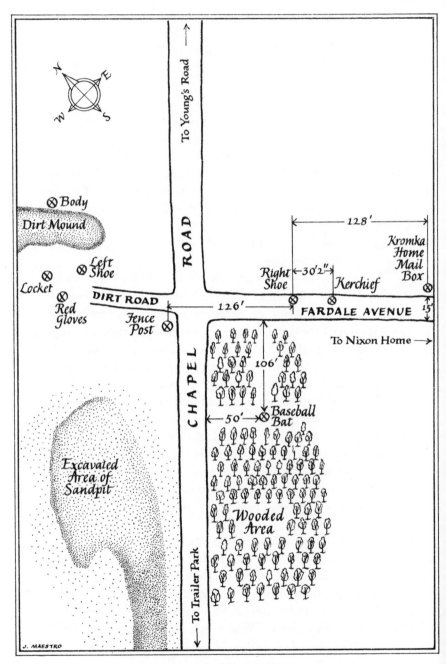

Map 2. The Murder Scene.

"How far is that?" Detective O'Har asked.

"Oh, about four or five hundred yards from where we turned," I replied. "There it is, up ahead, by the fence on the right."

O'Har pulled the car over onto the shoulder of the road and stopped at the beginning of a white rail fence. As he did so, I tried to think of how I would explain the condition of the pants when we found them. I had no doubt that we would find them.

"Right over there," I told Wickham, pointing to three garbage cans standing by the fence, "right by those cans—I think."

"Don't you know?"

"Well, I didn't stop. I had them rolled up on the seat. The car window was open, and when I came across the bridge I saw the cans and threw the pants in that direction."

"Are you sure these are the cans?"

"As sure as I can be. There are only two houses along here and the other one is back over the bridge, so there couldn't be any other cans."

"Okay, let's look around," Wickham said, opening the car door and stepping out. Each of us followed, Sinatra sticking to me like a postage stamp. As we watched, Wickham searched along the shoulder of the road for fifty or sixty feet on either side of the row of cans. He did not find the pants. "There's nothing here," he said. "You're sure you're not mistaken?"

"Hell, yes. They must be here somewhere. Maybe someone picked them up and threw them in one of the garbage cans. Take a look."

Each of the cans was empty. There obviously had been a garbage collection that day. It had never occurred to me that we would fail to find the pants. Perhaps, I thought, the garbage men had picked them up, or someone had found them and for some reason had not put them in the garbage; but neither possibility seemed likely, not with everyone in the area knowing of the murder. I was genuinely puzzled. Only one person knew where I had thrown them, and I could see no reason for *him* to have wanted to pick them up.

Wickham was furious. "They're not in any of the cans. They're all empty. What the hell are you trying to pull with us?"

"Look, goddammit, I told you where I threw them. If they're not here, it's not my fault." I was as angry as he, and twice as confused.

"Both of you take it easy," Detective O'Har ordered. "Let's take a look at the other place where you said you threw up, okay, Smith?"

"Yeah, sure, but keep this guy off my back."

Wickham, shining the spotlight in my face, asked: "That's over by the sandpit, isn't it?"

"You keep shining that goddam light in my eyes like that and I won't be able to find myself."

"Don't worry, Smitty," Sinatra said, putting his hand on my shoulder, "you aren't going to get lost."

The ride to the sandpit took four or five minutes. After returning to the car, we continued along Pulis Avenue, turned right on Chapel Road, and drove another half mile to the sandpit entrance. Again, the four of us got out of the car.

"Where was it you threw up?" Wickham asked.

"Right there by the entrance. Right along the side of the road where the driveway begins."

"Which side of the drive, right or left?"

"Left, I think."

"We'd better find something pretty soon," Wickham said as he began examining the ground with the spotlight.

The search revealed nothing but weeds and a couple of discarded cigarette packs. Looking up toward the sandpit, partly illuminated by the reflection of Wickham's spotlight, I could see several empty plaster-of-paris bags lying in the driveway, the ground near them sprinkled white where some of their contents had spilled. I knew what the presence of the empty bags signified—the police had been making plaster casts of impressions found in the ground. Obviously, Hommell *had* been trying to warn me about the tire tracks.

Wickham was still examining the ground when O'Har,

who had been leaning on the front fender of the car, called out: "Let's go, Captain. We're not going to find anything here."

"That's a good idea," I answered. "I'm freezing." I had not taken a jacket with me when I had left home, and during our searches I had been wearing only a light woolen shirt. The temperature must have been down around twenty-five, and a bitter cold wind was blowing.

O'Har and Wickham were silent as we drove back to Mahwah Police Headquarters. Sinatra, however, seemingly unperturbed by the entire affair, questioned me and asked me to repeat my story "one more time." By the time we had reached the police station, I was beginning to believe my own lies.

Gilroy was sitting at his end of the table when we walked into the courtroom. After telling me to sit at the other end of the table, and warning me not to talk to Gilroy—"If you want to talk, talk to the prosecutor"—O'Har and Wickham went into the office to report. Sinatra remained behind to guard the door to the stairs. Five minutes later Wickham returned and told me I was wanted in the office.

"Smith, we want you to go with Captain DeMarco and show him where you threw your shoes," Prosecutor Calissi said as I entered the room. "Mr. Galda, Captain DeMarco, Mr. Graber, and Lieutenant Haight of the Mahwah police will go with you. Is that okay with you?"

"It doesn't make much difference if it's not, does it?"

"Come on, Smith, let's get going," Galda said in response to my question.

There were six of us in the car on the second trip. Assistant Prosecutor Galda, Lieutenant Haight, and Captain DeMarco were in the front seat, the latter driving; I was squeezed into the back seat between Detectives Graber and Sinatra.

Ramsey was dark and deserted as DeMarco, following my directions, turned off the main street onto Mechanic Street, a one-way dead end leading to the railroad-station parking lot. The garbage cans, thirteen of them, still stood where they had been earlier in the day when I had thrown away my shoes. DeMarco waited until everyone had got out of the car before directing me to point out the can into which I had thrown my shoes.

"I wasn't paying that much attention. One of the cans near the middle, I think. Most of them were packed full."

The shoes were in the ninth can in from the street, just as I had left them. Captain DeMarco, taking the shoes out of the can and removing several bits of paper sticking to the soles, returned to the street, held them in front of the automobile headlights, and asked me to identify them.

"They're mine. You can see they're not much worth repairing."

"What's that on the side?" Galda asked DeMarco, indicating with his finger the outside of the right shoe.

"Yes, I noticed that," DeMarco answered, turning the shoe slightly.

I had been standing to DeMarco's left, Galda on his right, so it was not until he had turned the shoe over in the light that I could see what Galda had pointed to—a tiny spot of blood on the side of the shoe, behind the toe cap and just above the sole.

I started to speak, but Galda cut me off. "Let's go look around where you say you threw the pants." He was grinning from ear to ear.

For the next thirty minutes we repeated the trip I had made previously with Wickham and O'Har, searching unsuccessfully for signs that I had thrown up near St. Paul's Church, and again near the sandpit—I was sticking to that story; and searching on Pulis Avenue for my pants. Having failed to find anything, we returned to Mahwah, arriving there at about two-thirty. I was taken immediately to the office.

Galda, after a whispered conversation with the prosecutor, sat down behind the desk and said: "Okay, Smith, let's begin again. Tell us just exactly where you went and what you did last night."

"Oh, come on," I groaned, "I've told you three times already."

"So tell us again. We like listening to stories."

I told the same story as before, and when I had finished,

Prosecutor Calissi, who had been sitting on the side of the desk with his back to me, turned and asked me to describe the clothes I had worn the night of the murder.

"Well, I had on black shoes; work pants—*gray pants;* a black-and-red striped shirt, vertical stripes; and a dark-blue nylon jacket with white fleece lining."

"Were you wearing gloves?"

"Yes, brown leather."

"Where are those clothes now?"

"You have the shoes, the pants probably went with the garbage men, the shirt and jacket are at my mother-in-law's, and the gloves are probably at home."

"Gordon, you know where his mother-in-law lives. Go pick up the jacket, and make it a quick trip," the prosecutor told Detective Graber. "And look for the gloves," he added as Graber got to the door.

When the detective had gone, Calissi turned to me and asked: "Mr. Smith, would you be willing to take a lie-detector test?"

Two weeks earlier, I had read a newspaper article concerning the unreliability of such tests. The article suggested that the questions and conditions could be tailored to bring about any desired result. I decided to take no chances.

"Not this boy," I replied. "I don't trust you or those tests. I'd have to have my lawyer's advice."

"There's no need for that. If you didn't do anything, you have nothing to worry about. And it can't be used as evidence."

"That's what *you* say. I want to hear it from my lawyer."

Galda did not like that. "This man is the prosecutor of Bergen County," he said. "He knows better than any lawyer."

"That's what you say. I want my lawyer to tell me it's okay."

"What are you going to be, a goddam wise guy?" Galda asked angrily, his face looking like a pickled beet. "You don't need a lawyer."

I could not understand what was making Galda so jumpy. He had appeared supremely confident only a short while before when he had found my shoes. Perhaps that was it, I thought. Perhaps he had been certain that the case was in his hip pocket, but then when my shoes were found right where I had said they would be found, he could no longer assume that the rest of my story was a lie. Whatever it was, our last exchange had left him looking as if he were about to have a coronary. I decided to take a chance.

"If you're looking for a fall guy, why don't you grab Don Hommell?" I asked.

Nothing. Not even a flicker of an eyelid. Galda just sat there and looked at me. It fleetingly occurred to me then that they were interested only in grabbing the first "hot prospect" they got their hands on, and that I was it. They had not interrogated Hommell, I knew that, and now it looked as though they had no intention of doing so. The only alternative I had left was to stick to my story until I could get in touch with my lawyer. Until this moment, asking for my lawyer had been an automatic response, an excuse not to submit to a lie-detector test. Now, however, it was beginning to dawn on me that my lies were painting me into a corner, and that I really *needed* a lawyer.

It was 3:45 a.m. Prosecutor Calissi, seemingly uncertain what to do next, told Detective Garabedian: "Take this guy back and look for his pants. And look where he was sick. This is his last chance."

"Okay, Smith, let's go," Garabedian said wearily.

"Go, hell. You people are out of your minds if you think I'm going to walk around out there and freeze my butt again."

"You refuse to cooperate?" Galda asked.

" 'Cooperate' has nothing to do with it. I've been out there freezing all night, I'm tired, and I feel lousy."

"You're sick?"

"What the hell do you think I've been telling you? I feel rotten, and I've been up all day and all night. I'm not going out again with just this shirt on."

"Suppose I let you wear my overcoat?"

"Well—okay, but this is the last time. I don't understand

what sense there is in running back and forth all night. The garbage collectors must have picked up my pants."

"Fine," Galda said, taking his overcoat from the top of one of the filing cabinets, "take this, and don't ruin it or the state will have to buy me a new one."

"Let's go, Smith, we haven't got all night," Garabedian said.

With the single exception that a different combination of officers went with me—Garabedian, O'Har, and the omnipresent Sinatra—the third trip was similar to the first two. No traces of my having been sick were found, and the pants could not be located.

We had been gone for nearly an hour, and upon our return to Police Headquarters the questioning was resumed. Prosecutor Calissi had gone home, as had the chiefs and the local officers. Galda began speaking as soon as we entered the room: "Well, Mr. Garabedian, any luck this time?"

"Nothing at all," the detective replied. "We looked in all of the places Smith pointed out. Nothing."

"Okay, Smith, what do we do now?" Galda asked me.

"Look, I've been up all day and all night. I've hardly had a thing to eat in the past two days. I feel rotten. Except for riding around in the car, I've been on my feet all night. I don't know what you're going to do now, and frankly I don't give a goddam what you do. All I want is to see my lawyer and get some sleep."

Galda, not at all upset by my angry outburst, quietly said: "Those things can be taken care of later. Right now we want some better answers than we have been getting from you."

"Wonderful," I snapped back sarcastically, "tell me what answers will get you off my back. I'll make some up for you."

Galda did not bat an eye, but Detective Garabedian, who had been sitting on the wooden fence, jumped to his feet. "You're going to give us a wise answer once too often and we're going to kick that attitude right out of you," he shouted, his face a few inches from mine. "Do you understand?"

"Hold it. Sit down, Vahe," Galda said sharply, using

Garabedian's first name. "This guy wants you to slug him."

"If he wants trouble, he'll get it," the detective spat out, his face still close to mine.

"I told you to knock it off," Galda declared. He had got up from behind the desk and had both his hands on Garabedian's shoulders.

The detective, his face tight and flushed, turned and left the office. When he had gone, Galda pointed to a jacket lying on the desk and asked: "Is that the jacket you wore last night?"

I had noticed the jacket as soon as I had entered the room. "That's mine."

"The one you wore Monday night?"

"That's it."

"The night Victoria Zielinski was murdered?"

"I don't know when she was murdered."

"You know it was Monday night, don't you?"

"I don't know anything."

"You're a liar. You were there, and we can prove that you were there," he said. Then, lifting my jacket and revealing a pair of brown pigskin gloves, he asked: "Are these your gloves?"

"Where did you get them?"

"Don't worry about that. Are they yours?"

"They're mine. You can see where the palms are blackened from the kerosene," I said, turning the gloves over, palms up. "So what?"

"That's all we want to know. Now we want a sample of your hair. Captain DeMarco will pull out a few strands. Do you mind?"

"Do I have any choice?"

Captain DeMarco, usually content to stand silently in the background, smoking a cigar, came forward and spoke: "I told you once tonight that you don't get choices."

"I figured that, but I'll pull it out myself."

"No you won't," DeMarco said, "I'll do it."

As the captain pulled a few dozen hairs, a few at a time

from the area above and behind my right temple, Galda told me: "We're going to Hackensack now. Captain DeMarco and Detective Sinatra will take you with them."

"Hackensack? What are we going there for?"

"We've done all we can up here. We can all be much more comfortable and relaxed down in the prosecutor's office. And on the way down Captain DeMarco will take you for some breakfast."

"What about Gilroy? Is he going with us?"

"Gilroy has already gone home," DeMarco answered. "We can get him back if we need him. Why do you ask?"

"Just wondering, that's all." I had known that Gilroy's release would signal the shifting of the full light of suspicion to me. Now he had been released, and I realized that I must take my situation far more seriously than I had done so far.

## CHAPTER FIVE

**THE ROUTE TO THE PROSECUTOR'S OFFICE**
turned out to be a circuitous one. We left Mahwah at 5:30 a.m.,
Detective Sinatra driving. Our first stop was the home of Captain DeMarco, located in Wyckoff, a small town one mile
southwest of Ramsey, separated from Ramsey by the Fardale
section of Mahwah.

"I'm going to take a shower, shave, change my clothes, and
have breakfast," DeMarco told Sinatra as the latter turned the
car into the driveway and stopped. "That should give you and
Smith plenty of time to drive down to the diner in Midland
Park. Do you know how to get there?"

"No, I don't know the area too well."

"I know where it is," I said. "I'll show you if you think
you can trust me."

"I guess we can trust you that far," DeMarco said with a
laugh. Then, handing two one-dollar bills to Sinatra, he
added: "Here, have yourselves a good breakfast. And don't
forget, we have to be in Hackensack by seven o'clock."

The Midland Park Diner—Midland Park being the town
adjoining Wyckoff on the east—was a five-minute drive from
DeMarco's house. Few people were in the diner when we arrived, most of them delivery men and route salesmen, whose
trucks stood in the street outside. As I started toward a seat at
the end of the lunch counter, Sinatra grabbed my arm. "Over
there, in the end booth," he said, pointing.

"Suit yourself. The first thing I want to do is wash up," I
told him, "then have a cup of coffee. I'm beat."

"I'll go with you, but first we'll order breakfast. What do you want?"

"I don't know. My stomach is jumping all over."

The waitress took our orders as soon as we were seated facing each other—Sinatra was cautious—in the booth farthest from the door. The girl did not know who we were, nor why we had to be the only customers to sit in a booth, but she obviously was not pleased that we were forcing her to work by not sitting at the counter like the others. Ignoring the pained expression on her face, Sinatra ordered for us both—scrambled eggs, home-fried potatoes, toast, and coffee. When the waitress had gone, he said: "Okay, let's go wash up while she is getting the order."

The men's room, in the back of the diner, through a door at the end of the counter, was typical of men's rooms in most diners—paper towels, cold water, and no soap. I felt as dirty after washing as I had before, and looking in the mirror I could see I looked as bad as I felt.

On the way back to our booth, as we passed a public telephone hanging on the wall, I asked the detective if I could call my wife or my lawyer.

"Sorry," he replied. "I don't have the authority to permit that."

"Tell you what. My mother-in-law's house is only two blocks from here. How about if we stop on the way back? I could pick up some clean clothes and let my wife know I'm okay."

"Sorry. I can't take you anywhere but here and back to Captain DeMarco's house."

By the time I had finished expressing my opinion of his ancestry, and that of police officers in general, all of which he listened to with equanimity, our breakfast had arrived. It looked delicious, but as I began to eat the eggs, I found that my stomach would not hold them. Either I was still feeling the effect of the virus, or the cumulative tensions of the previous seven hours were beginning to take their toll. It had been a rough night. It would be a rougher day.

"What's wrong? I thought you were hungry," Sinatra asked when he saw me poking at the eggs with my fork.

"Can't eat. My stomach won't sit still."

"Drink the coffee, that will stay down."

I did as he suggested and found that with the coffee I was able to eat a couple of slices of plain toast, but the eggs were too much.

Captain DeMarco was out in the driveway, playing with his dog, a cocker spaniel, when we returned to his house. He appeared fresh and chipper as he approached the car and got in the front seat. He also had another cigar, a new but equally foul-smelling one, clamped between his teeth.

"Good news, Smith," he announced airily, taking the cigar out of his mouth. "Your pants have been found."

"Where, in the garbage dump?"

"Nope. Along the back road to the sandpit. The Ramsey police found them just after daybreak."

Ramsey police? I tried to digest that. Pulis Avenue was a mile from Ramsey. "What were the Ramsey cops doing on Pulis Avenue?" I asked. "That's in Mahwah."

"Oh no," DeMarco replied with a broad grin on his face. "They were found on one of the other roads, in the back part of Ramsey, right where you tried to hide them."

"You're out of your mind. They couldn't have been. I threw them on Pulis Avenue, and I wasn't trying to hide them."

"We'll see about that later. Right now we have to get to Hackensack," he said. Then, to Sinatra: "Let's get going, chauffeur. A nice morning ride will do us all a lot of good."

The ride to Hackensack took twenty minutes. Sitting in the back seat by myself as we drove along, I pondered the meaning of DeMarco's revelations. I was less concerned about the blood I knew was on the pants than by the fact that they had been found some distance from where I had thrown them. I had told the truth about having thrown them on Pulis Avenue, just as I had told the truth about where I had thrown the shoes. Clearly, someone had tried either to do what he thought was a favor to me, or was setting me up for a murder charge. I could not be certain which, but there was one person who knew where I had thrown the pants, and why. I now realized that I should have told the truth about him from the first. Now the police would not believe me and the only way left would be to say as little more as possible, keeping my fingers crossed meanwhile that my wife had enough brains to telephone my family or a lawyer.

DeMarco and Sinatra were silent, and left to my own thoughts I began wondering how much longer I could stick to my story. It had been twenty-two hours since I had got any sleep, and the all-night interrogation had worn me down more than I had realized. It was not until I had an opportunity to sit back and relax in the rear seat of the police car during the ride to Hackensack that I began to feel the weariness in my body. I felt lousy, ached all over, and I was cold.

My thoughts were interrupted by the realization that the car was stopping in front of a small, red-brick house located in one of the less desirable sections of Hackensack. DeMarco, turning to look at me as Sinatra parked the car in front of the house, read the quizzical expression on my face. "I have to stop and see someone," he told me. "You wait here with Detective Sinatra." I did not reply, nor did I believe him.

The captain was in the house for fifteen minutes. During that time, two other members of the prosecutor's staff—Investigators Nunno and Perrapato, the latter soon to become the Democratic mayor of Garfield, New Jersey—drove up. After inquiring as to the whereabouts of Captain DeMarco—"He's inside," Sinatra told them—they, too, entered the house. I did not like it. DeMarco had not stopped merely to "see someone," but all I could do was sit in the car and wait to see what could happen. I did not have long to wait.

DeMarco returned alone to the car a few minutes after the investigators had entered the house. "Smith," he said, "this is the office of Dr. Gilady, the Bergen County Medical Examiner. He is going to examine you to confirm that you have not been mistreated, and that you are not too seriously ill to undergo further questioning. It's just a precaution."

It would have been pointless for me to argue with him, since he had already twice assured me that I was not to be given choices. I had, moreover, reached that level of emotional fatigue at which one finds it easier to go along. So I went along.

Dr. Gilady, an elderly gray-haired man, was waiting for us in his office at the end of a hallway leading straight back from the front door. Investigators Nunno and Perrapato were with him when I entered, DeMarco and Sinatra trailing along behind me.

"Take off your clothes," the doctor commanded, his voice betraying his anger at having been awakened at such an early hour.

The examination was brief and superficial. When I had stripped naked as ordered, the doctor checked my blood pressure, temperature, and respiration, afterward examining me for injuries. The detectives, meanwhile, were examining and searching the clothing I had removed.

"Okay, put your things on when they are done," the doctor told me, indicating the clothing being searched by the officers.

There was no heat in the doctor's office at that hour of the morning, and after standing naked and barefoot on the cold tile floor for twenty minutes, I was shivering like a rabbit by the time my clothing was returned to me.

"A bit chilly, isn't it?" Detective Sinatra asked.

"You'd better believe it," I replied. "I'm freezing."

"We are going to the prosecutor's office now," he said, handing me my shirt. "You can sit in front by the heater when we get back to the car."

"Okay, let's get going," DeMarco ordered. "We haven't got all day."

# CHAPTER SIX

**THE BERGEN COUNTY COURTHOUSE, BUILT** in 1910, is situated a few hundred feet from the west bank of the Hackensack River—a slimy, black cesspool of sludge, garbage, and reeking sewage. We arrived at the courthouse at 8:30 a.m. No one had spoken during the five-minute ride from Dr. Gilady's office, but as Detective Sinatra parked across the street from the broad steps leading to the main entrance, Captain DeMarco cautioned me not to speak to any of the newspaper reporters who, he said, were "always hanging around the office." "I'll take you right into my office," he added. "You can wait there until we are ready for you."

"What do you want me to do?" Sinatra asked.

"You go home and get some rest. I'll call you if we need you for anything," DeMarco replied.

Sinatra, without another word, drove off as soon as DeMarco and I got out of the car. The detective had been my constant companion for eight hours. I did not mourn his departure.

"Let's go, Smitty," DeMarco urged, his hand on my arm.

The captain, his hand still on my arm, leading me across the street, up the steps, and through the main entrance, pointed to a long corridor leading away from us, directly across the rotunda from the door, and said: "That leads to the prosecutor's office."

The clerical staff had not yet arrived for work, and as we walked along, the sound of our footsteps on the marble floor echoing down the empty corridor, I could see to our right and left several empty offices. "Is this part of the prosecutor's office?" I asked.

"Yes," DeMarco replied, "all of these offices along here are part of it. These here"—indicating those on the right—"are the secretary's and legal staff's offices. They won't be in until nine o'clock. These here"—indicating several closed doors on the left—"are the investigator's offices. We go in here," he said, opening the next to last door on the left. "This is my office."

It was not much of an office: approximately eight feet wide and fifteen feet long; two large wooden desks covered with telephone books and a jumble of manila file folders; a couple of extra wooden armchairs, one standing alongside each desk; and two large windows overlooking the fifty or sixty feet of lawn separating the courthouse from the county jail. A detective sat behind the desk farthest from the door.

"Mr. DeLisle," the captain said, addressing the detective sitting at the desk, "this is Mr. Smith. He will wait here with you while I go talk to the prosecutor."

"Fine," the detective replied. Then, pointing to the chair beside his desk, he added: "Sit here, Mr. Smith, and make yourself comfortable. We'll have a little chat while we're waiting." I did as I was told. The detective, noticing that I was looking out at the barred windows of the county jail, asked: "Not a very pleasant view, is it?"

"Not much."

"Terrible place." he said, "I hope you never wind up in there. Would you like a cigarette or anything?"

"Yes. I'd like about three days sleep."

"How long have you been awake?"

"What time is it?"

"Eight-forty."

"I don't know. I guess I've been up twenty-four hours or so."

"Well, perhaps we can get this over quickly. It's up to you whether you cooperate or not."

"What does 'cooperate' mean?"

"Why don't you begin by telling me your story?"

"Man, I've told you people my story half a dozen times. I'm tired of telling it and tired of hearing it."

"But I wasn't with you earlier," he persisted. "I haven't heard it. I'd like to help you get this over with, but I can't if I don't know what you've told the others."

Whether I was stupid, or tired—I do not know which—I really believed that the detective wanted to help me in some way, so I began telling him what I had told the others. He was "Charlie Sincere" in person, nodding his head sympathetically and "yessing" everything I said. I had gotten to the part about throwing my pants away when DeMarco returned. With him was a young fellow carrying a camera—a four-by-five Crown Graphic, the press photographer's type of camera, with rear-loading film plates. The photographer was Ronald Ambler, of the *Bergen Evening Record,* who had been recruited by Chief Stewart to photograph Vickie's body in the sandpit. "This man is going to take some pictures of you, Smith," DeMarco explained. "We want to photograph the scrape on your finger and those on your knees."

Earlier, during the night's questioning, DeMarco had ordered me to roll up my pants legs, and he had found that both of my knees were scraped. The previous night, while pouring fuel oil into the tank of my trailer, I had slipped off a fence post on which I had been balancing on one foot in order to reach the tank. In falling, I had landed in the gravel driveway, scraping my knees.

"What are the pictures for?" I asked DeMarco.

"We merely want a record of your injuries to show that you had them before you came here," he answered. "It's just a precaution, as much for your protection as ours. Sit on the edge of the desk and pull up your pants legs."

I did as ordered, sitting on the desk with my feet on the chair in which I had been sitting.

"Good. Now, put your finger, the scraped one, right next to your knees, so we can get it all in one picture." Again I did as I was told, and the photographer, who had his camera ready to go, quickly snapped two pictures, then hurried from the room. When he had gone, DeMarco instructed me to follow him. "We're going to the prosecutor's office."

The prosecutor's office, at the end of the corridor, was not what one would expect of the office of a major county official. Square, about fifteen by fifteen, with dirty, paint-peeling walls, it looked little better than Captain DeMarco's office. The furniture consisted of a scratched, scarred, and cigarette-burned desk in the rear of the room, facing the door; a three-cushion, green plastic couch just to the right inside the door; and a wooden table about five feet long standing against the right-hand wall, under two windows overlooking a bank and gas station across Hackensack's main business street. Two other windows behind the desk provided a view of the county administration building, behind the courthouse. In the rear left-hand corner of the room, an open door led to an incredibly small, not too very clean lavatory. A red, threadbare carpet completed this picture of official dinginess.

Harry Voss, chief of police of Ramsey, was standing by the desk with Chief Smith of Mahwah when I entered the room. First Assistant Prosecutor Galda stood behind the desk, and was the first to speak: "Over here, Smith"—motioning me to approach the desk—"we want you to take a look at what we found."

I approached as instructed, DeMarco right on my heels, and as I did so, I noticed a small, brown-paper-wrapped parcel lying on the desk, amid a profusion of pencils, ball-point pens, papers, books, manila folders, and medicine bottles and boxes. The top of the desk was a garbage heap. "What do you want me to look at now?" I asked wearily.

Galda did not answer. Instead, clearly savoring the drama of the moment, he slowly and deliberately unwrapped the package, revealing a pair of neatly folded, military-style khaki trousers. He waited, but I stood silently, wondering what the game was. These obviously were supposed to be the pants I had thrown away the night of the murder, but I had worn gray trousers that night, just as I had told the police during the earlier interrogations.

When it became apparent that I had no intention of saying anything, Galda spread the trousers on the desk. The right leg, just above the cuff, was heavily stained with blood. "What about *that?*" he asked, pointing to the blood.

"What about *what?*"

"They're yours, aren't they?"

"The pants or the bloodstains?"

"The pants, goddammit," he roared. "You know goddam well what I mean."

The intensity of his anger brought me wide awake. I had been taking it for granted that he did not seriously expect me to identify the pants, but suddenly I realized that that was exactly what he did expect. I must have been much more tired than I had thought. "Never saw them before in my life," I told him. "They aren't mine."

Before Galda could open his mouth, Chief Voss leaned across the desk and shouted: "You son of a bitch, you know those are your pants. Admit it. We'll give you a break." I was much too tired to do anything but stand there silently.

Galda broke the silence. "Take him back," he told De-Marco. "Take him back. If he wants trouble, he came to the right place."


"All right now, Smith," DeMarco said when we had returned to his office, "we're done fooling around with you. We want some answers, and we want them right now. How did you get that blood all over your pants?"

"I've told you that those are not my pants. Now, I'm not talking about anything else unless you let me talk to my lawyer or my wife."

"Never mind that lawyer stuff, just tell us about the pants, then we'll talk about the lawyer."

"No good. I want my lawyer, then we talk. "

Without another word, the captain turned and left the room. Detective DeLisle, who had been sitting at his desk listening to my exchange with DeMarco, spoke up and suggested that it would be foolish of me to get the captain "all riled up."

"That's just too bad," I told him. "I want to talk to my lawyer and that's all there is to it."

"Who is your lawyer?"

"I want to call Judge Dwyer, from Ridgewood."

DeLisle, plainly impressed by the word "judge," sat erect in his chair. "What kind of judge is he?" he asked warily.

"He's not anymore. He used to be a Bergen County judge— District Court, I think—but everyone still calls him Judge Dwyer."

"Do you know him?"

"Yes. I went to school with his son."

Before DeLisle could reply, Captain DeMarco returned to the office with another detective, Walter Spahr, a younger man—tall, thin, with a hard, pinched face, and short blond hair.

"The prosecutor says you can call your wife to tell her you're okay, but no lawyer," DeMarco told me. "You don't need a lawyer."

"You told me that before, but I still want to call him."

"He says he wants to call a Judge Dwyer from up in Ridgewood. He says he knows him," DeLisle told the captain.

"We're not going to let you bother a lawyer when you don't need one," DeMarco told me. "You call your wife or you don't call. Make up your mind."

It was not much of a choice, so I agreed to call my wife.

"That's being smart. What's the number?" Spahr asked.

I told the detective the number, and when he had picked up the telephone book, I added: "She's at my mother-in-law's, in Ridgewood. It's under the name of Geraldine Johnson."

When Spahr had found the number in the book, he nodded to Detective DeLisle, who had written the number and the address on a piece of paper as I had given them. DeLisle dialed the number, waited until my wife had answered, then handed me the phone.

"Hello, Pat, this is Eddie."

"Hi, are you still in Hackensack?"

"How did you know I'm down here?"

"The police were here this morning. They told me. They think you did it. Are you all right?"

"Sure, I'm fine. Don't worry about me. Everything will be okay."

"But the police said it looks bad for you, Eddie. I'm afraid."

"Don't worry," I said, trying to reassure her. "I'm pretty tired, but I'll be okay. Now listen carefully. They are telling me to make this short, so I'll only explain once. Get yourself downtown to Judge Dwyer's office, Michael Dwyer, across from the movie theater. He has a sign on the office. Tell him who you are, Edgar Smith's wife, tell him what happened, and tell him to get me the hell out of here, or to send someone to get me out." DeMarco was gesturing to me to hang up, that I could not talk any longer, but I went on: "Don't worry about money. Just get down there quick and tell him what I said. Then you get back to your mother's and stay there. Understand?"

"I think so," she replied. "Michael Dwyer, right?"

"That's right. And don't worry. Once I get Judge Dwyer I'll be okay. I have to go now. They want me to hang up. Take care. Will see you soon."

"All right, Eddie. 'Bye now, honey."

Spahr took the phone from my hand and slammed it onto its cradle. DeMarco was displeased, obviously so, but Spahr was raging. "You bastard," he shouted. "What the hell are you bothering a lawyer for? We told you you don't need one."

"Sure you did, and I told you I wanted one."

DeMarco, after telling Spahr and DeLisle to check my story, again stormed out of the room, slamming the door behind him. It was a few minutes past nine, perhaps nine-fifteen, and I thought that if I could stall the detectives for another thirty minutes or so, my lawyer would be there to get them off my back. I was mistaken.

The questioning by Spahr and DeLisle was no different from the interrogation I had undergone all night long: Why did I borrow Gilroy's car? Why did I buy kerosene? What time did I get home? Where had I been sick? Why did I throw my pants away? Where did I throw them? By nine-thirty, I had been awake for twenty-five hours, and the interrogation had been going on continuously for ten hours. I was tired—"beat" would be a better word—and I was ready to fall on my face. My interrogators, who had gotten a few hours sleep during the night, were fresh and wide awake.

"Look, fellas, how about letting me sit down before I fall down?" I asked.

"Are you tired?" Spahr inquired.

"You're damn right I am."

"Just a few more questions," he told me. "You can sit as soon as we get some better answers than you've been giving us. Now, how about telling us how your pants got a mile away from Pulis Avenue?"

And so it went, the detectives asking the same questions, me giving the same answers. Finally, about thirty minutes after the telephone call to my wife, Captain DeMarco returned to the office. As the door opened and I turned my head to see who it was, my heart almost dropped into my socks; my wife was standing in the corridor with Detective Graber.

"What the hell is my wife doing down here?" I demanded. "What are you son of a bitches trying to do?"

"Calm down, Smith," DeMarco said. "Your wife is just here to corroborate your story, that's all."

"Is my lawyer with her?"

"I know nothing about your lawyer. Your wife came down in a police car with Detective Graber."

"You mean you grabbed her before she could get my lawyer for me, don't you?"

"We told you that you don't need a lawyer," DeMarco replied. "When *we* decide you need one, that's when you'll get one."

"Well, I want to talk to her now."

"I'm sorry, you won't be able to see her until we have completed our investigation."

"How long will that be?"

"That's up to you," Detective Spahr answered. "When you cooperate with us you can see your wife, and then she can go home. For her sake, you might as well stop being stubborn."

Leaving me to think that over, DeMarco, Spahr, and DeLisle went to the front of the office, by the door, and held a whispered conference. When it was over, DeMarco walked back to where I was standing and said: "Mr. Spahr is going to take you into the prosecutor's office. I would suggest that you pay very close attention to what he tells you." With that, he left the room.

Spahr, after waiting a few moments, said: "Okay, let's go, Smith." Taking me by the arm, his hand gripping my elbow, the detective led me down the corridor to the prosecutor's office. The corridor was crowded. Twenty-five or thirty newspaper reporters and photographers milled about, but my wife was nowhere in sight.

The prosecutor's office was empty when we entered. Spahr, still gripping my elbow, led me to the table standing against the right-hand window. Pointing to a row of approximately fifteen jars, he asked: "Do you know what that is in those jars, wise guy?"

The jars had not been there earlier when DeMarco had taken me to the office to identify my pants. Each was filled with what seemed to be sand or granular dirt. I had an idea of what they were, but I asked dumbly: "No, what are they?"

"Those jars are your ticket to the electric chair if you don't cooperate," the detective replied coldly. "They are samples of dirt from various parts of the sandpit, from Chapel Road to the dirt mound. We've checked your pants and shoes, and we've recovered bits of sand and dirt to match. We can not only prove that you were in the sandpit, but exactly in what parts you walked."

I did not know where the prosecutor's laboratory was located, or even if he had one. I could not, therefore, be certain as to whether the police could have completed spectroscopic and microscopic examinations in the short time the pants and shoes had been in their possession, but I did know that what Spahr was saying was theoretically possible, and I had to respect that possibility. Later, I would learn that he had been bluffing. No sand or dirt had been recovered from my pants or shoes.

"Well, are you going to cooperate?"

"What pants are you talking about? The pants you people have aren't mine."

"Smith, you must think we're stupid. Your wife wasn't brought down here for a tour of the courthouse. She's already identified your pants, and she is giving us a written statement. You thought you were going to get away with playing around with the Zielinski girl, didn't you? Well, now your wife is going to get even with you. Come on, let's go back to Captain DeMarco's office."

Once back in the other office with Detective DeLisle, Spahr shuffled through a stack of manila folders on one of the desks until he had found the one he was looking for. Holding it in front of my face, he asked: "What does that say?"

There were only two words on the front of the folder, printed in red block letters. "It says 'LEDWON—MURDER,' " I replied. "So what?"

"I'll tell you 'so what,' wise guy. This is the file on a guy who beat his brother-in-law to death in the street. Beat his brains out by banging his head against a curb. He should get the chair for it. I'd give him the chair, but he is getting a break, and do you know why he won't get the chair? He won't because he cooperated. Maybe he'll do a couple of years, three or four maybe, then he'll be back out on the street. We have a great, fair-minded prosecutor in this county. I know, I work for him, and this guy Ledwon knows because he got a break from him. The prosecutor is a great guy, a good Catholic, and a member of the Knights of Columbus. The only people he hates are bookies, so if you cooperate with us you'll get a break like Ledwon did. Now, what do you say?" he asked, almost out of breath. He had delivered his plea with near evangelical fervor.

"I want to see my wife or my lawyer."

"You really think you're tough, don't you? You think I'm going to play games with you all day, like the others did all night? Well, listen, boy, I don't play games with wise guys like you. I'll get some answers out of you one way or the other, but I'll get them. You'd better think it over. I'll be back." And with that he left the office.

When Spahr had gone, Detective DeLisle, who had been sitting at his desk listening to his partner's tirade, warned me: "Don't get that guy worked up. I'll try to help you out, but you've got to be more cooperative than you have been so far. Detective Spahr can get awfully rough when he's mad."

DeLisle had barely finished speaking when Captain De-Marco returned. Again, as he entered, I saw my wife standing in the corridor. Was this now-you-see-her, now-you-don't routine part of the interrogation? Were the police trying to remind me that she was in custody, and would stay in custody until I cooperated? That seemed at the time to be the idea.

"Well, Smith, Detective Spahr tells me you won't cooperate. What's the story?" De Marco asked.

"There's no story to tell. All I know is that I want to see my wife or my lawyer."

"No dice. If your lawyer shows up, we can't keep him from seeing you, but you aren't calling him, and you won't see your wife until you tell us what we want to know. She has been interrogated and is giving us a statement, and she will stay here until you cooperate with us. How long that will be is up to you."

"I don't know anything. What can I tell you?"

"Why don't you start by telling us what happened at the sandpit?" Detective DeLisle suggested.

"I've already told you. I threw up and went home."

"We know what you told us," DeMarco said, "and we don't believe it. We want the truth." Then, pulling over a chair and sitting down, he went on: "Listen, Smith, you know the area and the people up that way, maybe you can help us with that. Suppose you tell us how you think the girl was killed. Got any ideas?"

"Can I sit? My legs are killing me."

"Not now. Later you can sit all you want. How about it? What do you think happened to the girl?"

"I have no idea what happened, when it happened, where or why it happened," I replied. "I doubt if you do, either."

"Oh, we have a pretty good idea," DeMarco said, lighting a cigar. "Would you like to hear it?"

I shrugged, but DeLisle, hunching forward in his chair, elbows on knees, said: "Go ahead, Carl, I'd like to hear that myself."

"Well," the captain began, "I think the girl met someone she knew while she was walking home, someone who offered her a ride. I figure she was a pretty wild girl, and didn't object when the guy suggested that they go somewhere and park. She may have suggested it herself. Anyway, I think the guy was heading from Ramsey toward the Nixon home, so he just turned right and drove down and parked on the end of Fardale Road. But I figure this guy wanted more than just a little necking, that the girl objected, but maybe she let him get as far as unbuttoning her sweater. Then she tried to stop him, but the guy tore her bra. That scared her. She managed to get out of the car and tried to run, but the guy caught her, banged her head against the road, and knocked her out."

"And that's how she lost the shoes, kerchief, and other things on Fardale Avenue, right?" DeLisle asked the captain.

"That's the way I figure it. What about you, Smith?"

"I don't know anything about it," I answered, for in fact I did not know then that anything had been found on Fardale Avenue.

"Tell us, Carl, how did she get to the sandpit?" DeLisle asked. "Why did the guy take her there and kill her?"

"That's easy. After knocking her out, the guy put her in his car. The guy got all shook up when the girl didn't regain consciousness. He started to drive away, figuring to ride around till she woke up. When he turned on the lights of his car, they pointed straight up the dirt road to the sandpit, so he drove up there, parked, and waited for the girl to wake up. She did, and when she did she fought with him again. By this time the guy was probably as scared as she was. He dragged her outside the car, and when she continued to struggle, he lost his temper and killed her. Then he took off."

"Sounds good, Carl," DeLisle remarked when the captain had finished expounding his theory. "What do you think, Smith?"

"I think I still want my lawyer," I replied, expecting DeMarco to be outraged. Instead, after a minute or two of swiveling his cigar around in his mouth, he rose from his chair and left the room without saying a word.

Hardly had DeMarco closed the door when it flew open again and Detective Spahr charged into the room, fire in his eyes. "Take your clothes off," he demanded.

"What for?"

"Don't give me any of that 'what for' crap. Take your clothes off, or I'll take them off for you."

"Everything?"

"Every goddam thing."

"You'd better do as he says," DeLisle told me.

Had it been a few hours earlier, I would have refused, but by this time, ten o'clock, or a few minutes after, I was too worn down and exhausted to do anything but comply. When I had stripped as ordered, Spahr took my clothing, directed me to "stand right there until I get back," and walked out of the office, leaving me with Detective DeLisle.

The detective waited until Spahr was gone, then, pushing a chair over to me with his foot, he said: "Go on, Smitty, you can sit down now. He won't be back for a while."

It was cold in the room—even my shoes and socks had been taken. I was so glad, however, to be sitting down for a change that I did not care, but after the first few minutes I began to shiver and shake. Then Spahr returned. "Stand up, punk," he growled. "Nobody told you to sit down."

As I stood, Detective DeLisle interceded: "I told him to sit, Walter, he looks pretty tired."

"Are you?" Spahr asked, walking over to stand directly in front of me.

"I've been up since yesterday morning."

"Well, sit down," he said, at the same time putting his hands on my chest and shoving me backward. I was unprepared for the sudden push. As I stumbled back, I tried to put my hands on the arms of the chair behind me, to check my fall, but the back of my knees hit the edge of the seat. Both the chair and I landed flat on the floor.

Here we go again, I thought, now the rough stuff starts. Once before, when in high school, I had been slapped around by a Ramsey police officer—a sergeant—and a part-time deputy, who wanted me to tell them the names of the local boys who had perpetrated some Halloween pranks. I had been expecting the same treatment from the police this time, and when Spahr pushed me over the chair, I thought that signaled the start of the rough stuff. However, even before I had picked myself up from the floor, Spahr stalked out of the office.

DeLisle had remained silent while Spahr was in the room, except to say that he had permitted me to sit. Now, with Spahr gone, he said: "He's a short-tempered guy. You'd better do some cooperating before he really gets angry."

"That's okay. A little pushing around will wake me up."

"Go on, sit down," he said. "It's all right now."

I was a bit dubious, but I sat down anyway. My legs were becoming so sore from standing that I did not care what Spahr liked or disliked.

"Smitty—that's what they call you, isn't it?" DeLisle asked. I nodded my head and he went on. "Smitty, I don't know what you did or why, but I do know that you were at the sandpit with the girl. We can prove it, and you know we can prove it. If you deny it, we'll prove it, and you'll look bad for having lied. And the blood on your pants proves that something happened to the girl while you were there. What, I don't know, maybe just an accident, but something happened." I started to speak but he put up his hand. "No, let me finish. Your wife is outside asking to see you. If you'll cooperate with us we'll let you see her, then she can go home. You have a little baby. Your wife should be home with the baby, not down here answering questions you should be answering, but she can't leave until we get the answers. All you have to do is cooperate, that's all."

"How? What is all this 'cooperate' jazz?"

"It's very simple. Just give us a statement. If there are some things you don't want to say, you don't have to. You're a smart boy. You know you can say you don't want to talk about it, or you don't remember. That's an old trick."

"You've got to be kidding. You don't want cooperation, you want a confession."

DeLisle recoiled as if horrified by the word. "No, not a confession," he exclaimed. "We don't want *that*. Just a statement. You won't even be required to sign it. Think it over. I'll give you a few minutes."

"I'll think about it."

I began to consider seriously what DeLisle had said, but before I could reach a decision, Spahr returned. Looking at me sitting in the chair, then at DeLisle, he said: "I don't know why you're so damn soft on these punks."

"Oh, let him sit," DeLisle replied. "Smitty has been up all night. He's bushed. Besides, he's thinking of cooperating with us."

"Well, he damn well better think fast. I'm not going to wait much longer."

"Go on, Walter, leave us alone for a while. Smitty and I are getting along pretty good together."

"What time is it?" I asked after Spahr had gone.

"Ten-thirty," DeLisle replied. "Come on, Smitty, tell me what happened. You'll feel better, and then your wife can go home."

# CHAPTER SEVEN

**THE THINGS DETECTIVE DELISLE HAD BEEN** telling me, as contrasted to the tough-guy tactics of Spahr, seemed at the time to make a great deal of sense. If the police would be satisfied with nothing more than an ambiguous statement, I thought, one I would not be required to sign, I could tell them anything; and later, if necessary, I could repudiate it. I knew I would have to reach a decision of some sort, that I could not go on forever with the same story I had been telling them. Would it be possible, I wondered, to give them a misleading statement that would not get me in worse trouble. It seemed possible. All I would have to do, I thought, would be to say "I don't remember" whenever the questioning got too specific—as Detective DeLisle had suggested. DeMarco, in relating his theory of how the girl had been killed, had given me the impression that the police could prove that theory. Perhaps, I reasoned, I could tell them something different, something close enough to what they thought had happened to satisfy them, but far enough from the truth that they could not prove whether my statement was true or false.

As I sat there in Captain DeMarco's office, stark naked, staring at a spot of dirt on the wall, my reasoning seemed to me to be completely logical. Only later, in retrospect, would I realize that I had been thinking in precisely the manner in which the entire process of interrogation had been designed to lead me to think. Thus, when finally I made up my mind to give the police a misleading, ambiguous statement, to try to outsmart them, I was doing exactly what they were prepared for. My statement would in fact be an interrogation by a skilled, experienced prosecutor, who through carefully phrased questions would lead me into replies that would virtually guarantee a conviction for first-degree murder.

During the past eleven years, I have often looked back on what happened to me that long night and day. I prefer to think that now, knowing my rights and the limits to which the police can go to secure a confession, I could easily withstand the same type of interrogation; that I would realize that the police could not hold me and my wife forever; and that I would never "cooperate." But I am not certain. It is easy to say "I'd never confess to anything I didn't do," but it is not that simple when one is cooped up in a bare room, sleepless for many hours, listening to the same questions and giving the same answers over and over and over; when one is tired, hungry, unable to stand, sit, or even go to the bathroom except at the will of his interrogator; when he is being shouted at by one police officer and sweet-talked by another, threatened with the electric chair by the first and told that cooperation is best by the second; and all the while knowing that his wife is just across the hall in another bare room, and wondering if she is going through the same thing.

I honestly do not know if I could resist those pressures exerted upon me then if I were in the same situation today, and I doubt that anyone else knows what he or she would do in such circumstances. How much interrogation does it take to break a man's will, to make him cross that nebulous voluntary-involuntary line? No one can judge who has not been subjected to the full force of a police interrogation. Too many people think that the interrogation of a criminal suspect is a hit-or-miss affair, with the police playing it by ear and improvising as they go along. Actually, it is a clearly defined, highly sophisticated, relentless, grinding, degrading, pressure-packed process, designed to only one end: to extract a confession. It is a process so exact as to be nearly a science; it certainly is an art.

The officers assigned to the interrogation are not usually the old-timers with keen insights into the criminal mind, insights gleaned from years of experience. That is a myth fostered by fiction. Quite to the contrary, as I have learned, they are more often the younger, better-educated officers; and they are chosen not for their experience, but for their knowledge and appreciation of the techniques outlined in numerous textbooks on interrogative procedures, textbooks written by college law professors, psychologists specializing in criminal behavior, and teachers of police science. These textbooks, with sales and circulation of over 44,000—approximately one per four uniformed police officers—describe in detail, step by step, the various tactics to be used during the interrogation, and when, where, and how they are to be used.

The naïve might suppose that some of the things which took place during my interrogation—e.g., taking me to Captain DeMarco's office in the courthouse, taking away my clothing, the threat of physical violence when Detective Spahr pushed me over the chair, taking my wife into custody, the cat-and-mouse game played by Spahr and DeLisle, and DeLisle's plea for "cooperation" before Spahr *really* got angry—were things which "just happened." Well, in order that the naïve will not walk forever with their heads in the clouds, I shall quote briefly from some of the textbooks. Things do not "just happen" during police interrogations.

It was pointed out by the Supreme Court in *Miranda v. Arizona*, 384 U.S. 436 (1966), that the police are taught to eschew physical violence in favor of psychological means. The officers are told by the textbooks that the "principal psychological factor contributing to a successful interrogation is *privacy*—being alone with the person under interrogation." [1]

> If at all practicable, *the interrogation should take place in the investigator's office* or at least in a room of his choice. The subject should be deprived of every advantage. . . . In his own office, the investigator possesses all the advantages. The atmosphere suggests the invincibility of the forces of the law.[2] [Italics added.]

[1] Inbau and Reid: *Criminal Interrogation and Confessions* (1962), p. 1.
[2] O'Hara: *Fundamentals of Criminal Investigation* (1959), p. 99.

Undressing the suspect, allowing him to remain undressed, and threatening physical violence while he is in that condition, is an old police trick. As far back as 1945 it was openly defended by a New York prosecutor, who said that the technique "is some more psychology—let him sit around in a blanket [or less], humiliate him there for awhile; let him sit in a corner; let him think he is going to get a shellacking."[3] The stress always is to defeat the suspect psychologically rather than physically.[4]

Perhaps the all-time favorite interrogative technique, however, is the "Mutt and Jeff," or "Friendly-Unfriendly" ploy, used against me by Detectives Spahr and DeLisle.

In this technique, two agents are employed. Mutt [Spahr] the relentless investigator, who knows the subject is guilty and is not going to waste any time . . . Jeff [DeLisle] on the other hand is obviously a kindhearted man. . . . He disapproves of Mutt and his tactics. . . . He can't hold Mutt off for very long. The subject would be wise to make a quick decision. The technique is applied by having both investigators present when Mutt acts out his role. Jeff may stand by quietly and demur at some of Mutt's tactics. When Jeff makes his plea for cooperation, Mutt is not present in the room.[5]

In the event the suspect has the audacity to ask to speak to a relative or an attorney, the following advice is tendered:

The interrogator should respond by suggesting the subject first tell the truth to the interrogator himself rather than get anyone else involved in the matter. If the request is for an attorney, the interrogator may suggest that the subject save himself or his family the expense.[6]

However one reads these textbooks—I do not necessarily

[3] *Malinski v. New York*, 324 U.S. 401, 407 (1945).
[4] *Miranda v. Arizona*, 384 U.S. 436 (1966).
[5] O'Hara: op. cit., p. 104; Inbau and Reid: op. cit., pp. 58–9; *Spano v. New York*, 360 U.S. 315 (1959).
[6] Inbau and Reid: op. cit., p. 112.

refer only to those I have cited—one finds that the same general pattern emerges: get the suspect off balance psychologically, then use any trickery, any deception that might be effective. Taking the suspect's wife into custody and making the suspect's cooperation a condition for her release is another old trick.[7]

Whether or not the end result of these tactics is coercion is for the courts to decide—most courts have said it is coercion. I know only that at some point in the process a feeling of utter helplessness sets in, the subject is totally reliant upon his interrogators, and that he no longer cares about anything but getting himself out of the pressure cooker. And that is the point I had reached when I told Detective DeLisle: "Okay, I'll give you a statement if I don't have to sign it, and if I can see my wife."

Detective DeLisle did not take any chances on my having second thoughts. As soon as he had heard me say "Okay" he was on his way to the door to call Detective Spahr, who was standing outside in the corridor.

"Walter, Smitty is willing to give us a statement," DeLisle declared as Spahr entered the office.

"But only if I don't have to sign it, and if I can see my wife," I added.

"Good enough," Spahr replied. "You won't have to sign it if you don't want to. When it's over you can see your wife. I'll even promise you that if you cooperate and tell us everything you know, I'll fix it with the prosecutor for you to have visits with your wife in his office. That way she won't have to go into the county jail to see you. But if you back out on us, or don't tell the truth, I'll fix it so you'll get nothing but trouble."

"It's a deal."

"Good. Now we'll get you something to wear. A priest from Don Bosco High School is waiting to see you. We want you to see him before your statement." Earlier, I had told the police that I had attended that school, but the idea of seeing a priest did not appeal to me.

[7] *Haynes v. Washington,* 373 U.S. 503 (1963).

"Priest? What priest?"

"You know him," Spahr replied. "He is from Don Bosco."

DeLisle, who had left the office when Spahr entered, returned and handed me my shoes, socks, and a one-piece gray coverall, which later I learned was a county jail work uniform. Spahr waited until I had dressed, then said: "Let's go, the priest is waiting."

I was taken to the office next to the one I had been in, and there I was left alone with a somber-faced priest. I had never seen him before in my life—he had not been associated with Don Bosco High School while I was there—and to this day, more than ten years later, I still do not know his name.

"Hello, Edgar," the priest said, "I was told you wanted to see me. Can I help you?"

"Who said I wanted to see you?"

"The police officers. Didn't you ask to see me?"

"The only thing I've asked for is to see either my wife or my lawyer."

"But I was told you wanted to see me," the priest persisted.

"Listen, Father, I don't know what you were told, or who told you. If you want to do something for me, help my wife get out of here so she can call my lawyer. That's what I need—a lawyer, not a priest."

"I don't know what I can do for your wife," the priest said. "I understand that she isn't a Catholic. I was summoned to help you. I was told that you had admitted the crime and wanted to confess your sins."

"Father, I haven't admitted anything. As for confessing my sins, I can't remember the last time I was in a Catholic church. I attend the Episcopal church. I was married in the Episcopal church. My daughter was baptized in the Episcopal church. You couldn't hear my confession if I wanted to confess, and you know it."

"Yes, I know about your marriage. Technically, I suppose, you are excommunicated, but if you will confess that sin and permit me to arrange to have your marriage sanctified, then the Church will welcome you back. I can give you conditional absolution."

"I know I've been excommunicated. That's what I've been trying to tell you. I don't need my marriage approved by the Catholic Church. If I did, I would have gotten married there in the first place. As far as I'm concerned, my marriage is fine. I have nothing to repent."

"But what about this horrible crime? You can't die with *that* stain on your soul."

"I don't have that stain on my soul. I didn't kill the girl, and I'm not planning to die any time soon."

"But the police said you have confessed the crime."

"Did they tell you that?"

"Yes. The newspaper reporters asked me for details, but of course I told them nothing."

"Take my word for it, Father, I haven't confessed, and I'm not going to—now, tomorrow, next week, or any other time. I have nothing to confess."

"You should do all you can to cooperate with the police. They need your help. It is your Christian duty."

"My only duty," I replied, "is to get my lawyer and help myself. God helps those who help themselves. Remember?" ·

With a sigh and a rather sad look on his face—the priest rose, went to the door, and knocked. Detective Spahr, who must have been waiting for that knock, opened the door. As he did so, the priest departed. I never saw him again.

# CHAPTER EIGHT

FROM A PURELY PRACTICAL STANDPOINT, it would serve no useful purpose for me to reproduce here in its entirety my statement to the police. The statement, which covers forty-two pages in the printed record of my trial, is in fact a stenographically recorded interrogation, and as interrogations by lawyers tend to be, is exceedingly redundant. In many instances questions are repeated over and over for emphasis. What I have done, therefore, is to reduce the statement to its essential points by omitting the redundancies, as well as by omitting a number of irrelevant references which appear from time to time in the stenographic record.[1]

I was taken to the prosecutor's office at 12:45 p.m. First Assistant Prosecutor Fred Galda, who would conduct the entire interrogation, introduced me to the persons already present: Chief Harry Voss of the Ramsey police; Chief Charles Smith of the Mahwah police; Lewis Kalstad, a member of the panel of jurors available during that term of the county court, who was present as an impartial observer; Detective Walter Spahr; and Arthur Ehrenbeck, an official stenographic reporter for the county court. Prosecutor Calissi was not present. Forty-five minutes earlier he had called together the newspaper, radio, and television reporters, and he was giving them the specific details of the statement I had not yet made. The *Bergen Evening Record* actually would have the details of the state-ment in print and the newspaper on the street before the state-

[1] The quotations from my statement to the police, appearing in Chapters Eight and Nine, are taken verbatim from the record.

ment was half-completed. Besides being a "great, fair-minded guy," who "only hates bookies," it appears that Prosecutor Calissi is also a most remarkable mind reader.

Galda, who was standing in front of the desk, began the questioning at 12:50 p.m. "I am going to ask you some questions, Ed, concerning an incident that occurred in Mahwah, and one Vickie Zielinski. Speak loudly and clearly so we all can understand you." Now that I was cooperating, the "punk," "goddam wise guy," and "son of a bitch" had become "Ed."

After a number of questions dealing with my age, marital status, residence, and activities prior to borrowing Gilroy's automobile, Galda asked: "What automobile did you have at this time?"

"Joseph Gilroy's Mercury," I replied from my seat in a chair beside the desk. "It's a light-blue or aqua 1950 Mercury convertible."

"Then what happened?"

"I went to Reinauer's [service station]. It is in Mahwah, on Route 17. They didn't have kerosene. I went down the road to Moore's Truck Stop."

"Do you know the approximate time you got there?"

"I would say it was twenty-five to eight, twenty to eight, somewhere around there. I got there and got the five gallons of kerosene I needed. From there I went straight home. I went straight to my trailer, put the five gallons of kerosene in the tank and tried to light the heater. It wouldn't light. I told my wife and mother-in-law I couldn't get the heater going. I had to get more kerosene. So I went back to Ramsey, to Secor's. I got five gallons of kerosene there. On the time on that, I don't know. I would say it was somewhere around eight-thirty —twenty after eight, eight-thirty."

"By the way, what clothes did you have on then?" Galda asked.

"Gray khaki pants, black-and-red striped shirt, blue nylon jacket, white socks, black shoes."

"Right. And after you went to Secor's for the kerosene, what did you do?" Galda asked, after a brief off-the-record conference with Detective Spahr. Because they had whispered, it was impossible to tell exactly what it was about, but it obviously had something to do with the pants.

"I started back home. I got in the vicinity of Fardale Avenue, Mahwah. As I was riding along, I saw this girl walking. I knew her from meeting her in town."

"Did you recognize her?"

"Yes, I recognized her."

"Who was the girl?"

"Vickie Zielinski."

"Vickie Zielinski?"

"Yes. I was intending to keep on going. I don't recall whether she waved at me or yelled or said something—I pulled in the driveway down the road and came back up the road and stopped and she said: 'Give me a ride home.' "

"What time was this approximately?"

"About twenty to nine. It was somewhere around that."

"Did she get in the car?"

"Yes."

"What happened after that?"

"I headed back toward her house on Wyckoff Avenue. Just before her house she said her sister was coming to meet her. She didn't want her sister to see her riding in the car because she was in trouble with her family. She said: 'Go up and around again.' I turned up West Crescent Avenue, went up to what I think is Young's Road, down Young's Road to Chapel Road. When I got down by Fardale Avenue, there's a sandpit there. I pulled into this sandpit. I pulled to the end of the road and was smoking a cigarette. She was telling me about being in trouble with her family. It was a mix-up about the school sent her mother a note—she had cut school either that day or the day before—and she and her sister sent a return note to the school without her mother knowing it. She said something about: 'I am going to get out and walk home. I am going to tell my father. I am going to go home and tell him you are like the rest of the guys'—something like that. I didn't know what she meant. The first thing I thought of was I couldn't let her walk home. I had to take her home. She started getting out of the car."

"Was this in the sandpit?" Galda asked.

"This was in the sandpit. She opened the door and got halfway out. I reached across the seat and grabbed either her arm or her jacket or something."

"What clothing did she have on?"

"She had a heavy wool jacket of some kind. That's all I remember. I didn't notice her clothing at all."

"Did she have anything on her hair?"

"I didn't notice. I really didn't notice at all."

"When you held her arm, did she have any gloves on?"

"I don't think she had gloves on. I wouldn't say for sure, I don't think so. I think I had hold of her wrist. I wanted to pull her back in the car and take her home. She was almost completely out, and I worked my way across to the passenger's side of the front seat and tried to get out. I don't know what she said, but she started swinging at me and sort of slapping—you know."

"Did that make you upset?"

"All I remember is letting go of her arm and swinging with my right hand."

"Did you hit her?"

"I don't know. I imagine she hit me. I am not sure, but I didn't feel anything."

"Did she get back in the car with you?"

"No. Then that time"—at this point, for reasons that will be made clear later on, I had to be extremely careful—"whatever happened in between is vague to me. I don't know exactly what it is."

"What was the condition of the ground at that time?" Galda asked, changing the subject.

"Soft."

"And did you have your shoes on?"

"Yes, I had my shoes on, and the thing about the shoes is, after I had bowled in Paramus, I didn't lace the shoes because I had hurt my ankle bowling, and I didn't bother to lace the shoe on that foot. I didn't do either one of them. I left them loose."

"Then what did you do?"

"Next thing I actually remember is getting back in the car."

"Were you alone in the car?"

"Yes. I started to back the car out. It took me a few minutes. I couldn't see where I was going. I had to keep getting out of the car, looking to see where I was going. I finally backed the car right onto Chapel Road and turned south toward Pulis Avenue. I headed south on Chapel Road. I remember stopping forty or fifty yards down the road at the end of a wooded area. I remember seeing a Christmas tree I put there after Christmas."

"You had thrown the Christmas tree?"

"Yes. I guess some kids picked it up and left it in the road. When I came past a few days later, it was in the middle of the road. I picked it up and stood it up—on the edge of the wooded area."

"Do you remember stopping the car?"

"I remember stopping there. A couple of gentlemen have been asking me about her books and pocketbook. I am not sure I had them when I left the sandpit. I got home and went to the back door of my trailer. I only had one shoe on. I took off a pair of khaki pants and threw them outside on the patio outside the trailer. I asked my wife to bring me another pair of pants; I had been sick, I said. I put on a pair of gabardine pants, and my loafers, and went around and put in the five gallons of kerosene. Still I couldn't get the heater going. This was quarter after nine—ten after nine, quarter after. I told my wife: 'We will go down and stay at your mother's.' I still had the car belonging to Joe Gilroy. I called him up, told him I was sick, and that there was no heat, and asked him if he would ride me down to Ridgewood. He said: 'Fine.' I went back, told the wife I was going to get Joe. I picked up the khakis with the blood on them."

"Where were they at this time?"

"Lying outside on the patio."

"Where were your shoes at that time?"

"I had one shoe still in the trailer. I left that there. I got back in the car. I went down Chapel Road. I left the car parked on Chapel Road, got out, walked up into the sandpit with a lantern—a big spotlight. Right at the end of the road I turned it on, and I was almost standing on my shoe. I picked the shoe up.

"I saw a glove there, a red glove or red mitten. I didn't think anything of it. In fact, I kicked it as I walked away. I just kicked it off to the side a bit. I got back to the car. All of this is still vague to me. I don't remember driving through Ramsey at all. I remember when I got to Gilroy's house I tried to blow the horn. The horn didn't work. I turned around in the driveway across the street and pulled up in front of the windows. The family was watching television. Joe came out and got in the car. What strikes me now, by the time I had gotten into the car, I had completely forgotten about the whole thing. It wasn't on my mind at all. I drove back to Ramsey, got my wife. While I was getting my wife, I took the other shoe picked up at the sandpit—"

Galda interrupted: "You found the other shoe back in the sandpit?"

"Yes. We got the baby, and some baby food, and we got in Joe's car and went down to Ridgewood to my mother-in-law's. Exactly what time I got there, I don't know. We watched the end of a television show. I think it was probably about twenty to ten, quarter to ten, somewhere around there. We watched the end of the television show and went to bed. Just as I got in bed, the fight came on at ten o'clock. I knew it was ten o'clock then. I was already in bed. I got up the next morning about nine o'clock or so, and I told my wife I was sick. I had been sick for two or three days, I told her I was still feeling bad, so I stayed home that day."

"Did you do anything with your clothing?"

"I washed the jacket and shirt. I didn't have any reason other than they were dirty. I had been saying to my wife: 'I have to wash this jacket one of these days.' I threw it in the washing machine and washed it and hung it up in the cellar. Along about eleven-thirty I was sitting on the couch in the living room. I just heard one or two words of a radio program, on a radio in another room—something about Mahwah and Victoria—my wife heard the whole thing. She said: 'Do you know who that is?' I asked: 'Who?' She said: 'This girl Victoria Falinski?' That's how it was pronounced on the radio, spelled with an F. She said: 'She got killed in Mahwah last night.' I said: 'No.'

"Before I go any further, around eleven o'clock I had called Joe Gilroy and asked him if he would come down and ride me back to the trailer. He said he would be right down. I guess it was later on in the afternoon, one-thirty, two o'clock or something like that, I called Gilroy. He hadn't gotten there yet to pick me up. He had gone back to sleep. I asked him if he had heard anything on the radio. I said: 'Some broad from Ramsey got killed. It sounds like Vickie, but I don't know.' He said: 'To hell with it. I will be down later'—something like that. That's when it dawned on me that I had been with her the night before. Something snapped in the back of my head that I did it, but I couldn't convince myself."

"Can you identify these shoes, Ed?"

"They are mine," I replied, looking at the shoes I had thrown in the garbage the previous day.

"Are these the shoes you wore on Monday when you were up in the sandpit?"

"That's right."

"Is one of them the shoe you found when you went back in the sandpit the second time?"

"The right one."

"What did you do with these shoes, if anything?"

"Let me go in the sequence of things. Joe came down for us, but instead of coming down in his own car, he came down with another fellow—Don Hommell. First thing I said when I came out of the house, I said to this fellow Don: 'Was that Vickie that got killed?' 'Yeah,' he said. 'That place up there is swarming with cops, and they're checking the registration of every Mercury registered in Bergen County.' That's when it hit me that I must have been the one who did it. I rode back up to the trailer. My wife and I went to bed about seven o'clock. I was feeling pretty sick, and she wasn't feeling too well. She said she wanted to go down and stay at her mother's again. This thing had happened so close. We got to Ridgewood and watched a couple of television shows. My wife and I went to bed, and about eleven-thirty there were some people pounding on the door. I got up and there were a couple of detectives. They said they wanted to ask me a couple of questions."

"Ed," Galda asked, "are these the shoes you threw in the garbage can on Main Street?"

"They are."

"Ed, do you know whether it was the right or the left one you found in the sandpit?"

"The right one."

"You said you had on khaki pants that day?"

"Yes."

At this point in the statement, a recess was taken. I had gone to the men's room in the rear of the office and was just splashing some cold water on my face when Galda entered. "Ed," he asked, "what color pants did you wear Monday night?"

"Gray," I replied.

Galda appeared agitated. Earlier in my statement, when he had asked the same question, my answer that I had worn gray pants had startled him, and this had brought about the whispered conference with Detective Spahr. "What do you mean 'gray'?" he asked me.

"Look, I told you last night in Mahwah, and again just a few minutes ago, I wore gray pants. Gilroy and I got them from the uniform service that supplies Tony's Amoco."

"But you said 'gray khaki,'" Galda persisted. "That's two different colors. Which do you mean?"

"By 'khaki' I meant khaki-*type* pants, but not the color. The color was gray."

Galda walked out of the office. When he returned a few minutes later he said: "Ed, you must be mistaken. Your wife says that these pants we have are yours, so you must have worn them Monday night."

"That's what I thought when you showed them to me this morning, but these you have seem to be much bloodier than the ones I wore. That and my recollection of wearing gray pants makes me think these are a different pair."

"Well," Galda said, "they *must* be the ones you wore. You'd better back up the story your wife told us, for her sake. You can iron out your differences with her later."

The first thing the assistant prosecutor did when the taking of the statement was resumed, was to ask me to identify the pants. "Ed, are these your pants?"

"To the best of my knowledge they are," I replied in a reluctant fashion.

"I beg your pardon?" Galda asked, obviously upset.

"They are," I answered, adding: "To the best of my knowledge."

Galda was not satisfied. "Look at them, please. They *are* your pants?" It was more of a statement than a question.

"They are mine," I finally agreed.

My reluctance and hesitation must have been apparent. Galda pressed on: "And did you throw these pants away?"

"I don't know." I was not even sure they were my pants.

"I beg your pardon?"

"I don't know," I reiterated.

"Did you wear these pants when you were in the sandpit?"

"I did."

"Was Vickie bleeding at that time?"

"I don't remember."

"I beg your pardon?"

"I don't remember if she bled at all."

Galda, sensing that he was not going to get any better answers about the pants, abruptly changed the subject. "Now, you say you had on a blue jacket?"

I will never forget the stenographer's reaction when Galda

changed the line of questioning. He had been staring straight ahead, his fingers tapping away at the stenotype machine. Suddenly he looked directly at me and studied me with a quizzical expression on his face. Then he closed his eyes, and as he did so, one corner of his mouth lifted, leaving him with a half smile on his face. I am certain that he realized what I was trying to do, and that he knew his machine would not record a confession of guilt that day. And Galda knew it, also. Whatever his original plan may have been, he did not now dare to ask me: "Did you kill the girl?" Nor could he cut off the statement with a member of the jury panel present. The best he could do was to keep going and hope I would give some answers which might be incriminating—precisely what was to be done at my trial. He was an unhappy man, but he had an advantage: I was a very tired man.

I identified my jacket in response to the question. Then Galda asked: "Is this the shirt you wore Monday night when you met Vickie?"

"Yes."

"Is this the shirt you washed Tuesday morning?"

"Yes, I washed that with the jacket."

"I show you an undershirt, Ed, and ask you if you can identify it?"

"It's mine."

"Is this the shirt you wore Monday evening?"

"I can't actually recall whether it is. I won't say definitely."

"Now, what kind of socks did you have on that night?"

"White cotton."

"Do you know what you did with the socks?"

"No."

"I beg your pardon?"

"No. Somebody told me they were in the pocket of the pants."

Galda was becoming increasingly unhappy with the course my "confession" was taking. Apparently, he would have been happier if I had said that I had put the socks in the pocket, rather than saying what the detectives had told me. But he plodded forward. "Now, when she got out of the car in the sandpit, did she leave the books in the car?"

"That I will have to guess. I would say yes."

Then it was my turn to be surprised. Instead of asking me to identify the books, Galda changed the subject again: "Now, when you went back to the sandpit to look for your shoe, or whatever you went back for"—what did he mean by that?—"you say you saw a glove?"

"Yes, in the same vicinity as the shoe."

"Do you know how many gloves?"

"I don't know if it was a glove or a mitten. Something, red wool that looked like a glove."

"I show you what the reporter marked S-7," Galda said, taking a pair of gloves out of an envelope. "It appears to be a pair of gloves, and I ask you whether or not these are the gloves you saw by your shoe at the sandpit?"

"That I don't know."

"You say Vickie wore a heavy jacket?"

"Some type of heavy jacket, but I don't recall what it was."

"Would you recognize it if you saw it?"

"Well, from association with her, I would recognize whether she owned the jacket but not whether she had it on or not."

"Was it a solid-color jacket, if you know?"

"I don't know."

"Isn't this the jacket she had?" the assistant prosecutor asked. He was becoming more exasperated by the minute.

"I am not sure. I didn't observe that close to be sure whether it was or not. I know she wore a jacket like that. Whether it is the one she had on that night, I am not sure."

"What other clothing did she have on, a dress or pants?"

"I don't know." I was beginning to sound like a stuck phonograph record. "I think she had slacks of some sort. What kind—I don't know."

"Dungarees or jeans?"

"It was not a skirt or shorts."

Galda gave up on that line of questioning. "Did she have anything on her head?"

"Not that I can recall."

Again switching tactics, he tried a loaded question: "When you struck her in the sandpit, did you use your fist?"

"As far as I know, the only thing I remember is swinging with my hand. I am not sure whether I hit her or not."

"Did you tussle at all with her?"

"I don't know. Other than struggling and getting out of the car—once we were out of the car, I just don't know."

"Did you fall to the ground?"

"I am not sure of that," I replied. Then, thinking of my fall while pouring the kerosene, I added: "I fell somewhere."

"You fell somewhere. Did she fall?"

"I don't know."

"Did you at any time run up the bank in the sandpit?"

"I don't recall."

"Did you fall with your hands and knees on the bank?"

"I don't think so."

"I show you some type of kerchief," Galda said. "I ask you, isn't *this* the kerchief that Victoria wore when you picked her up and went to the sandpit?" Again, it was more statement than question.

"I don't recollect whether she was wearing one or not."

"Do you recall what type of shoes she wore?"

"No."

"I beg your pardon?"

"No."

The assistant prosecutor frowned at my refusal to give him the answers he desired. As I waited for the next question, he very slowly and carefully lifted from a box and set upon the desk a large, bloodstained rock. I estimated from his effort in lifting the rock that it weighed twenty to thirty pounds. Pointing to the rock, he said: "Ed, I show you what appears to be a boulder; will you come up and examine it, if you will, very carefully?"

Without bothering to leave my seat, I replied: "I don't recognize it."

"Did you strike or throw any article at her?"

"I don't know."

"You don't know?" Galda asked incredulously.

"I don't know at all."

"Your best recollection is that you don't know?"

"I don't know anything other than swinging with my hand."

Galda picked another slightly smaller rock out of the box. "Again, I show you what appears to be some type of rock. Do you recall anything concerning *that* rock?"

"No."

"I beg your pardon?"

"No."

"Are you familiar with that area?"

"Yes."

"Had you been there many times?"

"A few times. The last time quite a few years back."

Realizing that he was not going to establish that the sand-pit was a friendly, neighborhood lovers' lane, he switched back to the matter of Vickie's clothing: "You say Victoria wore a type of jacket. Do you recall whether or not she had any clothing on under the jacket?"

It was a stupid question that begged for a wise-guy answer—perhaps that was why he asked it—but I gave him a straight answer: "No."

"I beg your pardon?"

"No."

"When you held her wrist, what did you do?"

"I tried to pull her back toward the car."

"Do you recall which hand you held her with?"

"I think the left hand."

"Your left hand?"

"No, I held her with my right, her left," I answered, wondering where Galda was going with these questions.

"What if anything did you do with your hand?"

"Tried to get out of the car. I was trying to pull her in. I was off balance across the seat."

"Was she able to get out of the car completely?"

"Yes."

"Did you chase her at all?" he asked. Apparently, this was the question for which he had been trying to set me up.

"No. I don't think I did."

"Did you wear any gloves?"

"That I have to say I don't know. I had them in the jacket I wore. They were leather gloves, but whether or not I had those gloves on that night, I don't remember."

"I show you a left glove and ask you can you identify it?"

"That is mine."

"This appears to be a right glove. Can you identify it?"

"Mine."

"When Vickie said she was going to tell her father, did that make you angry?"

"No. I guess I was dumfounded"—Galda winced at that—"I couldn't understand why or what or anything. As far as I thought I would take her home because if she walked home from there, and she said I left her there, or something like that, I wouldn't know what to do."

"Why would she suggest to walk home?"

"I don't know."

"Did she say what she would tell her father?" Galda was pressing.

"Just something like you being like the rest of the guys or something like that. I don't know."

"Did you wash any clothing other than what you showed us so far?"

"Definitely no. No."

Galda, subtle as a bulldozer, switched the line of questioning again: "When you grabbed Vickie by the wrist, didn't she fight back?"

"As I recall it, she was pretty well out of the car. She was more or less—"

"Did you flop out of the car?" he asked, interrupting.

"Once I got over the kerosene can that was sitting in the middle of the floor, then I was able to scramble out of the car."

"Did she grab for your hair?"

"That I don't know. She was slapping. I let go of her wrist then. She didn't make any attempt to run, I don't think."

"How many times did you swing at her?"

"Once that I know of. I remember swinging once. I don't remember whether I hit her or not."

"And you don't know whether you struck her more than once?"

"No."

"Did she grab your hair at any time?"

"I wish I could tell you. I can't."

"When you went back to the sandpit for the second time, to look for your shoes, didn't you see Vickie then?"

"No, I didn't."

"Did you look for her?"

"No. I didn't even think about it. I just thought about my shoe."

"When you saw the glove, did you think anything about that?"

"No, I just gave the glove a glance and kicked it as I walked past. I think I kicked it over, or just walked past. All I remember was losing my shoe up there. That's the only thing I think I remember, about my shoe."

"Did you look for anything else?"

"No, I didn't."

"Did you go up on the bank?"

"No, I didn't. In fact, I didn't go all the way in[to] the sandpit. I went to the edge of the road, where the car was parked the first time."

"Did you leave your car out on the road?"

"Yes."

The assistant prosecutor, receiving a positive reply for a change, smiled broadly. "How long would you say you were in the pit with Vickie?" he asked.

"I want to think just a second. I would have to take a

guess." Until that moment, I had not considered the time element.

"Just as you know, Ed."

"With the time in between there, I don't remember—it seems like a minute or two, but it had to be longer—"

"Why would it have to be longer?" Galda asked. His smile had faded when I had replied "a minute or two," and now he was trying to compromise that reply. "Did you argue any length of time?"

"Time doesn't coincide in there. I don't know."

"Were you arguing for any length of time?" he repeated.

"No. I hardly said anything. I was smoking a cigarette."

"When she said she would tell her father you were like the rest of the boys—"

"Something *like* that," I said, cutting his question short and correcting him. "She had been raving on about the school, about cutting school and being in trouble—I don't remember."

"How many times did she hit you?"

"Two or three times."

"How many times would you say you hit her?"

That was the wrong question. "I don't know that I actually did hit her. I swung at her, but I don't know. I think if I had hit her, I would have hurt my hand. My hand didn't feel hurt or anything."

"Did you lift any heavy object at all while you were in the pit during this period?"

"I don't know."

"Was your mind still blank then?" he asked sarcastically.

"I don't know. That's all I remember until I remember getting back in the car, and the car wouldn't start right away, and it started up, and I backed out of the road."

"Prior to this swinging, did you kiss her good-night or anything?"

*"No. I didn't even touch her."*

"Wasn't the kerosene can on the floor?"

"It was more or less separating us," I explained. Then, since Galda had left the door open, I added: "She would have to climb up on the side for her to get near me, or for me to get near her. She raved on about school, cutting school, and this stuff about telling her father something—I don't know."

Undaunted, the prosecutor plunged forward. "Did you put your arms around her inside the car or outside the car?"

"No."

"Didn't you try to kiss her or—?"

"No."

"Did she try to kiss you, perhaps?"

"No, not that I remember."

"Did you feel any parts of her body?"

"No."

My negative replies, fired back as quickly as Galda could get the questions out of his mouth—and in the one instance before he could finish the question, had left him red-faced and angry. But I was dog-tired. The long hours of interrogation had left me ready to collapse.

"Do you know what type of clothing she wore?" Galda asked. He seemed to be running out of questions.

"Other than the jacket and the pants, that is all I know. She just had a heavy jacket and some kind of pants. That's all I know. I know what type of clothing she wears ordinarily, but that doesn't tell you what she had on that night."

"How do you account for all the blood on your pants?"

"I can't account for it. It's just there."

"When you left the pit the first time, did you leave hurriedly?"

"No. In fact, it took me a couple of minutes to back out of the pit. First the car wouldn't start. I finally got it started."

"When was the first time you missed your shoe?"

"When I got home. I was completely home when I missed the shoe. I got home. I realized I didn't have a shoe on." The prosecutor was about to ask the next logical question, but I anticipated him: "I don't remember how I lost it, or why I left it."

"Didn't you realize there was blood all over your pants when you got home?" he asked angrily.

"I think I knew it was blood but it didn't appear to me—I don't know."

That did it. With a weary sigh, eyes upturned in exasperation, Galda called for a recess. It was 2 p.m. I had been awake for twenty-nine and a half hours, and under constant interrogation for fourteen hours.

County Prosecutor Guy Calissi entered the room just after the recess was called, and as he held a quiet conversation with Mr. Galda, Detective Spahr approached me and said: "Come on over here, Smitty, I want to ask you something." Spahr pointed to the corner of the office, near the lavatory door, and when I had walked over there with him, he asked: "What's all this 'I don't know—I don't remember' stuff you're giving us?"

"I'm telling you people as much as I can or will tell you. What do you want me to do, confess?"

"That's what you're supposed to be doing."

"If that's what you expect, don't hold your breath. I may have to give you a statement to get to see my lawyer, and to get to see my wife, but if you are waiting for me to confess—that's going to be a snowy day in hell."

"Listen, Smith," Spahr exclaimed, "I warned you that there would be trouble if you backed out on our deal."

"The deal was for a statement which I wouldn't be asked to sign, nothing else."

Before Detective Spahr could reply, Prosecutor Calissi walked over to where I was standing and asked if I would mind taking a ride up to the sandpit. He said they wanted me to show them where I had parked the car, and where I had found my shoe. I agreed to do that. "Fine," Calissi said. "Now we will reopen your statement just for a minute to explain where we are going. Then I want you to shave. There are numerous reporters outside, and you look like something the cat dragged in." Then, turning to Detective Spahr, the prosecutor said: "Walter, get Smith's clothing, his own clothing. We can't take him out dressed like this." I was dressed in the prison coveralls given me earlier.

The statement was reopened at 2:13 p.m. Assistant Prosecutor Galda resumed the questioning: "What we are going to do now, on the places that you indicated to us, we are going to go to the area. It will be the same people in this room, and we are going in two cars, and you can point out these things you mentioned on the spot. Is that agreeable to you?"

"Yes."

"And while you were in the custody of the policeman and up at the Mahwah Police Headquarters, did anybody mistreat you or anything?"

"No, sir."

"Everybody treat you all right?"

Thinking of my prior experience with the police while in high school, and with Mr. Woods in the juvenile home, I gave Galda an answer which later would come back to haunt me: "Better than I expected."

"I beg your pardon?"

"Better than expected."

That was more cooperation than the assistant prosecutor had been expecting. He quickly dropped the subject, and after a few irrelevant questions concerning my whereabouts and activities on the afternoon of the crime, he said: "I believe we can state the time of the closing and the same people, together with the prosecutor of the County of Bergen, Mr. Guy W. Calissi, are going up to the scene."

This portion of the statement was ended at 2:15 p.m.

# CHAPTER NINE

**DURING THE SHORT PERIOD OF TIME THAT** the stenographer was packing his stenotype machine in its carrying case for the trip to Mahwah, Detective Spahr returned the clothing taken from me that morning, and Prosecutor Calissi gave me his electric razor to shave with.

The office was filled with detectives when, having changed my clothes and shaved, I returned from the lavatory. Captain DeMarco, Detectives Graber, DeLisle, O'Har, Spahr, Garabedian, and several others I did not recognize, all were present. Prosecutor Calissi was presiding over a meeting. "Walter," he said to Detective Spahr, "you take Smith in my car. Captain DeMarco will swing his car into the street behind you and block the road. Use your siren and don't stop for anything."

"What's up?" I asked Mr. Galda.

"Prosecutor Calissi will explain," he told me. "Wait just a minute."

Calissi was still talking. "I will go out to the car now. Spahr and Mr. Kalstad will come with me. In five minutes, the rest of you bring Smith out. As soon as Smith, Mr. Galda, and DeLisle get in the car, we'll move out. The others can follow with Captain DeMarco. He will bring the stenographer with him. We will meet at the Nixon home."

"All right now, Ed," Mr. Galda began, "I'd better explain. There are a number of photographers and reporters in the corridor. We will surround you and lead you through. Just keep moving straight ahead, don't stop, and don't talk to anyone. Understand? Don't talk to anyone at all. Just keep going. We will keep up with you."

"I guess so," I replied, somewhat dubious about the whole idea. The prosecutor's office suddenly seemed to be an attractive place to be in.

"Let's go," Galda shouted.

Despite the warning the assistant prosecutor had given me, I was totally unprepared for the shouting, shoving mass of people confronting me when the office door was opened. It was a madhouse. From the office to the courthouse entrance, packed wall to wall, there were what seemed to be a thousand reporters, photographers, and newsreel cameramen. The detectives surrounding me literally charged forward, shoving people out of their way. Galda, holding me by one arm, DeLisle by the other, followed the lead detectives, half-carrying me with them. One reporter, shouting "Why did you kill her? Why did you kill her? Why did you kill her?" tried to get close to me, but was pushed to the floor by a detective. A camera knocked from a photographer's hand was trampled by the mob. As we approached the end of the corridor, our path was blocked momentarily. Several photographers had moved a long wooden bench into position blocking the way, and they were standing on it to gain a better view. They did not remain standing. The detectives in the lead never hesitated. Grabbing one end of the bench, they dumped it and the photographers on the floor to one side, leaving just enough room for Galda and DeLisle to pull me through the crowd on the other side.

It must have taken us a full five minutes to reach the street. From there, it was no contest. Spahr, sitting in the front seat of the prosecutor's car, had the motor running. As soon as I had been yanked into the back seat between Galda and DeLisle, Spahr tramped down on both the gas pedal and siren button at the same time. We must have been doing sixty as we crossed the main street alongside the courthouse. Looking back, I could see that Captain DeMarco had swung his car sideways into the street behind us, blocking the way and very nearly causing a

*Bergen Evening Record* station wagon to become part of the bank on the corner.

By the time we had reached the highway a mile from the courthouse—having run two red lights and passed traffic on both sides of the road—there was little chance that we were being followed. Prosecutor Calissi, satisfied that we were in the clear, told Detective Spahr to "knock off the siren," and to radio back to Captain DeMarco. "Tell Carl to catch up with us," he instructed the detective. "He has the stenographer with him."

The remainder of the trip to Mahwah was uneventful. The juror, Mr. Kalstad, must have appreciated that. Both hands on the dashboard to brace himself, he had turned white in the face during our wild, siren-wailing escape from the court-house.

The statement was reopened at 2:55 p.m. Prosecutor Calissi had gotten out of the car upon our arrival at the Nixon home on Wyckoff Avenue, and his place in the front seat was taken by Mr. Ehrenbeck, the stenographic reporter. Assistant Prosecutor Galda waited until Ehrenbeck had the stenotype machine set up in his lap, then he began the questioning. "We are now, Ed, opposite the Nixon home on the corner of Wyckoff Avenue and Fardale. Is this area familiar to you?"

"Yes."

"Ed, we are going to ask you to direct us the route you traveled from this point. Would you talk as we go along, please?"

"All right."

"Point out the various things you recognize, and the route you traveled this particular evening with Victoria Zielinski," Galda directed.

Nodding in agreement to the prosecutor's order, I began explaining: "This is the point where I turned around and headed back in a northerly direction on Wyckoff Avenue to stop and see what Vickie was gesturing or shouting about. I continued up around this bend."

"The area of the Lehmann Construction?" Galda asked, pointing to a sign beside the road.

"Yes, I saw her standing and waiting. She got in the car and said she wanted to ride home. We continued on up this road in the direction of her house. She asked me how my wife was, how the baby was. She mentioned something about she was in trouble with her family and her sister was coming to meet her. We continued along this road."

"To what street?"

"West Crescent Avenue, about another three or four tenths of a mile. It's up a little way. I'll tell you where to turn. She said that she didn't want her sister to see her in the car because of the trouble she had been having. She said: 'Ride around one of the blocks or so.' We thought we could miss her sister. We turned left up West Crescent Avenue, up this road here."

Detective Spahr, at my direction, turned left onto West Crescent Avenue, left again onto Shadyside Road, then right onto Young's Road. We followed Young's Road to the point where it intersected with Chapel Road, at which time I said to Spahr: "At the base of this hill you turn left. This is Chapel Road." Spahr turned where I had indicated, and as we drove along, I continued to direct him: "Right up over the crest of the next hill, where the Mahwah police car is. That is the driveway to the sandpit."

"And is this the road you pulled in?" Galda inquired.

"I did. The fences and all have been ripped down."

Looking out of the car, I could see that someone had informed the residents of the Ramsey-Mahwah area of the prosecutor's intention to return me to the scene of the crime. Long lines of automobiles were parked on both sides of Chapel Road and Fardale Avenue, and curious spectators and photographers were everywhere. Most of the photographers, judging by their equipment, were professionals, but there were also a great many onlookers taking pictures as well. Something for the family album, one supposes.

Prosecutor Calissi, who had been following us in Captain DeMarco's car, approached ours on foot and asked everyone to get out. We did so, and as we did I noticed Donald Hommell's automobile parked on Chapel Road, a few hundred feet away. It seemed to be empty, and he was nowhere in sight. I could not imagine why he of all people would have wanted to be within a hundred miles of that place.

Prosecutor Calissi began to speak, but his words were drowned out by the roar of an airplane engine directly overhead. It was an airplane belonging to the New York *Daily News*. They were taking aerial photographs from an altitude of four or five hundred feet, and the noise of the engine made conversation impossible. We waited, and after ten minutes the plane climbed to a higher altitude. Then Assistant Prosecutor Galda resumed the questioning. "We are now at the intersection of Fardale Road and the entrance to the sandpit. Is this the sandpit you drove your Mercury in at approximately eight-thirty Monday evening with Vickie?"

Galda had the time wrong, but I let it go. "Yes, sir."

"How far into this pit did you drive?"

I pointed to an area where the road broadens out into the flat area above the sandpit. In response to other questions, I pointed out where I had been standing when I had swung my hand at her when she had gotten out of the car, where I had found my shoe.

"Did you run anywhere in the area?"

"I don't remember. There is not much distance to run—I think I remember running for some distance," I told him. Then I recalled something Detective Spahr had told me earlier in the day, and walking down the dirt drive, halfway to Chapel Road, I said: "Somebody during the day placed me out here. It is possible I ran out that road."

"The pants you had on, and the socks, had some sand on it. How do you account for that?" Prosecutor Calissi asked.

"The fact that I had lost one shoe."

"Did you run up on the bank?"

"I don't recall ever running up on the bank."

"Did you lift anything at all in this area while you were here?" Galda asked, picking up the interrogation.

"Nothing, except my shoe the second time I came back."

"How many times did you strike her?"

"I don't actually know if I did strike her at all. I swung once. That I really know, but other than that I don't know."

"What type of swing was it?"

"Pretty hard swing with my right hand."

Calissi gave up. "After that you got back in the car, is that correct?"

"Correct."

"Do you recall being on this bank at all?" he asked, pointing to the dirt mound. His question was nearly a plea.

"No, sir."

"When you got back in the car, were you alone?"

"Yes."

"When you backed out of the sandpit, what did you do then?"

"I started down Chapel Road for home."

"How far did you travel?"

"You see where that single tree sticks out by itself?" I asked, pointing down Chapel Road. Calissi nodded. "I went as far as that."

Assistant Prosecutor Galda, again taking me by the arm, led the entire group of us, with photographers trailing behind, down Chapel Road to the spot I had pointed out.

"You traveled to this particular spot and stopped?" Galda asked.

"Parked right across the street."

"Then what happened?"

"I walked over there."

"Did you throw anything in this area?"

"I don't know."

Several of the detectives accompanying us had walked into the woods on the south side of Chapel Road while Mr. Galda was questioning me. Detective Graber, who seemed to be in charge of the officers in the woods, waved to Galda, motioning

us to come forward. We walked in fifteen or twenty feet from
the road's edge and were confronted with Vickie's pocketbook
and schoolbook lying right where I had left them the previous
Monday night.

For reasons that will become apparent as this story
progresses, Vickie had left her belongings in my car, and since
I could not take them home with me—explaining Vickie's pocketbook to my wife would have been, shall we say, difficult—or
leave them in the car, where Gilroy would find them and want an
explanation, I had left them lying near a discarded Christmas
tree—a good marker, I thought—in the wooded area down the
road, where I would have no trouble finding them the next day,
to return them to Vickie.

I could not understand it. I had been certain that the
police had found these things during their searches for evidence
after the body was found; and I had wondered earlier, when
Galda was asking me to identify the girl's clothing, why he was
not asking me to identify the pocketbook. It was inconceivable
to me that these items, clearly visible from the roadway, could
have lain there a day and a half without being found by the
police, or by the hundreds of curiosity seekers, newspaper photographers, and reporters who had tramped through the area.
Before I could collect my wits, Mr. Galda asked: "Ed, there
appears to be a book, a brown leather bag. Do you recognize
them?"

"I recognize the pocketbook. I do," I stammered. "I do
recognize it, yes."

"Did you *throw* the bag?"

"I do recognize it."

Galda sensed my confusion and was moving in for the
kill. "Did you throw this bag Monday evening at about eight-
thirty?"

"I am not sure—I must have."

"You came down here?"

"Yes."

"You came down here?"

"Yes."

"You must have?" he pressed.

"I must have."

"Do you recognize what appears to be a red book?"

"No, I don't."

The assistant prosecutor, satisfied with my replies, handed the pocketbook and textbook to Detective Graber, instructing him to "take charge of these articles." Then, again taking me by the arm, he led me back to Prosecutor Calissi's automobile, parked at the sandpit entrance. "Tell us the route you traveled," he told me.

"Do I have to go back all the way to my home?"

"Just the route that you traveled."

"I was going to ask you, do we have to go all the way back to my trailer, in case the baby is there. I don't want all these hounds pouring in," I added, pointing to the horde of reporters and photographers following us about the scene. In the event that my wife had been released by the police, as promised, and if she had returned home, I did not want the reporters bothering her.

"I don't believe it is necessary," Galda replied. "If it is your desire not to do that, certainly we want to cooperate. I think that is a reasonable request. Let the record show that Detective Carl DeMarco is driving at this time."

With Galda's assurance that we would not have to go all the way to my house trailer, I pointed out the route I followed from the sandpit to my home—south on Chapel Road, left onto Pulis Avenue, and left again at the entrance to the trailer park. Without his assurance, I would have stopped talking right then.

As we approached the trailer park entrance, Galda asked: "Is it your desire not to go into the area?"

"I'd rather not."

"Very well. I think it is all right. We are about to describe the second trip to the sandpit. What did you do?"

"I left by the main road and turned right on Pulis Avenue. I followed Pulis down as far as Chapel Road and turned right."

"Did you go directly to the pit?"

"No, I went past it and I turned around somewhere."

"We have now returned to the sandpit," Galda remarked as Captain DeMarco stopped the car by the end of the driveway, facing north in the direction of Oak Street, where my pants had been found.

"I didn't go directly to the sandpit," I told the assistant prosecutor. "I went past on Chapel Road in a northerly direction."

"You went to the end of the road and made a U-turn?"

"Yes, go straight up. I went up here."

"We have come to the intersection of Young's Road and Chapel Road," Galda stated for the record, "and we are making a U-turn and are headed back in a southerly direction on Chapel Road."

"That's right," I said. We were now headed in a direction away from Oak Street, and away from where the pants had been found.

"Where is the five-gallon can?"

"At my house trailer."

"We will now proceed to the trailer to see if we can locate the can, and we will close the record until we arrive there."

I argued with Galda, pointing out his prior agreement not to go near the area with so many reporters and photographers following us. I suggested that he could just as easily send a couple of detectives to pick up the can, but the assistant prosecutor brushed my arguments aside. His earlier agreement seems to have been a "Look at how nice we treated Smith" ploy, which would look good on the record.

"We are now at the trailer home," Galda said, to reopen the record. "We are pointing to a Great Lakes Superior forty-five-foot house trailer, and is this your home?"

"That's right."

"We are in front of a patio. Is this where you threw your pants?"

"I threw them right out the back door."

"Also, alongside the entrance there appears to be a five-gallon green can. Can you identify that?"

"That's the can I used last night."

"Is this the can that was in the Mercury in the sandpit when you and Vickie were in the area?"

"That's the can."

"Is that the can you had to climb over to get out the right side of the automobile?"

"Yes."

The emphasis on the identification of the can made no sense to me. As I pondered Galda's fascination with trivia, and wondered when he was going to get around to asking me how my pants had gotten from Pulis Avenue, where I said I had thrown them, to Oak Street, where the police had found them, he turned to the stenographic reporter and said: "I believe now that completes the two trips, and we will close the questioning. Will you indicate the time?" It was 3:45 p.m. I had been without sleep for thirty-one and a quarter hours, and under constant police interrogation for sixteen and a quarter hours. I was not asked to sign the statement.

When the first assistant prosecutor indicated that the taking of the statement was being concluded, I was flabbergasted. It was obvious since my denial that I had struck Vickie, or that I had lifted any heavy objects while with her, that Galda was not going to take a chance on asking me if I had killed the girl —my negative reply would have destroyed the statement. But his failure to inquire into the matter of when or where I had disposed of my pants was incomprehensible. My earlier statement that I had thrown them on Pulis Avenue still stood, and the police had no evidence to dispute that story. It was essential, therefore, to obtain from me a declaration that a) I had thrown the pants on Oak Street where they were found by the Ramsey police, or b) at some time subsequent to the murder I had traveled on Oak Street. Yet no attempt to obtain such a declaration was made.

At one point Galda did ask whether I had thrown the pants away, and I had replied: "I don't know." He did not, however, ask whether my story about having thrown them on Pulis Avenue was true, whether I had thrown them on Oak

Street, or whether I had traveled on Oak Street. In fact, throughout the two-hour-and-fifty-five-minute interrogation, Oak Street never once was mentioned by anyone, nor was I ever taken to the spot where the pants had been found. The only conclusion I can draw, in light of the fact that I was taken to all of the places even remotely connected with the crime, such as Galda's big production about the location and identification of the oil can, is that the prosecutor feared that I would reiterate my story of having thrown the pants on Pulis Avenue, and that he knew he would not be able to disprove that claim. Moreover, such a claim, being inconsistent with the prosecutor's theories, would tend to show that my statement was not a confession of guilt by a conscience-stricken murderer, given after consultation with his spiritual adviser—as the prosecutor would later describe the statement to a jury.

There is, of course, another possible explanation for the prosecutor's failure to ask the $64,000 question, and that is that he knew I had not killed the girl—or at the very least doubted that I had killed her—and as a result had to be satisfied with a statement which involved me in the crime, which he could offer to the jury as a "confession," but which in fact was no confession at all. From the prosecutor's point of view, an incriminating statement involving me in the crime would not be perfect, but it would be better than having me cut the ground out from under him by denying that I had killed the girl, or that I had thrown my pants on Oak Street.

## CHAPTER TEN

**MAHWAH POLICE HEADQUARTERS, WHERE** my ordeal had begun sixteen and a half hours earlier, was as much of a madhouse when we arrived there as the corridor outside the prosecutor's office had been. All the reporters and photographers we had eluded in Hackensack were waiting for us in Mahwah, and in addition a clamorous mob of at least a thousand spectators had gathered in the parking lot to contribute to the general bedlam. Someone, no doubt the prosecutor, must have made a public announcement of where and when I would appear, for the sensation seekers certainly knew where to be to catch a glimpse of the man already being described in the newspapers as the "sex-killer" of Victoria Zielinski.

The prosecutor cannot deny that his office informed the public of the fact that I would be taken to the scene of the crime—the presence of hundreds of spectators proves that. The information could have come from no other source. And one can easily imagine how far in advance notice was given of my itinerary when one considers the fact that the New York *Daily News* had sufficient time to send their photographic airplane to the scene, and to time its arrival to coincide with my appearance on the scene. And finally, the presence of great numbers of sightseers, photographers, reporters, and newsreel cameramen from the metropolitan area television stations, proves that the time and place of my arraignment was also well publicized far in advance. Prosecutor Calissi was playing the publicity angle to the hilt.

The second-floor courtroom of the Municipal Building

was only slightly less crowded than the parking lot. The same group of detectives who had convoyed me out of the county courthouse were waiting at the side door to the Municipal Building when we arrived, and after a pushing, shoving dash up the stairs and through the courtroom—during which I was half-dragged and half-carried by Galda and DeLisle—they managed to deliver me all in one piece to the office at the rear of the courtroom.

It was relatively calm and quiet in the office. Most of the detectives who had brought me through the crowds had left the room. Only Prosecutor Calissi, First Assistant Prosecutor Galda, Chiefs Smith of Mahwah and Voss of Ramsey, Captain De-Marco, and Detective Spahr were present. While the others conferred on the matter of the arraignment procedure to be followed, Spahr took me to one side and explained what was to take place next.

"We are going to let some photographers in here. They will be kept on the other side of the fence there," he said, pointing to the wooden fence dividing the room. "After they get a couple of pictures, we are going to have the building cleared of all but a few reporters from the local papers, people we trust. Then we will take you before the magistrate and proceed—"

"Hold on. Just hold it right there. If you want me to go before a judge without my lawyer, you are going to have to carry me."

"Don't get excited," Spahr said. "Calm down. You aren't going before a judge, it's only a local magistrate. It's only a formality. You won't need your lawyer for this. Just don't say anything to the magistrate. It will be over in a minute. He will refer the case to the grand jury."

"Who is the magistrate?"

"A Mr. Young, I believe."

"Frank Young?"

"I believe so. Do you know him?"

"Hell, yes, I know him. He is a regular at Herbie Pelzer's gin mill down the street."

Herbert Pelzer was a local tavern owner. His tavern, down the street from the Municipal Building, was at one time the abandoned house which had inspired Joyce Kilmer's poem, "The House with Nobody in It." A year after my trial and conviction, Pelzer would come forward with an affidavit tending to support my trial testimony.

My conversation with Detective Spahr was interrupted by Mr. Galda, who directed me to stand in the rear of the office and face the door. When I had done so, the door was opened and twenty-five or thirty photographers were permitted to squeeze into the room. The photographic session lasted ten minutes, until someone shouted that the magistrate was ready. Hearing this shout, Prosecutor Calissi immediately ordered Captain DeMarco to have the office and courtroom cleared of all unauthorized persons.

The courtroom was nearly empty when I was ushered in to be arraigned. Less than a dozen newspaper reporters had been permitted to remain, and these were required to stand in the back of the room. At least twice that number of county detectives, state police officers, and uniformed officers from Mahwah and Ramsey stood about the room in small groups.

The magistrate, Frank Young, a short, rotund man of about fifty, sat behind the long table at the front of the room— the same table at the opposite ends of which Gilroy and I had sat the previous night. To the right of the magistrate sat a woman stenographer, who would take shorthand notes of the proceedings. Fred Galda, representing the county prosecutor, stood just behind and to the left of the magistrate.

"Hello, Smitty," the magistrate said as I was led up to the table by Chief Smith and Detective Spahr. "Got yourself in a jam, didn't you?"

"Sort of," I replied.

"Well, this will be over in a minute. I will read the complaint and ask you to plead. You don't have to answer because a plea of not guilty is mandatory, and I am required by law to record that plea and remand you to the county jail without bail, for action by the grand jury. This is just a formality to bring the complaint against you. No evidence will be heard or admitted. Do you understand that?"

"I'm not pleading to anything, Frank. I'm not taking part in any legal stuff until my lawyer is here."

"Are you represented by counsel?"

"I want Judge Dwyer from Ridgewood—you know him. These people have been telling me all day and all night that I don't need a lawyer. You're the judge, can't you postpone this till I get my lawyer up here?"

Before the magistrate could reply, Assistant Prosecutor Galda, who appeared to be irritated by our friendly exchange, bent over and whispered something to him. I could not hear what Galda was saying, but he surely was saying it with some degree of insistence. The magistrate nodded a few times, then began examining a section of a lawbook on the table in front of him.

The magistrate spent two or three minutes scanning the book, once cross-checking a point in a second book. He did not seem to be entirely satisfied with what he found, but finally he looked up at me and said: "Eddie, the county prosecutor wants to get on with this. He tells me you will be permitted to speak with your lawyer as soon as it can be arranged. So we are going to go ahead. A complete record of this proceeding will be kept for your lawyer to examine. Now, you just stand there. You needn't say a word."

The magistrate began by reading the complaint prepared by Detective Spahr and signed by Chief Smith, alleging that on or about March 4, 1957, in the Township of Mahwah, State of New Jersey, I had "willfully, feloniously, and with malice aforethought, killed and murdered one Victoria Zielinski." The stenographer at his side was taking notes of everything he said. *That record has since disappeared.*

As instructed, I remained silent throughout the reading of the complaint, and at the end of some half-mumbled legal jargon, the magistrate looked up and said: "That's it, Smitty. I've entered the mandatory plea of not guilty for you. Now, the county prosecutor will take you back to Hackensack."

"What about my lawyer?"

"It's out of my jurisdiction, Smitty. It is a county court matter now," he replied. Then, scooping up his books and a few sheets of paper, he hurried from the courtroom. The time was 5:30 p.m.

As to whether or not my arraignment was fairly and properly conducted, the following is excerpted from the *Rules of Criminal Procedure for New Jersey Courts:*

RULE 3:2-3. PROCEEDINGS BEFORE THE MAGIS-TRATE.
(a) APPEARANCE. An officer making an arrest under a warrant issued upon a complaint shall take the arrested person, without unnecessary delay, before the court or the magistrate named in the warrant. *A person making an arrest without a warrant shall take the arrested person, without unnecessary delay, before the nearest available magistrate and a complaint shall be filed forthwith and a warrant issued thereon. A preliminary hearing shall be held forthwith.*[1] [Italics added.]

In my case, the governing portion of the rule is that portion concerning an arrest without a warrant. And for the purpose of compliance with the rule, the "nearest available magistrate" was any of the county or superior court judges available in the courthouse in Hackensack, where I had been all morning and part of the afternoon. Taking me to Mahwah to be arraigned might have been good publicity for the prosecutor, but it was not a practical or legal requirement. Prosecutor Calissi could just as easily have walked me down the corridor from his office at 9 a.m., into the first courtroom he came to, and had me arraigned right then and there, "without unnecessary delay."

[1] *Police Manual of New Jersey Statutes and Court Rules* (1956 edition) (Newark, N.J.: Gann Law Books), p. 215.

RULE 3:2-3.  STATEMENT BY THE MAGISTRATE.

(b) *The magistrate shall inform the defendant of the complaint against him, of his right to counsel or, if indigent, of the privilege of having counsel assigned, and of the right to have a preliminary examination. The magistrate shall allow the defendant reasonable time and opportunity to consult counsel.* He shall also inform the defendant of his right to make a statement not under oath as to the charges against him, and that he is not required to make such a statement. . . .[2] [Italics added.]

The magistrate's failure to comply with the rule is self-evident. He knew of my desire to have counsel present, that I wanted the proceedings delayed until my attorney was present, and that the required delay would be a brief one. Yet notwithstanding this knowledge, he proceeded with the arraignment, refusing to "allow the defendant reasonable time and opportunity to consult counsel."

The Bergen County Courthouse was deserted when we returned to the prosecutor's office at 6 p.m. Detectives Spahr and DeLisle had gone off somewhere as soon as we had returned, leaving me in the office with Prosecutor Calissi, Mr. Galda, and Chief Smith of Mahwah. I asked Calissi when I would be permitted to see my wife.

"You'll have to take that up with the warden of the county jail," the prosecutor replied. "Your wife has been sent home."

"But Spahr and DeLisle said I could see her as soon as I gave you a statement."

"I'm sorry, Smith, I know nothing about that. I didn't promise you anything, did I?"

"Ask Spahr about it. He can tell you."

"I know nothing about that. Did Mr. Galda promise you anything?"

"No. It was Spahr and DeLisle. You two weren't around when they were bugging me with questions all morning. Why don't you ask Captain DeMarco? He was there and told me the same thing."

[2] Ibid.

"I didn't promise you anything, Smith. You'll have to talk to the county jail warden about seeing your wife. Right now I'm going across the street to the State Restaurant. When Mr. Spahr returns, he will bring you across. We will have dinner before we take you to the jail. I will see you over there."

Prosecutor Calissi left the office immediately after speaking, leaving me with Mr. Galda and Chief Smith. A minute or two later, Detective Spahr entered the room and said: "Let's go, Smitty. I don't know how you rate around here, but Mr. Calissi is buying everyone dinner."

"What's the deal about my wife?" I asked Spahr. "Either I see her or I deny everything I said."

"Just a moment, Ed," Mr. Galda said. "If Detective Spahr promised you anything, he will speak to the prosecutor about it. Isn't that right, Walter?" My threat to deny my statement had shaken Galda.

"Of course I will," the detective stated. "I'll speak to the prosecutor at dinner."

"Where is my wife now? Is she all right?"

"Sure, she's just a bit shook up. One of the women from the office has driven her home. Tomorrow morning I will bring her down here myself, and you can see her here in the office just as I promised. Now, let's go eat."

"Okay. But you'd better not be giving me a run-around."

Assistant Prosecutor Galda remained behind when I left the office with Chief Smith and Detective Spahr. As we reached the street, a photographer from the Newark *Star-Ledger* rushed up and requested a picture of me standing between the officers. Spahr declined to have his picture taken, telling the photographer that anonymity made his work easier, but Chief Smith was only too happy to pose for a picture, even going so far as to suggest that the photographer should use the courthouse as a background. Then, as the man was ready to snap the picture, Smith threw his arm around my shoulders and assumed his best fatherly look. I almost threw up.

The State Restaurant, directly across Main Street from the courthouse, was a small bar and grill frequented by the courthouse regulars—judges, lawyers, detectives, reporters, and administrative personnel. The restaurant was nearly empty when we entered. Prosecutor Calissi was nowhere in sight.

"We'll sit over here in a side booth until the prosecutor arrives," Spahr said, pointing to one of the booths along the wall.

When the waitress arrived, Chief Smith ordered scotch and water for himself. Spahr ordered Seagram's V.O., after asking me if I wanted a drink. "If the prosecutor comes in," he told me, "push the glass in front of me."

"Don't worry," I replied, "it won't last that long, I need something to keep me awake."

Prosecutor Calissi arrived ten minutes later. By then, the drink Spahr had given me was only a warm glow in my stomach as we moved from our booth to a large table at the rear of the restaurant. Calissi ordered chicken soup, lobster tails, french fries, salad, and coffee for everyone. The soup was terrible, and the prosecutor, claiming it was rancid, personally returned it to the kitchen. The rest of the food was not much better, but since it was the first food I had seen since the toast and coffee with Detective Sinatra twelve hours earlier—it seemed as if it had been twelve days earlier—I tried to eat, but it was too much for me. A woman reporter, invited to the table by Calissi, offered to eat it for me. I do not remember her name. All I can recall is that she was fat, wore a horrible print dress that I would not have used to shine my shoes, had a head of hair that looked as if it had been set by the Roto-Rooter man, and that between mouthfuls of lobster meat and french-fried potatoes she asked me a million asinine questions about myself. She ate the leftovers from the whole table.

We finished dinner a few minutes before seven o'clock. The time stands out in my mind because Prosecutor Calissi wanted me out of the place before the seven o'clock news came on the television in the bar. He did not want the people in the restaurant and bar to see my picture on television and recognize me. Handing me two of his cigars, he told me that I would be taken over to the county jail by Chief Smith and Detective

Spahr. Then he added: "Mr. Spahr has told me of his agreement to permit you to see your wife. He will arrange transportation for her tomorrow, and I will make my office available to you."

At 7:15 p.m., March 6, after nineteen and three-quarter hours in police custody, and having gone thirty-four and three-quarter hours without sleep, I was committed to the Bergen County Jail on a charge of murder. Within ten minutes, I was sound asleep on a filthy, sweat-stained mattress.

# CHAPTER ELEVEN

**DETECTIVE SPAHR SURPRISED ME. ON** Thursday afternoon, the day after my arrest, two prison guards appeared at the door to my cell and told me that I was wanted in the prosecutor's office. They did not know what it was about, but when I had been taken to the basement of the jail, from which a narrow tunnel connects the jail to the courthouse, two uniformed county court attendants entered the jail through the tunnel and informed me that my wife was waiting to see me.

Detective Spahr was alone in the prosecutor's office when I entered with the court attendants. Curiously, although the prosecutor's detectives had not handcuffed me during the entire time from my arrest until my commitment to the county jail, I was handcuffed for the walk through the tunnel, as I would be every time in the future. With two guards escorting me, and with guards and locked steel door at either end of the tunnel, one wonders where they thought I might go if unrestrained.

Detective Spahr ordered the court attendants to remove the restraints as soon as he saw them. They demurred, but Spahr, stating that he would assume responsibility for me, again ordered the handcuffs removed, adding that he wanted the officers to wait outside in the corridor.

"Your wife is outside," the detective told me when the court attendants had, with obvious reluctance, left the room. "It's been awfully busy around here today, and Mr. Calissi needs his office, so we will have to hold this down to a few minutes. Next week we will try to work out a better arrangement. Okay?"

"Sure," I replied. "How is she?"

"Well, you know, still a bit shook up. It's been a big shock to her. When I bring her in, I'll wait over by the door. I have to keep an eye on you, but you'll be able to talk in private. You ready?"

"Okay, bring her in."

Spahr went to the door and said a few words to a young woman standing outside. The woman went away, but returned in a minute or two with my wife. As soon as my wife saw me she began crying, and it was a few minutes before I could calm her down enough for her to speak. Her first words were: "Why did you do it, Eddie?"

"I didn't," I told her. "Don't believe anything you've heard. Whatever else you want to believe, you can. Just believe I didn't do it. Try to trust me that far."

"But you confessed," she protested. "It's in all the papers, on television, everywhere. The detectives told me yesterday, before they took me home. Everybody says you admitted it." She began crying again.

"Listen, Brat," I said, using her nickname, "don't believe anything like that. I haven't seen the papers, so I don't know what you've read, but you can take my word for it that I didn't confess. In fact, I didn't even sign the phony statement I made to get them to release you."

"I don't know, Eddie, they said you signed a confession."

"They, whoever 'they' are, are lying. I didn't sign a goddam thing. Nothing. Not a thing. Now, tell me, what did Judge Dwyer say yesterday?"

"I didn't get to see him. After you called, I got ready to drive downtown as you told me to do, but the police, a detective, Garber or Grabber, or something like that"—she meant Gordon Graber—"came to the house and insisted that I had to go with him. They brought me down here to identify your pants."

"Did you identify them?"

"I'm sorry, honey. I thought I was helping you."

"That's all right," I said, trying to reassure her. "Don't worry about it. It's not important. How long did they hold you?"

"All day. They took me home to get your shirt about three o'clock, then they brought me back. A woman took me home finally, about four-thirty."

"I saw you, but they wouldn't let me talk to you."

"I know. I saw you, too. They kept on bringing me out in the hallway, outside the office you were in. I saw you every time the door was opened, but they wouldn't let me talk to you, either. When I wanted to call Judge Dwyer, and when they took me home for your shirt, they said you didn't need a lawyer. That's what they kept telling me all day, every time I asked if I could phone him for you. They wouldn't let me call anyone or leave."

"So you never did call him?"

"When I finally got home at four-thirty, your mother was there. She called Judge Dwyer, and he put her in touch with a criminal lawyer. Your mother said to tell you he would see you in a day or two. Is that all right?"

"What's his name?"

"I can't remember. Gaudelly, or something like that."

"Okay. Don't worry about it. Everything will work out when I get the lawyer. I only asked for Dwyer because he was the first lawyer I could think of at the time."

"Eddie, I'm afraid. What's going to happen?"

"It will work out, honey. Just try not to worry too much."

"Are you sure you'll be all right?" she asked dubiously.

"Positive," I lied. "Just trust me. As soon as this is over we will take a nice long vacation."

That promise seemed to brighten her spirits a bit. After a few more words about our daughter, and my wife's plan to remain at her mother's house, Spahr approached and said he had to end the visit. "The boss wants his office back."

My wife was crying again as we said good-bye. She was "shook up," as Spahr had told me, but she was a good kid, and I was certain she would be all right. That was the important thing, I thought, as I was led back to the county jail. Once I could be certain that she would be taken care of, then I could get to work extricating myself from the mess I was in. The police knew only half the story. With the assistance of a lawyer, things would work out fine—or so I thought at the time. I was wrong. More than eleven years later, I am still waiting for things to "work out."

Prosecutor Calissi did not waste any time setting in motion the legal machinery. Two days after my arrest, Friday, March 8, he went before the grand jury, and before lunchtime, after the testimony of one witness, DeLisle, he had obtained the following indictment.

Indictment No. S-276-56
(Filed March 8, 1957)
Superior Court of New Jersey
Bergen County—Law Division
September Term A.D. 1956
Second Stated Session

---

The State of New Jersey,
v.
Edgar Smith,
Defendant.

---

The Grand Jurors of the State of New Jersey, for the County of Bergen, upon their oaths present that EDGAR SMITH on or about the 4th day of March, 1957, in the Township of Mahwah, in the County of Bergen aforesaid, and within the jurisdiction of this Court, did willfully, feloniously and of his malice afore-thought, kill and murder VICTORIA ZIELINSKI, contrary to the provisions of N.J.S. 2A: 113-1 and N.J.S. 2A: 113-2 and against the peace of this State, the government and dignity of the same.

Guy W. Calissi
County Prosecutor

A True Bill
William S. Davis
Foreman

The following day, in an effort to forestall a defense of insanity, temporary or otherwise, Prosecutor Calissi had me brought to his office for an examination by two psychiatrists retained to represent the state. It was at this time that I first met the attorney recommended to my family by Judge Dwyer. He was Joseph Gaudielle—lawyer, philosopher, gourmet, Beau Brummel of the legal fraternity, and for many years one of the most respected criminal defense attorneys in the state. He had been summoned to the prosecutor's office by Mr. Calissi who, in observation of his profession's code of ethics, would not permit the doctors to examine me without the consent of my attorney.

> A lawyer should not *in any way* communicate upon the subject of controversy with a party represented by counsel . . . but should deal only with his counsel.[1] [Italics added.]

Mr. Gaudielle advised me that it probably would be in my best interests to cooperate—I was beginning to hate that word— with the doctors. Then, taking me to one side, he asked me if I had signed a confession.

"No," I replied. "I didn't sign a thing."

"Did you initial the stenographer's notes?"

"No. I didn't sign or initial anything. I told them in advance that I wouldn't, so they didn't ask afterwards."

"Wonderful," the lawyer exclaimed. "I had heard through friends that the newspaper accounts of your signing were inaccurate, and I have so advised your parents and your wife, but I wanted to hear it from you."

"I haven't read the papers, so I don't know anything but what my wife told me the other day. I told her that I didn't sign anything, and that I didn't confess to anything."

"What do you mean, you didn't confess to anything?"

"Just what I said—I didn't confess. They didn't ask if I killed the girl, and I didn't say I did, and I wouldn't have said so if they had asked."

"Let me be certain that I understand. Are you telling me that you were never asked whether you had committed the crime? Is that what you are saying?"

---

[1] Canon 9, Canons of Professional Ethics, *New Jersey Court Rules* (1958 edition) (Newark, N.J.: Gann Law Books).

"Precisely. At one point, Galda, who did the questioning, seemed to be working up to the question, but when I denied ever having seen or handled the rock he showed me, and denied so many other things, I think he chickened out."

"You admitted attacking the girl with your fists, did you not?"

"No. Galda asked me that about a dozen times. Every time he asked, I admitted swinging at her when she slapped at me. It was just a reflexive action; I only swung once, and I told Galda I couldn't even be sure that that one swing hit her."

"Well, that certainly is not the story the authorities have given the newspapers. According to the authorities, you admitted punching the girl in the face after she had resisted your attempts to molest her, but you claimed that you were unable to remember how you killed her."

"I don't give a damn what Calissi says. I'm telling you what I *didn't* say."

"You claim now that you are innocent of the crime?"

"You're goddam right I do."

"That creates a much more complicated picture. I must hold further discussions with your family. I shall see you again Monday or Tuesday. We can review your story at that time. Meanwhile, Edgar, you may cooperate with these doctors. I know them, and I know they are honorable gentlemen. As for your confession, or statement, however, you must refuse to sign it if the authorities ask you to do so. Tell them you are acting upon my instructions. Do you understand?" I nodded, and he went on: "Under no circumstances are you to sign or initial any document, no matter what the authorities tell you. I doubt if Mr. Calissi would seek to interrogate you without my permission, but if he does, or if anyone does, insist that I be summoned."

"Okay, you're the boss. I'll tell them to go to hell and take the statement with them."

Mr. Gaudielle smiled broadly at my comment. After a few more comments about taking it easy and not worrying, he departed, leaving me with Prosecutor Calissi and his psychiatrists.

The medical examination took fifteen minutes. The doctors asked a number of superficial questions concerning my schooling, military service, and my arrest. Then they asked me to stand with arms outspread, close my eyes, and touch the tip of my nose with my index fingers. Apparently satisfied with my ability to comply, the doctors ended the examination. They did not testify at my trial—sanity was not an issue—so the reader will have to draw his own conclusions as to whether the doctors, had they testified, would have sworn that a) I was sane; b) I could touch the tip of my nose while standing with my eyes closed; or c) because I could (b), I must, therefore—*therefore?* —have been sane.

On Monday morning, March 11, five days after my arrest, I was taken before Judge Arthur J. O'Dea of the Bergen County Court for arraignment on the indictment, and to enter a formal plea. My attorney, who appeared with me, entered a plea of not guilty. Judge O'Dea promptly scheduled my case for trial one month later. The prosecutor was not letting up on the pressure; public emotions, inflamed by the virulent publicity, were not allowed to cool down.

I was returned to my cell on the second floor of the county jail immediately after the arraignment. A few minutes later, I was informed that someone from the prosecutor's office wanted to speak to me downstairs, and I was taken to a room on the first floor, at the back of the jail. There was nothing to indicate to me that what was about to take place would be, for the prosecution, the key to my subsequent trial and conviction. Had I known then what I know now—one of the world's oldest and saddest laments—I would have refused to take one step outside my cell. But I did not know, and as a result, I walked right into the prosecutor's neatly laid trap.

Detective DeLisle was sitting at a table when I entered the room. The guard, after asking if he would be needed, and having received a negative reply, left me alone in the room with the detective.[2]

---

[2] The following conversation is reconstructed from affidavits filed in the United States District Court, District of New Jersey.

"Hello, Smitty, how are you getting along?" DeLisle inquired when the guard had gone.

"Okay. I'll live."

"Fine, glad to hear that. Smitty, I have here two typewritten transcripts of your statement of last Wednesday. Mr. Calissi asked me to come over and have you sign them. We only want you—"

I did not permit him to finish. "You can quit right there. I've told you before, I'm telling you now, and I'll tell you tomorrow—I won't sign anything."

"Why not, Smitty?"

"I want my lawyer, Joe Gaudielle, to be here."

"Yes, I know Mr. Gaudielle is your attorney. And he is just about the best. But why do you need him?"

"Because he said I should not do anything unless he is present."

"And you won't sign your statement?"

"My lawyer told me not to sign anything."

"Yes, I know that you refused to sign a receipt for the indictment on your attorney's advice," DeLisle stated. Three days earlier, Detective Garabedian had stormed out of the jail in a rage when I would not sign for a copy of the indictment.

"Well, if you already know, don't ask."

"Oh, I wouldn't pressure you to disobey your attorney's advice. However, there is no harm, is there, in reading it over to be certain that we haven't misinterpreted or misrepresented your statements? It's for your protection as well as ours."

"I don't remember what I said. There would be no sense to my reading it."

"Well, just look it over anyway," DeLisle said, sliding a copy across the table to me. "It might come back to you."

I thought about that for a few minutes. I recalled that Prosecutor Calissi had not allowed the psychiatrists to say a word to me until he had obtained the consent of my attorney— as the Canons of Professional Ethics require; and for that reason, I was under the impression that Mr. Gaudielle must have been informed of DeLisle's intention to visit me. So, seeing no harm in reading the statement, I agreed to look it over.

I did not read the statement in its entirety. Rather, I scanned it as one would scan a book one was considering purchasing, thumbing through it and stopping occasionally to read an interesting portion. At one or two points, I found statements which sounded different when reread than when they were made. I asked DeLisle if I could delete them, or change the wording.

"I have no authority to permit that," he replied.

When I had finished skimming through the statement, the detective suggested that he might take a chance and permit me to make corrections in one of the two copies he had with him, provided that I initial the corrections and sign both copies. I declined the offer, saying that I would not sign.

"Listen, Smitty, Prosecutor Calissi will be burned up if I don't bring this back signed. He would probably cancel your special visits with your wife.[3] How about it? I don't want the boss thinking I didn't try hard enough."

"I told you I'm not signing the goddam thing," I responded angrily. I was beginning to lose my temper. "If you're worried about Calissi, call the guard in and he can be a witness."

"All right, Smitty, don't get upset. We don't need witnesses. I can tell the boss that Mr. Gaudielle ordered you not to sign. Maybe he will let me off the hook if you'll just tell me whether the statements you made are accurately reported here. How about that? Have we misrepresented anything?"

"I don't know. I suppose the stenographer is honest. I didn't see anything wrong in the little bit I read."

"Well, that's just fine," DeLisle remarked with a big smile, "just fine." I would find out exactly how fine two months later at my trial.

The detective and I chatted a few minutes longer. I was fascinated by the workings of the stenotype machine, and I asked DeLisle how so few symbols on a small roll of paper

[3] That's precisely what happened.

tape could record so many words. He did not know how the machine worked. Finally, thirty minutes or so after our meeting began, DeLisle departed, and I was returned to my cell just in time for lunch. Two hours later, I was again summoned to the room at the rear of the jail. There, instead of a detective, I found Mr. Gaudielle waiting.

The lawyer waited until the guard had left us alone, then he asked: "What did Detective DeLisle want this morning?"

"He wanted me to sign the statement. What did they do, tell you he was coming over?"

"No, they did not tell me. I must speak to Mr. Calissi about that. He should not contact you without your attorney's permission. He knows better than to do that. You did not sign the statement, did you?"

"No. I told him I wouldn't sign anything. I wouldn't even have talked to him except that I figured he had asked you, like he did last Saturday with the doctors."

"You should not have spoken with him, but I cannot blame you for not knowing that. You should have requested that I be called to appear."

"I did, but he said I didn't need to bother you."

"That is the old story they tell everyone. If the authorities return—I doubt they will—insist upon the presence of your attorney. I should like to see that statement."

"Can't you get a copy?"

"Oh, no. They never permit defense counsel to read those things until they are offered in evidence. The prosecution does not wish to afford defense counsel the opportunity to prepare. I must rely upon your memory."

"I'm not going to be able to help you much. I don't remember half of what I said. I was really beat at the time, making it up as we went along. I had been awake a day and a half, and they were coming at me with questions all night and all day."

"Well, do not worry too much about that. As long as the statement is unsigned, it is useless to them. The conditions under which it was given would be pertinent only where there was to be an attempt to offer the statement in evidence. As it is, without your endorsement, the authorities might as well have a sheaf of blank paper. Now, Edgar," he went on, "I have an appointment with your mother this afternoon. I have visited you only to ask you one question, and to see how you are getting along."

"Shoot, I'll answer if I can."

"Good. First, however, I must impress upon you that you are in a very dangerous position. The public is demanding speedy action against you. People are outraged by the brutality of the crime. Wild rumors are circulating that you murdered another young girl in the same fashion in Japan, Hawaii, California, Texas, or Ohio—depending on which version of the story one hears. The pressure on the prosecutor is enormous. It will prove exceedingly difficult, if not impossible, to obtain a fair trial before an impartial jury at this time and in this county. I have, therefore, discussed the matter with Mr. Calissi —he is a very reasonable and honest man; and he indicates that he is prepared to accept a plea of guilty to second-degree murder, on the assumption that this was a crime of passion. He would require, however, that you make that plea and render a full confession in open court. Even with the imposition of a maximum sentence, which you would have to expect from Judge O'Dea, you would be a free man in eight to ten years." The lawyer paused, and when I did not reply, he asked: "Do you desire that I should arrange such a plea?"

As the saying goes, I did not know whether to laugh or cry. The only comment I could make was: "You've got to be kidding."

Mr. Gaudielle was taken aback by my reply. "No," he assured me, "I most certainly would not jest about so serious a matter. I must have your decision."

"My reply," I said slowly, "is that you should go back to the prosecutor and tell him to shove his plea." The lawyer was obviously dissatisfied by both the substance and the intemperance of my response, but I went on: "I am not going to plead guilty to something I didn't do. If you think you are going to talk me into something like that without ever hearing my story, you're playing in the wrong ball park."

"Please, Edgar, don't misunderstand me. I will—if I accept your case—I will most assuredly hear everything you have to say. But as of now, I cannot say your decision is a wise decision. You are being quite unreasonable, and under the circumstances I shall be forced to reconsider the acceptance of your case."

"I thought you *were* my lawyer."

"In a manner of speaking, I am. However, in my agreement with your mother, I stipulated that I would be free to withdraw if, subsequent to discussions with you, I concluded that I could not do my best for you. If you refuse to take my best advice, which I conceive of as accepting the proffer of a plea, then I shall have to reconsider. I cannot help you if you will not cooperate."

"You've just said the wrong word. That 'cooperate' stuff is what I listened to from Calissi's people for a day and a half. You sound like you're working for him."

"I do not work for anyone but my clients. I resent the implication, and I shall not sit here and be vilified. If you refuse to take my advice, I shall be forced to speak with your mother."

"Listen, Mr. Gaudielle, let's get a few things straight. You can discuss any goddam thing you want with anyone you want. The answer is still going to be No, N–O, No. I am not going to plead guilty to something I did not do. If you are going to give me the choice of pleading guilty or getting a different lawyer, well, so long, it's been nice knowing you."

"Very well, Edgar, if you refuse even to consider the matter, I shall re-evaluate my own position. I may not be back to see you for a few days, so please try to be patient. Do not think I have forgotten you. Do you need money for cigarettes or anything?"

"No, I'll be okay. Sorry if I lost my temper a bit. Give my best to my mother and my wife."

"I shall do that. Call me if you need me."

# CHAPTER TWELVE

MR. GAUDIELLE DID NOT RETURN TO SEE ME
until two weeks after I had refused to plead guilty to second-degree murder. When finally he did return, it was for
the purpose of informing me that he was withdrawing from my
case. He did not explain fully his reason for withdrawing—
there was something about one of his law partners having died
—but I had the impression that my refusal to accept the plea
was his primary reason. Seven or eight years later, when I had
occasion to correspond with him concerning an incident that
took place during the period of time he was representing me,
he did not pass up the opportunity to say, in effect: "I told
you so. If you had taken the plea, you would be a free man by
now."

The attorney who replaced Mr. Gaudielle was John E.
Selser. A former first assistant prosecutor of Bergen County
(1944–9), Mr. Selser brought with him to my defense forty
years of experience in criminal law. As both a prosecutor and
defense attorney, he had been involved in dozens of murder
cases. He was a heavy-set man, with thinning gray hair combed
straight back, and a rather gruff, direct manner of speaking
which belied his gentle nature.

What struck me as curious about him, as compared to what
I was accustomed to, was his formal manner of speaking; like
Mr. Gaudielle, Selser could sometimes make "hello good-bye"
sound like a writ of habeas corpus. This, I realized, was the
result of his legal training; but still it was disconcerting to

hear someone begin an everyday conversation with "whereas" and end it with "hereintofore."

My first visit with my new attorney took place three weeks after my arrest. It was a brief meeting, just long enough for him to tell me that my trial had been postponed until May 13. He had hired an investigator, he told me, but information was difficult to obtain. The local police departments involved had been ordered by the prosecutor not to give us any information. The investigator, a man by the name of Andrew Nicol, had visited the prosecutor and had requested certain basic information, such as the precise location of the scene of the crime; the location of the place where the body had been found; the cause and time of death; and the names of witnesses, if any. The prosecutor had refused to divulge the information, instead sending the investigator to Judge O'Dea. The judge agreed that we were absolutely entitled to the information, but he refused to order the prosecutor to supply it until we had made a formal application in court. Mr. Selser and the investigator were forced to give up. The lawyer did not have the time to drop the preparation of my defense to prepare, have notarized, and to serve upon the court and the prosecutor copies of petitions for information, and then to appear in court to argue the matter. It was easier, and faster, though less reliable, to obtain the information from a local newspaper reporter. As it developed, the lack of precise information regarding the time of death would prove to be the single most significant factor contributing to my conviction.

My first lengthy meeting with Mr. Selser took place on the morning of April 7, 1957, a Sunday. As usual, I had been brought from my cell to the back room of the jail. I knew in advance that Mr. Selser would visit me that day, and I had resolved that he was not going to get away without hearing my story in all its details.

"Good morning, Mr. Selser," I said as I entered the room. "Are we going to have time for more than a 'hello good-bye' visit today?"

"Yes," he replied. "We have all the time we require. What's bothering you?"

"I want to ask you a question. I haven't read the papers— I can't get them, and the prosecutor's people didn't tell me much. So I want to know, exactly what killed Vickie?"

"What killed her? What do you mean? Don't you know?"

"I want you to tell me."

"All right, if you insist," he said, giving me a strange look. "I have not seen the medical report, but from what I gather, her skull was crushed by a large rock."

"Crushed? What does 'crushed' mean? Fractured skull? What?"

"No, Ed. Her skull apparently was totally destroyed. Her brains were found lying on the ground. The whole back of her head—if we accept the newspaper accounts—was missing."

Taking a pencil from his pocket, Mr. Selser began to sketch a human form on the bottom of a cardboard box which had been standing in the corner of the room. When he had completed the sketch, he explained that it represented the position in which Vickie's body had been found. "The cause of death was a total loss of the brain," he concluded.

"Then there isn't a chance that I could have been responsible," I declared. "Not a chance."

"What do you mean by that?"

"Well, I've been telling you, and before you Mr. Gaudielle, that I didn't kill the girl, but I've always had a lingering doubt. You see, Vickie was injured when I was with her, and I left her that way. I thought she might have died from those injuries."

"You mean you did not know her skull had been crushed?"

"I saw that in the first newspaper report, before my arrest, but you know how exaggerated newspaper reports are. A crushed skull could mean anything from bone being depressed in a limited area to what happened to Vickie. Hell, I saw a kid in service get his fingers crushed under a tank of oxygen. All of the bones were mashed, but his fingers were not even cut. He didn't lose a drop of blood."

"Ed, you'd better start right at the beginning. Tell me everything that took place in the sandpit."

"Okay, but you might as well make yourself comfortable. It's a long story."

"That's all right. Take your time and don't leave anything out. We have all day."

"Well, Mr. Selser, you and Nicol have been pestering me about covering up for someone. Nicol is convinced that I am, and he is right. You see, when I left the sandpit, I left Vickie there with Don Hommell."

Selser took my statement as calmly as if I had told him that the sun was shining. It was as if he had expected me to say what I did, and his only reaction and response was to light a cigarette and ask: "Was she alive when you left her with Hommell?"

"Sure she was. But I'd better start at the beginning, or you'll never understand. It was like this: I was on the way home from Secor's with the kerosene when I met Vickie. She was walking toward her home, walking on the east side of Wyckoff Avenue, about two hundred yards north of the Nixons'. I had Gilroy's car. She didn't know the car—she didn't know Joe, either—and the lights of the car were in her eyes, so she couldn't have seen who was driving. But she waved and yelled something as I came abreast of her. I went down to a drive across from Nixons', turned around, and went back to where she was waiting. She opened the door and asked me to drive her home. I had to move the kerosene can closer to the hump on the floor, so there would be room for her legs. As I leaned over, another car passed and the driver blew the horn."

"Whose car was it?" Selser asked.

"I didn't see it. The kerosene can was heavy—five gallons weighs a bit over thirty pounds. I leaned over with my right elbow on the seat, lifting the can with my left hand. While I was bent over, the car went by."

"Which direction?"

"Toward Ramsey. The same way I was going."

"All right. Go ahead."

"Vickie got in the car and—"

"Hold it a minute, Ed. Did you meet Vickie by some plan?"

"No, of course not. I didn't even know she was at the Nixons'."

"But you did know Vickie?"

"Yes. Pat and I both knew her. I gave her a ride home several times before."

"When was the last time prior to March 4?"

I thought about the question for a few moments. "I think the Thursday or Friday before." I finally replied. "I remember it was in my car, just before the transmission trouble. Vickie and another girl asked me to drive them home. I had met them in Robbie's Corral."

"Who was the other girl—Barbara Nixon?"

"No. A kid named Ann Ramera." [1]

"Who is she?"

"A local girl we call Eveready. She is one of the town sweethearts—everybody's, anybody's, anytime. So we call her Eveready."

"How do you know about her, Ed?"

"Everybody knows about her. She is the most available girl who ever lived."

"And she was a friend of Vickie's?"

"No. I doubt they were friends, but they were in the same class in school. They were both going the same way. One of the girls asked—Vickie—and this other girl said, 'Me too.'"

"All right. What happened when Vickie got in the car on the night of the fourth?"

"Well, we headed toward her home. She told me that her kid sister was coming to meet her—that shows there was no plan for us to meet. As we approached West Crescent Avenue, just before her house, she said to go around the block, back around toward Fardale Avenue. She said she had to tell me something, and that she didn't want Myrna to see her with me."

"Why not?"

"Myrna, from what I gathered from Vickie and Mary, was

[1] This is a fictitious name.

a momma's girl, with a big mouth. Mary would cover up for Vickie when she dated guys she wasn't supposed to, but Myrna wouldn't."

"You knew Mary Zielinski?" Selser asked, his voice betraying his surprise.

"As well as Vickie. Mary was a really nice girl. Quiet, but nice. She had asked me some months ago to get her a date with one of the guys from town, but I didn't like the guy. I told her she would be better off with the guy she had been going with."

"What happened after you turned onto Crescent?"

"We went up to Shadyside Road, stopped for a minute or two where the side of the road was being dug up, then went—"

"You say the road was being dug up?"

"The side of the road, left side going west. They were digging a ditch. They had a Payloader, one of those front-scoop tractors, backed onto the road," I explained.

"Keep going."

"Well, after this machine pulled out of the way—it took a minute or two, I went down Shadyside to Young's Road, followed Young's Road to Chapel Road, then turned left on Chapel Road."

"Stop right there. What time did you pick up Vickie?"

"About a quarter to nine."

"What time did you reach Chapel Road?"

"Five or six, maybe seven minutes later."

"All right, go ahead."

"Well, let's see, where was I?"

"You had turned onto Chapel Road," Selser prompted.

"Oh, yes, I remember. As you enter Chapel Road, the road dips, then rises. There is a depression of some twenty-five feet, I'd guess. As you go back up over the rise, the road begins gradually to drop off again. Is this clear?"

"Go ahead."

"Well, Vickie had been telling me she wanted to tell me something, but up to then had said nothing but that she was in trouble for cutting school. Pat and the baby were waiting for me in the cold trailer, so just before Fardale Avenue I stopped—this was on Chapel—and I asked Vickie what she wanted to tell me. She hesitated, said: 'Wait a minute.' Well, I was parked just over the rise in the road, and if anyone came high-balling over the rise, I'd have to pluck him out of the trunk of my car. So I told Vickie I'd pull into Fardale Avenue, she could tell me what it was she wanted to say, then I'd take her home. She was still talking about her school troubles. I started the car, then she noticed the dirt drive to the sandpit, pointed, and said: 'Pull in there.' "

"*She* said, 'Pull in there'?"

"Yes. It was, I suppose, a spur-of-the-moment thing. I doubt she had ever seen the place before."

"The sandpit was a regular lovers' lane, was it not?"

"Hell, no. That's ridiculous."

"I went there with Mr. Nicol," Selser explained, "and found many automobile tracks and beer cans, as one might expect to find in a place the press describes as a well-known lovers' lane."

"The tire tracks and beer cans are probably from the truck drivers and shovel operators. Empty beer cans are the most commonly found item around construction sites. Remember, this was a working sandpit area, with trucks hauling out dirt. The excavated area to the left of the dirt road changed shape and dimension every day. The dirt road went to the area above the excavation, where the job foreman usually parked his pickup truck. Nobody in his right mind uses a place like that for a lovers' lane. Who the hell could be sure at night where the edge of the excavation would be? The ground where a guy parked one night might not be there the next night. Eventually, the entire area where Vickie was killed and her body was found will be a hole in the ground. Anyway, Mr. Selser, if a guy from Ramsey wants to park with a girl, he doesn't go to Mahwah. He parks in one of the regular places in Ramsey. When the police come along, they recognize the car and keep going."

"The police are that permissive?"

"Look, Mr. Selser, it's a small town. Small towns keep their business to themselves. If I want to park with a girl, all I have to do is stop the police car, tell the cop I'm going to be parked up at the abandoned trolley tracks, or wherever, with so-and-so, and he closes his eyes when he drives past."

"All right, Ed, what happened in the sandpit?"

"I pulled in to the end of the road, where the road broadens out into the flat area, and stopped the car. Vickie was talking about her school problems, then she abruptly shifted gears and told me that she heard from one of the guys from Tony's Amoco that Patricia, my wife, had been playing around with a friend of mine."

"Was she?"

"No. Take my word for it that she wasn't involved with anyone, and especially not with the guy Vickie heard about."

"All right, what happened then?"

"Well, at first—"

"Wait, Ed. Why would Vickie say that? Did she know Patricia?"

"Sure, Pat and I both knew her. I told you that before. I suppose Vickie was at that gossipy age for girls. She always wanted to talk about who was doing what with whom."

"Vickie dated Hommell, didn't she?"

"Yes. But she did it secretly. How did you know?"

"We have been investigating Hommell," Selser replied. "I will explain later. Now, continue with your story. Vickie had just told you about your wife."

"Okay. At first, I thought Vickie's statement was pretty damn funny. I told her she was crazy to believe that. Well, instead of listening to me, Vickie said: 'Your wife is probably as bad as Ann.' That made me angry."

"Ann? Who is she?"

"Ann Ramera. Eveready—remember?"

"Oh, yes. All right, Vickie made you angry. What did you do?"

"I slapped her."

"How hard did you strike her?"

"Not hard. Not with my fist. The open hand. I slapped her and told her to get the hell out and walk home."

"Did she get out of the automobile?"

"Yes. You have to try to picture the situation. She was probably scared stiff, startled by the slap, and I was hot under the collar. If we both had counted ten, it would have been over. But we didn't. She jumped out of the car and ran toward Fardale Avenue, and I started the car to leave. I hadn't yet made up my mind whether to let her go or to pick her up and apologize." I paused.

"Keep going, Ed," Selser insisted impatiently. "Go on."

"Okay. The dirt road to the sandpit is quite narrow, just room for one car, and there is a ditch on either side—not really a ditch, more of a depression a foot or so deep. Gilroy's car had no back-up lights, so I opened the door and leaned out to see—one hand on the door handle, the other on the wheel. Well, just as I began to back the car out, I heard a commotion down toward Chapel, or Fardale Avenue, where Vickie had headed."

"What sort of commotion?"

"Voices, a girl and a man. It sounded like an argument."

"What did you do?"

"I was leaning out of the car, as I have explained. When I heard the commotion, I yanked the emergency brake handle, letting the car stall, and bailed out. My left foot was where a running board would be in an older car. I just put that foot on the ground, let go of the door, and twisted around in the seat. There must have been a hole in the ground, or I put my foot on a stone or clod of dirt. Whatever it was, the ground was uneven, and my left ankle, which I had hurt bowling, gave way. I tried to pull my right foot out of the car quickly. As I did, my foot hit the edge of the seat, the corner, or the door frame. My shoe came off."

"How had you hurt your ankle, Ed?"

"Bowling, the afternoon of the fourth. I'm right-handed. I was trying something different and hit my ankle with the ball."

"Was your ankle cut or swollen?"

"Both. I got some ice from the bar and put that on it. When I changed back from bowling shoes to street shoes, I didn't bother to lace them. That's why the shoe came off so easily."

"Did you pick up the shoe?"

"I didn't even look to see where it landed. I was in too much of a hurry getting out to see what the commotion was."

"All right, go ahead."

"As I got to my feet alongside the car, I could see the figures of two people just starting up the dirt road, and I noticed a car parked on Chapel, just south of the dirt road entrance."

"Whose car was it?"

"Let me tell it my way."

"All right, Ed, go on."

"This car must have come down Chapel or Fardale with its lights out. I hadn't seen or heard it till I got out of the car."

"Wait, Ed. How could you fail to see or hear it?"

"With Vickie talking, I wouldn't have heard a car come down the road very slowly. And Gilroy's car, a convertible, had a rear window that was discolored, fogged up. You could be riding along at night and never notice a car behind you if its lights were out."

"What about the rear-view mirror?"

"The inside mirror was useless because of the back window, and there was no side mirror. Someone had broken it."

"All right. Did you recognize the car?"

"Yes, no, then yes. It was a Ford, '53 or '54, a two-tone job. I could tell the make from the silhouette. The top was light, the bottom dark, but I couldn't make out the colors in the dark. Right away I figured it was Mary, Vickie's sister. Then I saw Vickie coming up the road with a guy holding her arm. I could hear her saying: 'Let me go, let go of me.' These things happened in seconds, almost all together, much more quickly than it takes to tell it. When I saw the guy, my first thought was that it was Vickie's father. He often used Mary's car. I knew he checked up on the girls, and that he was supposed to have threatened to kill Hommell, and—"

"When did he threaten Hommell?"

"I heard about it from Vickie a few weeks before. Hommell went up to the Zielinski house, parked in the driveway, and blew the horn for Vickie. Something like that. She said the father went out to the car and threatened to kill Hommell if he went near Vickie. The old man had a mean reputation. Well, I wasn't about to stand there like a jerk, so I grabbed a baseball bat out of the back seat. I walked around to the back of the car, then I realized that the guy with Vickie was Hommell."

"What was he doing with Mary Zielinski's car?"

"He wasn't, that's the point. It was *his* car."

"What type of automobile does Hommell have?"

"A '54 Ford, two-tone, dark bottom, light top."

"The same as Mary Zielinski's," the lawyer commented.

"Precisely. And both cars are two-tone green. In the dark, at a distance, both look alike."

"And both are the same as the station wagon from the drugstore. Had you thought of that?"

"What drugstore?"

"The Wyckoff Pharmacy," Selser replied. "The place where Hommell works. Their delivery vehicle is a 1954 Ford station wagon, two-tone green, dark body, light roof. Didn't you know?"

"I didn't know he was working anywhere. The job must be new. Just a couple of weeks before, he was trying to get a job at a liquor store in Ramsey, and a few days before that at a trucking company in Mahwah. As for the station wagon, I know nothing about that, either."

"With three vehicles of the same year, make, and color, could you have confused one for the other in the dark?"

"Anything is possible, especially with things as hectic as they were. On the way out, I did glance at the license plate—it's a habit I have—and it was a four-digit number. Hommell's plate is four-digit, but then so are the plates of delivery vehicles—the commercial plates."

"Do you recall the number?"

"I couldn't even guess at it. Numbers usually stick in my mind, but just offhand, I don't even remember Hommell's number."

"All right, Ed, what happened when Vickie and Hommell approached you?"

"Hommell was angry as hell. He was burned because I was with Vickie. She was crying. Hommell said she had fallen, tripped on the road and hit her head. She was bleeding like a pig."

"Describe the injury, as best you can."

"The left side of her head, her left, was bleeding, above the ear. With all of the hair on her head, and in the dark, it was impossible to see exactly what it was, but assuming she fell on the road, I figured it was a severe abrasion. The blood was running down the side of her face, around the ear. You know how profusely a scalp wound bleeds. The skin is so thin that all the blood vessels are near the surface."

"How do you know that?"

"About scalp wounds? We had a basic medical course in the Marines. Besides, I was pretty good in biology and anatomy in school."

"Did Vickie tell you how she had been injured?"

"No. She was scared and asked only that I take her home. I told her to get in the car, that I'd take her to a doctor who would patch her up without asking questions."

"What doctor was that? A Ramsey doctor?"

"I'd rather not say. We didn't go to him, so who he is isn't important. He is just a doctor some of us know we can go to, no questions asked."

"Did Hommell know him?"

"No. Hommell originally was from Florida. He wasn't really one of the local boys in that sense. Very few guys, mostly guys my age, know the doctor. He wouldn't have said 'Hello' to Hommell."

"All right. Continue the story. What happened next?"

"Vickie got in the car. The door was open. Hommell suddenly grabbed the kid by the jacket, at the shoulder, and yanked her out. She fell on the ground on her side, her legs still in the car, and grabbed me around the legs as she fell. When she was lying on the ground with her head against my right leg, the blood got on my pants. This is why there is blood only on the right leg. For a minute, things got hectic. She was clinging to my leg, telling me to make Hommell leave her alone; I was trying to get her to stand; Hommell was trying to push me away. Vickie was pretty hysterical."

"Did you fight with Hommell?"

"No. He finally calmed down. I got Vickie up and tried to calm her down."

"How long did all this action take?"

"About a minute or two."

"Go on, Ed."

"Well, Hommell said he would take care of her. She didn't want me to leave her with him, but I figured she would be all right, and Pat and the baby were home waiting for me. I got in the car, backed out, and took off for home."

"Now, Ed, how is it you couldn't see Vickie's wound in the car's headlights? You said you were backing out when you heard the commotion, and I take it you did not stop to turn off the lights when you scrambled from the car."

"The lights were not on. It's easier to back up with the lights out—no glare or false shadows."

"What about your shoe? Did you pick it up when you left?"

"You know I didn't. I looked on the ground when I went to get back in the car. I didn't see it. Perhaps I thought it didn't fall out of the car. I'm not certain. With so much going on, I wasn't thinking clearly, and an old shoe wasn't much to worry about. I just wanted to get the hell out of there."

"Now, what about the baseball bat?"

"I left it. When Hommell said the kid was hurt, I dropped the bat on the ground. I didn't remember it till I was on the way out of there. I thought Hommell would pick it up."

At this point Selser, a chain smoker who had run out of cigarettes, suggested a break for lunch, promising to come back at one o'clock so as to finish up that day.

# CHAPTER THIRTEEN

**THERE IS VERY LITTLE I CAN SAY ABOUT MY** stay in the Bergen County Jail. The second floor, on which I was confined—the third if one counts the basement—had four cell blocks, each with seven cells, fanning out from a circular hub. The first cell in each block contained a shower, which inmates were free to use at any time during the day. The cells in which inmates were confined from 7 p.m. to 7 a.m., were five feet wide and eight feet long, with riveted and welded steel walls. There was no hot water in the cells, and no light. The cots were supplied with one sheet, a thin, dirty mattress, and a blanket very much resembling khaki-colored cheesecloth.

Coincidentally, the windows of the cell block in which I was confined were in a direct line with the windows of Captain DeMarco's office in the courthouse, where I had been interrogated by Detectives Spahr and DeLisle, so that I could sit in my cell day after day and watch the comings and goings in that office.

Boredom was the greatest problem in the jail. There was no radio or television, and books, magazines, and newspapers were virtually nonexistent. Not even a set of checkers was allowed. "It's a matter of security," the warden told me when I offered to buy a set. Playing cards were allowed, however, and poker games, with packs of cigarettes as the stakes, ran from morning till night, seven days a week. It was not unusual for one inmate to win sixty or seventy packs one day, and before a week had passed, to lose and win the same cigarettes half a

**169**

dozen times. The cigarettes moved from cell to cell as frequently and easily as the mice and roaches.

No form of physical exercise or recreation was provided—facilities did not exist, and the cell blocks were too small for anything but walking—it was sixteen steps from one end of the cell block to the other. Even walking proved difficult, however, because of the narrowness of the area and the poker game usually in progress on the floor. There were no tables or chairs.

Personal visits were permitted twice a week, for thirty minutes at a time. The inmate receiving a visit was taken to the basement of the jail and placed in a steel booth the size of a voting booth, on one side of which was a tiny window, approximately three inches high and six inches wide. Below this window, a small screened mouthpiece packed with steel wool was built into the wall. The ostensible purpose of the steel wool was to prevent anything from being passed through the mouthpiece. It was a rather senseless security precaution, since the steel wall of the booth was not properly fitted to the floor, and objects up to three eighths of an inch thick could be passed beneath. A visitor could pass not only a hacksaw blade in that manner but an entire package of blades.

Visitors were brought into the jail on the other side of the booth. One could look through the window or talk through the mouthpiece below, but doing both at once was impossible. It was generally believed that the visitation booths were fitted with listening devices which permitted the authorities to monitor the conversations. Most inmates preferred, therefore, to correspond with visitors by means of notes slipped beneath the booth. This delivery system—"going under the wall," in jailhouse vernacular—was the primary source of the pornography which circulated throughout the jail—easily the most readily available reading material.

The food served in the jail was surprisingly good, but scarce. All meals were served in the cell blocks. Breakfast, served at 7 a.m., consisted of one tin cup of coffee and two slices of plain white bread. Lunch, served at 11 a.m., was the big meal of the day, and might be hamburgers, hot dogs, stew, or fish, with another tin cup of coffee. The entire meal was served in a six-inch metal bowl. On Friday, for instance, lunch, which never varied on that day, consisted of mashed potatoes, fish, and creamed corn—in that order, in one bowl, one on top of the other. It was delightfully disgusting. Supper, served at 4 p.m., was either a bowl of watery soup or a cheese sandwich, with the usual tin cup of coffee. No knives or forks were permitted—everything was eaten with a tablespoon. No fruit or dessert was ever served.

There were no means, within the rules, to supplement the foregoing meals. In most jails, county and state, as I have learned, the inmates are permitted to purchase supplemental foodstuffs—cookies, cakes, candies from an inmates' commissary or from an outside source. But not in the Bergen County Jail. There, the only food available from the inmates' commissary, if it can be called that, was cherry-flavored cough drops. I must have eaten a million. In three months, I lost thirty pounds.

Things were not so difficult for the guards in the jail. They were served hotcakes, or bacon-and-egg sandwiches on toast, for breakfast, along with various types of cakes—crumb cakes, fruit rings, cinnamon buns, and the like. In addition, midway through each shift, the guards on duty were served snacks, usually coffee and cake. It probably is an unfair generalization, but based upon my personal observations over the past eleven years, I do not hesitate to suggest that this country's smallest minority is made up of underweight prison guards. They are as scarce as ALL THE WAY WITH LBJ placards at Berkeley.

I have mentioned that an inmate of the county jail could not, within the rules, supplement his diet. If, however, an inmate had money smuggled to him—usually under the wall of the visiting booth—he could always find a guard willing to sell an egg sandwich in the morning (fifty cents), or coffee and cake during the day (fifty cents). Several mornings each week, I would purchase an entire crumb cake, or a large fruit ring (one dollar each), and share it with the other fellows in the cell block.

The jail's religious facilities were similar to the recreational facilities, that is, they were nonexistent. So were religious leaders. I was in the county jail for exactly three months, and during that time, not once did I see or hear of a minister, priest, or rabbi being in the building. To the best of my knowledge, the only religious people to enter the jail during those three months were two members of the Salvation Army, from a mission across the street from the courthouse.

My friends, or at least those persons I had thought were my friends, ceased to exist at the moment of my arrest. With a single exception, that of my former high-school football coach, not one person I had regarded as a friend made even the smallest effort prior to my trial to send me a card or a note, or to contact my family, to wish me luck; nor have any of them done so during the eleven years that have elapsed since my conviction. The attitude of those people may cast a dreary reflection on the quality of the friendships I had formed, but I have never permitted myself to become demoralized by it. Rather, it has enabled me to better appreciate, and to value more highly, the very few genuine friendships I have found in recent years. Today, I can count the number of my friends on the fingers of one hand, and all but one of these persons were completely unknown to me prior to my arrest; yet each in his or her own way means more to me than all my former friends combined.

My family, apart from certain aunts, uncles, cousins, and my father—all of whom dropped me completely—rallied to my side and did all they could to buoy up my spirits from the very beginning. One expects that from one's mother, and from those other family members with whom one has been especially close, but it was my wife who really opened my eyes.

I do not wish any other man to find himself in the position I was in, but if one does, he will be a lucky man if he has a wife as loyal and trusting as mine was. She was magnificent: never once missing an opportunity to visit me; never expressing the slightest doubt that I was completely innocent; always cheerful despite the flood of vicious and often obscene letters and telephone calls to which she was subjected during those first few trying weeks; and never letting on to me that it was only through the constant care of a doctor, who kept her well supplied with tranquilizers, that she was able to keep going. Preoccupied as I was with my own misery, it took me a long time to realize how very much personal courage, faith, and loyalty it took for a nineteen-year-old girl to be so steadfast in adversity. For this I shall always be grateful to her.

# CHAPTER FOURTEEN

MR. SELSER RETURNED AT TWO-THIRTY THAT afternoon. I had spent most of the intervening time lying on the bunk in my cell, thinking back over our morning conversation, and trying to fathom Selser's attitude of total equanimity while listening to my story. It was as if he had known in advance the things I would say. I knew that our investigator, Andrew Nicol, had been hard at work for two weeks, and that he suspected that Hommell was somehow involved in the case, but he could not have learned exactly *how* Hommell was involved. Yet the more I thought about it the more obvious it seemed to me that Selser had been prepared for the story I had related during the morning visit, which in turn indicated that Nicol must have learned something that even I did not know.

As before, Selser was waiting in the back room when I was brought downstairs from my cell. He was the first to speak.

"I am sorry I could not return earlier, Ed. I have been discussing with Andy Nicol your disclosures of this morning. I shall shortly make application to Judge O'Dea for a court order permitting Nicol to accompany me when I visit with you. As you know, he is limited to visiting you in the visitation booths in the basement, just as if he were a personal visitor."

"Yes, I know."

"Very well. Now, Ed, if I remember correctly, you had just backed out of the sandpit when we broke for lunch. You had left your shoe and the baseball bat at the sandpit. Is that correct?"

"That's right."

"All right. Did you go directly to your home?"

"I told Calissi I stopped on Chapel Road to dump Vickie's pocketbook, but that's not how it happened. It was on the floor of the car, by the kerosene can. I didn't realize it was there until I returned home and went to take the can out of the car. That's really why I went back to the sandpit. The shoe wasn't important. I thought Hommell and Vickie might still be there, so I went back to give her the pocketbook. When I found they were gone, I put the pocketbook and things in the woods, where I could pick them up the next day and return them to her."

"You threw her things by a Christmas tree you had discarded?"

"Yes. How did you know that?"

"It was in the newspapers. Why did you say you stopped when you didn't?"

"The question, Mr. Selser, is why did I say anything."

"All right, why did you?"

"Let's go one step at a time. To begin with, I was so damn tired I might have said anything in that statement. I didn't think it made any difference when I had dumped the pocketbook. I thought the police had searched the area and had found it after the body was found. When I pointed out the spot, the last thing in the world I expected was that those things were still there. It is unbelievable."

"Why do you say that, Ed?"

"Well, the pocketbook and things could be seen from the road, and for a day and a half the police, spectators, and press had been tramping through the area. When Hommel went past there the next day, there were cars parked all along that side of the road, yet the things were never noticed—if they were there."

"What do you mean?"

"Look, Mr. Selser, you were a prosecutor, think about it. The police must have asked the Zielinskis about Vickie's clothes and things, and so must have known she was carrying a pocketbook and schoolbooks. They didn't find those things in the sandpit, nor did they find them on Wyckoff Avenue where Vickie obviously disappeared. And they were not found on Fardale Avenue by the kerchief and shoe. So what would you have done if it had been your investigation? You would have instituted a thorough search of the entire area. What would have been the most obvious place to begin a search? In the small patch of woods across the street. Right?"

"That seems likely, but what are you getting at?"

"Just this. When I walked down the road to the Christmas tree with Galda and Calissi, Detective Graber and a couple of the others already were standing in the woods by the pocketbook. They waved to us to come into the woods as we approached the area. Looking back on it, I think the whole thing was staged. I think the things were found during the initial investigation, and that they were put back there for me to lead them to during my statement."

"Let's forget that for now, Ed. What happened when you reached home?"

"Okay. First thing I did was go in the back door, take off my pants, drop them outside, then put on clean pants and another pair of shoes."

"Where was your wife?"

"She was in the front, in the kitchen. You see, there is a living room, kitchen, bedroom, bath, then the back bedroom where I was."

"Go on."

"Well, after changing my clothes, I went to the kitchen and told Patricia I had thrown up, to explain the clothing change. She knew I hadn't been feeling well for a couple of days. Then I went out the front door to the car. I checked the floor to make certain that the shoe I had lost wasn't still in the car. That's when I found the pocketbook. I left that in the car, took out the can of kerosene, and went around the opposite side of the trailer to fill the fuel tank."

"The side opposite the door?"

"Right. We had been in the trailer only two months or so, and were still using a temporary fuel tank consisting of a fifty-five-gallon fuel drum on a four-legged steel stand about nine feet high. The drum was mounted on its side, the filler cap at the top. Next to the tank—well, actually a few feet away —was a split-rail fence. The fuel truck could back right up my driveway to the tank, and by standing on the truck the tank could be filled easily."

"Is this important, Ed?"

"Yes, you'll see in a minute."

"All right, go on."

"Well, for me to pour the five gallons from the can into the tank took some acrobatics. First, I put the can on the top of the corner post of the fence, then I got up on the top rail. Then I picked up the can and stepped up on top of the post. There was room for one foot, so with my right foot on the fence, my left in mid-air, the can in my right hand, I leaned forward and put my left hand against the tank. Now I am five feet up, looking like I am posing for a statue of Mercury. Then I lifted the can and tried to pour the fuel in the tank. The can has a handle like a pail, so I put the bottom of the can on the top of the tank, tilted it with one hand on the handle, and in doing so spilled the first quart or so all over the tank's outside. As you know, kerosene, because of the high oil content, is slippery stuff. Well, my left hand on the side of the tank was right where the spilled kerosene was running down. My hand slipped, and I lost my balance—all my weight was on that hand—and I landed in the gravel driveway, scraping my knees all to hell."

"What is the importance of this, Ed?"

"Calissi had photos taken of my knees. When he was taking my statement, he asked how I had injured my knees. He asked if I had fallen in the sandpit, or on the dirt mound."

"What did you say?"

"All I said was that I fell somewhere—not on the dirt mound—but I didn't say where."

"Why didn't you tell him what you have told me?"

"I thought it would be better to tell him as little as possible."

"Did you finally fill the fuel tank?"

"Yes. I got back up and filled it. Then, when I went back inside, the heating system still wouldn't work. I then phoned Gilroy, and he agreed to drive me, Pat, and the baby to my mother-in-law's."

"What time did you phone Gilroy?"

"Nine-ten, nine-fifteen."

"What time had you gotten home from the sandpit?"

"I told Calissi it was nine o'clock, a few minutes either way. Pat said she looked at the electric clock in the kitchen when she heard me come in the back door. She said it had been three minutes to nine."

"How long would you say you were at the sandpit?"

"Well, let's guesstimate. I picked Vickie up between eight-forty and eight-forty-five. I was home at eight-fifty-seven. That's twelve to seventeen minutes. From where I picked her up, to the sandpit, took about about seven or eight minutes, including the time to stop, turn around, and pick her up. From the sandpit to home, three or four minutes. That's ten to twelve minutes traveling time. Subtract that from the total and it comes to two to five minutes in the sandpit, roughly."

"That's not very much time for all the prosecutor claims you did up there," Selser commented.

"No, it's not. And that is a liberal guess, favoring Calissi."

"All right, Ed, what did you do after phoning Gilroy?"

"I picked up my pants, threw them in the car, grabbed a portable spotlight, and returned to the sandpit."

"Via Chapel Road?"

"Yes. As I approached the sandpit, I saw that Hommell's car was gone. I continued to the end of Chapel, made a U-turn at Young's Road, came back and stopped at the sandpit entrance. I walked up the dirt road, flicked on the spotlight, and was nearly standing on the shoe I had lost."

"Did you see anything else?"

"Yes. I told Nicol, and I'm sure he doesn't believe me. The baseball bat was lying there, also a white cloth, perhaps a man's T-shirt."

"Did you pick up the bat?"

"No. It was badly split, not worth having."

"Was it split when you left it there?"

"I really didn't notice, but I doubt it."

"Why?"

"If the bat were slightly split, Joe might have kept it. You can wrap tape around a minor split and still use the bat. Joe wouldn't have kept the bat the way I saw it in the sandpit—it was shot to hell. I took it for granted that Hommell had broken it for spite. That's his way."

"Have you heard that he smashed all the pool cues in Pelzer's Tavern?"

"I've heard that. Like I said—that's the sort of thing he would do. He has a wild temper."

"So you left the bat lying there?"

"Yes."

"Ed, why would you leave the girl with Hommell if you knew, as you say you did, of his propensity for violence? Is that logical?"

"Well, to begin with, she was his girl. He had been dating her quite regularly and everyone took it for granted she was his girl. If anyone had driven by, seen us, and called the cops, there would have been hell to pay. Remember, we were in Mahwah, not Ramsey. I couldn't stand there all night arguing with him."

"Did you not fear for the girl's safety, leaving her with a man you knew was of a violent nature?"

"I didn't even think about it. Looking back on it I think differently, but at the time I figured she would be okay."

"All right. What did you do then?"

For a moment, I sat there and looked at the lawyer. Then I exploded: "Goddam, Mr. Selser, you're just like Nicol. You don't see the point."

"What point, Ed? I am sorry if I have missed something. By all means, tell me."

"The baseball bat. Don't you see? Calissi doesn't know anything about it."

"Do you mean the police did not recover the bat?"

"Exactly. They don't even know it exists. Hommell must

have gone back for it later, after I left. Or else someone else was there later that night."

"Are you certain the police do not have the bat?"

"Positive. It was never mentioned. And again, that is the point. If Calissi tries to claim I confessed, the answer is that if I were confessing and telling the truth, baring my soul, I would have told them about the bat. But I purposely did not say a word about it. That is the big hole I left in the statement."

"Yes, Ed, now I see your point. But where is the bat?"

"That's for Nicol to find out. Gilroy can establish that a bat is missing from his car. He knows how many bats he had."

"Yes. I shall put Nicol to work on that. But let's go back for a minute. Do you know if Vickie's body was in the sandpit when you returned?"

"I have no idea. If it was, I couldn't see it from where I was standing."

"How bright was your light?"

"Bright? It was a twelve-volt, sealed-beam emergency light, the type fire departments use to penetrate smoke. You could probably read a newspaper by its light if you were a mile away. It lit up the whole sandpit area."

"But you couldn't see over the dirt mound, beyond which Vickie's body was found, could you?"

"No. It wasn't an X-ray light."

"On the other hand, Ed," Selser commented, "the very brightness of that light seems to show that you had no fear of being seen in the sandpit."

"That's right, Mr. Selser. If I had gone back there after having killed Vickie, I wouldn't have lit a match."

"Let's go back some more, Ed. When Vickie accused your wife of cheating, might not that have caused you to lose your temper sufficiently to lead you to murder her in a fit of temper?"

"You're saying I killed her?"

"No. I am asking what the prosecutor might ask."

"That's silly. I was momentarily angry because she was repeating what I had told her was untrue. You don't kill someone for that. She was just a kid, trying to act old and wise about such things, teasing me to see how I'd react. Maybe she was a bit angry, too, because I had laughed off what to her seemed like a real big deal. As for believing her, if I had believed the story, which I knew was untrue, I still wouldn't have killed her. If I was going to kill anyone, it would have been Pat, not Vickie. All Vickie did was tell me what she had heard. Can't blame her for that."

"Yes, I see what you mean now. Your anger would have been directed toward the accused, not the accuser. All right, Ed, what did you do after retrieving your shoe?"

"Now we have a problem. During my interrogation, Detective Spahr had me draw a number of diagrams showing the various ways of getting from the trailer to the sandpit to Gilroy's house. I drew one showing a route north on Chapel Road, stop at the sandpit, continue north on Chapel, turn right on Young's Road, left on Shadyside, right on Oak Street, left on Wyckoff Avenue. Got that?"

"Go ahead, Ed."

"Okay. Next, during my statement, Galda trotted out the diagram I've just described, but not the others. I told him it was wrong, that I went north on Chapel, made a U-turn at Young's Road, and back south on Chapel to the sandpit.

"As you have told me today?"

"Not quite. I told Galda that after picking up the shoe, I backed into Fardale Avenue, then went north on Chapel again, over the route in the diagram."

"Why did you say that?"

"I was hoping to confuse things a bit."

"That was stupid."

"I know it was," I admitted, "but after the hours of interrogation, I wasn't thinking too brightly."

"All right, Ed. What's done is done. Tell me what you actually did when you left the sandpit. Which route *did* you follow?"

"Let me finish. When Galda got me up at the scene, during my statement, he asked how I had made the trip from the trailer to Gilroy's. He told me to direct Captain DeMarco, who was driving. I thought I'd confuse things a bit more. I took them north on Chapel, made the U-turn at Young's Road, then back south on Chapel to the sandpit. At that point, Galda gave up and stopped asking questions about the route.

"Galda did not ask you to show them how you had gotten to Gilroy's after finding your shoe?"

"No."

"Did he ever ask you to show him where you had thrown your pants?"

"Not once."

"Did he ever ask you if you have traveled on Oak Street, where the pants were found?"

"No."

"In other words, Ed, your only statement regarding the pants is that you threw them on Pulis Avenue. Is that correct?"

"That's right. I think Galda was afraid to ask if I threw them on Oak Street."

"Why would he fear to ask that?"

"Because I had been insisting that I threw them on Pulis, and he didn't want me to repeat that in my statement. After all, if I denied throwing them on Oak Street where they were found, that would destroy the illusion of me giving a confession."

"Explain that, Ed."

"Look. If Galda had asked, I would have repeated that I had thrown the pants on Pulis. The prosecutor claims that is untrue. So if he had that in the statement, he would have to admit that part of the statement is untrue. But if he admits that a part is untrue, who can say what other parts are not actually untrue? Prosecutor Calissi has to contend that all of it is true, so Galda couldn't afford to ask about the pants."

"I see. That is interesting. But how *did* you get to Gilroy's?"

"Well, as I said, I went up Chapel Road, saw that Hommell and Vickie had left, made the U-turn, then came back south on Chapel. I picked up my shoe, got back in the car, and continued south toward home. I couldn't leave the pocket-book in the car—Gilroy would ask questions—and I obviously couldn't take it home with my wife there. Then I remembered the Christmas tree I had thrown away, so I stopped and put Vickie's things in the woods. I figured the tree was a good marker. The next day I would know right where they were. I could pick them up and get them back to Vickie."

"That sounds logical. Go ahead."

"After dumping the books—I didn't throw them away; I carried them in and placed them together on the ground—I got back in the car and headed for the trailer. I was going to drop off the shoe and the spotlight, so Gilroy wouldn't ask questions. As I turned onto Pulis, it dawned on me that if I did that, Pat would ask questions. I hoped to keep her from knowing about any of this, from learning that I had been with Vickie. I decided to leave the shoe and the light on the floor in back, figuring that Joe would never notice. I continued up Pulis Avenue, over the stone bridge, threw out the pants, continued on to Wyckoff Avenue, turned left, and followed Wyckoff Avenue into town. That's when I met Hommell."

Once more, Selser reacted as if he had expected me to say precisely what I had said. He merely lit a fresh cigarette and asked: "Where did you meet Hommell?"

"You act as if you've heard all this before. How much of this do you know?"

"Continue your story, Ed. I have learned some things, but if I tell you now, I shall never know if you are tailoring your story to fit what I know."

"Okay, Mr. Selser, you're the boss. Hommell was sitting in his car, parked in front of the bank."

"Across the street from Tony's Amoco?"

"That's right. I pulled up alongside and asked how Vickie was. He said that I should keep my mouth shut about her, that if I said anything about what had happened, he would take it out on Pat and the baby."

"What did you say to that?"

"I laughed. I thought he was making a big deal out of

nothing. Even if Vickie's family called the police, nothing had been done intentionally. It would be settled quietly. I figured she would have more trouble with her father than Hommell and I would with the police."

"You were not worried about being reported to the police?"

"No. It could have been smoothed over."

"Were you worried about Hommell's threats?"

"Not then, no. I just thought he was making a big deal out of nothing."

"Did you discuss anything else?"

"Well, I mentioned to Hommell that Vickie had been bleeding like hell. I said something like: 'Boy, she was bleeding like a stuck pig. My pants were a mess. I had to throw them away.'"

"You *did* tell Hommell you had thrown away your pants?"

"Yes. Why?"

"Did you tell him where you had thrown them?"

"Yes, in a way. He asked where I had thrown them. I said: 'By the stone bridge on Pulis.'"

"What did Hommell say?"

"He told me that was a stupid thing to do."

"Did he say why it was stupid?"

"No. I told him I had to pick up Gilroy, that I'd see him the next day. Then I took off up Main Street, to go to Gilroy's house."

"Now, Ed, I had to hear you say it without prompting from me to indicate that it was important. You see, we have a witness who saw Hommell searching for your pants by the stone bridge at eleven o'clock the next morning. Apparently he is the one who found them and put them on Oak Street, right near your family's home."

"Why didn't you tell me before today?"

"Don't you see, Ed, if I had told you, and then you had said that you had told Hommell about the pants being near the bridge, I could never be certain that you were not making it up to fit the knowledge I had of Hommell's search. The very fact that you told me your story without your knowing of Hommell's search, indicates to me that you are telling the truth. Now, what happened after you picked up Gilroy?"

"Well, I picked Joe up about nine-thirty. On the way back to the trailer, I wondered if Joe would notice that I had changed my pants. I didn't want him to begin to ask a lot of questions if my wife mentioned the pants when she got in the car, so I told him I had gotten sick, messed up the pants, and had thrown them away."

"Did you tell Joe where you had thrown them?"

"Now you've got me. I think that after we picked up Pat and the baby, on the way to her mother's house, she asked about the pants. Whether Joe was paying attention when I told her, I really don't know."

"All right, Ed. Now, what time did you arrive at your mother-in-law's home?"

"Before ten o'clock. The Gil Turner–Rudy Gwin fight came on television after we had arrived. Turner won by a knockout in the fourth. By then, I was already in bed."

"Did you remain in bed all night?"

"Yes. Till eight-thirty the next morning."

"Did you sleep well?"

"Fine. I figured everything had worked out just fine."

"You thought Hommell had taken Vickie home?"

"That's right."

"What happened the next day?"

"Well, about eleven o'clock, I was in the living room, Pat in the kitchen. She came in and asked if I had heard about the murder."

"What did you say?"

" 'What murder?' I hadn't heard the radio report she had heard on the kitchen radio. She said: 'Victoria Falinski, or something like that. I couldn't understand the name. It was up in Mahwah.' "

"What did you say to that?"

"Nothing. You see, nobody ever called Vickie by any other name, so Victoria meant nothing to me. Also, I never was too sure of her last name, except that it was some Polish name, and the radio announcer had mispronounced it. But what really misled me was the location. You see, the main part of Mahwah is north of Ramsey, the Fardale section of Mahwah is south of Ramsey. Except for a thin section to the west, Ramsey all but cuts Mahwah in two. To get from one section to the other, you go through Ramsey. The Fardale Section, to the south, where Vickie was killed, was never referred to as Mahwah. It was simply called Fardale, and I suppose a lot of people thought it was a separate town. No one ever said: 'I'm going to the Fardale Section of Mahwah.' You either said, 'I'm going *over* to Fardale,' or 'I'm going *up* to Mahwah'—if you meant the northern part."

"So, Mahwah, to you, meant the area to the north?"

"Right. If anybody were to ask me where my trailer is located, I'd say Fardale. Anyone from up that way would know just what I mean."

"So you did not know that the radio announcer was talking about Vickie?"

"Not right away. I had no reason to suspect she hadn't gotten home all in one piece. I listened to the twelve o'clock news. They still had the name wrong, but I was beginning to wonder. And I felt that if it were Vickie, I was responsible."

"Why did you think that, Ed?"

"Well, I thought that if it were Vickie, she must have died from the head injury, though I couldn't see how. But if she had, it was my fault. She wouldn't have run down the road and fallen if I hadn't slapped her, and she wouldn't have died if I had taken her to a doctor instead of leaving her with Hommell."

"Did you think the head injury was that serious?"

"I didn't know. Head injuries are crazy things. Sometimes the reaction is delayed. I didn't know. Perhaps shock, or loss of blood, something like that—she was bleeding like hell. I phoned Gilroy and asked him to pick us up and take us back to the trailer. I asked him if he had heard about the murder, and if it was Vickie."

"What did he say?"

"He said: 'To hell with it.' He also said he would come down for us."

"What time did he get there?"

"Well, Joe always goes back to sleep after the first call. I called again at one o'clock or so and woke him. He arrived at two o'clock with Hommell."

"Continue the story, Ed. What happened then?"

"When I heard the horn blow, I went outside. I was surprised to see Hommell. I asked him: 'Was that Vickie that was killed?' He said it was, then he said the police were looking for a Mercury. I damn near fell over."

"Why, Ed?"

"Well, besides the shock of knowing I must have been responsible for her death, because of my failure to take her to a doctor, I was flabbergasted that Hommell would mention the thing about a Mercury in front of Gilroy. I think now that Hommell said that to put me on my toes not to say anything more in front of Joe. I remember going back into the house to get Pat and the baby, and I was thinking to myself that I had done it, but I just couldn't believe it."

"You had done what that you couldn't believe?"

"I remember thinking to myself: 'Boy, you really did it.' It's just an expression. You do something like—well, suppose you dropped the cigarette you're smoking and burned your suit. You might say: 'Dammit, now I've done it.' That's what I meant, but I found it hard to believe. I just couldn't convince myself that I had been stupid enough to get in a mess like that."

"Did you say these things in your statement to the police?"

"I might have. I don't remember half of what I told them."

"All right. Did Hommell drive you and your family up to the trailer?"

"That's right."

"What did you talk about on the way? Did you discuss the murder?"

"No. I don't think we did. Once, however, just when I don't recall, Hommell told me that he had seen Myrna Zielinski walking along Wyckoff Avenue."

"Did he volunteer that information?"

"Yes. I was watching his face in the rear-view mirror. He looked right at me in the mirror and said: 'It's a good thing I didn't stop. The cops would have been after me by now." I took that to be his way of tipping me off that the police had not questioned him."

"What did you do when you got home?"

"Well, Hommell pulled into my driveway. I got out his side, the driver's side, and as the seat was tilted forward, a lipstick rolled out."

"Where did the lipstick come from?"

"Under the seat, I believe. The driveway is inclined, oh, fifteen degrees or so. The lipstick rolled out. I picked it up, handed it to Hommell, and made some wise remark about the lipstick not being his shade."

"Did he say anything?"

"He said something—I'm not sure of the exact words—about the lipstick being Vickie's, and that he'd better get rid of it."

"What did he do with it?"

"I don't recall. I took Pat and the baby inside. The oil man had been there, and the heater—I had left the valve wide open —was flooded. I picked up my old shoes, the ones I had worn the night before—wait, that's wrong. I had two pairs of shoes exactly alike, both the same age, and both shot to hell. I took the two best, which happened to be one of each pair, and took them out to the car. Hommell and Joe were waiting."

"Why did you take one of each pair, Ed?"

"Both pairs were shot, but I thought if I had soles and heels put on the two best shoes, they would be good enough for work shoes."

"Did you go with Hommell and Gilroy?"

"Yes. The afternoon was warm, so I told Pat I would get a ride into town while I could, then come back and get the heater going later. Pat needed some things from town for supper, and she was driving me crazy to get a haircut."

"So you went with Hommell?"

"Yes. When I came out, Hommell said he was going to throw the lipstick in my garbage can, alongside the driveway. He didn't. I don't know what he eventually did with it. I got in the car. We took the back road—Chapel, Young's Road, Oak Street, that way—past the sandpit."

"Whose idea was that?"

"Hommell's."

"Did he give you a reason?"

"No."

"Did you discuss the murder?"

"Well, Joe asked Hommell what a sadist was. Hommell didn't know. I explained it to Joe."

"Why did Joe ask that?"

"He said the newspaper said the murder was done by a sadist."

Selser thought for a moment, then asked: "I thought you said Gilroy was not interested when you asked him on the telephone about the murder. Didn't you say that?"

"Yes. Joe said: 'The hell with it.' "

"Obviously, Gilroy had enough interest to stop and read the newspaper account of the crime before going with Hommell to pick you up in Ridgewood," Selser commented. "By the way, how did you know what a sadist is?"

"We discussed de Sade in school. His name came up in a discussion of the moral and theological ramifications of the French Revolutionary period—which I must confess was way over my head."

"Did anyone say anything else about the murder during your trip to Ramsey?"

"Yes. Joe said they would hang the guy who did it."

"What did Hommell say?"

"Nothing. But I was sitting in the back, leaning over the front seat. I looked in the mirror at Hommell and said: 'He will probably plead insanity.' "

"Why did you say that?"

"I enjoyed needling Hommell, telling him he was a screwball. The story around town was that he was psycho'd out of the Navy, and he acted that way from all I heard."

"What happened when you reached town?"

"Well, Hommell and Gilroy went to buy a pair of sneakers. That was supposed to be the reason Hommell drove Joe to Ridgewood. They came straight back to pick me up. I think he told Joe that story about needing to go to Ridgewood to buy sneakers just to have a reason to see me, to remind me to keep my mouth shut about him."

"What did you do in Ramsey?"

"First, I went to the shoemaker—Nick, the old guy in the center of town. He said the shoes were not worth fixing, so I went across the street to Robbie's Corral, had a cup of coffee, went out Robbie's side door, through the alley, and threw the shoes in a garbage can. Then I walked back across Main Street and met Gilroy and Hommell. They wanted me to play basketball. I told them I had to get home to fix the heater."

"Then what did you do?"

"Went and got a haircut, bought the groceries Pat asked for, then went over to Tony's Amoco and asked one of the guys to drive me home."

"Who was in Tony's?"

"Just the guys who were usually there. Tony, as usual, was playing the bigshot. He was telling everyone he had the inside dope that the murder would be solved in twenty-four hours."

"Did you say anything about that?"

"Damn right. I offered to bet him a hundred bucks that he was wrong. He didn't want to bet."

"Why did you want to bet?"

"I figured Hommell and I wouldn't say anything, so the police couldn't get anywhere. I still don't know how the cops got around to me and Joe."

"You don't know that Joe went to the police and reported

the blood he found in his automobile?" Selser asked incredulously.

"What blood?"

"The blood on the front seat."

"I don't know anything about it, but if there was blood on the seat, it got there when Vickie got back into the car."

"Didn't the police ask you about it?"

"This is the first I've heard. You mean there was blood in Gilroy's car, and that son of a bitch ran to the cops?"

"Yes, Ed, I thought you knew."

"That dirty little bastard."

"What would you have done if you had been in his position?"

"Goddam, Mr. Selser, if my best friend were involved, I'd at least give him a chance to explain. Joe knew where to find me. If it were my car that Joe had borrowed, and no one else knew about the blood, I'd probably have cleaned it up and kept my mouth shut. Damn, over the past two years, I could have put half of the guys I know in jail—if I were a son of a bitch like Gilroy."

"I thought you knew, Ed. Haven't you seen the reports in the newspapers?"

"I told you, Mr. Selser, I haven't seen the papers in here, that's why I asked about Vickie's injuries this morning."

"All right, Ed, after you returned home from Ramsey, what did you do?"

"I've already told you that much. I got the heater working, but then Pat was afraid to stay in the trailer, so her mother picked us up. We went down to her house. About eleven-thirty, Detective Graber picked me up."

"There was a report that you had washed some of the clothing you wore the night Vickie was killed. Did you?"

"Yes. You see, we hadn't been in the trailer too long, and hadn't gotten a washer or dryer installed. So, Tuesday, while at my mother-in-law's, I thought it was a good time to throw my shirt and jacket in her washing machine. The jacket was filthy, and both the shirt and jacket were stinking from the kerosene I had spilled on the sleeves."

"Now, Ed, I want you to tell me why you didn't tell the prosecutor the story you told me today."

"Primarily, I suppose, because I was too stupid. But I didn't realize just how stupid I was. You see, it wasn't until after I knew Vickie was dead that Hommell's threat made sense."

"You mean about getting Pat and your child if you brought his name into things?"

"Right. At first, as I said, I didn't know what he was talking about, so I didn't take him seriously. Then, when I found out the kid was dead, I knew what he meant."

"Did you believe he would take some sort of revenge if you disregarded his warning?"

"You're damn right I did. I've known Hommell for a couple of years. From what I've seen and heard, I think the guy is off his rocker, a real straitjacket case. I wouldn't turn my back on him for a second. Once, just after the police picked me up, I said to Galda: 'If you want a fall guy, why don't you grab Don Hommell?' He acted as if he had never heard of Hommell."

"Why did you say that if you believed Hommell's threats?"

"I thought Galda would at least be curious enough to have Hommell picked up for questioning. Once he was in custody, then I could tell what had happened. But Galda didn't bite. He didn't want to hear about Hommell."

"Ed, aren't you worried about telling this story now?"

"Yes and no. Pat tells me she never sets foot out of the house alone, so I figure she is okay. Besides, I've *got* to tell you. My neck is on the chopping block."

"Didn't you think the police would have protected your wife?"

"Don't give me that routine, Mr. Selser. What would they have done, sent a car past the house every few hours? I know those cops up that way. I went to school with some of them, and the others I've known for years. You should know what they are like. From what I gather from talking to you, Mr. Nicol, and some others, the police knew all night long that Vickie was missing and didn't even bother to look for her. They were probably sitting in a diner on the highway drinking coffee most of the night. That's where you can usually find them."

"You had no confidence in the police?"

"They didn't do a very good job of protecting Vickie, did they?"

"All right, Ed," the lawyer said with a sigh, ignoring my question, "it's been a long day. You realize, don't you, that I am bound to report to the prosecutor the story you have related to me?"

"I guess so."

"Ed, would you be willing to take a truth-serum test?"

"You name the date. I'll be there."

"Fine. I shall discuss the matter with Mr. Calissi and Judge O'Dea. Now, I must leave. There is much to be done."

# CHAPTER FIFTEEN

PROSECUTOR CALISSI FLATLY REFUSED TO believe my story as related to him by Mr. Selser; and as the days stretched into weeks, every indicator pointed to my being tried for the murder of Vickie Zielinski.

In the four weeks following my attorney's report to him, the prosecutor 1) refused to give any credence to the testimony of the woman, Mrs. Wood, who said she had seen Hommell searching for my pants the day after the murder, notwithstanding the fact that the woman had identified Hommell from a group photograph, picking him out without hesitation; 2) made no effort to locate the baseball bat, or to ascertain whether a bat was in fact missing from Gilroy's automobile; 3) made no effort to obtain and have examined the clothing Hommell had worn the night in question; 4) made no effort to have the interior of Hommell's automobile examined by laboratory technicians; and 5) made no known effort to compare with the tires on Hommell's automobile the plaster casts of the tire tracks found on the dirt road to the sandpit.

It was not until one month after Mr. Selser had reported to him, and then only as a reaction to the results of a "truth serum" examination, that the prosecutor moved to investigate my story. And when he did move, having given Hommell four weeks' notice of my accusations, the prosecutor acted as if the very last thing in the world he desired was to find evidence to substantiate my story.

By May 3, with the scheduled start of my trial ten days away, Selser and his investigator, Nicol, had been unable to find any evidence to support my contentions; and those witnesses who might have helped, including Vickie's older sister, Mary, were reluctant to stand up in court and repeat the statements they had made in private. Selser, not knowing where to turn, finally petitioned the Bergen County Court for a "truth serum" examination. Judge O'Dea, who heard the petition, insisted that I take the witness stand and testify under oath to my willingness to submit to such an examination. I did so.

The prosecution, represented by First Assistant Prosecutor Galda, at first bitterly opposed the examination, claiming that we were trying to "delay and confuse" the proceedings against me. But when it became apparent that Judge O'Dea was prepared to grant the petition, Galda, certain that I would not dare agree, asked me on cross-examination if I would stipulate in advance that the results of the examination could be put in evidence at my trial. I would give a thousand dollars to have a picture of the expression on his face when I agreed, absolutely and without preconditions. Judge O'Dea, however, came galloping to Galda's rescue, ruling that the results would not be admissible.

The prosecutor was not finished. He insisted that doctors representing the state be present and be allowed to participate during the examination, that the examination be followed within a few days by a lie-detector test, and that a member of the prosecutor's staff be present during the examinations. Judge O'Dea granted the first request, I agreed to the second, and the third was denied. The judge ruled that neither attorneys nor police officials would be permitted to observe either the "truth serum" examination or the lie-detector test. As with the record of my arraignment in Mahwah, the record of the hearing on the "truth serum" petition has disappeared.

The "truth serum"—$7\frac{1}{2}$ mgs. of sodium amytal, followed by 10 mgs. of benzedrine sulphate—was administered to me on Sunday, May 5, in a doctor's office in the county jail. Present, besides myself, were Drs. John H. Cassity, Chief of the Department of Criminal Psychiatry at New York City's Bellevue Hospital; Nelson C. Policastro, a practicing psychiatrist from Hackensack; Ralph S. Baney, a New York City psychiatrist; and Fabian L. Rourke, another New York City psychiatrist. Drs. Cassity and Policastro had been retained by Mr. Selser; Drs. Banay and Rourke represented the prosecutor. Following the injection of the drug, one of the prosecutor's doctors switched on a tape recorder, which until that time had gone unnoticed in the back of the office. Neither I nor my doctors had been aware that the examination was to be recorded. Had I known before the injection of the drug, I would have refused to proceed without the approval of my attorney. In retrospect, it appears that the tape recorder was the prosecutor's means of circumventing the court's instruction that attorneys and police officers were to be barred from the examination.

The day following the examination, May 6, Mr. Selser received from Drs. Cassity and Policastro brief medical reports related solely to my mental condition. The doctors' reports contained no mention of my statements while under the influence of the drug. As Mr. Selser was to state later, in an affidavit dated February 26, 1965, and filed in the United States District Court, District of New Jersey, on July 14, 1965:

> I at no time knew, nor did I ever consent that a tape recording of the examination of the defendant would be made by the doctors representing the State. I was never informed that it was the purpose of the State to make a recording and as a matter of fact I did not learn that a tape recording was in fact made until a long time after the trial of the defendant resulting in a judgment of guilty.
>
> I was never provided a verbatim copy of the interview with the defendant while he was under the influence of the so-called "truth serum." I did receive reports from Dr. Cassity and Dr. Policastro, but there was no mention made to me in such reports of the fact that a tape recording had been made. . . . My recollection is very clear, however, that there was no verbatim statement of the conference, nor was there any reference to the fact that a tape recording was made, but the reports confirmed my belief that the defendant denied participation in

the murder and did confirm, while under the influence of the drug, the statements he had made to me. I never consented to an examination other than to get confirmation of the statements given to me by the defendant and certainly it was never known to me that the examination proceeded beyond the scope intended by me in my representation to the County Prosecutor and to the Court. I never learned that there was an inquiry about, nor statements given with regard to a "baseball bat" which allegedly had some part in the murder. I had no reason to believe that any information solicited from the defendant was designed to be used at the trial of the defendant and certainly I was never informed by anyone that information was secured from the defendant with regard to the baseball bat.

No transcript of the interview was available to me at the trial or at the time of the appeal, either a tape recording, a transcript thereof, or handwritten notes. As a matter of fact, when I learned quite accidentally that a tape recording had been taken, I demanded a copy of a transcript thereof or the original tape recording and I was informed by the County Prosecutor, and his statement was made in court at the time of my application to the Court for an Order, that *no transcript of the tape recording was available and the original tape had been destroyed.* [Italics added.]

The prosecutor, however, did not suffer the same lack of information. His statement to the court was correct in the sense that he did not have a verbatim transcript of every word spoken during the examination; but he did have, and he eventually admitted having, a partial transcript of the essential portions of the examination. The fact is that the day following the examination, a secretary from the prosecutor's office went to New York City with a detective, and was permitted by the state's doctor to make stenographic notes of the tape recording before it was destroyed. This secretary, believed to be a Miss Rosemary Buzzoni, then returned to the prosecutor's office and prepared a typewritten transcript of her stenographic notes, which were waiting on Prosecutor Calissi's desk when he came to work the morning of May 7.

When the prosecutor read the transcript of the "truth-

serum" examination, things began to happen. Detectives were
sent to question Hommell, and to obtain from him for laboratory analysis the clothing he claimed to have worn the night of
the murder. This was an obviously futile defensive gesture on
the prosecutor's part. Calissi really could not have expected to
find anything on Hommell's clothing two months after the
crime, and more than four weeks after Hommell learned that
I had implicated him—assuming of course a fact which I
challenge: that Hommell gave the police the clothing he had
worn on the night in question.

Further study of the transcript of the examination convinced the prosecutor that my story about having left a broken
baseball bat in the sandpit was true. Gilroy was brought in to
examine his impounded automobile, and he confirmed that one
of his baseball bats was missing. By Wednesday afternoon there
was no doubt in the prosecutor's mind that a baseball bat was
somehow involved in the case, and that it would prove to be a
problem at trial if he could not explain to the jury what had
become of the bat. Then the unexpected happened: First
Assistant Prosecutor Galda came up with an idea. Taking all
the available detectives and investigators with him, he went
to the sandpit and began a systematic search of the entire area.

Investigators George O'Har and Carmine Perrapato were
assigned to make a foot-by-foot, walking search of the stand of
woods across Chapel Road from the sandpit—the same wooded
area searched by Mr. Zielinski after finding Vickie's shoe and
kerchief, and the same area in which her pocketbook had been
found. O'Har found the bat within minutes. It was lying on
the ground, in plain view, fifty feet from the edge of Chapel
Road.

No one ever would be able to say how long the baseball
bat had been lying there, who had put it there, or why. If, as
the prosecutor was compelled to assert, the bat had been lying
there for two months, it certainly is a damning indictment of
the sloppy, superficial nature of the original investigation of
the crime. If one looks back and considers the evidence found
at the scene of the crime—shoes, kerchief, tire tracks, footprints,
red gloves, locket, bloody stones, the pocketbook, the baseball

bat—one cannot help but notice that all this evidence was pointed out to the police by non-policemen, and that not a single piece of the evidence was located as the result of independent action by the investigating officers. What possible excuse was there for failing to search the entire area surrounding the sandpit? Even Mr. Zielinski, after sending his wife to call the police, instinctively realized that the wooded area, only fifteen feet across the road from where he had found the shoe and kerchief, was the most logical place to begin his search.

Mr. Selser visited me Thursday morning, May 9. From the expression on his face and his apologetic manner of greeting me, I knew that the news was bad. The prosecutor, Selser explained, had refused to believe my story regarding Hommell, and the lie-detector test, ordered by the court, had been canceled at the prosecutor's insistence.

"Can't you do anything?" I asked the lawyer. "Isn't there anyone who could tell us what we need to know?"

"I'm sorry, Ed. Hommell claims he was in Pelzer's Tavern until ten o'clock, and that he was home in bed shortly thereafter. There is some indication that Pelzer could refute that, but he apparently fears to speak. He claims to have been threatened with the loss of his license, for serving minors, if he testifies in your behalf. I do not believe him. I shall subpoena him."

"Well, I believe him. They know Pelzer served Hommell, and he is only twenty, a year under age. And I'm sure Rockefeller, who also drinks there, is under age. Pelzer also has a record for making book on the horses. He is the kind of guy they could scare to death."

"Yes, I know that, but the problem goes beyond Pelzer. We need other testimony, Ed, but people will not help us. They either refuse to talk to us, as Gilroy has done—he threatened to throw Nicol out of the house—or they claim the prosecutor has instructed them to remain silent. We know, for instance, that Mary Zielinski could help us break Hommell's alibi. She is not, we think, as violently opposed to you as one might expect, but she seems to be more concerned not to incur the wrath of her father."

"Mary is a nice girl."

"Yes, she seems to be. I understand she soon may marry George Self. Perhaps when she is free of her family she will speak up."

"That's no help now."

"No, it isn't. But it is something we can fall back on."

"Tell me this, Mr. Selser—how can Calissi explain the baseball bat?"

"From what I understand, the prosecutor will merely alter his theory to fit. Instead of claiming that you chased Vickie, fought with her, forced her to return to the sandpit, and then killed her with a rock, he will say that you chased her with the baseball bat, struck her down on Fardale Avenue, threw the bat into the woods, dragged her body back to the sandpit, and then crushed her skull."

"Christ almighty! He could fit anything into that theory."

"Yes, I suppose he could," Selser answered with an air of resignation. "Whatever you say, the prosecutor will alter his theory to fit it."

"So, what happens now?"

"We go to trial Monday. The prosecutor and the judge are dead set against any delay."

"What are my chances?"

"I don't know. I honestly don't know. We are not as well prepared as we should be, but there is nothing we can do about that this late in the game. We can only go to trial and hope for the best."

"Okay. If that's it, that's it."

"Just a couple of more points, Ed. I have heard that the medical report will establish that Vickie was a virgin. Do you know about that?"

"I wouldn't *know* one way or the other, but I'd guess she was."

"Have you ever heard, or do you know, that she had engaged in abnormal sexual practices?"

"Nobody is perfect."

"That isn't what I asked you," Selser said angrily. "I asked if you had heard that."

"I'm sorry. No, I hadn't heard, and I'm not too sure I'd tell you if I had heard. It wouldn't do anyone any good to bring that up."

"Oh, I would never raise that issue," the lawyer exclaimed. "Never. I wanted to know just in case the prosecutor raised the question. Now, Ed, there was a report, either in the press or in one of Mr. Nicol's memos, that you told the police that Vickie threatened to report you to her father. What could she have told him if you did not do anything to her?"

"What you probably mean is when I told Galda she said, 'I am going to tell my father you are like all the guys,' or something like that. I don't recall her exact words."

"Yes, that's it. That is the statement."

"Well, you see, Mr. Selser, her father seems to have drilled into her the idea that all men are bastards, all interested only in getting in her pants. So when I slapped her, she said that, and I guess that what she meant was that she would tell her father she had learned he was right, all guys *are* bastards. To tell the truth, I didn't understand what she was talking about right then, but with a month or so to think it over, I guess that is what she meant. But it really makes no sense. All I did was slap her, and her father was the last guy in the world she would have told."

"Why do you say that, Ed?"

"If there was anything she wouldn't do, she wouldn't tell him she had been picked up in a car by some guy. She was scared stiff of him. She wouldn't have told him if she had been raped. From what I heard from her, the old man would have told her she deserved it, then would have kicked her ass around the house."

"Then perhaps it was an idle threat?"

"I don't know. It made no sense, and I said in my statement to the police that it made no sense. Like I said, I've been thinking about it for a month, and I'm seriously beginning to wonder if she didn't say she would tell all the guys I was like her father. That might have made some sense, like telling them that I was a son of a bitch."

"All right, it's really a minor point. Now, are you certain you made no attempt to molest her in any manner?"

"Hell, yes. Look, we've discussed the time factor, that I was with her only a couple of minutes, less than five. How fast can I be? Seriously, think about it. I wasn't even there long enough to chase her all over the place with a baseball bat like Calissi claims I did, so where in hell do you figure I found time to molest her? If Calissi claims I did that, too, where is he going to dig up time for the killing? He can't say I chased her with a bat in one hand while I molested her with the other, on the run."

"Yes, Ed, I suppose the time factor is a strong point in your favor. We must stress that. Now, just one more thing. You say you left Vickie with Hommell because she was his girl, and that notwithstanding your knowledge of his prior violent acts, you could not foresee him killing the girl?"

"That's right. Maybe a psychiatrist might have expected him to do something like that, but it never occurred to me to figure on such a thing."

"All right, Ed, but will Hommell deny in court that she was his girl friend?"

"Of course not. Take the names of all the guys who hang around Tony's gas station, pick one name out of a hat, and I guarantee you will have someone who has seen Hommell and Vickie together. Don't worry, Hommell won't deny it in court. Too many people know."

"Fine. Now I must be going. There is much to be done before Monday morning. I may not see you before then."

"That's okay. If anything comes up before then, I'll have Pat or my mother phone you."

"Good. Keep your chin up. We will give them a good fight."

CHAPTER SIXTEEN

PROSECUTOR CALISSI: "IF THE COURT
please, the State moves the case of the State of New Jersey v.
Edgar Smith, Indictment Number S-276-56."

Judge O'Dea: "Defendant ready?"

Mr. Selser: "Yes, sir."

With that simple formality, my trial began at 9:30 a.m.,
Monday, May 13, 1957, just sixty-eight days after my arrest.

The courtroom in which my trial was held, officially
known as Room 326, was the largest available. The spectator
seating area, as in most theaters, was divided into three sections:
a large center section flanked on both sides by aisles; and two
narrow sections along the side walls, but separated from the
walls by aisles, where spectators were permitted to stand.

In addition to the seating arrangements on the main floor,
a wide, horseshoe-shaped balcony ran around both sides and
the rear of the room. Here, too, spectators were permitted to
stand. When all the seats were filled, and all the available
standing room taken—as it would be every day of my trial—the
room's capacity was approximately five hundred persons.

In the high ceiling of the courtroom, functioning as sky-
lights, were three stained-glass windows. I recall that one of
the windows, with the words "Mosaic Law" across the bottom,
depicted the tablets upon which the Ten Commandments had
been inscribed. A second window—the center window if I recall
correctly—depicted the Pilgrims' meeting with the Indians. A
third stained-glass window in the ceiling dealt with, I believe,
the theme of Civil Law, but I cannot recall the specific design

**203**

of that window. The well of the courtroom, set apart from the spectator area by a polished wooden railing, was furnished with a long table, at either end of which were chairs for the defendant and the opposing attorneys. Another table of the same size, in front of and below the raised judge's bench, was used to display the evidence. To one side of this area, to the judge's left, was the jury box, consisting of twelve wooden swivel chairs, their columnar bases bolted to the floor. The jury box was not a box in the strictest sense, as one is accustomed to seeing in motion pictures involving courtroom scenes; there was no partition in front of, or enclosing, the jurors' seats. An attorney could not, therefore, as they do in the movies, lean on the jury box and have a folksy conversation with the jurors, à la Clarence Darrow.

In the corner of the courtroom, next to the jury box, was the door to the room into which the jury would retire to deliberate and reach a verdict. In the other corner, directly across from the jury, was another small room reserved for the use of the defendant and his attorney, providing a nearby refuge for having a cigarette and a conference during a recess.

The witness stand was built onto the side of the judge's bench, between the judge and the jury. At the opposite end of the bench sat the clerk of the court. The court reporter, using a stenotype machine, sat just below and in front of the witness stand. It had been arranged in advance that two court reporters would be employed at my trial. One reporter would record the proceedings for an hour or so, then would leave to prepare a typewritten transcript of his notes while the second reporter took his place in the courtroom. By alternating thus, a typewritten transcript of the proceedings would be available to the prosecutor and the defense attorney at the end of each morning and afternoon session.

Judge O'Dea, who presided at both my arraignment on the indictment and the hearing of my petition for a truth-serum examination, had only recently been appointed to the county court bench, and this was to be his first criminal trial of any great significance. A brusque, florid Irishman, he had never before presided over a first-degree murder trial, nor in fact over any criminal proceeding involving such widespread publicity and public interest. This lack of experience in such matters, besides the fact that he, himself, was the father of a young girl the victim's age, may account for what seemed to me his emotional involvement in the issue, to a point that may well have impaired his ability to function impartially without his being aware of this. Indeed, at one point in the trial, while viewing color photographs of the victim's mutilated body, he would find it necessary to call a recess when he felt himself "overcome"—the word he used to describe his reaction—by the evidence.

Therefore, while I passionately disagree with his judicial decisions, it is for precisely the foregoing reasons that I hold no "grudge" toward Judge O'Dea. Even while I find fault with the manner in which he conducted the trial, I recognize that he was an honest, sincere man caught up in an extremely difficult situation. In later years, having acquired greater experience and judicial maturity, he has come to be respected by many, including myself, as one of the better county judges in the state.

The first order of business was the selection of the jury. The law in New Jersey, as in most other states, requires that not less than twelve jurors shall hear a murder case. It is the practice in New Jersey, therefore, to select fourteen jurors at the outset of the trial, to ensure that the minimum number will be on hand in the event one or two jurors are lost during the course of the trial due to illness. Later—after all of the evidence has been introduced, the attorneys have said all they have to say, and the judge has explained the law to the jury—the clerk places the names of all fourteen jurors on folded slips of paper in a box, from which he then draws twelve names. These twelve jurors make up the deliberative body, the others are dismissed. One of the interesting problems facing the judge in my case was that the jury box had only twelve seats. He solved the problem by seating the thirteenth and fourteenth jurors behind the railing, out among the spectators.

The jury in my case was selected from a special list of one hundred names, drawn at random a week earlier from the master list of all jurors available during that session of the court. After excuses for illnesses and hardships, however, the original list of one hundred had been reduced to seventy-four before selection of the trial jury began.

The selection of the jury required two days. The persons selected to serve were, with two or three exceptions, much older than I, at least twice my age. Twelve of the fourteen conceded during questioning that they had read the newspaper accounts of the case, some the night before the trial began. One juror had a brother-in-law who was a police officer with whom I was acquainted; another had three nephews who were police officers, one a New Jersey state policeman; and finally, a juror who had read about the case the night before the trial knew personally, and had worked with, Anthony Zielinski, Vickie's father.

The question is, of course, why jurors such as these were accepted. I do not know. Perhaps my attorney, a man in his sixties, was overly fatigued from the sixteen- to eighteen-hour days he had put in preparing for the trial. Once, during the first day of jury selection, he had found it necessary to request a brief recess, so that he could sit down and rest a few minutes. His fatigue became so evident as the trial progressed that at the end of the trial, in a request which Judge O'Dea denied, he asked permission to leave rather than await the verdict. Then, too, had he been younger and more alert, or if he had had an assistant, he might not have made some of the catastrophic mistakes I shall point out as the story of my trial progresses.

It is possible also that Mr. Selser realized that the selection of an impartial jury to hear my case was a near-impossible task, and for this reason was content to select what he thought were the best of the lot. I do not know if that was the case, but I do know that had I seen the newspaper accounts of my arrest, I would have 1) demanded a postponement; 2) demanded a change of venue to some other section of the state; and 3) appealed the denial of either demand.

At this point I must clarify my position toward my trial lawyer, to forestall any imputation of personal ill-feeling. His errors in conducting my defense happen to be an essential part of the story; they cannot be ignored. But ever since the time of the trial, when Mr. Selser and I became friends on a first-name basis, we have remained so. He is one of the kindest, gentlest, most loyal human beings I have ever known, and in many respects has treated me more as a son than as a client. He took my case when few other attorneys would have done so, and did his best in a near-impossible situation; for this I shall always be grateful. My criticisms, harsh as they may be at times, are of his judgments, often made in moments of great stress, and should not, therefore, be misread as animadversions upon the man.

The flood of newspaper reports that inundated the public immediately following my arrest—some newspapers devoted entire pages to the story—was as overwhelming as individual and specific reports were inaccurate. Throughout the New York–New Jersey metropolitan area the story of my arrest was front-page news. The *Bergen Evening Record* gave the story such disproportionate treatment in relation to its actual importance that, at the end of 1957—the year in which another fifteen-year-old Bergen County girl was raped and murdered; Senator Joseph McCarthy died; the British tested their hydrogen bomb; President Eisenhower sent federal troops to desegregate the Little Rock schools; and in which the Soviet Union launched the first Sputnik—the editors of the *Record* chose to designate the story of my arrest and conviction as the top news story of the year.[1] But of even greater significance to the issue of whether my trial jury would be unduly influenced by the pretrial pub-

[1] *Bergen Evening Record,* December 30, 1957, p. 3.

licity was the inaccuracy, rather than the extent of the newspaper reports.

It is difficult to judge whether the newspaper reporters decided to follow the old axiom that "nothing will spoil a good story more quickly than a few facts"; or whether individual reporters, too lazy to verify the statements emanating from the prosecutor's office, allowed themselves to be misled. It seems that a conscious effort was made by the prosecutor and his staff to prejudice beyond redemption any defense I might offer; and to attain that end, the press was given a distorted, and at times totally false, picture of the case against me. The alternative, that the reporters, and all the newspaper editors of the area, having been given the truth by the prosecutor and his staff, joined together in a single-minded plot to publish the same misquotations, the same falsities, the same twisted and distorted "facts," is too implausible to believe. I reach this conclusion not merely because a similar story line appeared in all the newspapers at the same time, but because I cannot conceive of any way in which the newspapers stood to gain by publishing false, juror-prejudicing accounts of the case, as opposed to publishing the truth. On the other hand, the benefit accruing to the prosecutor from having such reports published is too self-evident to require elaboration.

Having read the significant portions of my statement to the police, the reader will find the following excerpts from a few randomly selected newspaper reports to be especially illuminating and illustrative of the phrase "prejudicial pretrial publicity."

A mold of a tire track near the scene of the tragedy indicates the killer drove a Mercury, *police said*.[2] [Italics added.]

This statement was published while I was being interrogated in the prosecutor's office. The statement was untrue. Tire molds were made of a single set of tracks found on the dirt road, but the automobile which left those tracks has never

[2] Ibid., March 6, 1957, p. 1.

been identified; or, if identified, its identity has never been made known by the police. This false report, however, given to the press prior to the announcement of my arrest, left the public with the notion that the police had an airtight case against me, since the follow-up reports describe the automobile I drove as a Mercury.

> A 23-year-old Mahwah father of one child shortly after noon today confessed to having killed 15-year-old Victoria Zielinski. . . . He is Edgar Smith. . . . He made his formal confession in the Prosecutor's Office in the presence of a priest he requested.[3]

This report must have come as a great surprise to the priest.

> Smith questioned since early yesterday morning, finally signed a statement. . . .[4]

The statement was never signed, but it always helps the prosecutor when the public thinks he has a signed confession.

> Calissi . . . announced at noon yesterday that Smith was being charged with murder on the basis of his statement and other evidence.[5]

Amazing. At noon, the prosecutor announced that I was being charged on the basis of a statement that did not begin until one hour later.

> The other evidence includes . . . a blood-spotted automobile floor mat.[6]

The spot on the floor mat was found eventually to have been kerosene.

[3] *Herald-News*, Passaic, N.J., March 6, 1957, p. 1.
[4] *Bergen Evening Record*, March 7, 1957, p. 1.
[5] Ibid.
[6] Ibid.

## CAN'T REMEMBER KILLING RAMSEY
## GIRL, SMITH SAYS [7]

The only thing I cannot remember is the prosecutor sum-
moning the nerve to ask whether I had killed the girl.

. . . Calissi . . . announced that Smith had signed a statement
in which he admitted everything up to the actual killing.
    According to police and detectives, Smith said he grabbed
the girl by the wrist and that she slapped him. Smith then struck
her, and in a scuffle both fell from the car.[8]

Assistant Prosecutor Galda: "How many times would you
say you hit her?" Smith: "I don't actually know if I struck her
at all." Galda: "Did you fall to the ground?" Smith: "I am not
sure of that." Galda: "Did she fall?" Smith: "I don't know."

During questioning, Smith identified all of the Zielinski girl's
clothing.[9]

Galda: "What clothing did she have on?" Smith: "I didn't
look very close. I didn't notice her clothing at all." Galda:
"What other clothing did she have on besides the jacket, a
dress or pants?" Smith: "I don't know at all."

. . . He admitted to detectives he felt better after making his
statement.[1]

I did not say that, but I will now: getting the police off
my back after sixteen and a quarter hours *was* blessed relief.

Calissi said that Smith signed a statement in which he admitted
punching the girl, but said he could not remember crushing her
skull with a 25-pound rock. . . .[2]

[7] Ibid., p. 2.
[8] Ibid.
[9] Ibid.
[1] Ibid.
[2] *Herald-News*, March 7, 1957, p. 1.

The fact is that, when asked, I specifically denied having lifted any "heavy object" with which her skull might have been crushed, or that I had ever seen or handled the rock in question.

Galda: "Ed, I show you what appears to be a boulder." Smith: "I don't recognize it." Galda: "Again I show you what . . . appears to be some type of rock. Do you recall anything concerning that rock?" Smith: "No." Galda: "Did you lift anything in this [sandpit] area while you were here?" Smith: "Nothing except my shoe. . . ."

. . . When taken yesterday to the spot where the girl's body was found, he cringed and even refused to look at it . . . he readily pointed to the mound where he fought with the girl.[3]

Galda: "Did you run up the bank?" Smith: "I don't recall ever running up on the bank." Calissi: "Do you recall being on this bank at all?" Smith: "No, sir." Galda: "Did you go up on the bank?" Smith: "No, I didn't.

After his confession to a priest, Smith signed a transcript of his statement taken by a court stenographer.[4]

Sheer fantasy.

### ADMITS HE "PUNCHED" SCHOOL GIRL
### KNEW VICTIM
### SAYS SHE RESISTED ADVANCES

The suspect, Edgar H. Smith . . . virtually confessed . . . claims he "blacked out" after hitting the girl in the face when she tried to resist his advances.[5]

When did I say *that?*

. . . Calissi termed the killing "the act of a fiend and a sadist." [6]

---

[3] Ibid.
[4] Ibid.
[5] *Hudson-Dispatch,* Union City, N.J., March 7, 1957, p. 1.
[6] Ibid.

Warming up the prospective jurors.

The autopsy later disclosed that although the girl's slayer had attempted to molest her, she had not been raped.[7]

The autopsy showed no such thing, and the judge would so rule at the end of my trial.

Smith reportedly admitted trying to make love to the girl.[8]

Galda: "Did you put your arms around her in the car or outside the car?" Smith: "No." Galda: "Did you try to kiss her?" Smith: "No." Galda: "Did you feel any parts of her body?" Smith: "No." Galda: "Did you move any of her clothing?" Smith: "No."

. . . Becoming enraged, he punched his fist into her face and began tearing at her clothes.[9]

Pure invention as is all the following:

. . . The trousers Smith discarded were also found to bear scratch marks on the knees and tiny pieces of gravel were imbedded in the cloth.[1]

Calissi said he had also received information that Smith was actually observed at the murder scene Tuesday afternoon.[2]

### FAST ACTION, TEAMWORK
### BEAT CLOCK ON MURDER

Press time for the Home Final, 12:50, was near when McHenry got his confirmation Smith had confessed. His story was in fact correct, needing only a few changes in attribution. It had been

[7] Ibid., p. 2.
[8] Ibid.
[9] Ibid.
[1] Ibid.
[2] Ibid.

readied in advance and by 1:30 p.m., the page was cast, and the press run, held for 40 minutes, began.

The West Bergen Edition went to press at 2:45 p.m., carrying the full story but no picture. West Bergen residents got their home-delivered Record about a half-hour later than usual. . . . The Record was first with the full facts of the confession.[3]

The *Record* certainly was "first with the full facts," so "first" that when the reporter, McHenry, "got his confirmation" that I had confessed, my statement to the police had not yet begun. And when the *Record* went to press at 2:45 p.m. with the "full facts," my statement was only half complete. Where and how the *Record* got the "full facts" of a statement not yet made is almost as interesting a question as how the *Record* could report that I had led the police to Vickie's pocketbook—isn't that one of the "full facts"?—before I had done so.

### PAL SAYS VICTIM FEARED SUSPECT

The best friend of suspected murderer Edgar Smith told this newspaper yesterday that Victoria Zielinski had been afraid of the Mahwah man . . . "One time when Vickie and Barbara were walking along the street, Edgar and I drove past. He said something to Vickie and Vickie said she would tell his wife if he didn't leave her alone." [4]

That makes a nice story. It is, however, untrue; and the words are not Gilroy's. No one, but no one, with the exception of my mother, had ever called me Edgar. Throughout several hours of extensive direct testimony and cross-examination at my trial, not once did Gilroy refer to me as Edgar. But aside from the language not being Gilroy's, the fact is that he would not have recognized Barbara Nixon if he had tripped over her, and neither Barbara nor Vickie knew him. So fallacious is Gilroy's story that not even the prosecutor believed it. The prosecutor's entire theory depended upon Vickie having been friendly

---

[3] *Bergen Evening Record,* March 6, 1957, p. 1.
[4] Ibid., March 7, 1957, p. 1.

enough toward me to accept a ride on a dark, lonely road. Significantly, Gilroy did not repeat his tale at my trial.

> Gilroy gave this theory of what had taken place the night of the slaying: "After Edgar dropped me off on Ramapo Valley Road at 8:30 p.m., he probably went to look for a girl. He saw Vickie walking along Wyckoff Avenue and asked if he could take her home. She said yes, but instead of driving straight ahead he turned down Fardale Avenue to lover's lane. Edgar made advances and when he got fresh she slapped him and ran from the car. He pursued her and a struggle took place.[5]

Remarkable. At my trial Gilroy testified that I had dropped him off on Lake Street at 7 p.m. As for Vickie accepting an offer of a ride home, that would hardly seem to fit his picture of a girl who was afraid of me. Moreover, the language again is not Gilroy's. Terms such as "made advances," "pursued," "got fresh," "a struggle took place," were not his style. One need only compare these expressions with the language he used when he reported to the police in Mahwah to see the inconsistency. The language there is taken directly from his testimony at my trial.

I cannot ascribe to Gilroy a motive for making these statements—if indeed he did make them. The newspaper clipping from which they were taken was first brought to my attention on May 18, 1967. My first impression was that Gilroy had displayed a remarkable knowledge of the prosecution's theory of the crime, particularly since he is reported as having made the statements on March 6, the day of my arrest. It would seem likely, one supposes, that Gilroy was being carried away by having been thrust suddenly into the limelight; and that to make himself appear important, he permitted a story-hunting newspaper reporter to put words into his mouth.

### STILL GETTING AWAY WITH MURDER!

The horrible murder of a pretty Ramsey High School girl, 15, Monday night, as she was on her way from visiting friends in

[5] Ibid.

Mahwah and the arrest of her alleged slayer, has again focused public attention on New Jersey's "save-the-criminal laws" and the deterioration of JERSEY JUSTICE that allows slayers TO GET AWAY WITH MURDER.

SWIFT PUNISHMENT, retributive and exemplary, is the greatest deterrent to crime, yet A MURDERER WHO COMMITS HIS CRIME IN NEW JERSEY has probably a 99 to 1 chance of NEVER PAYING THE SAME PENALTY EXACTED OF HIS VICTIM.

In the last 5 years 12 MURDERERS HAVE PAID WITH THEIR LIVES FOR TAKING THE LIVES OF OTHERS. During that five years more than 300 men, women and teenagers were SLAIN. Many escaped the electric chair because of effete prosecutions while others escaped because juries were too "chicken-hearted" to find the killers guilty of first-degree murder WITHOUT RECOMMENDATION OF MERCY.

Under our "save-the-criminal laws," a murderer cannot be sent to the electric chair if the jury recommends mercy to the trial judge. ALL THAT THE JUDGE CAN DO IS TO SENTENCE THE SLAYER TO A TERM IN PRISON THAT MAY BE FOR ONLY $14\frac{1}{2}$ years. Yet under New Jersey's deteriorated Jersey Justice this is called a "life sentence." What mockery!

Is there any wonder that killers commit bestial crimes in New Jersey without fear of ever paying the supreme penalty?

In the past year and a half probably 100 murders were committed throughout the state BUT THERE WAS ONLY ONE KILLER WHO WENT TO THE ELECTRIC CHAIR. That was in August 1956.

Yet there are murderers in State Prison who have been living on the taxpayers for years. They have been saved by clever lawyers who take advantage of loopholes in the statutes, often put there by lawyer-legislators, and JERSEY JUSTICE HAS LOST ITS ONE-TIME MEANING when a life was demanded for a life.

What is the Legislature going to do about it? Abolish the electric chair and let the penalty for MURDER BE ONLY $14\frac{1}{2}$ years in State Prison? That would be a direct invitation to potential murderers to commit their bestial crime. WHAT PROTECTION WILL THE PEOPLE HAVE IF THIS INSANE BILL INTRODUCED BY Assemblyman C. William Haines, Burlington Republican and a Quaker, ever becomes law? It would abolish the death penalty.

But the electric chair has all but been abolished through the

BREAKDOWN OF LAW ENFORCEMENT, THROUGH THE TRICKY
STRATAGEMS USED BY DEFENSE COUNSEL AND THROUGH THE
FAILURE OF CHICKEN-HEARTED JURIES TO DO THEIR FULL DUTY.

Does it amaze you that 2 slayers of a special policeman
back in 1951 in a Newark supermarket are still being kept by
the taxpayers in State Prison, DESPITE THE FACT THEY WERE
SENTENCED TO DIE FOR MURDER IN 1952? Clever lawyers,
through one technicality after another, exhausted the tolerance
of the state courts, and now have the case tied up in the federal
courts. What a mockery of JUSTICE! Why, you may ask, is this
allowed? The answer is simple—because our lawmakers have
made the "save-the-criminal laws" so that, if a murderer has
enough money to have the cleverest lawyers, he might be able
to defeat the death penalty even after being sentenced to the
chair. Every lawyer recognizes the beneficence of time in behalf
of his client, even after being convicted. The longer a convicted
murderer is kept alive the more the likelihood he will be eventually freed.

With this deterioration of New Jersey JUSTICE, the KILLER
HAS WHAT SEEMS TO US TO BE a 99 to 1 chance to "get away
with murder," although he might be sentenced to serve 14¾
years.[6] [Emphasis in original. The "2 slayers of a special
policeman" referred to in the foregoing editorial were granted
a new trial by the United States Court of Appeals for the Third
Circuit, five months after the editorial appeared. The grounds
for reversing the conviction were that a juror had concealed the
fact that he, himself, had been an armed robbery victim. The
state appealed, and the United States Supreme Court permitted
the lower court decision to stand. The two men were reconvicted
at their second trial. They are serving life sentences. They were
not set free in fourteen and three quarter years. No one ever is
released in the minimum time. The "average" life sentence in
New Jersey is seventeen years.]

This editorial, and the excerpts from news reports, are but
a fractional part of the adverse publicity my case received
during the time I was preparing for my trial. These are not the

[6] Editorial, *Hudson-Dispatch*, March 8, 1957.

most extreme examples. They are, in fact, merely the output of three newspapers over a three-day period. Similar articles appeared during the two-month period between my arrest and trial in the Paterson (N.J.) *Evening News;* the Paterson *Morning Call;* the Ramsey *Journal;* the *Ridgewood* (N.J.) *News;* the Newark (N.J.) *Star-Ledger;* the Newark *Evening News;* the New York *Daily News;* the New York *Post;* the New York *Herald-Tribune;* and in several of the so-called "detective" magazines—all distributed in the Bergen County area from which my jury would be chosen. One of the detective-magazine articles, complete with photographs from the files of the Mahwah Police Department, appeared under the byline of Charles E. Smith, Chief of Police. He denied having written the article. He claimed that a reporter asked questions, and he said: "I gave him some information. . . . He wanted to know if it would be okay to use my name on the article, and I told him it would be." A few weeks after giving the reporter "some information," Chief Smith refused to give my attorney and my investigator *any* information whatsoever about the crime. Perhaps *they* should have promised to write an article, and to put the chief's name on it.

On April 24, 1967, in response to a question I had put to him, my trial attorney, John E. Selser, of Hackensack, wrote to me: "There is no question in my mind at all that the publicity prior to trial and during the trial was very harmful to your interests."

During the course of selecting the jury to hear my case, sixty-four persons were questioned "in depth" as to their qualifications to serve. Of these, fifty-two (81.2 per cent) were asked whether they had read the newspaper accounts of the case, and forty-two (65.6 per cent) admitted that they had done so. Of those forty-two persons who had read the newspaper accounts, seventeen (40.4 per cent) openly admitted having been prejudiced by those accounts, with the degree of prejudice ranging from "some" to "definitely" prejudiced. The breakdown follows:

| | |
|---|---|
| Questioned as to qualifications | 64 |
| Asked if they had read the newspaper accounts | 52 (81.2%) |
| Did read newspaper accounts | 42 (65.6%) |
| Admitting prejudice | 17 |
| Percentage of total (64) admitting prejudice | 26.5% |
| Percentage of newspaper account readers (42) who admitted prejudice | 40.4% |

The next question is whether the jurors selected to hear the case had read the newspaper accounts. Yes. Of the fourteen jurors selected, twelve had followed the case in the newspapers. Three—including the man who had worked with Vickie's father, as well as the man whose three nephews were policemen—had followed the newspaper accounts right up to the night before the trial began.

Prosecutor Calissi knew as well as anyone that the murder of a young girl always arouses the public emotions, and doubly so when the newspapers have given the gory details maximum front-page coverage, portraying the crime as a "sadistic sex murder." Right from the opening gun, therefore, in a jam-packed courtroom, the prosecutor played to the emotions of the judge, jury, and spectators.

May it please the Court, ladies and gentlemen of the jury: From the evidence the State will show that the victim, Victoria Zielinski, was a fifteen-year-old schoolgirl. . . . Victoria left the Barbara Nixon house at 8:30. . . . Smith passed her going in the opposite direction. . . . He pulled down a short distance, backed into a driveway, came back and picked her up. . . . Smith turned on to Crescent Avenue, Young Road, and went down to what is called the sandpit. . . . He went right into the sandpit. They talked. Victoria talked about school but the defendant, *Edgar Smith, did not have school problems on his mind. He molested this girl immediately. He ripped up her sweater and fondled her breast, this 15-year-old girl. She refused his advances* and she tried to get out of the car. He grabbed her . . . but she still released herself and started running. He ran after her. . . . He finally caught up with her down on Fardale Avenue and he struck her with a blunt instrument, which we will offer into evidence, which the defendant at that point tried to discard and hide.

He got her back into the sandpit. He wanted to silence this girl, and while *he was trying to molest this girl* in the car she said: "You are like all the other men. I am going to tell my father."

He was afraid of being exposed, and this man had to silence this girl. *She ran from him refusing his sexual advances.* He got her back in the sandpit and crushed her skull with a very heavy implement. . . . Her brains were scattered on the sand. In the sandpit he took that body, that mutilated body—he took it to the top of a knoll and dumped it. . . .

. . . [We] will prove that this murder was an intentional, willful, premeditated murder, *a murder in the course of attempting to have sexual relations* with this girl, Victoria Zielinski, a fifteen-year-old schoolgirl. . . . We will show that it was premeditated, that he intended to kill her, to silence this girl. We will show you that this was a brutal, a savage, a sadistic killing.

If we produce that evidence then I will ask this jury to render a verdict of guilty in the first degree without a recommendation of mercy, thank you.

There it was for all to hear: Prosecutor Calissi had committed the state to proving a felony murder. Under New Jersey law, a killing resulting from the commission of, or the attempt to commit, a felony, automatically rises to first degree murder, notwithstanding the fact that the killing was neither intentional nor premeditated. The prosecutor had put the court, the jury, and Mr. Selser on notice: he was going to seek to establish attempted rape, a felony. It would be exceedingly important, therefore, for Judge O'Dea to keep his eyes and ears open, so that when the time came for him to charge the jury as to the applicable law, he could tell the jury whether the evidence was sufficient to sustain a felony-murder conviction.

My attorney's opening statement to the jury was three times longer than the prosecutor's. It is not necessary for me to cite any of that statement here, since Mr. Selser confined himself solely to a repetition of my version of the events at the sandpit, as I had described them to him four weeks earlier in the back room of the county jail.

The jury listened attentively to all of this, but by the time Mr. Selser had finished, I could see that some of the jurors were beginning to fidget in their swivel chairs. They, like the spectators, the vast majority of whom were, oddly enough, teen-agers, were anxious to see the proof and hear the witnesses, not listen to speeches by the lawyers. Always, always, always better a dull witness than a dull lawyer.

When Selser had finished, a brief recess was taken to give him and the prosecutor the opportunity to agree on the admission into evidence, without proof of when or how they were made, several maps and aerial photographs of the scene of the crime. Selser agreed to allow the exhibits to go into evidence without objection, and thereby made his first mistake.

One of the maps, depicting the Ramsey-Mahwah area, was inaccurately drawn. Had I been permitted to examine the map before Selser gave his consent to its admission, I could have pointed out that some of the roads did not run in the direction, and did not follow the contours, in which they were drawn; other roads depicted on the map did not in fact exist; and still other roads which did exist, including the street on which my family had lived for many years, were not shown on the map.

The second map, which depicted the sandpit area in scales of 1 inch : 40 feet and 1 inch : 10 feet was dated March 29, 1957, twenty-five days after the murder. With the thought in mind

that this was an active sandpit from which soil was constantly
being taken, and considering the fact that distance and lines
of sight would be important in the context of the case, I would
have objected to the map unless and until the prosecutor had
established that it depicted the scene as of March 4 and 5, not
March 29. What the sandpit looked like twenty-five days after
the murder was totally irrelevant.

I would have had similar objections regarding the aerial
photographs. It is clear from a glance at those photographs that
they were not taken on either the fifth or sixth of March; and I
would therefore have required proof that they depicted the
scene as it was at the time of the crime.

This concern with photographs and maps representing the
scene as of the time of the crime is not in any sense nit-picking.
Shortly after the trial opened, Prosecutor Calissi sought to have
the jury taken to the sandpit to view the area, but Judge O'Dea
properly denied the request on the ground that the prosecutor
had failed to establish that the scene at the time of the trial was
the same as when the crime occurred, and that the appearance
of the scene at any time other than when the crime occurred
was irrelevant.

# CHAPTER SEVENTEEN

**THE STATE'S FIRST WITNESS WAS MYRNA** Zielinski. Myrna began by describing her arrangement to walk Vickie halfway to the Nixon home at seven-thirty, and to meet her sister again at eight-thirty.

"Did you walk all the way to the Nixon house?" the prosecutor asked when she had finished.

"No, I didn't."

"How far did you walk with Victoria?"

"I left Vickie at two houses before Barbara's house."

"Then what did you do, walk back home?"

"Yes."

"Then what did you do?"

"My mother told me when I was doing my homework that I was supposed to start to meet Vickie. I was already ten minutes late."

"So what time did you start toward the Nixon house again?"

"I left my house at twenty of nine."

"What time did you get to the Nixon house at this particular time?"

"About ten of nine."

"Then what did you do."

"Then I left her house and walked back home."

"Did you see anybody in an automobile?"

"Yes, I did."

"Who did you see?"

"I saw Don Hommell. I was four houses from my home when I saw Don."

"And which way was Don going?"

"Going toward Ramsey."

"Going slow or fast?"

"No, he was going very fast."

"Well, do you know approximately what time it was when you saw Don Hommell?"

"Between five and ten after nine."

At this point, Prosecutor Calissi did something completely unnecessary, but from the standpoint of its emotional impact upon the jury, very smart: he brought out, piece by piece, Vickie's blood-soaked clothing for young Myrna to identify. Obviously, the only relevant identification of the clothing would have been that of Barbara Nixon, who was the last person to have seen Vickie alive. The prosecutor, however, intended to wave those bloody clothes before the jury at every opportunity, and Myrna was the first opportunity.

The first item to be brought out was Vickie's pocketbook. Myrna took one look and burst into tears. Judge O'Dea called a recess.

When Myrna had regained her composure, she quickly identified the pocketbook and a bookkeeping textbook. She was barely holding back the tears, and her voice was so low and hoarse that several times the judge had to ask her to speak up so that she could be heard by the jurors, two of whom were, as noted, sitting out in the spectator area. Then Calissi gave the knife another twist, asking Myrna to identify Vickie's jacket. The sight of that jacket, the inside of which was a horror of dried blood, strands of hair, and tiny bits of bone, was too much for Myrna. Again a recess had to be called until she had calmed down.

By the time Calissi had finished with the witness, after many more tears and short rests for her to regain her composure, she had identified her sister's black loafers, white woolen socks, coral-color cardigan sweater, and blue jeans. Then it was Mr. Selser's turn to cross-examine.

Selser's first point was to establish the distance from the
Zielinski home to West Crescent Avenue. Myrna said it was
four houses away. Since it had been four houses from her home
that she had seen Hommell, she must therefore have been
walking past West Crescent Avenue at that time.

Mr. Selser then began questioning Myrna about the route
she and Vickie had followed to the Nixon home, and at one
point she stated that while returning home alone, she looked
back and saw Vickie under a streetlight in front of the Nixon
home. The lawyer did not seem to realize, however, that there
is a sharp bend in the road just before the Nixon home. For
Myrna to have seen Vickie under the streetlight, she would
have had to be on the Nixon side of the bend in the road, which
in turn would indicate that she was not telling the truth. If
she had seen her sister under the streetlight, she must have
walked almost to the Nixon home; if she had walked only halfway as she claimed, then the bend in the road would have made
it impossible for her to see her sister under the streetlight.

The cross-examination turned to the question of Donald
Hommell. Selser asked Myrna if she knew Hommell.

"Yes."

"You knew that Don was friendly with your sister Vickie,
didn't you?"

"She knew him," the girl replied defensively.

"Had he come to the house for Vickie at any time?"

"He never came—he never took her out."

"He *never* did?"

"No."

Again changing the line of questioning, the lawyer asked
whether, at eight-forty, Myrna had seen any automobiles on the
road while walking toward the Nixon home to meet Vickie.
Myrna said she had not. On the way home, after failing to meet
Vickie, she repeated, she had seen Hommell.

"Now, did I understand you to say that Hommell was
driving very fast?" Selser asked.

"Yes, he was driving very fast."

"How fast would you say he was going?"

"About maybe sixty or so."

"What kind of a car was Don driving?"

"A Ford."

"A two-tone green Ford?"

"Yes."

"That is all, Myrna. Thank you very much."

Myrna Zielinski's testimony, though interesting, was not especially important. The testimony of the prosecution's next witness, Barbara Nixon, was very important, however, since much depended upon establishing the precise time that Vickie had departed from the Nixon home.

Prosecutor Calissi began the direct examination of Barbara, a tall, husky blonde, with a series of questions designed to establish that Vickie had gone to the Nixon home on the night she was killed, that she had worked on her bookkeeping lessons with Barbara—"She copied some of my work from school"—and that she had been wearing clothes identified by Myrna. Barbara also testified that Vickie had arrived at her home at 7:45 p.m.

"How long did you do homework?" the prosecutor asked.

"I guess about three quarters of an hour."

"Then what did you do?"

"We talked for a while, and we turned the radio on."

"And did Vickie stay at your home all night?"

"She left my home at about eight-thirty."

How, I wondered as I listened to Barbara's testimony, did she arrive at that conclusion? If Vickie had arrived at seven-forty-five, and had done homework for forty-five minutes, then it must already have been eight-thirty before they began talking and listening to the radio.

Prosecutor Calissi did not go any further with the time element. Satisfied with the eight-thirty estimate, he dropped the subject and began dragging out the bloodstained clothing for Barbara's identification. When Barbara had identified the clothing, Calissi turned the witness over to Selser for cross-examination.

Mr. Selser wasted no time. His first question was directed

toward the manner in which Barbara had fixed the time of Vickie's departure from the Nixon home.

"Well, she said that she had to meet her sister, start meeting her sister, at eight-thirty, and so she left my house around eight-thirty," the Nixon girl responded.

"Well, did you look at a clock to see if it was eight-thirty?" Selser asked.

"I don't remember."

"You said you had been listening, I think you said, to the radio, or was it television?"

"Radio."

"Radio. Was there a change of program?"

"I don't remember."

"The only reason then you say eight-thirty is because she said that is the time she wanted to leave?"

"Yes."

"You really don't know whether it was that time or not, do you, Barbara?"

"No."

"Was there a clock in the room?"

"Yes."

"You didn't look at it at all?"

"I don't remember."

"Do you remember what radio program was on?"

"No."

"Do you remember whether it went off?"

"No."

Selser, realizing that Barbara would not cooperate if he were to question her till hell froze over, gave up, apparently satisfied with the girl's statement that she could not be certain that Vickie had left at eight-thirty. He should have confronted Barbara with her earlier statement that she and Vickie had done homework for forty-five minutes before turning on the radio. Whatever her reply, the jury would have got the point from the question.

"The State calls Mary Zielinski, the mother," Prosecutor Calissi announced.

Mrs. Zielinski—tall, dark-eyed, her curly brown hair cut close to her head—she had once been a very pretty woman, that was obvious; but her sad face showed plainly the signs of a hard, worrisome life. Every eye in the courtroom followed her as she walked to the witness stand.

The mother's voice was surprisingly clear and calm as she related, in response to the prosecutor's questions, the details of Vickie's plan to visit Barbara Nixon, and as she described in great detail the clothes the girl had been wearing that evening. Except that her descriptions were more detailed, she added nothing to what was known from the testimony of Myrna and Barbara.

"All right, what time did Myrna leave the house to meet Victoria as was prearranged?" the prosecutor asked.

"She left the house at twenty minutes to nine."

"And did Myrna return to the house then?"

"Yes, she did."

"And did Myrna say anything about Victoria?"

"No, she went up to the Nixons' and didn't see anything of Vickie, and Barbara's sister, Laura, told her that Vickie had gone ten minutes ago."

Mrs. Zielinski's reply, fixing Vickie's departure from the Nixons' at eight-forty, had been neither expected nor wanted by the prosecutor. He had been careful to avoid asking Myrna what she had been told when she had got to the Nixon home, and the mother's unexpected statement caused him to frown. He remedied the situation by changing the subject.

"When did you see Victoria after you had seen her when she left at seven-thirty to go to Barbara Nixon's?"

"At the sandpit," the mother replied, the words catching in her throat, "when she was murdered."

"And as a result of having seen your daughter at the sandpit, what did you do?"

"What would any mother do?" she cried out in a flood of tears.

As before, Judge O'Dea called a recess until the witness could compose herself. Mr. Selser, sitting beside me at the end of the counsel table farthest from the jury, leaned over and whispered to me that he would not cross-examine the mother. The jury, he said, might be alienated, thinking he was badgering her. I agreed that she had it tough enough already.

Prosecutor Calissi, on the other hand, had a job to do, and the best way to do that job was to put aside his concern for Mrs. Zielinski, and to sustain the emotional level of the trial. Thus, when the recess ended, he went right back at it, again dragging out the already twice-identified, blood-drenched clothing. He began with the girl's shoes.

"I show you S-14 and S-15, and ask whether you can identify them?"

"Those are Vickie's loafers."

"Did you go up to the sandpit and make any identification?"

"I did. I went up there."

"What did you see?"

"I saw her red gloves, and just a couple of feet away I saw her locket broken, and I saw—it was horrible—I saw her brains scattered on the ground. Then I looked over at my husband and he said: 'There she is . . . ' "

"Did you recognize Victoria?"

"I would any place. . . . Her campus jacket was not on her, it was alongside her, and her bra was off, but it was hanging down, and her breast was exposed."

"Where was the brassiere on her body, Mrs. Zielinski?"

"Down around her midsection. And her sweater was up around her neck."

"I show you a brassiere and ask you if you can identify it?" Calissi asked, holding up for the first time a torn, blood-stained brassiere.

"That is Victoria's."

"How far away from the dirt mound did you see the brains?"

Mr. Selser objected to the manner in which the question had been phrased, but Judge O'Dea replied laconically: "I will allow it." The mother, however, was unable to estimate the distance.

"Mrs. Zielinski," the prosecutor went on, "I show you a jacket and ask if you can identify it?"

"That was Victoria's campus jacket."

"Are these the gloves Victoria had with her on the night of March 4?"

"They are," the mother replied, identifying the red gloves found in the sandpit.

"And can you identify these pants and belt?"

"Those are Vickie's."

"And can you identify this sweater?"

"That was her coral sweater."

The prosecutor, sensing that Mrs. Zielinski's identification of the bloody clothing had made a great impression on the jury—not to mention Judge O'Dea—turned to Selser and said: "You may cross-examine."

"No questions," the lawyer replied.

The prosecution's fourth witness of the day was Anthony Zielinski, the murdered girl's father. A squat, heavily muscled, craggy-faced man, forty-five years old, he was the sort one might expect to see laboring in the coal mines of northeastern Pennsylvania, whence the Zielinski family had come.

Mr. Zielinski's reputation for precipitous action apparently had preceded him, and as he walked down the aisle toward the witness stand, several uniformed court officers rose from their seats at one side of the room and placed themselves in a position to be between the father and me. I did not consider that to be a proper action to be viewed by the jury, and when later I inquired about it, one of the officers told me: "Those were our orders." He refused to say who had issued the orders.

The prosecutor's first few questions were concerned with Mr. Zielinski's movements and activities between the time his oldest daughter, Mary, awakened him to tell him that Vickie was missing, and the time when he and his wife discovered Vickie's shoe and kerchief lying on Fardale Avenue. It was dur-

ing this preliminary questioning that the father stated that at
two o'clock in the morning he had suspended the search for the
girl. "Well, there was nothing else to do but sit around," he
told the prosecutor. "It was too dark to look around, but I
stayed up all night."

The questioning eventually turned to the discovery of the
shoe and kerchief.

"We went up Oak Street," the father said, describing the
search he began after daybreak. "We went all the way through
Oak Street to Shadyside Road. From there to West Crescent.
Then I doubled back again, and I went all the way down on
Young's Road. I was on Young's Road, and I doubled back. I
got on Chapel Road. Then when I made a left-hand turn on
Fardale Avenue, that is where I discovered the slipper."

"What time was this?" the prosecutor asked.

"That was approximately ten minutes to nine, nine o'clock,
somewhere around there."

"What did you do?"

"I looked out the window, and I seen the slipper. Then I
looked up about twenty feet further, and I seen a babushka—a
kerchief, I guess they call it."

"Did you get out of the car?"

"I got out one side and my wife got out the other. I said:
'You better go call the police,' so she did."

"After you saw the slipper and the scarf, what did you
personally do?"

"Well, we were going due east . . . Well, I went to the
right-hand side of the road to search for whatever I could find."

"Where did you go from there?"

"I crossed the wall. Not where the slipper was, on the
other side. There's a growed-up area, it's growed up in the
brush, and I searched in there for a while before my wife came
back."

Sitting at the counsel table listening to Mr. Zielinski's
story, I had difficulty at first understanding what he was saying.
But when I realized that the "other side" of the road from the
shoe and kerchief meant the south side, I turned to my attorney

and whispered: "That is the wooded area he is talking about. If he went in there to look around until his wife came back, why didn't he find the baseball bat? It must have taken her at least five minutes to call, and that is where you told me they found the bat."

Selser nodded his head, but said nothing as the prosecutor continued the direct examination.

"Did you make any observations in the area you are talking about?"

"I didn't. I came back and went up to the sandpit. I discovered a pair of red gloves. I left them lay right where they were and I came back."

"Did you recognize those gloves?"

"I didn't, no, I didn't. I didn't recognize the gloves."

"Now, then, what did you do?"

"I came back to the car, and I seen a police car pulling in."

"Who was in the police car?"

"Captain Wickham. We walked and kept searching both sides of the road. . . . Captain Wickham happened to discover the gloves, and he bent down and looked at the gloves."

"What did you do, sir?"

"I turned to the right . . . I looked around and I seen where it was scuffed, it was all scuffed up, very freshly so. I said: 'Gee, it's funny.' I looked at the bottom of the pit, and I seen some stones with blood on it."

"Would you describe this for us, this particular part?" the prosecutor asked, pointing to the outline of the dirt mound drawn on a map.

"That is the mound where they [?] drove up in here. This is a flat area in here, and there was a mound up on the right-hand side, it went up for about six or seven feet. Then it had a little flat surface where it widens out. So when I got up on top of the pit I discovered the foot marks. . . ."

The prosecutor did not pursue the matter of the footprints. After eliciting from the father his description of how he had found his daughter's corpse, and having had the man identify various photographs of the sandpit area, Mr. Calissi released the witness to Mr. Selser, who thereupon proceeded to astound everyone present.

"You said that the shoe on Fardale, according to your estimate, was about 120 feet from Chapel?" Selser asked.

"Well, approximately, yes."

"And I think you said the scarf or babushka was about twenty feet further away from Chapel?"

"In that radius."

"That is all I wanted to straighten out, sir, thank you."

Incredible. Here was a witness who might have shed some light on three important points: he had driven along Oak Street searching the sides of the road for some sign of Vickie, yet he had not seen my pants, which were found there the following morning; he had searched the wooded area where the baseball bat was not found until two months later; and he had found footprints on top of the dirt mound, only a couple of feet from the body. Yet all my lawyer wanted to know was whether the shoe or the kerchief was farthest from Chapel Road when found.

Prosecutor Calissi, quite rightfully expecting a lengthy cross-examination, had no sooner got comfortably settled in his chair when Selser's "That is all" brought him to his feet again. Judge O'Dea, seeing the expression of disbelief on the prosecutor's face, and sensing that the state was unprepared to call its next witness, declared a ten-minute recess.

I knew nothing of law and procedure, but it seems to me that a much broader cross-examination of Vickie's father might have elicited some favorable information. There is, after all, little cause for concern that an extensive cross-examination would have alienated the jury, as it might have done in the case of Mrs. Zielinski; and I am quite certain that it was at this point in the trial that the seeds of doubt began to germinate in my mind: doubt that my attorney was prepared for the trial; doubt that he was capable of handling the task without assistance; and doubt that he had the right mental attitude, the confident expectation of victory one must carry into any contest.

Prosecutor Calissi had recovered his aplomb and was prepared to proceed when court reconvened. His witness was Captain Wickham of the Mahwah police, dressed for the occasion in civilian clothes, his gold badge pinned to the breast pocket of his gray tweed sports jacket.

Led on by the questions of the prosecutor, Captain Wickham described how he had been called to meet Vickie's parents at the intersection of Fardale Avenue and Chapel Road, and what had taken place upon his arrival at that location.

"I met Mr. and Mrs. Zielinski. . . . They pointed out a scarf and a loafer or moccasin which was on the side of the road on Fardale Avenue. . . ."

"Don't tell us what he said," the prosecutor cautioned. "As a result—"

"As a result, on top of the mound of dirt, Mrs. Zielinski and I found the body of the girl. It was on the north side, down an embankment about six foot."

"What was the position of the body?"

"The body was in a semi-crouch, mostly on the back, with the legs up toward the stomach. The clothing had been pulled up around the shoulders, and it had blue dungarees on, and no shoes, and white socks."

"Did you notice anything else in the sandpit at the time?"

"Yes. On the way in we noticed, I noticed, tire marks."

That was not the answer Prosecutor Calissi wanted. He did not then, or at any subsequent time, care to discuss tire marks. Brushing aside the reference, he asked Captain Wickham if he had observed anything else.

"I observed a large rock with a large mound of blood on it, which was partially up on top of the bank, and up on top, also near the rock, was a large clump of blood, and a white substance which looked like brains to me. The body of the dead girl had a large hole in the head of it. The whole skull was missing."

"What did you observe about the clothing?"

"The clothing had been pulled up over the shoulders, leaving the middle section of the body bare, and the brassiere was hanging down around the waist.

By the time Captain Wickham had finished describing the finding of the body, it already was mid-afternoon. The remainder of the day, until the four o'clock adjournment hour, was consumed by the dull, tedious process of having the officer identify, one by one, so that they could be admitted into evidence, dozens of photographs of the scene. Finally, at four o'clock, Prosecutor Calissi suggested to the court that the trial be adjourned until the next morning.

Judge O'Dea agreed, but first he called Mr. Selser to the bench and announced: "I have given permission to the court officers and the jury tonight for their entertainment to see the *Spirit of St. Louis* at the Park Lane Theatre in Palisades Park. Seats have been reserved for them in the rear. . . ."

Mr. Calissi: "I have no objection."

Mr. Selser: "I think it is perfectly proper."

Judge O'Dea: "We will recess now until tomorrow morning at nine-thirty. . . ."

I was handcuffed and returned through the tunnel to the county jail immediately after the recess had been called. Mr. Selser did not visit me that evening, and consequently I had plenty of time to meditate upon the day's events. It had all been very unreal, as if I had awakened suddenly to find myself in another world.

Criminal trials in real life are not as they are in motion pictures, or in Perry Mason shows on television. Rarely does a witness do or say anything spectacular or unexpected; hardly ever does a canny defense attorney trap a witness in a web of lies—prosecutors prepare and coach their witnesses too well for that to happen; there is very little shouting or arguing, and almost no surprises; and never, at least not that I have heard of, never does a spectator leap to his feet and blurt out a confession at the last crucial moment to free the accused. Generally speaking, a courtroom in which a murder trial is being held is one of the best places in town to catch a few hours of uninterrupted sleep. The judge, jury, witnesses, and the attorneys will in all probability be too bogged down in minutiae to notice or care.

I must concede that I was not totally discouraged by the

first day's events, but I was appalled by my attorney's concern with irrelevancies. More often than not, when he should have been probing matters such as the footprints Mr. Zielinski had found on top of the dirt mound, Selser was wasting five full minutes questioning Captain Wickham regarding the mutilation of the face of a photograph. The "mutilation" was merely an indentation caused when someone with a heavy hand had written the words "Prosecutor's Office" on the back of the photograph.

# CHAPTER EIGHTEEN

THE TRIAL RESUMED AT NINE-THIRTY
Thursday morning, and for two hours Captain Wickham continued to identify photographs of the sandpit area, and of the
body. Much of this time was dissipated in technical arguments
concerning the quality of various color enlargements depicting
the body. When at last the identification of the photographs
had been completed, Prosecutor Calissi put the trial back on
the tracks by asking: "Could you tell us whether or not you saw
Edgar Smith at any time on March the fifth?"

It was the first time my name had been mentioned in the
trial—except for the opening statements—and as Captain Wickham painstakingly recounted the searches for my pants, and
for signs that I had thrown up, the jury displayed a marked
increase in attention. Backs straightened and heads cocked as
the jurors leaned forward in their seats, better to hear every
word.

Midway through his description of the searches, the officer
was rather vague in his placement of the section of Pulis Avenue on which the search for the pants had been concentrated.
Mr. Selser, from his seat next to me at the counsel table, interrupted the prosecutor's questioning to ask Captain Wickham:
"That location you are pointing to . . . is a stream going
across Pulis, aren't you?" The lawyer presumably desired to
establish that I claimed to have thrown the pants in precisely
the area in which Donald Hommell was seen searching the
morning after the murder.

"Yes, sir," Captain Wickham replied.

"And at that particular location what did you do?"

"We searched the area and found no pants."

The prosecutor asked a few more questions regarding my claim of having been sick, then turned the witness over to Mr. Selser for cross-examination.

Mr. Selser began his cross-examination by asking Captain Wickham if anything other than the shoe and scarf had been found on Fardale Avenue.

"There was a wad of hair," Wickham replied. "The hair was found west of the shoe, or about six or eight feet closer to Chapel Road. In other words, the hair first, then the shoe, then the scarf."

Directing Captain Wickham's attention to the tire tracks found in the sandpit, Selser asked the officer where exactly the tracks had been found.

"They were on the driveway and beyond the driveway, both."

"How far beyond the driveway?"

"Approximately fifty feet, I would judge, or better."

"Running in what direction?"

"Running in a westerly direction."

"How close would you say the nearest blood was that you noticed, to any of those tire marks?"

"About twenty-five feet."

While Captain Wickham and the lawyer were discussing the tire marks, I turned to Andrew Nicol, the investigator, who was sitting behind me, and I suggested to Nicol that in light of the prosecutor's assertion that Vickie had been struck down on Fardale Avenue with a baseball bat, Selser should ascertain whether any markings were found on the dirt driveway, such as would be expected if Vickie had been dragged back to the sandpit. Nicol passed the suggestion on to the lawyer, who in turn asked the officer if any blood had been found between Fardale Avenue and the sandpit area, including the dirt driveway.

"None that I noticed," he replied.

Mr. Selser, apparently satisfied, indicated that he had no further questions to ask.

The prosecutor's next three witnesses were: Ronald Ambler, the *Bergen Evening Record* photographer pressed into service by Chief Stewart when color photographs of the body were desired; and Alvin P. Freeman and Thomas Germenn, both of the Technicolor Corporation, the firm which had processed the color enlargements. The enlargements, close-ups of Vickie's body, sixteen by twenty inches, were two of the worst horror pictures ever seen. Selser had objected to the photographs for two reasons: 1) they were merely color renditions of black-and-white photographs already in evidence, and therefore served no purpose other than to inflame the jury; and 2) the photographer had used a type of film which, when used under daylight conditions, had the effect of exaggerating the color red. This, Selser claimed, heightened the bloody appearance of the girl's injuries.

Mr. Selser, an expert in the field of photography, engaged in a forbiddingly technical discussion with each of the three witnesses, during which they used such terms as dye transfer print, matrix, silver image, relief image, Kelvin temperature, red separation negative, gelatin emulsion, scale value, photomechanical, Chromas, and color balance. I doubt if anyone else in the courtroom, including Judge O'Dea, knew what the lawyer and the witnesses were talking about. The result was that Judge O'Dea overruled all of Selser's objections, admitted the enlargements into evidence, and permitted each of the jurors in turn to examine them.

The afternoon session following a one-hour recess for lunch, opened with the prosecutor calling Howard Sneider, the mortician who had removed Vickie's body from the scene to the funeral chapel. Once again the prosecutor paraded the bloody clothing before the jury, as he asked the mortician to identify it, piece by piece, as the clothing he had found on the body. But other than to establish that the medical examiner had begun the autopsy at one o'clock on the afternoon of March 5, Mr. Sneider's testimony was strictly routine, and the prosecutor quickly moved on to his next witness, James Stewart, the chief of the county detectives.

"On March 5, 1957, were you assigned to go to Mahwah?" the prosecutor inquired.

"I was. I received a call at nine-forty-six, and as a result of that call I arrived in Mahwah with Detectives Ridgway and Graber at about ten-thirty-five at the scene."

"What did you do upon arriving?"

"I took the whole area in and had it guarded, had it protected. I immediately requested that a photographer be sent up from the Bergen County Police. . . . I directed that measurements be taken. . . ."

"All right, Chief, what else did you do?"

"As we proceeded in [to the sandpit] we noticed on the right at the end of that path . . . you have got it marked a dirt roadway . . . [to] the right of that there was a rock that was blood-covered. It looked to weigh about twelve pounds, and I would say it was probably thirty-five feet away from where the gloves were, in a northerly direction. . . . Going west and slightly north there was another rock of a much larger size. It looked like it might weigh about twenty-five pounds, and that was also heavily smeared with blood. . . . Now, between where those two rocks were was weeds and small brush and all. . . . The weeds and the brush were down and was blood-smeared the same as if you would drag something over it. . . . Now, as I reached the top of the knoll, to my right was one of the other loafers that matched the one we had found on Fardale Avenue, and to the left of it was a clump of brains, I would say about that big, it would fill my two hands."

Mr. Calissi: "You may cross-examine, Mr. Selser."

My attorney, who had not questioned the previous witness, the mortician, asked the chief of detectives one innocuous question concerning the position of Vickie's jacket at the time her body was found, then dismissed the witness. I was becoming increasingly unhappy with Mr. Selser's lackluster performance, and I feared that the defeatist attitude I detected would be sensed also by the jury.

Prosecutor Calissi's next witness was to be County Detective Russell Ridgeway, the officer who had been detailed by Chief Stewart to take measurements of the scene of the crime. There were, however, but a few minutes remaining in the trial day. It was decided, therefore, that after identifying himself, the detective would draw a sketch of the sandpit area, then the trial would be recessed until the following day.

Detective Ridgeway returned to the witness stand at nine-thirty Friday morning and began to explain his diagram, drawn in black crayon on a large sheet of white paper. It is impossible to determine with any certainty which was more unintelligible, his diagram or his testimony. He had begun, he said, by taking measurements from a fixed position, the fence post at the end of the dirt road; but in going along, he had taken the measurements from one article of evidence to another. The result of this ridiculous procedure was that we know, for example, that a certain rock was five feet west of another rock, which was twelve feet in some unspecified direction from a black loafer, which in turn was thirty-seven feet from [the edge of?—the center of?] a "shuffled area"; but there was no way to determine the distance of any of these items to, say, the fence post, or Chapel Road, or the top of the dirt mound. Moreover, in a post-trial examination of the detective's diagram, it was determined, by using known distances between clearly defined fixed objects, which served as control points, that the diagram drawn by the detective was highly inaccurate.

Prosecutor Calissi, seemingly as confused as anyone, eventually brought Ridgeway around to the subject of the collection of the evidence.

"Who gathered up the evidence, do you know?"

"Chief of Detectives James Stewart, Detective Gordon

Graber, Garabedian, and myself. . . . I then noted Lieutenant Abrams arriving on the scene, who I noted making plaster casts of some tire tracks and footprints that were found in the area."

As before, the prosecutor did not care to hear about the tire tracks. He changed the subject quickly, asking Ridgeway if he had clocked the distance from the Nixon home to the Zielinski home.

"I clocked it in my car, and it was eight tenths of a mile."

Detective Ridgeway must have found mathematics to be an elusive subject. The distance between the two homes was, in 1957, and still is in 1968, seven tenths of a mile, as clocked by three different automobiles, as well as by measurement on a scale map of the area.

The prosecutor's final questions of the witness concerned his activities during the time I was being interrogated. The witness stated that he and Lieutenant Haight of the Mahwah police had gone to my house trailer at 2:15 a.m. on the night of March 6. No one was home, he said, so they had entered and searched the trailer, seizing at that time a pair of brown leather gloves, which Prosecutor Calissi was offering into evidence. Mr. Selser did not object to the admission of the gloves into evidence because, as he later explained to me, the Fourth Amendment prohibition against illegal search and seizure did not apply in state courts. It does today, but not retroactively.

Very little was accomplished when Selser was given the opportunity to cross-examine, and when he had finished with the witness, the prosecutor called Joseph Gilroy.

Joseph Gilroy was a diffident witness. He may have felt quite at ease acting important for the press on the day of my arrest, when he was expounding his theory of the crime; but slouched in a witness chair in a crowded courtroom, under the searching eyes of a jury, he was a shrinking violet, whose replies to the prosecutor's opening questions were barely audible.

"You are not speaking up loudly," Judge O'Dea told him. "Sit up straight, and hold your head up and speak."

Thus admonished, the witness described the events of

March 4; how he had permitted me to borrow his automobile at seven o'clock that evening, and how later that evening I had telephoned him and asked him to drive me to my mother-in-law's home in Ridgewood.

"What time was that?"

"Approximately ten or fifteen after nine. It was ten or fifteen after nine o'clock."

"What time did [Smith] pick you up?"

"About a quarter of ten."

"From your home to the trailer, did you have a conversation?"

"Yes. Well, he told me he was sick, and he threw up on his pants, and he had to throw them away . . . I dropped Eddie and his wife and baby off at their mother-in-law's."

"You took your car then?"

"Yes, sir."

"Would you describe the interior of your car to us, referring of course to the car?"

"I have blue seat covers . . . and in the back there was a whole mess of stuff. There was a couple of baseball mitts . . . a couple of baseball bats . . . and a lot of junk was back there."

"What time did you arrive in Ridgewood?"

"Oh, about quarter after ten."

"When did you hear from Smith again?"

"The next day. Oh, about twelve o'clock," Gilroy replied, going on to explain that afterwards he and Donald Hommell had driven to Ridgewood to pick me up, and that upon their arrival Hommell had told me the police were looking for a Mercury.

"And what did Smith do?"

"He had a startled look on his face. Then he brought his wife and baby out. They got in the back seat and we went toward Ramsey."

"On the way toward Ramsey, did you have any conversation with Smith?"

"Well, I don't know, but Eddie or his wife picked up a

lipstick. I don't know which one it was, and they handed it to Donnie [Hommell].

Under Prosecutor Calissi's further questioning, Gilroy explained that he had seen me take along an old pair of shoes when, after dropping off my wife and child, he and Hommell had driven me to Ramsey.

"Eddie had the shoes one minute, and then the next minute he didn't have them. I started to suspect him. I wasn't sure. I couldn't believe it."

For the next few minutes, the prosecutor had the witness pointing out on the seat cover, which had been placed in evidence, the spot he had found. It was a very small spot, so small in fact that it does not show up in color photographs of the seat cover. There was much confusion over which was the front and which was the back of the covering, and I must admit that although Gilroy claimed the spot was on the driver's side, I was not certain. I have studied carefully a series of enlarged photographs taken of the seat cover while it was still in the car, taken from both sides and a dozen angles, as well as photographs taken of the seat covers after removal. I cannot say which side the spot was on.

Following the confusion involving the spot on the seat cover, Gilroy identified the floor mat from his automobile, pointing out a circular oil stain, approximately twelve inches in diameter, on the passenger's side.

"I show you S-68 for identification, Mr. Gilroy, and ask whether you can identify it."

"That's the brown baseball bat that was in the back of the car."

"And what about the other bat?"

"It was a white bat."

Prosecutor Calissi removed from a paper wrapping a severely discolored, once white, baseball bat. The cracks, each approximately fifteen inches long, ran down the bat's centerline.

"I show you S-69 for identification and ask whether you can identify it?"

"That is the bat I *think* was in the back of the car."

"Pardon me?"

"That was the bat that was in the car."

"Is this the condition the bat was in on the night or day of March fourth?"

"I couldn't be sure of that. We might have cracked it playing. I don't know."

"What about the color of the bat?"

"It wasn't dirty like that. It was white."

"Fine. You may cross-examine, Mr. Selser."

My attorney had assured me that he would be questioning Gilroy at great length, so as he began his cross-examination, I settled myself comfortably in my chair to listen to what I hoped would be a good job.

"Now, Mr. Gilroy, while you were bowling at the Paramus Bowling Alleys on the afternoon of March fourth . . . did anything happen to Ed's foot or leg?"

"When he was bowling, he crossed the ball over and hit his ankle with the bowling ball."

"Was the skin broken at the point where he hit the ankle?"

"Yes, it was cut a little."

"Cut?"

"Yes."

Changing the subject to the afternoon of March 5, when Hommell had made the statement about the police looking for a Mercury, the lawyer asked Gilroy: *"Had you told Hommell that you had loaned Eddie your Mercury?"*

"Well, I think—I don't know where—no I *didn't, I don't think so."*

"When you got to Ridgewood to pick up Smith . . . what did Ed say to Hommell, or when he saw Hommell?"

"He said: 'Did you hear about the murder?' That's what Hommell said to Eddie."

"Hommell said it?"

"Yes."

"And did not Ed say at that time: *'Was that Vickie?'* "

"Well, I think so."

"What?"

"Yes."

"Now, this lipstick that was found in the automobile. . . . Didn't Hommell then say: 'It looks like Vickie's'?"

"No, sir."

"Did Hommell take the lipstick in his hand?"

"Yes, sir. He said: 'Maybe it was Vickie's . . .' "

"He said maybe what?"

"He said: 'Maybe it was Vickie's.' He threw it out the window."

"When did you first examine the back seat of your car . . . to see whether or not the baseball bat and the other items were still in there?"

"I didn't examine the back seat of my car."

"Do you know whether they were or were not still in your car when you went to the police?"

"I presume they were in the back of my car."

Mr. Selser asked Gilroy a great many other questions, but most were intended merely to clarify portions of his earlier testimony, or to stress certain points the lawyer considered important. It was, I thought, a shame that Selser had not objected to the admission into evidence of the baseball bat when he had had the opportunity to do so, during the prosecutor's direct examination. I was quite certain then, and I am absolutely certain today that Gilroy, if pressed, could not identify *that* baseball bat as being the one from his automobile, and his failure to identify it as such would have destroyed its value as evidence. But that opportunity had been lost.

Prosecutor Calissi was able to get through three more witnesses before the one o'clock recess for lunch.

William Hoehne, an attendant at Secor's Service Station, testified that I had been there on the night of March 4; that I had purchased a can of kerosene; and that I had departed "about eight-thirty."

The second witness, Gloria Kanreck, a young girl, testified that on the evening of March 4 she had got off a bus on the highway in front of Secor's, that she had entered Secor's, and that she had seen me leaving with a can of kerosene at "about eight-thirty."

The third witness, Detective George O'Har, stated that on May 8, at about three-thirty in the afternoon, he had gone to the intersection of Fardale Avenue and Chapel Road. He was, he stated, "assigned with Carmine Perrapato, an investigator, to search the area south of Fardale Avenue and east of Chapel Road."

The search, the detective added, uncovered the baseball bat. ". . . [He] took one side and I took the other, going back and forth continuing the search through the woods. I found a bat."

"How many feet south of Fardale Avenue?" Judge O'Dea inquired.

"One hundred and six feet . . . fifty feet east of Chapel Road."

"One hundred and six feet south of Fardale?"

"Yes."

As Detective O'Har stepped down from the witness stand, Judge O'Dea called the afternoon recess for lunch.

"That baseball bat was found more than a hundred and twenty feet from the shoe and kerchief on Fardale Avenue," Selser remarked. "That's a long way."

"Considering that Calissi claims it was thrown that far," I replied, "it's a hell of a long way."


The afternoon session opened with Detective Gordon Graber being called to testify.

Graber stated that on the night of March 5, at eleven-thirty, he and Detective Garabedian had been sent to Ridgewood "to take Mr. Smith with us back to headquarters for questioning."

"And did you do that?"

"Yes, we did."

"And subsequent to the interrogating, what did you do, if anything?"

"I went with Mr. Smith, Mr. Galda, and Captain De-Marco . . . to Ramsey, Mechanic Street in Ramsey, where Mr. Smith showed us the garbage can where he had put his pair of black shoes."

"Can you tell us which garbage can it was?"

"It was the ninth garbage can. There were thirteen in a row. . . ."

"How did you ascertain that the shoes were in the garbage can?"

"Mr. Smith directed us to it."

"Can you describe the shoes you testified about?"

"They were a pair of black Oxford shoes."

"Then what next did you do, Detective?"

"From that point we proceeded to the crime scene where Mr. Smith was going to show us where he had gotten sick. He told us . . . he had gotten out of the car and thrown up at that particular point. We searched that particular point. . . . We could not find any evidence of anyone throwing up at that particular point. We walked back to the gravel pit and Mr. Galda shone the light over to the knoll and asked Mr. Smith if he knew what was over there. Mr. Smith said he had never been over in that section at all. . . ."

"By this vicinity you [mean] what?"

"I am talking of the knoll, the rise of ground. . . . He said he did not know what was over there. He said he had never been back in that vicinity."

"In addition to searching the sandpit . . . did you make any other discoveries or searches?"

". . . [He] told us he had thrown his pants away . . . along Pulis Avenue there is a little bridge. . . . We searched that vicinity. . . . We could not find his pants."

Prosecutor Calissi, pointing to a map, asked Detective Graber to indicate the area he had searched for the pants.

"Right in the vicinity of this little stream there is a little bridge in here, and there is a house. . . . We had searched all in this vicinity where he said he had thrown it."

"Then what did you do subsequent to that?"

"Subsequent to that . . . about three-thirty a.m., I went to his mother-in-law's house in Ridgewood, and I searched the blue jacket that he stated he had been wearing on the night previous."

"Did you see Smith . . . subsequent to the time that you picked up the jacket?"

"Yes. I was present when Edgar Smith was taken to the crime scene again, after he had made a statement in the prosecutor's office. . . ."

"What did you do when you arrived there?"

"I was going with Mr. Galda and yourself and Mr. Smith. . . . He pointed out the spot on Wyckoff Avenue where he saw [Vickie] walking toward her home."

"Did Smith . . . point out the exact place where he had driven into the pit?"

"Yes. He did."

"While Smith was in the sandpit, and in your presence, did he say what had occurred and what had happened?"

"Yes. He told us he had driven Victoria Zielinski back into the sandpit, and that she had slapped his face. . . . She then jumped out of the car, and he said he fell out the right side of the car. . . ."

"And from the sandpit, where did you go with Smith?"

"We came out of the sandpit, and he directed us south on Chapel Road about 350 feet. . . . We stopped the car, and we got out of the car, and Mr. Smith directed us across the road where there was a Christmas tree. We looked over in the field, and we discovered a pocketbook and some schoolbooks . . . lying in the woods."

"Do you recall who first pointed out the items that were found at that particular location?"

"As we walked across the road after getting out of the car . . . as we were walking across there, we could observe the books and the pocketbook lying directly ahead of us."

"Was there any conversation pertaining to the number of times that Smith was at the sandpit?"

"Yes, sir. He said that he went to the trailer court and changed his pants, and he returned after he secured a flashlight to search for his missing shoe. . . ."

"You may cross-examine, Mr. Selser."

My attorney had been making notes on a scratch pad throughout Detective Graber's testimony, and as he advanced toward the witness stand to cross-examine the officer, he had those notes and a photograph in his hand.

"Now, I have here, sir, a photograph. . . . I ask you whether you can identify that as a photograph of the area on Pulis Avenue where the stream crosses the road. Where the search was made for Smith's trousers?"

"That shows just one part of the scene. I believe the search started from across the bridge—"

"But this is the general area . . . and the place where Smith indicated to you the night of March 5 as the place?"

Mr. Calissi: "I object."

The Court: "I will allow it."

"Yes, this is the vicinity that we searched that night, and where Smith showed us he had thrown the pants."

"How far in off the hard pavement of the road would you say these things, the pocketbook and the books, were found?"

"I would say approximately twenty-five feet."

"That is all, Detective."

"The State calls Donald Hommell."

Mr. Selser: "May I ask the Court whether or not the Court can find it within reasonable convenience to recess at this time? Very frankly, sir, I am very desirous of an extensive cross-examination of this witness Hommell, and I would rather that his examination not be broken into parts, and very honestly sir, I am tired . . . I am exhausted, and I should so much be grateful to the Court were we at this time allowed to recess."

Judge O'Dea: "Well, I am aware of your situation Mr. Selser, but I am concerned about using our court time, and taking advantage of the recess tomorrow and Sunday for the rest we all need."

Mr. Selser: "We have but twenty minutes or so left, sir."

Judge O'Dea: "Twenty-five minutes."

Mr. Selser: "I am saying to Your Honor I am tremendously exhausted. I am not looking for any consideration by reason of this, but there comes a limit, sir, to a man's endurance, and I have reached it."

Judge O'Dea: "That is why I took the long recess, Mr. Selser."

Mr. Selser: "I appreciate it. I told Your Honor at noontime that this is so."

Judge O'Dea: "Well, under the circumstances of this application for recess, I will grant it."

Mr. Selser: "Thank you, sir."

Judge O'Dea: "Until Monday morning at nine-thirty."

# CHAPTER NINETEEN

THE TRIAL RESUMED MONDAY MORNING
with Donald Hommell on the witness stand. The weekend
recess had given me an opportunity to evaluate the events of
the first week of the trial, and I was not at all pessimistic as I
watched Prosecutor Calissi shuffle through a stack of paper on
the table in front of him. I knew little would be accomplished
during Selser's cross-examination of Hommell, however long
and competent that examination might be; the prosecutor and
his legal staff had spent several evenings and most of the weekend with Hommell, going over his forthcoming testimony and
preparing him for Selser's attack. The boy had been groomed,
preened, and briefed as thoroughly as a Miss America con-
testant facing her big night. But I was not relying upon the
cross-examination to expose the flaws in the circumstantial evidence against me. The key to the trial would be the testimony of
the medical examiner, who would tell us the time and cause of
death.

Donald Hommell was a small fellow, five-ten, about 135
pounds, with blond, crew-cut hair brushed straight up. His
cold, blue-gray eyes, set close together in a usually expression-
less narrow face, were constantly moving from side to side,
taking in the scene about him. They moved in their sockets
like a pair of matched ball bearings, and seemed to contain
about as much feeling.

The prosecutor began by asking Hommell to give his address.

"92 Snyder Road, Ramsey."

"How long have you lived at 92 Snyder Road?"

"Approximately three years."

"Prior to that time where did you live?"

"Vero Beach, Florida."

"Now, on March 5, 1957, did you have occasion to see Joseph Gilroy?"

"Yes, sir."

"When was the first time you learned that Smith was driving Gilroy's car on the fourth of March?"

"In a conversation between Joseph Gilroy and Anthony Saveriano. . . ."

"When was that?"

"Well, that was approximately between noon and one o'clock."

"On the basis of, or as a result of that conversation, what did you do, if anything?"

"After the conversation, I left for Ridgewood with Joseph Gilroy, to pick up Eddie Smith."

"Whose car did you use?"

"Mine."

"What did you do in Ridgewood?"

"We picked up Eddie Smith."

"Did you have any conversation with Edgar Smith when you met him in Ridgewood?"

"Yes."

"What did you say?"

"I winked at Joseph Gilroy, and I said: 'I hear they think it is a Mercury and are checking out all of the Mercurys in Bergen County.' "

"What did Smith say?"

"Well, he just had a funny look on his face, and he didn't say anything."

"Tell us about the discussion about the lipstick. What was all that about?"

"Well, when Eddie Smith or his wife got in the car, I guess one of these picked up the lipstick and handed it over the front seat to either Joe or I. Kiddingly it was said it could be Vickie's."

"Who said that?"

"I don't know."

"Was it you?"

"I can't remember, sir."

"What happened to the lipstick?"

"I just threw it out the window."

Prosecutor Calissi asked Hommell a few more questions to bring out the fact that he had dropped my wife and child off at the house trailer, after which he had driven me to Ramsey, as stated by Gilroy. Then, in a transparent move to limit Mr. Selser's range of cross-examination, the prosecutor declared that he was finished with the witness.

My lawyer was dissatisfied with having so little testimony upon which to question—cross-examination is limited to those things brought out on direct examination, but he went ahead.

"With regard to the lipstick," Selser began, "you knew that was Vickie's, didn't you?"

"No, sir."

"When did it get in the car?"

"I don't know, sir."

"Whose lipstick did you recognize it to be?"

"That I couldn't say."

"As a matter of fact, the lipstick was found in your automobile when the front seat was moved, wasn't it?"

"I don't know, sir."

"Wasn't the lipstick found when the front seat of the car was moved back, and the lipstick was forward of the front seat?"

"I could not say."

"In the front compartment of the car?"

"I cannot say. I didn't see it being found."

"Where was it you threw the lipstick out of the car?"

"I couldn't say."

"You had been out with Vickie, had you not?"

Prosecutor Calissi leaped to his feet, objecting vehemently to the question, but Judge O'Dea overruled him.

"Casually, that is all," Hommell replied.

"She had been in your car?"

"Yes."

"When next before the night of March fourth had Vickie been in your car?"

"I would say approximately a month before that time."

"Not since that date?"

"That I couldn't say. I don't think so."

"Of course, you knew Vickie pretty well, didn't you?"

"Casually I knew her."

"How many times would you say Vickie went out with you?"

Again Prosecutor Calissi was on his feet objecting, but after a long argument with Judge O'Dea, he was once more overruled.

"Very few times," Hommell said.

"Can you tell me how many times?" Selser pressed.

"I would say approximately ten times at the most."

"What time did you leave [your place of employment] on the night of March fourth?"

Mr. Calissi: "I object to the question, sir."

Judge O'Dea: "I will allow it."

"Approximately five after nine," Hommell answered.

The prosecutor continued to object, and a long argument between Selser, Prosecutor Calissi, and Judge O'Dea ensued. The argument became so loud and heated that Judge O'Dea finally had to excuse the jury from the courtroom.

When the jury departed, Prosecutor Calissi resumed the argument, telling the judge: "If Mr. Selser believes that that question pertaining to whether Hommell had any *direct* [sic] connection with the killing should be asked, I have no objection whatever if Mr. Selser will ask him that question."

Selser was outraged: "And make him *my* witness so I

can't attack it? This man is a psychopathic liar. I *know* what his answer would be."

Mr. Calissi: "Now, I think that is very unfair."

Mr. Selser: "It is outside the presence of the jury."

Mr. Calissi: "It doesn't make any difference. It is in the presence of the people here, in the presence of the judge. . . ."

Judge O'Dea: "Don't you think in fairness to the Court that you should withdraw your question?"

Mr. Selser: "All right, I shall withdraw it."

Mr. Calissi: "Just a minute now. In view of the fact that Mr. Selser made a statement about a psychopath, which I think is an unfair low blow, I will withdraw any objections of any kind. . . . He can ask him anything, starting from the Book of Genesis, as far as that is concerned."

Judge O'Dea: "Let us resolve this impassionately."

Mr. Calissi: "How can you?"

Mr. Selser: "I will withdraw my examination at this time."

Judge O'Dea: "You will withdraw your statement about the witness being a psychopath?"

Mr. Calissi: "How can you withdraw a statement like that impassionately, when counsel calls the witness a psychopath?"

Judge O'Dea: "We all know that in the course of heated argument in trials we say a lot of things that we inconsiderately would not have said."

Mr. Calissi: "Well, I have a sixteen-year-old boy, and I wouldn't want my boy to be called a psychopath."

Mr. Selser: "I wouldn't call your boy such."

Mr. Calissi: "I don't know about that."

From the audience, a man, later said to have been Hommell's father, shouted: "I don't want him to call mine one either."

The trial was obviously getting out of hand. Judge O'Dea was uncertain as to how the matter should be resolved, and it was only when Selser agreed to withdraw his question that the issue was settled. Then, to the surprise of everyone, Selser announced: "I have no further cross-examination of this witness at this time." It was a brilliant move.

My lawyer's announcement, which he had withheld until the jury had returned to the courtroom, put the prosecutor in a tough spot. The jury had heard the cross-examination cut short by Calissi's objections, and it must have appeared to the jury that the prosecutor was protecting the witness by preventing Selser from asking important questions.

Prosecutor Calissi did the only thing he could do: he reopened the testimony himself.

"Where do you work, son?"

"Wyckoff Pharmacy."

"What are your hours of employment?"

"That night it was six to nine."

"What time did you leave that night?"

"About five after nine."

"Well, now, on this particular night of March fourth, where did you go after you left the drug store?"

"To Pelzer's, to Pelzer's [Tavern] in Mahwah."

"What time did you get to Pelzer's that night?"

"About nine-fifteen or nine-twenty."

"When you got to Pelzer's, who was there, if anyone was there?"

"Charles Rockefeller."

"When you traveled the route from the drugstore to Pelzer's, did you see anyone on the road whom you recognized?"

"Myrna Zielinski."

"Did you see Edgar Smith, the defendant, at any time during the evening of March 4, 1957?"

"Definitely not, sir."

"You may cross-examine now, Mr. Selser."

Hommell, seated in the witness chair throughout the prosecutor's clash with Mr. Selser, had remained utterly impassive in the face of the accusation that he was a "psychopathic liar"; but as Selser advanced toward him to conduct the second phase of cross-examination, Hommell squirmed a bit, his demeanor betraying a wariness and insecurity not previously apparent. The questioning undoubtedly was about to go beyond that which the prosecutor had anticipated, and for which he had painstakingly prepared his witness. And clearly, though Hommell had maintained a stolid silence during the lawyers' arguments, he had been shaken badly by the passion with which Selser had delivered his accusation. The wariness of the witness would manifest itself in his replies under the pressure of cross-examination.

"Now, sir, Mr. Gilg is the pharmacist where you are employed, is he not?"

"Yes, he was," Hommell replied.

"And he was the man who was on duty the night of March fourth, wasn't he?"

"I can't possibly remember whether he was or he wasn't."

"Now, the pharmacy where you are employed is on Wyckoff Avenue, isn't it?"

"I believe so."

"And the drive from the pharmacy to, say, the Nixon home, at the speed of twenty-five miles an hour, takes how long?"

"That I couldn't say, sir."

"Would you say that it takes more than three and one half minutes?"

"It might."

"How much longer would you say it takes?"

"That I couldn't say."

"Would it take as long as four minutes?"

"I don't know, sir."

"At what speed would you say you were driving along Wyckoff Avenue?"

"About sixty."

"You were in a hurry?"

"No, I just normally drive that fast."

"Now, you say you went directly to Pelzer's?"

"Yes."

"Was Mr. Pelzer there?"

"I believe he was. I couldn't positively say."

"Don't you know that when you arrived at Pelzer's it was a quarter to ten?"

"No. It wasn't a quarter to ten."

"You say you got there at a quarter after nine?"

"Approximately a quarter after nine. It could be twenty after nine. I couldn't say."

"How long did you stay at Pelzer's?"

"I couldn't positively say, sir."

"What did you do at Pelzer's?"

"I sat around and talked to Rockefeller for a few minutes."

"Rockefeller was playing pool when you got there, wasn't he?"

"I believe so. He may have—and then again I can't say he was actually there."

"From Pelzer's, where did you go?"

"Well, I think I went to Pellington's, or then I went directly home. I couldn't positively remember."

"Who did you meet at Pelzer's other than Rocky?"

"I think Rocky was the only person in the place at the time."

"You didn't see anybody else in Pelzer's?"

"I don't think so, not that I can remember."

"Which Pelzer was behind the bar?"

"Either his wife or Herbie [Pelzer]. I don't remember."

"Now, at Pellington's what time did you get there?"

"I couldn't say for sure."

"Was it after ten?"

"No, I would say it was before ten, if it was I don't remember."

"Who did you meet at Pellington's?"

"I do not remember if I was there or I wasn't. I can't say."

Before he had begun the cross-examination of Donald Hommell, Selser had asked me to prepare a list of Hommell's friend's, and to note which of these usually frequent Pelzer's and Pellington's. Now, with the witness on the defensive, and hiding behind an allegedly bad memory, Selser drew my list from his pocket, studied it for a moment, then set about to pin Hommell to the wall.

"Let's see if we can refresh your recollection," he began, with all the sarcasm he could muster. "Do you remember Tommy Doyle being at Pellington's?"

"He could have been. I don't remember."

"Do you remember asking Tommy Doyle whether or not he would go with you to Herbie's place?"

"I might have said it. I don't remember."

"Do you remember Dick Schlott being at Pellington's?"

"No, I don't, sir."

"Do you remember John Metzger being at Pellington's?"

"No, I don't, sir."

"Do you remember asking John Metzger whether he would go with you to Pelzer's?"

"I say I didn't—I don't remember if I did."

"Were you or not over on Pulis Avenue on the morning of the fifth, at the area where the stream crosses Pulis Avenue?"

"Definitely not, sir."

"Do you remember Mrs. Woods who lives immediately adjoining the area?"

"Never seen the lady before, nor heard of her."

"And you told her to mind her own damn business?"

"Never seen the woman or never heard of her."

"When did you find out that Smith had thrown his trousers away?"

"I believe March fifth, that night, I think, sir."

"How did you learn of that?"

"I think it was from one of the police officers—or I read it in the paper, I don't remember. . . ."

"Do you remember saying to Rocky: 'Be sure you don't mention my name'?"

"No, sir. I never said that."

"Do you remember when you said to Smith and Gilroy in your car: 'It's a good thing I didn't pick up Myrna because I would have to take the next boat out of the country'?"

"Not that I remember."

"When had you left the Navy?"

"September 11, 1956."

"How long were you in it?"

"Approximately nineteenth months, six days."

"You had a nervous breakdown, didn't you?"

"No, sir. I had a skin rash, a nervous skin rash."

"Now, on the fifth, you talked to Mr. Gilg of the pharmacy, didn't you?"

"I believe so, yes, sir."

"Do you remember asking Mr. Gilg about a solution that would remove bloodstains?"

"No, I asked him about a solution to test bloodstains."

The matter of a solution to remove or test bloodstains was a surprise to me, and I tried desperately to signal Mr. Selser. Hommell had left himself wide open. Joseph Gilroy had stated in his testimony that he had left Hommell at about 5 p.m. on the fifth; that when he arrived home he had found the bloodstains in his car; and that he had not seen Hommell from that time until eighty-thirty or nine o'clock—after the bloodstains had been reported to the police and the automobile impounded. It was clear, therefore, that when Hommell went to work at 6 p.m., he did not know Gilroy had found the bloodstains, so he could not claim that he had wanted a solution to test those stains. But Mr. Selser did not see my signals and proceeded to change the subject.

"Do you remember talking to Mr. Nicol, my investigator?"

"Yes, sir."

"Do you remember telling Mr. Nicol that you had washed your trousers?"

"Definitely not, sir."

"Do you remember when Mr. Nicol asked you about the lipstick you said none such was found in your car?"

"I don't remember, sir."

"Well, do you say you didn't say that to him?"

"I won't say I didn't, and I won't say I did."

"And do you remember he said: 'Why did you throw the lipstick out of the car?' and you said: 'What the hell do you think I would do with it?' "

"I don't remember. . . ."

"Do you say you didn't?"

"I won't say I did, and I won't say I didn't."

"Didn't you tell Nicol you saw this girl just at the Nixon house—I am talking about the sister?"

"I don't think so, no, sir."

"Do you say you didn't?"

"I don't say—I say I didn't."

"You know that Fardale Avenue runs directly from the sandpit right out to Wyckoff Avenue at the Nixon home?"

"I have never seen the sandpit until after this happened."

"You drove your car directly to it, didn't you?"

"Definitely not, sir."

"I am talking about the fifth?"

"Oh, the fifth. Yes, sir."

"Are you familiar with this baseball bat which is marked S-69 in evidence?"

"I don't know, sir."

"This baseball bat?"

"I can't remember, sir, no."

"Do you remember after the police had possession of the automobile asking whether or not you could get into the car to get the other baseball bat?"

"I believe so. There was something to that effect."

"You were with whom when you went up there?"

"Charles Rockefeller."

"How did you know there was only one remaining baseball bat in the car?"

"I didn't know there was one remaining. I don't know how many."

"Why did you ask about the *other* baseball bat?"

"I didn't know how many were in the car."

"But you did do that, didn't you?"

"I believe so, sir, yes."

Mr. Selser paused, looked at the witness for a few moments, then said: "That is all at this time."

My belief that little would be accomplished during Hommell's cross-examination had proved correct. His evasiveness had been apparent to everyone in the courtroom, but the fact that he had been evasive did not prove that my claims regarding his presence at the sandpit were true. More than ever before, I knew, the testimony of the medical examiner would be the crucial testimony in the trial.

The trial moved much more quickly after the testimony of Donald Hommell. In rapid succession, Prosecutor Calissi called Lieutenant Arthur Abrams of the Bergen County Police; Anthony Saveriano, owner of Tony's Amoco; Captain Carl De-Marco; Investigator Vahe Garabedian; and Patrolman Ulric Fairbanks of the Ramsey police.

Lieutenant Abrams testified that he had found "markings" in the dirt at the sandpit; that these markings were a set of footprints 125 feet in from Chapel Road, and five feet from the sandpit end of the dirt road. Earlier testimony had placed Vickie's red gloves 175 feet into the sandpit, or fifty feet beyond the footprints. Based upon the maps of the scene, the footprints were forty to fifty feet from the dirt mound.

The lieutenant made plaster casts of the footprints, he said. No mention was made of the footprints Mr. Zielinski had found on top of the dirt mound. Nor did the lieutenant mention the tire tracks on the dirt road, or the plaster casts he had made of the tire tracks.

My attorney blithely announced that he had no questions to ask the officer. At the very least, Selser should have asked if the police had attempted to identify the tire tracks.

Anthony Saveriano provided little information, and none of a substantial nature. He was quickly dismissed.

Captain Carl DeMarco testified at great length, but his testimony was essentially a rehash of Detective Graber's. He described my interrogation; the searches for my pants and for signs that I had thrown up as claimed; the finding of my shoes;

the medical examination at Dr. Gilady's office; the recording of my statement; and the finding of the pocketbook.

Mr. Selser questioned Captain DeMarco with regard to all of his testimony, but nothing new or significant was brought out.

Vahe Garabedian, an investigator in Prosecutor Calissi's office, repeated much of what DeMarco and Graber had stated. He also testified that the distance from Secor's Gas Station to the Nixon home was 3.2 miles, and that he had driven the distance in seven minutes.

Mr. Selser's only question concerned the rate of speed at which Garabedian had made the trip, and brought a reply of "thirty-five to forty."

Ulric Fairbanks, the Ramsey patrolman, stated that he had found the pants on Oak Street, Ramsey, during a search to which he and another officer had been assigned. The pants had been found, he said, at 6:20 a.m.

On cross-examination by Mr. Selser, the officer stated that the pants were found approximately fifty feet from the road, but that they were "clearly visible" from a passing automobile, spread out as they were on the ground. The spot where they were found was only a few hundred yards from my family's home, hardly the place I would have thrown them.

Dr. Raphael Gilady, the Bergen County Medical Examiner, followed Patrolman Fairbanks to the stand. For days there had been rumors that the time of death would be estimated to have been approximately ten o'clock on the night of March 4. If so, the prosecutor was in trouble. By 9:15, according to Gilroy, I was at home talking to him on the telephone; and by ten o'clock I was in Ridgewood, eight miles away, without an automobile. The prosecutor had, therefore, provided me with a perfect alibi for the time after 9:15. I did not have to say a word. All, however, depended upon the doctor's estimate.

Dr. Gilady's qualifications were conceded, and following

a brief period of questioning concerning his examination of me the morning of March 6—"I found him to be in normal health"—the prosecutor turned to the real issue:

"Now, Doctor, on March 5, 1957, were you called to Van Emburgh's Funeral Home?"

"Yes."

"When you got there would you explain to us exactly what you did?"

"I performed a complete autopsy on the body of Victoria Zielinski. The body revealed on inspection a total crushing of the skull . . . the brain was absent . . . the subject was decerebrated, total loss of brain . . . her left eye was totally destroyed and there were numerous bruises right around the eye, especially on the lower surface . . . her lower jaw and her upper jaw had multiple fractures . . . the nose was fractured in two or three places, and bleeding from the mouth. Her teeth, most of them were loose in her mouth. There was not a single mark on her elsewhere. . . . *I found very pure immaculate white silk panties, or nylon panties, that had not been stained or mutilated . . . there were no marks or bruises on her thighs* . . . her hands were clutched . . . they were covered with blood, and her fingernails were bitten very severely. . . . I also did a rectal examination which was entirely normal . . . there was no bleeding from the vagina or the vulva and the hymen was intact. . . . I concluded that the cause of death was due to a total crushing of the skull with a decerebration, traumatic."

Selser was grinning broadly. The doctor's testimony had destroyed the prosecutor's attempt to prove a felony murder, committed in the course of an attempted rape; he had one foot on a banana peel.

"Now, can you, Doctor, establish the time of death from your examination?" Calissi asked.

"At the time I did the post [autopsy], which was early noon, I believe, *I put that down,* but you see, the time of death in winter with rigor mortis is a very moot problem. The prevailing weather has a great deal to do with the setting in and dissolution of rigor mortis, and I estimate she was dead about twelve hours, give or take an hour."

I very nearly ran over and kissed Dr. Gilady when he said twelve hours. The entire courtroom sat in stunned silence, but no one had been more stunned than Prosecutor Calissi. If Judge O'Dea had not come to his rescue, Calissi might still be standing there today, his mouth hanging open like a mother kangaroo's pouch.

"What time did you make that examination?" Judge O'Dea asked the doctor.

"I would say it was between twelve-thirty and one, Judge. Between twelve-thirty and one. I got there early, but I believe I started to work at one o'clock."

Prosecutor Calissi, having regained his composure, quickly asked the doctor how certain his estimate could be.

"Well *as I said before,*" Gilady explained, *"about twelve hours before I started the autopsy, give or take an hour,* but I must emphasize that it is a very difficult question to decide with the prevailing weather, because it was cold. The body will set in with rigor mortis much earlier in cold weather than it would in warm weather."

"Well, assuming, Doctor, that the weather on March fourth was twenty-four degrees, how long would it take for rigor mortis to set in?"

The prosecutor was doing his best to compromise or impeach the testimony of his own expert, but Dr. Gilady would have none of that. He carefully explained, step by step, the process of rigor mortis, as if lecturing an exceptionally thickheaded schoolboy; then, for the third time, he stated: "Therefore, I would say that approximately twelve hours, or an hour or two less as the time of death because of the cold weather."

The prosecutor, clearly defeated, gave up. Vickie had been killed at one o'clock in the morning, or an hour or two later; and the prosecutor's own witness, Gilroy, had given me an airtight alibi. There was only one thing that could save the state's case against me: a mistake by my own lawyer. Unless Mr. Selser needlessly cross-examined the doctor, the time of death would stand at one o'clock, and Judge O'Dea would have no choice but to dismiss the charge. This was precisely the fatal error Selser made.

There are certain unwritten rules of cross-examination which should not be broken except in the direst of circumstances. One of these, reduced to simplest terms, is: *Leave well enough alone.* In my case, that meant not to try to improve the doctor's testimony. What did it matter whether the doctor said one o'clock, two o'clock, or five o'clock? All we had needed was for him to say the girl died after nine-thirty or ten; how much after was unimportant. Any kid right out of law school could have seen that; but my lawyer, with forty years of experience, had to seek to improve the unimprovable.

"Doctor, from your examination made, you have established that the time of death occurred somewhere around midnight of the fourth of March?"

"About, give or take an hour."

Midnight. What was Selser talking about? The doctor told the judge one o'clock, or twelve hours before the autopsy.

"So that in your judgment," Selser went on, "I would take it that you would be of the opinion that the brain was separated from the head of the girl somewhere in the area of midnight?"

"Yes," Dr. Gilady replied for the fifth time, "give or take an hour."

There was still time for Selser to sit down and shut his mouth, but he kept pressing.

"So it was, in your judgment, not later than eleven o'clock—not earlier than eleven o'clock, I mean, or perhaps not later than one?"

I was beginning to doubt that Selser had any idea of what he was talking about. First midnight, then eleven o'clock. He was, I thought as I listened to him, doing a better job for the prosecution than the prosecutor.

Dr. Gilady, now as confused as Selser, replied: "It *could* have been earlier than eleven o'clock. . . ."

My lawyer had managed to snatch defeat from the jaws of victory.

It did not help much that Selser asked the doctor again if death had occurred "about midnight of the fourth, give or take an hour," or that the doctor had replied: "It is a matter of record. I put it down." The damage had been done.

Detective Charles DeLisle was called to testify regarding my interrogation on the morning of March 6, in the prose· cutor's office. His testimony was routine until the prosecutor asked whether the detective had ever discussed with me my statement to the police.

"Yes, sir," DeLisle replied. "On the eleventh of March."

"I show you a [document] and ask whether or not you can identify it?"

"This is the statement, the transcription of a statement given by Smith and taken by a court stenographer. I took this statement and some copies of the statement over to the jail at about ten o'clock in the morning of March eleventh, and I asked Smith to read them."

"Did Smith read it?"

"He did read it, sir."

"How long did he take to read it?"

"About thirty-five minutes. Smith said that—I asked Smith to sign the statement. He said he wouldn't sign the statement. I asked him why and he said his lawyer told him not to. I asked him if the statement was accurate, and he said: 'Yes, it is accurate.' "

Selser, given the opportunity to cross-examine, asked two questions:

"Who was his lawyer then?"

"I think Mr. Gaudielle."

"I was not his lawyer then, was I?"

"I don't think so."

"No further questions."

During the recess which followed DeLisle's testimony, Selser and I had a violent argument. It seems that under the law in New Jersey, a statement need not be signed to be admitted into evidence. If the accused reads it and admits its accuracy, the law considers that the equivalent of a signature. That I denied reading the statement was irrelevant. The detective said I had, and it was my word against his. In such cases, the police always win. Hence the reason DeLisle had not wanted witnesses present when he brought the statement over to the county jail.

Selser was boiling with anger. "Why didn't you tell me about this?" he demanded, when we were alone in the conference room used during recesses.

"Why the hell didn't you ask me? If you lawyers had had enough brains to warn me about this half-assed law, I would never have talked to DeLisle. All you meatheads said was 'Don't sign.' Well, I didn't sign, so don't come around blaming me."

"Don't blame me," Selser fired back. "I wasn't your attorney at that time."

"No, you weren't. But have you ever asked me what happened? Hell no! All you ever asked was whether I had signed. Well, I didn't, and I didn't read it either."

"Well, it's too late to argue about it now. Detective DeLisle said you read the statement, and Judge O'Dea will take his word for it."

"Yes, and it's too late *not* to cross-examine Dr. Gilady, also," I snapped back sarcastically.

The lawyer did not reply, but he knew just what I meant.

The trial moved very quickly after the testimony of Detective DeLisle. My statement was offered into evidence, and over Selser's objections, Judge O'Dea admitted it as a concession of guilt. Then over a period of nearly two hours, Prosecutor Calissi read to the jury the statement Detective DeLisle swore that I read in thirty-five minutes. The statement covers forty-two pages in the trial record, and that record reveals that it took the prosecutor sixty-eight minutes to read the last twenty-six pages, as timed by the clock on the courtroom wall.

The last important witness was John Brady, owner and director of Edel Laboratories in Newark, and the official, according to his way of seeing himself, chemist and toxicologist for a number of New Jersey counties.

Under questioning by the prosecutor, Mr. Brady stated that he had found three small spots of blood on my black shoes, but it was "impossible to determine the type of blood." My pants and the socks found in the pocket were heavily stained with blood, he said—the pants "very heavily stained down on the right leg in front." The blood on the pants and socks was type O.

Vickie's sweater, the chemist stated, was very heavily stained with type O blood, human tissue, hair, and small sections of bone. Her jacket was stained with type O blood, human tissue, hair, and pieces of bone.

The largest stone in evidence was stained with type O blood, human tissue, and hair.

Vickie's brassiere was stained on both the inside and outside with type O blood. Her red gloves were heavily stained with type O blood and hairs.

The lower legs of the girl's jeans were stained with blood, type not specified, hair, human tissue, and pieces of bone.

The sweepings from the floor mat from Gilroy's automobile reacted to tests for blood, but it was impossible to determine even if it was human blood. The seat cover from the automobile did have a spot of blood on it; but ironically, in view of the fact that the blood on the seat cover provided the first break in the case, the chemist was unable to determine the type of that blood.

My gloves, shirt, and jacket had been tested, and had been found to be entirely free of blood.

The baseball bat found in the woods was stained with blood, but its origin and type could not be determined. Neither the baseball bat, nor any of the rocks in evidence, revealed finger or hand prints.

When asked if he had compared the plaster casts of the footprints with my shoes, the witness said it had been impossible to compare them "by measurements." Instead, from the sole section of each cast, he had made a composite sole section; and from the heel section of each cast, he had made a composite heel section. The newly made composites were then fitted together, and from them the laboratory fabricated "the semblance of a third." This fabrication, a third-generation hybrid, was compared with my shoes, and lo and behold, the single hybrid cast exactly "fitted" *both* shoes, right and left.

The witness's choice of language was appropriate. My shoes did not fit the original castings, so castings were made which "fitted" the shoes. In all humility, I suggest that given five pounds of plaster and a bucket of water, I could turn out a casting to fit the footprints of the Abominable Snowman.

Perhaps the chemist's most significant testimony concerned the clothing. Vickie's sweater, jacket, and jeans showed traces of hair, human tissue, and chips of bone; but my clothing was totally free of these things. Vickie's kerchief, sweater, brassiere, jacket, gloves, jeans, and shoes were bloodstained—in short, blood from head to toe; but only my shoes, socks, and my pants below the knees—where I claimed the girl grabbed my legs, were bloodstained. And Gilroy's automobile, into which I am supposed to have gotten after the murder, was free of bloodstains, with the exception of the tiny stain on the seat cover, the type of which could not be determined.

The prosecutor rested his case soon after the testimony of the chemist. Mr. Selser, not yet fully aware of the damage he had done while questioning Dr. Gilady, moved for a judgment of acquittal based upon the fact that I had not been present at the time of Vickie's death, and that I must therefore be innocent, notwithstanding any evidence to the contrary.

Judge O'Dea was put on the spot by Selser's motion. The doctor's testimony, taken as a whole, was that death had occurred at approximately one o'clock in the morning, but if Judge O'Dea had to throw out of court a case which had so greatly aroused the public's appetite for vengeance, the press would have crucified him, and he was not inclined to volunteer for martyrdom. So he called a recess and went to look for a loophole in the medical examiner's testimony. It took more than an hour, but thanks to my lawyer, O'Dea found the loophole, rather a small one, to be sure, but it would serve the purpose.

On motion for judgment of acquittal . . . the defendant urges that on the testimony of Dr. Gilady as to the cause and time of death and the whereabouts of the defendant on the night of March 4 the State has demonstrated that it would have been impossible for the defendant to have administered the fatal blows.

A review of Dr. Gilady's testimony does not support the defendant's contention in this regard.

He said . . . in answer to a question: "I estimate she was dead about 12 hours, give or take an hour."

. . . [A]gain . . . the doctor said: "Well, as I said before, about 12 hours before I started the autopsy . . . but I must emphasize that it was a very difficult question to decide. . . ."

Then . . . the doctor said: "Well that again I say rigor mortis usually sets in between two and four hours. . . . Therefore, I would say that approximately 12 hours, or an hour or two less. . . ."

And . . . on cross-examination: "It could have been earlier than 11 o'clock because the prevailing weather was so cold. . . ."

Now, that testimony of the doctor, and taking all of the testimony of the doctor as to the exact time of death, the exact time of decerebration, it is clear that the exact time of death could not be established from his examination . . . and according to his own estimate it could have occurred earlier than 11:00 o'clock that night. Therefore, the time the fatal blow was struck is a question for the jury to determine from all the evidence.

. . . [T]herefore the motion is denied.

# CHAPTER TWENTY

MY DEFENSE, SUCH AS IT WAS, WAS AN UN-mitigated disaster. It was, fortunately, brief, lasting but a day and a half.

Mr. Selser had not prepared me for my testimony. When called to be the first witness in my own defense, I had no more idea of what my lawyer would ask than I had of what the prosecutor would ask. And it showed. I was a weak, ineffectual witness. But I cannot place all of the blame for my poor showing on my lawyer. I am by nature—as my writing surely must indicate—a transcendently unemotional, matter-of-fact individual, the antithesis of what a man testifying in his own behalf, with his life at stake, should be.

The story I told on the witness stand was, in all its essential details, exactly the same story I had told my lawyer in the county jail two weeks before Easter; and the same story which, several years later, both the prosecutor and the New Jersey Supreme Court would concede was, and I quote the prosecutor verbatim, "exactly the same story he [Smith] had given these four doctors while under the truth serum." The trial jury, however, was never to know of the truth-serum results.

After describing how I had met Vickie on the road, Selser's questioning led me through the drive to the sandpit, the accusation against my wife, the face-slapping incident, and Vickie's threat to walk home. Then, as I began describing the arrival of Donald Hommell at the sandpit, the spectators in the courtroom stirred noticeably. For the first time, my version of the events was being told in public in all its details. The jury, however, the people who held my life in their hands, showed little interest as I told of leaving Vickie with Hommell, and as I explained that, after all, she *was* his girl friend, and I fully expected him to take her home. The reaction of the jury, or more properly the lack of reaction, left me feeling that I might as well have been reading the Yellow Pages of the phone book to them.

Notwithstanding the cold reception my testimony was being accorded, however, things were moving swiftly and smoothly until Selser asked: "What was your knowledge of Don Hommell's activities with respect to violence?" Then the fireworks began anew.

The words were hardly out of the lawyer's mouth when Prosecutor Calissi was on his feet screaming: "Objection. Objection. I object to the question as being irrelevant."

Judge O'Dea: "All right, we will excuse the jury."

Subsequent to the retirement of the jury from the courtroom, Mr. Selser stated: "I most respectfully urge upon the Court the thought that I have the right to explain . . . the state of mind and basis of fear in support of the statement already made . . . that Hommell had threatened to kill his child if he mentioned Hommell's name, and it is upon this theory that I offer the evidence."

Judge O'Dea: "Isn't that already in? He has already made that statement, that Hommell so stated. . . ."

Mr. Selser: "I have the right to show the basis of the fear. . . . If I were to say to someone alongside of me: 'I would kill your child,' they certainly would not believe it and would not be justified in a fear, but if Don Hommell, knowing Don Hommell as this man does, Don Hommell says it, there is basis for fear and the state of mind which is hereby prompted in this man. . . ."

Mr. Calissi: "If the Court please . . . This is merely an attempt to paint Hommell as a rascal, as a vicious person, not to show the basis of fear. . . ."

Judge O'Dea: "All this is a matter for cross-examination."

Mr. Selser: "I intend to develop, sir, first of all that this man knew that Hommell was discharged from the Navy under circumstances indicating he was a psychopath."

Mr. Calissi: "I think that is absolutely wrong. I don't think you have a right to ask this witness . . . whether a man is a psychopath."

Mr. Selser: "I intend to show by this witness that Hommell without provocation beat up a series of youngsters. I intend to show that Hommell . . . ran into Dr. Canning's car, and I have Dr. Canning who will testify that it was done deliberately, and that Hommell said to Dr. Canning: 'I'll bash your skull in.' I will show that this man was with Hommell one night . . . when Hommell drove his automobile onto Dr. Canning's garden, and when Dr. Canning came out to complain about it, Hommell said in this boy's presence: 'You crippled son of a bitch, I'll kill you.' I will show that Hommell deliberately, without provocation, at Pelzer's Tavern smashed the pool cues and deliberately committed acts of violence, showing that he is a dangerous, psychopathic creature."

Mr. Calissi: "I object."

Mr. Selser: "It's true, Mr. Calissi . . . I will show that he deliberately threw catsup . . . on the walls of the [Robbie's] Corral, that he did this without cause, without reason. These are acts which raised in this man's mind the thought that the threat made was one which the man was capable of committing. . . ."

Mr. Calissi: "And I object."

Mr. Selser: "I am not only prepared to prove the state of mind . . . I am prepared to prove the facts."

Mr. Calissi: "And I object to it. We could bring in any young man . . . go through his life history . . . and we could find in this man's character and in this man's reputation something for which he could not be canonized . . . so this business of trying to paint this Hommell as vicious, malicious, a poisonous type of individual is not proper in this case. . . . Mr. Selser . . . is speaking for the press."

Mr. Selser: "Speaking for the press is a strange practice, isn't it, confined to me?"

Judge O'Dea, recognizing that the "discussion" was getting out of hand, stepped in. The question regarding Hommell's propensity to violence would not be permitted, he ruled. The judge gave no reason for so ruling, and Selser lodged no objection to the ruling.

The prosecutor, when given the opportunity to cross-examine, had me repeating my version of the events over and over and over, all day Thursday. He was particularly interested in my description of the clothing Hommell had been wearing when I claimed to have seen him at the sandpit—dark trousers and a light-green or light-blue sports shirt, open at the neck. Other than that, however, his cross-examination, despite its great length, was a desultory affair. He seemed confident that he had already won.

The most important event of that day took place outside the courtroom. From the first day of my trial, the row of spectator seats directly behind the counsel table had been filled with detectives and legal assistants from the prosecutor's office; but by mid-morning Thursday, those seats were empty, and by noon, First Assistant Prosecutor Galda, and most of the press corps, had disappeared. At one o'clock, when the recess for lunch was called, Selser gave me the bad news; a fifteen-year-old girl, missing for six days, had been found raped and strangled with her own belt, a few miles from the courthouse.

My lawyer, in a classic of understatement, told me: "This girl's murder will hurt us if the jury learns of it."

I was followed to the witness stand by Mrs. Rosella Wood, an elderly lady who lived alone in the house by the stone bridge on Pulis Avenue. Selser got to the point quickly.

"Mrs. Wood, I want to direct your attention to the morning of Tuesday, March fifth, at about eleven o'clock in the morning. What if anything happened at that time?"

"I stepped out my door onto my porch and saw two young men opposite my home as if they were searching for something.

I asked if they had lost anything, and with that one turned and full face to me said: 'Oh, mind your own business.' "

"Do you see that young man in this courtroom?"

"Yes. Yes sir."

"Where is he, point him out?"

"Sitting in the first row."

The witness pointed directly to Donald Hommell, and after he had been ordered to stand, the woman said: "That's the boy. I didn't know him by name."

Prosecutor Calissi did his best on cross-examination to break down the woman's story, but she remained steadfast in her identification. She could not identify the person Hommell was with, she said, but Hommell, she was certain, was the boy she had seen.

"Had you ever seen Hommell before?" Calissi asked.

"Never before that time. I don't know of another boy that looks like Hommell."

"Could it be possible you saw Hommell before?"

"No. It couldn't be possible."

Mrs. Wood went on to explain that shortly after the crime she had been shown four photographs taken at a party, and that she had identified Hommell in two of the photographs.

My wife, who was the next witness, supported my claim that I had returned home at 8:57 on the night of March 4, and that Gilroy had driven us to Ridgewood, dropping us off there before ten o'clock.

On cross-examination by the prosecutor, she confirmed that I had told her I had thrown my pants by the bridge on Pulis Avenue. She also stated that she had identified the pants while she was being held in the prosecutor's office, but that the pants had been folded up so that she had not seen all of them.

The trial ended Friday afternoon. Final arguments, Judge O'Dea declared, would be heard at nine-thirty Monday morning, after which the case would go to the jury. From where I was sitting, the jury appeared ready to give a verdict right then and there. Compared to the jurors at the conclusion of my case, the defendants at Nuremberg had appeared cheerful.

Mr. Selser was the first to address the jury on Monday morning. He began with a lengthy discussion of the relative duties of the judge, jury, and the attorneys; then he turned to the facts:

> I believe that there is a basis for your finding that this case has been brought on for consideration before this crime of murder has been solved, and I believe sincerely that there is a basis for your finding that the truth of the matter is not yet established, factually or otherwise.
>
> You will recall that the entire area about the sandpit where the body was found, where the blood existed upon the clothing of Vickie, upon the rocks, upon everything there existing, there were: type O blood, human tissue, and pieces of bone. . . . On Eddie Smith's trousers there was no human tissue. There were no pieces of bone. . . . There were tiny little spots of blood on Ed's shoes, not blood-soaked, but a tiny little spot of blood, no tissue, no bone. . . . Here was a gory area filled with blood, human tissue, and bone that Eddie Smith is supposed to have been walking over . . . and none of these things which absolutely must have been present, were present. How could it be possible?
>
> Is it possible that he could have walked through the gore and left upon the shoes as little blood as was found?

In any other case, or before any other jury, Selser would have scored heavily with that argument. Its logic could not be ignored. But in my case, the jury had long since assumed a let's-get-this-over-with appearance.

Turning to my pants, which I claimed to have thrown on Pulis Avenue, the lawyer noted:

> They were no longer over on Pulis Avenue because eleven o'clock of the morning of the 5th day of March, Don Hommell with some other person . . . is searching in the area where the trousers were cast, and when the lady who saw him asked if she could help she was told to mind her own damn business. . . .
>
> And then where are they found? On Oak Street, in such a position that a policeman riding on the street could see them

. . . thrown there that they might be seen, not that they might be concealed; in plain view of the officers riding along Oak [Street].

Regarding my statement to the police, the lawyer said:

If a man were a willing offender, desirous of clearing his soul right after, they say, he had a conference with [a] priest, why did he not say: "I killed Vickie," and how "I killed Vickie" he would outline. But no, he doesn't.

Immediately, immediately after he has seen a priest—I don't know what inference you are supposed to draw from the fact that he had seen a priest—but he did not confess to having killed Victoria Zielinski at all.

There was much emphasis placed by the lawyer upon Dr. Gilady's estimate of the time of death. Then, almost as an afterthought, he added:

I may also add that her hands were clutched . . . her fingernails were bitten very severely.

"Now, before I pass it to go on with the reading of the testimony, Vickie's fingernails were chewed off. This was not something that happened in a couple of seconds or minutes. Whatever happened to Vickie took a long period of time because there could not have been the destruction of the fingernails to the extent described by Dr. Gilady. . . ."

Mr. Selser went on talking for two more hours, carefully, though not methodically, sifting through the evidence, weighing claims and counterclaims, and pointing out much that was illogical about the prosecution's theory; but when at last he sat down, I could not help but feel he had been wasting his time.

Prosecutor Calissi's approach to the jury was entirely different. His method was to picture the victim as an innocent young schoolgirl, lured to her death by a vicious, sex-crazed maniac, meaning me, of course:

Now, I am not sure of what the defense has done here, because in summation I gather now that we have not solved the crime. I thought that the defense had solved the crime for us in naming Hommell. I thought that was the purpose of the defense to show that Hommell had committed this crime . . . and the foulest, dirtiest, legal trick that was ever pulled by a defendant was pulled when it named his friend as the person to whom we should point the finger and say that he murdered Victoria Zielinski.

Sympathy should go to Hommell and his family. What a disgraceful thing to have to cope with, a friend pointing his finger at you and saying to you: "You committed this crime." [Who said that?]

Now, how under God's sun can you blame a thing like that on Hommell? What kind of a character, what kind of malicious and vicious mind must a person have to concoct and to invent that kind of a story?

It is an attempt by a malicious, vicious mind. . . . Straws. Straws. That's what they are hanging on, and why all these lies.

This is a very intelligent and cunning person we are dealing with, cold as a cucumber. Persons might have cried during the course of this trial, but not Smith, not Smith. He sat here like this was a Hollywood production. . . . Could any of you jurors, if you were innocent of this crime, sit there cool, calm, and collected like that? That's the kind of mind we are dealing with. . . .

It took the prosecutor nearly a full hour to do it, but eventually he did get around to discussing the evidence, or what in his mind passed for evidence:

What has the State proved? You have to understand that cases of this kind [?] are not always judged on direct evidence. . . . He [Smith] went into the sandpit . . . he ran down, or might have run down. . . . Sure, he ran down Fardale Avenue, he admits grabbing a bat. . . . He chased her with the bat and he struck her on Fardale Avenue with the bat, and then he threw the bat away.

That there did not exist a single shred of proof to support

his theory, never bothered the prosecutor; he said it, and the jury was expected to accept it as gospel.

> Here was a girl 15 years of age in the car. The clothing . . . indicates her entire top was exposed. . . . What do you think Smith was doing in the car? What in the light of human experience do you think he was doing in the car? Why would her clothing be all the way up? You know why . . . because this fellow was making violent love to her. . . . Where was the brassiere of the girl? Down around her stomach, down around her stomach.

Calissi was not giving up. He intended to press the theory of attempted rape, thereby establishing felony murder.

> Now, what happened? He crushed her skull. Now, with regard to the gloves that Mr. Selser talked to you about, Dr. Brady said there was blood on these gloves. . . . The gloves are S-57 and S-58.

The prosecutor, having falsely accused me of lying, falsely told the jury that blood had been found on my gloves. Dr. Brady had found nothing on my gloves but kerosene and dirt.

> Smith had the bat with him when he chased Vickie down Fardale Avenue. He struck her in the head and got rid of the bat [Why?] and then brought her back into the sandpit [How?] and then he completed his mission [?] because he was going to be exposed. . . . She had not conformed—she had not acquiesced to his desires . . . this is a terrible, terrible crime.
>
> Again I say . . . this has been a horrible, despicable attempt on the part of the defendant to create a doubt by concocting, by fabricating, by inventing this terrible story about a friend. . . .
>
> We are dealing, I say again, with a very cunning man, who sits for over two weeks, doesn't bat an eyelash, shows absolutely no sign of sympathy or remorse, and believes that this is just one of those things.
>
> My stomach and my heart feels, well, it feels the way I

know it feels. . . . The eyes of the people of the State of New
Jersey, and particularly the eyes of the people of Bergen
County are . . . shifting onto your shoulders. You have a duty
to perform.

The people of this county are looking to this jury. Shall the
teen-agers of the county, the schoolgirls of this county walk the
streets without fear? . . . I again repeat to you that the eyes of
Bergen County, especially, are now on this jury. I ask you to do
your sworn duty.

Calissi had finished with the same plea to emotionalism
he had used to open the trial. There was, however, one significant difference: a second murder of a schoolgirl had occurred
during my trial, and sequestered or not, the jury knew about it.
It is impossible to keep fourteen people in a public hotel, and
to transport them twenty miles each day from hotel to courtroom to hotel, without having them read the headlines, hear
the gossip, and learn of what has been happening in the world.
The jury knew of that second murder, and Calissi knew they
knew it. His schoolgirl plea was directed straight at that knowledge.

It was late in the day when the prosecutor ended his summation, and Judge O'Dea, not wishing to have the jury deliberate at night, put off his charge to the jury until Tuesday morning.

Throughout my trial, Judge O'Dea had given me the
impression, an impression shared by many others, that he was
not quite the detached, impersonal arbiter a judge should be,
particularly a judge in a capital case. There is no single event
in the trial I can point to as evidence of his lack of detach-
ment. Rather, it was a combination of things: his attitude and
tone of voice when dealing with certain witnesses; his taking it
upon himself to ask witnesses questions the prosecutor had
failed to ask; his refusal to allow Mr. Selser to examine the
records of the drugstore in which Hommell worked—not be-

cause the examination would be improper or irrelevant, nor because of any objection by the prosecutor, but solely because it would take too long, perhaps ten minutes; and his calling a recess so that he could compose himself after looking at color photographs of Vickie's injuries. But nothing in the trial prepared me for his charge to the jury.

One of my former attorneys, in a petition to the United States Supreme Court, said of the charge: "It is highly significant to note that this judge's charge was the most vicious and brutal summary of prejudice and hostility imaginable and not within counsel's scope of knowledge and experience of over twenty years at the Criminal Bar."

Judge O'Dea was not content to recite, repeat, and repeat again, in the most inflammatory terms, the state's case against me, citing the prosecutor's claims as if they had been proven apodictically; but he had to compound the unfairness by not once in his entire two-hour charge, not once, citing my counterclaims.

Some of the judge's opening remarks were, to a jury of laymen unfamiliar with legal jargon, who could not sit and study the words on paper, utterly unintelligible.

> You determine from the evidence according to the law what are the true facts as nearly as you can ascertain the truth from the evidence adduced from the evidence you have seen and heard elicited from the witnesses at this trial.
>     You may draw proper and legitimate inferences of fact from the facts which you find and with your conclusions of fact, the conclusion of fact that you draw. . . .

I doubt whether anyone, hearing that read one time from a piece of paper, and not having time to think it over, would have the slightest notion of what it means. After years of reading it, I still do not understand it.

> The statutes mentioned in the indictment . . . 2A:113-1 and 2A:113-2 provide: "If any person, in committing or attempting to commit arson, burglary, kidnapping, rape, robbery, sodomy,

or any unlawful act against the peace of this State, of which the probable consquences may be bloodshed, kills another, then such person so killing is guilty of murder.

Murder which is perpetrated by means of poison, or by lying in wait, or by any other kind of willful, deliberate and premeditated killing, or which is committed in perpetrating or attempting to perpetrate . . . rape . . . is murder in the first degree.

There are other provisions in this statute . . . which I have deleted because they have no part in the case.

The fact is that the statutory references to attempting to commit rape had no part in the case either, but Judge O'Dea read them twice. These references were, however, minor annoyances compared to what came later.

I will refer to the facts from the evidence, from the testimony . . . I am merely taking the facts from the case *to show you the jury, how you* . . . *take the facts* and apply the law to the facts or the facts to the law . . . when I discuss the facts, *I take them at random.* . . .

You have this case, if you find it credible, evidence that a body, the body of Victoria Zielinski, was found *decerebrated, torn, crushed, mutilated, clothing torn away, breasts exposed, shoes off, clothing bloodstained, human blood,* the same type as her own, *brains separated from the head, skull crushed, face bashed in, bloody area, bloodstained area, blood-drenched rocks nearby, blood-marked baseball bat* in the area of the scene, medical testimony as to the death and cause of death, decerebration.

So that you make your determination from the evidence, from the facts. . . .

I thought that Judge O'Dea had outdone himself with that selection of "facts" taken "at random," but as it developed, they were merely his warm-up.

. . . [T]here is evidence direct and circumstantial . . . that the victim was killed as a result of severe mortal blows, *the de-*

*fendant contended* [?] *with her, struggled with her, was annoyed, startled, alarmed by her remarks, she fled or sought to flee, they travelled on foot at the scene, he took the time to retrieve a baseball bat from the rear of the auto, the rear seat of the auto. There was evidence of her hair, clothing, a distance from the scene of her body, blood-drenched rocks,* near the scene of her body, *the bloodstained, split and broken baseball bat* a distance from her body, *blood-drenched foliage* at another point . . . all sufficient for the jury if they find the testimony to these facts credible. . . .

What testimony? The prosecutor's claims are fairly well recited, but where do we find the testimony?

*I have pulled out the facts at random.* . . . I am calling that to your attention, citing *these* facts solely *for the purpose of showing you, helping you, guiding you in your deliberations* . . .

If you find . . . that he murdered Vickie Zielinski the night of March 4, 1957, then you determine whether *the murderous act, the killing, the bashing and crushing of her head, the braining* . . . were committed with intent to take her life. . . .

If you find there was no intent to take her life in dealing the mortal blows, *in braining her at this lonely dark scene* . . . then your verdict shall be guilty of murder in the second degree.

If you find there was intent to kill her . . . *by bashing in her face and head, with wilfull, deliberate death-dealing blows* . . . that there was sufficient time and thinking in the mind of *Smith as he retrieved a baseball bat from the back seat of the car at the scene, as he pursued the victim who sought relief from his clutches, as he traveled about the scene of the murder* . . . then your findings shall be murder in the first degree.

Having finally completed his random selection of the facts, the judge turned to another problem:

Now, what do we mean by moral certainty? You don't have to be as sure of guilt, as certain of guilt, as you are that

two plus two are four. . . . You don't have to be as sure as you
are of death. . . . A moral certainty is something less than
those kinds of certainties, and you have to be satisfied only
to that lesser certainty.

So, a moral certainty is something less than death, less than
two plus two equals four. All right, now we know what is *more*
than a moral certainty, what is "something less"? What is the
"lesser certainty"? Judge O'Dea did not say.

Now, as to another point of testimony . . . Dr. Gilady's
testimony as to the time of death. First, let me say . . . *the
element of the time of death is not an essential element* of the
proof of the State . . . *the time of the killing on the element
and essential element of the offense is not material or important.*

That did it. Judge O'Dea, with that statement, completed
the job Selser began when he had foolishly cross-examined the
doctor. When I heard that, I knew that all that remained was
for me to pack my bags for the trip to the Death House. It did
not matter even when the judge added that the time of death
had been brought in to "affect proofs of the state," an asinine
statement. The doctor was a state witness.

Judge O'Dea's random selection of facts had failed
somehow to select the fact of my testimony regarding Hommell; the fact that never once had I vacillated in my story of
having thrown my pants on Pulvis Avenue, the fact of Mrs.
Wood's positive and uncontradicted courtroom identification
of Hommell as the person she had seen searching where I had
thrown the pants; the fact of the prosecution's failure to identify the tire tracks on the sandpit driveway, or the tire tracks
on Fardale Avenue alongside Vickie's shoe and kerchief; the
fact of the failure to identify the footprints Mr. Zielinski had
found on the top of the dirt mound, only a few feet from the
body; the fact that my clothing, in direct contrast to the scene
of the crime and the clothing on Vickie's body, was totally free
of human hair, human tissue, and pieces of bone; or the fact

that my clothing was free of bloodstains above the lower leg of the pants, although the scene of the crime, and every stitch of Vickie's clothing, was soaked in gore.

The judge should have qualified his charge by noting that his facts were taken from the state's case alone, and did not represent a fair balance of fact or claim. And such phrases as "the defendant contended with her"; "was annoyed, startled, alarmed"; "they traveled on foot at the scene"; "as he [Smith] pursued the victim, who sought relief from his clutches"; "as he traveled about"; had no place in the charge. Such phrases were not drawn from testimony or direct evidence; they represented the claims, the theories, of Prosecutor Calissi. For Judge O'Dea to offer them to the jury as facts—and he did exactly that when he said "as he pursued the victim," rather than "if you find the state has proved that he pursued the victim"—was the height of irresponsibility.

The jury retired for its deliberations at 11:30 a.m. After they had been escorted from the courtroom, the following dialogue took place:

Mr. Calissi: "The State contends that there was sufficient evidence in this particular case . . . to indicate that there was evidence at least to go to the jury of a felony murder."

Judge O'Dea: "Under what felony?"

Mr. Calissi: "Rape."

Judge O'Dea: "Rape?"

Mr. Calissi: "Attempted."

Judge O'Dea: "With your own State's testimony that the girl from the waist down was virginal, clean and pure, her pants were spotless, her belt untouched? There wasn't sufficient evidence, or any evidence, on which I could let this go to the jury on a felony rape. . . . I gave that consideration and say for the record I found no evidence to support an attempted rape. . . ."

The judge's statement for the record begs four questions: 1) Why, if he did not intend for the jury to consider attempted rape, did he twice read to the jury the felony murder statute mentioning rape and attempted rape? 2) Why did he randomly select for the jury's consideration the fact that Vickie's clothing was torn and her breasts exposed? 3) Why did he not advise the jury to disregard the prosecutor's comments, in his summation, alluding to Vickie's attempts to resist my alleged advances? 4) Why did the judge, after hearing both the prosecutor and Mr. Selser complain about the charge, fail to return the jury and say: "Look, folks, you are not to consider rape or attempted rape. The Court has found that there is no evidence of felony murder"?

The jury returned its verdict at 1:50 p.m.

The clerk: "Members of the jury, have you agreed upon a verdict?"

The foreman: "We have, sir."

The clerk: "What do you find?"

The foreman: "We find the defendant guilty of murder in the first degree."

From the moment the jury returned, there was no doubt regarding the verdict. Each and every one of the jurors, as they filed back into the courtroom, had carefully averted his or her eyes. Not one of them had so much as glanced in my direction.

Although the verdict had been expected, the speed with which it had been rendered was shocking. No one knows the precise length of time of the deliberations, but from the time the jury had retired, until the verdict was announced—two hours and twenty minutes—the jury had deliberated; had eaten lunch; a messenger had been sent to a restaurant to notify Selser, who was having his lunch; and court officers had been sent to bring me from the county jail, where I was awaiting the verdict. Unofficially, the jury reached the verdict *and* had its lunch in one hour and fifty-one minutes.

Judge O'Dea appeared to be totally pleased by the verdict, and when the formality of polling the jury had been completed, he said: "In discharging you, ladies and gentlemen of the jury, I first want to commend you on your verdict. . . . I would have found the same as you found, and I say that for whatever personal satisfaction it may be to you as the jurors in this case."

Sentencing was postponed until one week later, June 4, and during that week Selser gave me everything but a written guarantee that the conviction would be reversed on appeal. But something else occurred that week, something which at the time seemed far more important: Mary Zielinski, Vickie's older sister, and George Self, Mary's boy friend, were finally beginning to tell us what they knew of Hommell's whereabouts the night of the murder. Selser spoke to Judge O'Dea regarding the statements made by Mary and George, and requested that the sentencing be postponed; but the judge denied the request, and on June 4, 1957, four months to the day after Vickie's death, I was sentenced to death. Two days later, three sheriff's deputies delivered me to the state prison.

# CHAPTER TWENTY-ONE

"**THIS IS THE DEATH HOUSE, SMITH, THIS IS**
where you'll be living for a while."

The Death House, a drab, virtually windowless, cinder-block structure, was a separate building within the twenty-two-foot-high red sandstone walls of the state prison, located in an old residential section of south Trenton, the state capital.[1] Set off in one corner of the prison's inner compound, the Death House was, for security reasons, completely isolated from the main buildings of the institution. I use the past tense because a new Death House has since been opened, a matter for later comment.

As the prison officer who had spoken led me into the building, first through an outer door of bars and thick steel mesh, then through an inner door of solid steel plate, I had my first opportunity to observe the elaborate security precautions reserved for those the state considers its most dangerous, desperate prisoners. The outer door, I observed, could be unlocked only from the outside; the inner door, after the appropriate signal had been given, and those seeking to enter had been identified, could be unlocked only from the inside, by the guards on duty.

Inside, the building was not much to look at: to the right, two tiers of cells, nine cells on each tier; a small shower room opposite the last cell on the bottom tier; and at the far end of

---

[1] I am the second of my family behind the walls of this prison. The first, a great-uncle, served as the warden of the prison in the early twenties, having previously served as the chief of police of Jersey City.

the narrow building, a solid steel door, painted green, which led to the execution chamber. With the exception of the doors, which were painted a darker shade, the entire building inside was painted a sickly pale green.

The cells, larger and brighter than I had expected, were seven feet wide and eight feet deep, and each was furnished with a washbasin, toilet, and a steel bed, painted white. The reason for the brightness of the interior, I noticed, was several large lighting fixtures hanging from the ceiling. The lights in the Death House burn twenty-four hours a day.

Six of the cells were also furnished with a condemned man in each. I was taken down the line and introduced:

Larry, under sentence for a year. A Negro, he shot his wife to death in the street.

Joe and Silvio, partners in a cop-killing. Both white, they had been under a death sentence for five years, the longest Death House confinement in New Jersey history, until I broke their record in 1963.

Gene, Bland, and Willie, partners in a murder during a robbery. All Negroes, they had been under sentence three months.

The amenities completed, I was locked in the third cell from the door, and the rules were explained:

"You have a set of earphones here, Smitty, and a switch with three positions. This is the radio: one music station, one sports, and one for whatever the radio-room operator puts on. Radio hours are seven in the morning till midnight. Meals are seven, eleven, and four. You eat if you want, or not, it's up to you. You get up when you want, sleep when you want. There are books in the prison library. The guard on duty has a catalogue you can order from. If you have money and want newspapers, magazines, or books, you can subscribe to them. Visiting is once a month, half hour per person—wife, mother, father, sisters, brothers, and kids over sixteen."

"You mean I can't see my daughter?"

"Not till she is sixteen. Now, on mail—you get eight relatives on your list, plus your lawyer. Each relative can write five letters per month. You can write a total of ten. Split them up however you like. You won't leave this building for any reason except a new trial, if you're lucky, or after you're burned, if you're unlucky. The doctor comes in every day. If you need the dentist, he will come down here. You get out of your cell for fifteen minutes every Friday, for a shower and a shave by the barber. Once a month we shave your head, as we did when you came in this morning. You'll get used to having a bald head."

"What about visits? Where do we have those?"

"Right here. We bring the visitor in. A wire screen is put over the front of your cell. The visitor sits five feet away, and a guard sits next to the visitor to listen."

"What about lawyer's visits?"

"The same rules."

"Friday is the only time we get out of the cell? No walking around or anything?"

"That's right, Smitty. That cell is your home. You don't leave it except for a haircut, shower, new trial, or to be executed."

The first year was the most difficult. I could not understand why month after month after month passed with no action on my appeal, and there were times when I felt that my attorney did not care how long I spent in my tiny cell. It had taken less than four months to put me on trial and to convict me; so why, I wondered, should it take so long to hear an appeal.

Mr. Selser visited me often and did his best to explain the necessity to have the trial record properly printed; to research the applicable case law; to write and have printed the legal briefs—a task which could not be done until the printed trial record was available; and to be absolutely certain that everything would be done correctly. The explanations were reasonable, but all I could understand was that I was locked in a barren cell, cut off from the world, and unable even to see my daughter. It was rough.

Two things sustained me that first year: the confident expectation, based upon Selser's assurances, of the reversal of my conviction on appeal; and the spirit-lifting faith and devotion of my family. They never missed an opportunity to write or visit, and after the first few months, Selser arranged for a court order permitting visitation with an aunt and uncle who had always been like a second set of parents to me.

For my wife, who had observed her twentieth birthday during my trial, the passage of time was especially hard to bear. She had been left with the task of raising our daughter in a fatherless home, yet she bore her burden without complaint, always arriving smiling and cheerful for our monthly visits. It never dawned on me that the smiles and cheerfulness were for my benefit, to cheer me up, and to keep me from worrying. I did not know that she cried all the way home.

The appeal finally was argued before the State Supreme Court in May 1958, and the decision was handed down on June 6, exactly one year after I had entered the Death House.

> The crime involved is not pleasant, nor is the punishment inflicted, but such is the law as it stands upon our books, vigorously and challengingly upheld by the trial jury. The record leaves no room to disturb the jury's findings. Our conclusions support it.
>
> The judgment of conviction is affirmed.[2]

I could hardly believe my ears when the news came over the radio. I had been utterly convinced that the conviction would be reversed. Selser, who also had been overly confident, was so disconsolate that he was unable to visit me until two weeks after the court's decision. "I'm sorry, Ed," he told me, "I just didn't have the heart to come down sooner."

The points raised on appeal had been that: 1) the enlarged color photographs of Vickie's injuries were inflamma-

[2] *State v. Smith*, 27 N.J. 433 (1958).

tory and should not have been admitted into evidence; 2) Judge O'Dea had made technical errors of law in his charge to the jury; 3) it had been prejudicial error to tell the jury that the time of death was neither material nor important; 4) my unsigned statement should not have been admitted into evidence; and 5) the jury's verdict had been the result of passion and prejudice. The court rejected every point raised.

The weeks following the denial of the appeal were hectic indeed. Judge O'Dea, conscientious as ever, immediately after receiving official notice of the affirmation of the conviction, set August 19 as the date for my execution; and the state came close, exceedingly close, to carrying out the judge's order.

By August 18, there was every likelihood that Edgar Smith would become the *late* Edgar Smith. Selser was in a quandary. He had asked then Governor Robert Meyner to commute my sentence to life imprisonment—an appeal made without my consent—but that application was denied within an hour. Another lawyer, a friend of the family, went to the attorney-general and requested a temporary stay of execution; but that, too, was denied. Selser applied to the Appellate Division of the New Jersey Superior Court for a stay of execution pending the filing of a new appeal. That was denied. An attempt was made to obtain a stay from the State Supreme Court, but the justices were either on vacation or at a judicial conference in San Francisco. Selser gave up. He was unfamiliar with federal court appeals, and could think of no way in which a state conviction could be taken to the federal courts.

Time was running out. Only a few hours and a single green door stood between me and the electric chair when my family retained two new attorneys, recommended as specialists in federal appeals. As quickly as a brief application for a stay of execution could be typed, Judge Mendon Morrill of the United States District Court, District of New Jersey, signed the order canceling the execution. I was having my last visit with my wife when the notification was telephoned to the prison. I had come close to the electric chair for the first and, hopefully, the last time.

It is amazing the amount of activity one federal judge can generate. When word of his action was publicly reported, first by the wire services of the Associated Press, Selser received unofficial suggestions from both Judge O'Dea and the State Supreme Court that they would consider applications for stays based upon a new appeal, and the attorney-general announced that the state had stayed the execution just moments before Judge Morrill had done so.

It was a perturbed federal judge who held a hearing three days later, ostensibly to determine the disposition of an application for a writ of habeas corpus filed by my new lawyers. The judge was, however, mainly interested in unraveling the matter of the multiple stays of execution. Selser had filed a motion for a new trial based upon newly discovered evidence, but Judge O'Dea had denied the motion. Since that denial had not been appealed to the State Supreme Court, the federal court judge decided to dismiss my habeas corpus action until the State Supreme Court had first settled the appeal of Judge O'Dea's denial. If that appeal was denied, then I would be free to return to the federal court.

The solution was satisfactory to all parties, but there remained the problem of the multiple stays. Judge Morrill was concerned lest the State of New Jersey "play games with the life of this boy," so he demanded, and was given, through Prosecutor Calissi, on-the-record assurances from the attorney-general that the state would make no attempt to execute me until I had been given the opportunity to return to his court, if that became necessary.

A hearing on the motion for a new trial was held in the Bergen County Court, before Judge O'Dea. The motion was based upon three points: 1) That a series of signed statements we had obtained contradicted Hommell's trial testimony as to his whereabouts the night of the crime, and supported my testimony regarding the clothing he had worn that night. 2) That other statements indicated one of the jurors had prejudged the case, and that the jurors had been aware of the murder of another young girl during my trial. 3) That Dr.

Gilady be ordered to state under oath whether in all reasonable probability death could have occurred prior to 9:30 p.m. The doctor refused to give a formal opinion unless permission for him to do so had been obtained from the prosecutor.

George Self, who married Mary Zielinski after the trial, had given a signed statement on May 20, 1957, indicating that he had seen Hommell in Robbie's Corral, and had seen him riding around town in his automobile after the time that Hommell had sworn he had been home in bed—eleven o'clock. Self's statement was witnessed by his commanding officer at the missile base.

Called to testify in support of his statement, Self stated that he had seen Hommell in Robbie's Corral at about midnight, and again near the Ramsey police station at about 1 a.m., two hours after Hommell was supposed to have been home in bed.

Self's wife, the former Mary Zielinski, testified in support of her husband's statement. She, too, had seen Hommell in Robbie's Corral at midnight.

In my trial testimony, I had stated that Hommell had been wearing a light-green or light-blue sport shirt when I saw him in the sandpit. Hommell insisted that he had worn a red sweater that night, a sweater he wore practically every day. If I had been making up my story, the logical thing for me would have been to say Hommell had been wearing his red sweater. The odds were 1,000 to 1 that I would have guessed correctly. But I did not say that, and at the motion for a new trial, both George and Mary supported me, testifying that Hommell had been wearing a light-blue sport shirt.

Judge O'Dea rejected the testimony of the Selfs, ruling that Hommell's whereabouts "is not material to the issues."

For some reason known only to my former attorneys, no use was made of a signed statement by one Covell Potter, dated June 1, 1957, which read in part:

> I, Covell Potter . . . state that on or about May 13th, and several times since then, I have had direct conversation with Anthony Zielinski in Basile's Tavern in Ramsey. At these times,

Mr. Zielinski told me, in the presence of Mrs. Helen Basile, Jasper Zinmeister, her husband and Samuel Basile, and others including myself, and stated that his daughter Mary and the soldier had been downtown looking for Victoria the night she disappeared, and they saw Hommell sitting in Robbie's Corral talking to Robert Friscia, at 11:45 p.m., the proprietor, and he had on different clothes than what was produced at the trial. Tony [Zielinski] told me his daughter said it was a blue sport shirt Hommell was wearing at the time. Tony said Mary did not get out of the car, but could see Hommell and what shirt he had on.

On another occasion during the trial, I was in Basile's Tavern when Mr. and Mrs. Zielinski came in—it was when Dr. Gilardy [sic] had testified, and both Mr. and Mrs. Zielinski stated that they had doubt about Smith's guilt, and they were not sure they had the right man.

With regard to Hommell's claim that he had been in Pelzer's Tavern the night of the murder, a statement was obtained from the proprietor, Herbert Pelzer, dated July 8, 1958, and witnessed by Andrew Nicol, my investigator, and one Joseph P. Kuznick. The Pelzer statement read in part as follows:

I, Herbert Pelzer . . . owner of a tavern located at the same address, known as Pelzer's, state the following without promise of reward as my own voluntary act:

That on the evening of March 4, 1957, I was operating my tavern in the normal pursuit of business. That on that particular night, March 4th, Charles Rockefeller, known as "Rocky," was in my establishment at 7:30 p.m., when his father came to pick him up, and they both went out of my tavern. I did not see Charles Rockefeller again that night. Also, a man named Donald Hommell was not in my place of business on March 4th at any time. However, on Tuesday, March 5th and thereafter, Donald Hommell was constantly after me to say that he and Rockefeller were in my tavern from 9:30 p.m. and on during the evening of March 4th. . . . I wish this last and final statement to be accepted as the whole truth because I thought originally that everything would work out and the truth would be told, but now I see Edgar Smith is going to die, I cannot withhold the God's honest truth hereby given.

Mr. Selser testified at the hearing, stating that he had not called Pelzer to testify during my trial because Pelzer had been drinking heavily before coming to court, and that Pelzer threatened to say he could not remember anything because if he testified his tavern license would be taken away by the prosecutor.

In his testimony at the hearing, Pelzer denied having been drunk during the trial. He also stated that he had not seen Rockefeller leave with his father at 7:30 p.m., but had assumed that it was his father who had come for him; and that Hommell was not "constantly after me" to say he was in the tavern on March 4. It occurred, Pelzer testified, "only a few times."

Judge O'Dea dismissed Pelzer's testimony as incredible, ruling that the witness had lied so often he could not be believed. It must be noted, however, that no action for perjury or false swearing has ever been taken against Pelzer. My opinion: the prosecutor did not dare bring such charges. He could not risk having a jury acquit Pelzer, since an acquittal would have established, at least by inference, the truth of the statement.

One wonders how Judge O'Dea would have looked upon the statements of the Selfs, and upon Pelzer's affidavit, had he been aware of the character and medical history of Charles Rockefeller, Hommell's only alibi witness.

Prosecutor Calissi had called Rockefeller to the witness stand after the presentation of my defense had been completed, to rebut my testimony regarding events at the sandpit. Rockefeller told the jury that Hommell had been in Pelzer's Tavern shortly after the time I claim to have left Vickie with him. As it developed, Rockefeller was the only person in the entire Ramsey-Mahwah area that Hommell could name who had seen him from the time I say he was at the sandpit, until sometime after 10 p.m. Hommell was unable to provide any other witness who had seen him in Pelzer's Tavern that night, although Pelzer stated that at least three other persons, including Frank J. Young, the Mahwah magistrate, were present at the time in question. The issue, therefore, is whether Rockefeller is a reliable witness. Was he to be believed? Can his testimony stand against mine, Pelzer's, and that of Mary and George Self?

Charles "Rocky" Rockefeller, Hommell's and Prosecutor Calissi's "ace in the hole," was a twenty-year-old former mental patient who had previously been confined in the Greystone State Hospital in New Jersey for psychiatric treatment including shock therapy—an experience he often described to his friends. Those of us who knew him well considered him to be a likable though highly unstable personality, the last fellow in town any of us would want to rile. Six feet tall, 220 pounds, he was extraordinarily strong, though generally meek as a lamb, readily amenable to suggestion, and easily dominated. When harried and under pressure, however, or when drinking, he became a tiger: illogical, erratic, and virtually incoherent. His friends recognized his moods and knew when to "stay away from Rocky today."

When it became apparent that Rockefeller was to be called as a last-minute witness to rebut my testimony, Hommell's only alibi witness, I communicated the fact of his medical record to Mr. Selser, as did my family and Andrew Nicol, the investigator. We all assumed that Selser would introduce the fact when cross-examining Rockefeller, to destroy his credibility as a witness. He did not. Mr. Selser did not ask the witness a single question.

Immediately following the day's testimony, my mother accosted Selser in a corridor outside the courtroom and demanded to know why the lawyer had not attacked Rockefeller's reliability and credibility. Selser's reply was that he had not had the heart to embarrass the boy, or to "hurt his feelings." My mother, as might be expected, commented bitterly: "Because of you I can now bury my son." Selser, I am told, broke down and wept. He was a defeated man.

Following the dismissal of Pelzer's testimony on the

grounds that it was incredible,[3] two signed statements were introduced to establish the prejudice of the juror. The first statement, dated June 5, 1957, and witnessed by Andrew Nicol, and the witness's husband, stated in part:

> I, Mrs. Catherine Ferber . . . wish to give the following state-ment without promise of reward of any kind. . . .
> On May 24th, 1957, while in Wyckoff Economy Shop . . . I got into conversation with a woman named Mrs. Hundemann. . . . We sort of drifted into talk about the Smith trial. Verdict was due that day. . . . Mrs. Hundemann remarked to me in the presence of a store clerk . . . that "he is guilty and will get what is coming to him." I told her in my opinion it looked like the State did not prove its case against Smith. I felt he was not guilty. . . . She explained to me that her husband was on the jury and in her conversation with him he had told her that "they"—meaning the defense witnesses—"were lying in their teeth." When I said to Mrs. Hundemann that I had read no one was in contact with the jurors, that they were locked up, she explained to me that she had spoken to her husband and a guard over the telephone. . . . She also said that the Zeitler murder would not help Smith, and that when her husband talked to her on the telephone he already knew about the Zeitler murder.

The "Zeitler murder" referred to by Mrs. Ferber in her statement was the rape-murder which occurred during my trial. Ruth Zeitler was the fifteen-year-old victim.

Another signed statement, dated June 10, 1957, in part confirmed Mrs. Ferber's statement:

> I, Mrs. Marie Brewer . . . hereby give the following statement:
> Sometime during the trial of Edgar H. Smith, and before the case went to the jury, I heard Mrs. Theodore Hundemann state she had spoken to her husband. I do not know the nature of that conversation.

[3] The documentation and/or confirmation of the Rockefeller medical history can be had from Andrew D. Nicol, Detectives, Inc., 144 Hopper Street, Hackensack, N.J.

    She mentioned the above when she was in the Economy
Shop. . . .

    A third statement affirmed Mrs. Hundemann's presence
in the Economy Shop.

    Judge O'Dea, after hearing Mr. Hundemann, the juror,
testify that he had not spoken to his wife, ruled that the evidence of prejudice was "insufficient." The motion for a new
trial was denied.

    My new attorneys were not admitted to practice law in
New Jersey, so it was decided that Selser would take the
appeal to the State Supreme Court. That appeal was argued
May 7, 1959. It was denied a month later.[4]

    The State Supreme Court ruled that the evidence regard-
ing Hommell was insufficient. It probably would not, the court
held, have changed the jury's verdict. The fact that a number
of witnesses supported my trial testimony regarding the clothing Hommell had worn on the night of the killing, and that
none supported his story, was completely ignored by the court.
The matter of Mr. Hundemann, the juror, was not raised on
appeal. No reason has ever been given me for the failure to
do so.

    On the question of time of death, the court admitted that
the autopsy report stated:

> I hereby certify that I, R. Gilady, M.D., have performed
> an autopsy on the body of Victoria Zielinski at H. Van Em-
> burgh's on the 5th day of March 1957 about 12 hours after the
> death. . . .

    The court conceded also that it was "arguable that some
of his [Dr. Gilady's] testimony was susceptible of the inference that it might have happened around midnight," but the
court pointed out that in answer to one of the many questions
he was asked, the doctor had said it *"could"* have been earlier
than eleven o'clock. This single deviation from the autopsy

[4] *State v. Smith*, 29 N.J. 561 (1959).

report, and from his otherwise consistent trial testimony, the court held, was sufficient to leave the time of death in doubt. The court rejected without comment my contention that doubt in a criminal case, and especially in a capital case in which the doubt bears on the question of guilt or innocence, must be resolved in favor of the defendant. That, I had pointed out, is a fundamental tenet of the American system of jurisprudence.

Specifically, the State Supreme Court ruled that the jury had resolved the doubt by finding that I had killed the girl, and, therefore, that she had died at the time I was present. That, of course, was a manifestly inane conclusion.

Time of death was not related to whether I *had* killed the girl, but to whether it was *possible* for me to have killed her. According to the State Supreme Court, the jury had reasoned as follows: a) Smith killed the girl; therefore, b) it was possible for Smith to have killed her; and, therefore, c) she must have died before nine-thirty.

Such reasoning is obviously putting the cart before the horse. To find that I had committed the crime, the jury would have had to reverse the reasoning process, finding: a) that Vickie probably had died before nine-thirty; and, therefore, b) Smith could have killed her. Then, and only then, could the jury find that I *had* killed her. They could not find the fact before the possibility.

An appeal was taken to the United States Supreme Court, but the court declined to review the case.[5] Then, in November 1959, we returned to the United States District Court, applying for a writ of habeas corpus.

The key point in the federal court appeal was that my statement to the police had been given involuntarily; Selser had never bothered to ask me about the manner in which I had been interrogated, and in the course of the trial had failed to ask questions which would have brought out the facts of denial of counsel, denial of requests to see my wife, the non-stop interrogation by relays of police officers, the hours I had gone without sleep, the taking away of my clothing, the holding

[5] *Smith v. New Jersey,* 361 U.S. 861 (1959).

of my wife in custody to prevent my obtaining counsel, or the promises and threats. These matters were being raised in the federal court by my new attorneys, but we faced the difficult problem of not having the facts in the trial record.

A secondary issue raised in the federal court was the matter of the truth-serum examination. Judge Morrill sent questionnaires to each of the four doctors who had attended the examination. Each responded that normal and established procedures had been followed. Dr. Cassity stated in his written response that he did not know the examination was being tape-recorded until "after the administration of the serum." He also stated:

> After receiving a written request from defendant, Edgar Smith, in and about May of 1959, I questioned Dr. Ralph Banay about the tape-recording made at the time of the truth serum examination and he stated then that he could not release it since it was confidential. I recently and on January 14th, 1960, at the request of William Richter, the present counsel for Edgar Smith, spoke to Dr. Banay about the said truth serum tape-recording and he now replied that it was not available since it was erased. . . .

Judge Morrill took the appeal under consideration. Months passed, then a year, then a year and a half. I was beginning to wonder if the judge had forgotten me, and in my frustration I was seriously considering writing the judge a letter: "Dear Judge: What the hell are you doing? Sincerely, Smith." I did not have the opportunity to write. In the spring of 1961 I received the word: Judge Morrill had dropped dead. A year and a half of my life had gone down the drain.

In April 1961, the case was reassigned to Judge Arthur S. Lane, and two months later the matter was reargued. Judge Lane gave his decision in January 1962. It was "No." [6] He had considered the trial record, and only the trial record, and had found that my statement to the police had been given volun-

[6] *United States ex rel Smith v. New Jersey*, 201 F. Supp. 272 (N.J.D.C., 1962).

tarily. None of the facts of denial of counsel—the taking of my clothes, the taking into custody of my wife, the promises and the threats of Detective Spahr, the refusal to permit me to see my wife, in short, none of the facts of my interrogation—had been considered.

Judge Lane's denial brought me face to face with two crises, one legal, one personal.

The legal crisis was easily solved. My family, who had been paying my attorneys for their services, had reached the bottom of the barrel. There was no more money to be had; so the lawyers, with a tip of the hat and a few words of encouragement, rode off into the sunset.

Left without an attorney, and without the means to retain one, I decided to ask the federal court to appoint an attorney to represent me. Everyone I asked about the procedure to be followed in making such a request told me the same thing: the federal courts do not appoint lawyers to represent state prisoners. Had anyone ever asked a federal court for a lawyer? No one seemed to know.

I wrote to the United States Court of Appeals, in Philadelphia, explaining my situation. Three days later, a lawyer was appointed to represent me. I was the first Death House inmate in New Jersey to have a lawyer appointed by a federal court.

The personal crisis did not pass as easily. Three weeks after the denial of my appeal in the United States District Court, my wife visited me for the last time. It was a difficult visit for both of us, and I must confess that at the time I was quite bitter. For several months, she had been determined to obtain a divorce if my appeals continued to fail. She wanted a real home, with a real father for our daughter, she told me, and the longer she put off the final decision the more difficult it would be for all concerned; but right up to the moment I received the divorce papers from her Reno attorney, I did not really believe she would go through with it.

My bitterness lasted for several months, then I began to

do something I had waited twenty-eight years to do: I began growing up. I faced the fact, first of all, that what my wife had done had been the right thing—right for herself, and right for our daughter. Time has proved that. Today, she is living in a Western state, and with her second husband has found happiness and a new life. I wish her well.

The second stage of my growing-up process was a bit more difficult and unpleasant. For the very first time in my life, I took a good look at myself, and I did not like what I saw. I was a thoroughly indolent, immature, half-educated drifter. Five years in the Death House and all I had accomplished had been to read a lot of cheap novels, listen to the radio, and get fat. It was time, I decided, that Edgar Smith set about to straighten out his messed-up life.

The first task facing me was to complete my high-school education. A check with the prison education office revealed that there were two methods I could employ: I could obtain free textbooks, study, and eventually take the high-school equivalency tests, or I could take the tests without study. The latter method, I was advised, would be exceptionally difficult for one away from the classroom as long as I had been. That was the method I chose.

The tests were administered over a period of three mornings and two afternoons. Two weeks later, my diploma was delivered. The education officer stated that my test scores were the highest he had ever seen, double the average score required for a diploma.

The prison had neither the funds nor the facilities for educational work above the high-school level. I was, however, given a list of colleges and universities offering correspondence courses carrying credits toward a degree, but I was told I would have to pay my own tuition. Luckily, I had saved some money from my Veterans Administration compensation during the first five years of my confinement, and I was curious to see how well I could handle college work. By the time my money ran out, I had taken courses in accounting and economics from Pennsylvania State University, and in English and history from the University of Illinois, for which I received twenty-three semester hours of credit. My grade average was 4.33 on a scale of 5.

My experience with college-level studies, and the ease with which I was able to achieve relatively high grades with a bare minimum of effort, emboldened me to seek membership in Mensa,[7] an international society headquartered in London. Mensa has but a single qualification for membership: one must have a tested IQ greater than that of 98 per cent of the general population. Money, social position, and academic achievement mean nothing; the tested IQ is everything. In this sense, at least, Mensa has been described by one prominent critic—who probably failed to qualify for membership—as a "little cult of snobs."

I had always been aware that my IQ rating was rather high, but even I was surprised when the scores of my preliminary tests exceeded 154, sufficiently high to qualify for membership. At this point, however, institutional red tape and regulations took effect, and I was prevented from actually becoming a Mensa member.

It was during this period of study and the reorientation of my life that I first came into contact with William F. Buckley, Jr., the editor of *National Review* magazine. The circumstances were unusually fortuitous.

A newspaper reporter for an obscure North Jersey weekly, whom I had known prior to my arrest, wrote an article in which he mentioned some of the magazines I had been reading. One of the magazines mentioned was *National Review*, and somehow a copy of the article found its way to Mr. Buckley's desk. A week later, I received a letter from him, offering me a complimentary subscription, an offer I gratefully accepted.

One thing led to another, and before long Mr. Buckley had obtained permission to write regularly. At first, our letters

---

[7] *Mensa* is the Latin word for table. It symbolizes the society's purpose of providing, through its magazine and regular meetings, a forum, or round table, for discussion, correspondence, and the free interchange of ideas between persons of exceptional intelligence.

dealt primarily with the facts of my case and with my efforts to win a new trial; but as time went by, a more personal relationship developed. So well did our friendship develop that today, five years later, Bill Buckley is the closest and most trusted friend I have ever had, or ever hope to have. But that is getting ahead of my story.

# CHAPTER TWENTY-TWO

**THE ATTORNEY ASSIGNED BY THE FEDERAL**
court to represent me was Stephen F. Lichtenstein, a brilliant
young lawyer from Trenton, whose offices are located only
a few blocks from the state prison. A graduate of Washington and Lee University, where he had been elected to Phi Beta
Kappa, and the New York University School of Law, Lichtenstein proved to be a careful, methodical worker who prepared
himself down to the smallest detail.

My new attorney argued my appeal before a three-judge
panel of the United States Court of Appeals for the Third
Circuit, in Philadelphia, in the fall of 1962. Ten months later,
in July 1963, the court rejected the appeal by a 2–1 vote.[1] We
had come awfully close.

The court ruled that the manner in which my statement
to the police had been obtained was not a violation of the then-
existing constitutional standards; but in reaching its decision,
the court relied upon the trial record alone, and had not considered those facts of the circumstances of my interrogation
which were not a part of the trial record. Nor did the court
rule upon my attorney's argument that Detective DeLisle had
acted improperly in attempting, without the knowledge or consent of my attorney, to obtain my signature upon my statement.
Lichtenstein had argued that an indicted person, represented
by counsel, as was I, cannot be questioned by the police outside
the presence of counsel.

[1] *United States ex rel Smith v. New Jersey*, 322 F. 2d 810 (3 Cir. 1963).

The majority's reluctance to rule upon this issue was not shared by the dissenting member, Judge J. Cullen Ganey, who issued a blistering denunciation of the actions of the prosecutor, concluding:

> . . . To take this undue advantage of a youth and one unlearned in the law, in spite of his informing the detective of his counsel's advice, is a shabby piece of police work which this Court should not lend sanction to, or permit to go unchallenged.[2]

The judge also considered this "subtle, coercive conduct" as corroboration that the statement had been obtained "from an overweary, distraught mind after hours of questioning solely for the purpose of convicting him." On petition for rehearing, Judge Biggs joined Judge Ganey in voting for rehearing, but five judges disagreed.

As a court-assigned lawyer, Mr. Lichtenstein received no compensation for his services, and his assignment ended with the completion of the appeal. He would have been entitled, therefore, to withdraw following the rejection of the appeal. But Lichtenstein felt that the 2–1 vote gave me some hope for victory in the United States Supreme Court; so, at his own expense, he took my case to Washington.

The Supreme Court, in February 1964, by an 8–1 vote, Justice William O. Douglas dissenting, refused to accept the case for review.[3] Three months later, on another case, the Supreme Court ruled that the interrogation in the absence of counsel of indicted persons is unconstitutional.

Mr. Lichtenstein advised me that he could not continue on my case at his own expense. He promised, however, to keep in touch, and to give me whatever advice I needed. I was faced with another legal crisis.

Strange as it might seem, at the end of seven years in the Death House, I knew no more about legal principles and procedures than I had when first arrested. Legal matters were something I had always left to the lawyers, and they in turn

[2] Ibid.
[3] *United States ex rel Smith v. New Jersey*, 376 U.S. 928 (1964).

never made much of an effort to keep me informed. Suddenly
I no longer had a lawyer to leave things to, and the only solution I could see was for me to drop everything and become a
"jail-house lawyer."

It was not an easy thing to do, but somehow I managed
to put together appeals to Judge O'Dea and the state supreme
court,[4] which were rejected, and by the fall of 1964 my legal
efforts had brought me back to the point at which the next
court in line was again the United States Supreme Court. Now
an appeal to the Supreme Court is not the easiest thing in the
world to prepare, and there are many experienced lawyers who
would hesitate to attempt to prepare one without expert assistance. And to make matters worse, I had exactly ninety days to
file the appeal. Somehow I made it, but in February 1965, the
Supreme Court once again declined to review the case.[5] Another
year had gone down the drain.

Although my appeals had been unsuccessful, two very
interesting events did take place during that year, events which
I believe tell a great deal about the character and methods of
the prosecution in my case.

The first event took place in the state supreme court, where
I had argued that it was only after the prosecutor had received
a transcript of the tape recording of the truth-serum examination, which confirmed my story regarding the baseball bat, that
he had conducted the search for the bat. It was my contention
that the finding of the bat resulted directly from the truth-
serum examination, and that since Judge O'Dea had ruled the
results of the examination inadmissible, the bat, one of the
results, should not have been admissible. I pointed out that
the examination was conducted May 5, and the bat was found
May 8.

To my complete surprise, the state supreme court's written
opinion, in which the court denied my appeal, alluded to the
prosecutor's having found the bat by accident. Detectives had
gone to the scene of the crime, the prosecutor told the court in

[4] *State v. Smith,* 43 N.J. 67 (1964).
[5] *Smith v. New Jersey,* 379 U.S. 1005, rehearing denied, 380 U.S. 938
(1965).

a brief filed without my knowledge, and had thrown some large stones about the area, searching where the stones had landed. By pure chance, he claimed, one of the stones had landed near the bat.[6]

Winston Churchill would have called the prosecutor's story a "terminological inexactitude." George O'Har, the detective who found the bat, testified at my trial that he and another officer had found it after pacing back and forth through the wooded area across the street from the sandpit. There had been *no* throwing of stones, *no* chance discovery.

The second event occurred in the United States Supreme Court. I had minced no words in my petition in taking apart the prosecutor's "discovery" of the bat, and so he changed his story. Instead, the prosecutor told the Supreme Court that the baseball bat had been found on March 8, not May 8, and thus the discovery could not be connected to the truth-serum examination.[7]

The second "terminological inexactitude" was even more outrageous than the first, and it gave me great satisfaction to tack the prosecutor's hide to the wall. He never had a chance, and on February 19, 1965, an assistant to Prosecutor Calissi wrote to me and stated: "I must concede that the baseball bat was found May 8, not March 8." The prosecutor did not, however, forward a copy of his letter to the Supreme Court, which still had my appeal under consideration, nor did he take any other steps to retract his false statements.

As noted earlier in this narrative, my relationship with William F. Buckley, Jr., which had begun with his letter offering me a free subscription to *National Review,* soon grew into a close personal relationship; and by the spring of 1965 I had come to regard Mr. Buckley as my most trusted friend and adviser. It was in this context of our relationship that he offered to consider means of raising the funds necessary to retain a lawyer for me.

[6] *State v. Smith*, 43 N.J. 67.
[7] *Smith v. New Jersey*, 379 U.S. 1005, Brief for the Respondent (Prosecutor), p. 5.

An application was made to Judge O'Dea for a court order permitting Mr. Buckley to visit me, and over the vigorous objections of the attorney-general, the prison authorities, and Prosecutor Calissi, the order permitting a single visit was issued.

The visit took place during the second week of March, and a course of action was laid out. At my own suggestion, I would file another appeal in the state courts, placing on the record all the legal points necessary for another appeal in the federal courts. In the meantime, Mr. Buckley would make an effort to raise the funds to retain a lawyer to take over when my appeal reached the federal court.

"What lawyer would you like to have?" Buckley asked.

"Steve Lichtenstein," I replied without hesitation. "He is the best lawyer I've ever known, and he has the added advantage of being already familiar with my case."

Some months later, Mr. Buckley told me that I could have had any lawyer I wanted. My reply was that Steve Lichtenstein was not only the attorney I wanted, but the best available, bar none.

My new round of appeals began before Judge O'Dea. In one year's time, I had so mastered the intricacies of legal practice that, in his denial of my appeal, Judge O'Dea described the petition for a writ of habeas corpus I had filed as having been "prepared and drafted with the consummate skill of a seasoned practitioner." [8]

I filed a motion for leave to appeal to the state supreme court, pointing out that Judge O'Dea had set a new execution date, and asking the court for prompt action. The court did not reply. Another letter explaining the exigency of my situation was similarly ignored. With one week to go before my scheduled execution, I wrote to both the court and the attorney general, explaining that further delay followed by a denial would leave me insufficient time to seek a stay of execution

[8] My term paper in English at the University of Illinois was an exposition setting forth the rules and procedures to be followed when petitioning the United States Supreme Court for a writ of certiorari. I received an "A" for both the semester and the paper.

from a federal court. I advised the court and the attorney general that I would wait a few more days before asking the federal court to take jurisdiction from the state. By return mail, the court advised me that permission to appeal had been denied. Two days later—on Good Friday, appropriately— Associate Justice William J. Brennan of the United States Supreme Court, in response to my petition, issued an order halting the plans for my execution, scheduled for the following Tuesday.

While acting as my own attorney during 1964 and 1965, there came into my possession a voluminous file of old documents related to my case—outdated court orders, rough drafts of petitions and briefs, and a batch of miscellaneous correspondence between attorneys and persons involved in my case. These documents seemed now worthless, but before discarding them, I spent an entire afternoon going through them one by one. That is when the issue of the truth-serum examination was revived.

Among the correspondence was a letter dated January 15, 1960, in which Dr. John H. Cassity, the doctor who had supervised the truth-serum examination, stated:

> . . . *I will state that the defendant spoke truthfully under the sodium amytal,* though he was somewhat evasive and defensive on the examination I had prior to the administration of the drug.

The doctor further stated that he had made fragmentary longhand notes of my responses while I was under the effect of the drug. I was astounded. Not only did it seem likely that a partial record of the examination was available, but I held in my hand a signed letter attesting to the reliability of the examination, to the fact that I had spoken "truthfully."

It took me several months to locate Dr. Cassity, and to obtain the notes he had made. In the meantime, a statement made by the special assistant prosecutor assigned to oppose my appeals came to my attention.

On June 5, 1961, in the United States District Court, District of New Jersey, the special assistant prosecutor, in the course of oral arguments regarding the truth-serum examination, had stated to the court that:

> *It seems very peculiar that at the trial he* [*Smith*] *related exactly the same story he had given these four doctors under the truth serum.*

*Peculiar?* It was more than simply peculiar. If it could be shown that I had spoken "truthfully" while under the effect of truth serum, and then it could be shown that I had "related exactly the same story" at my trial, then it would follow that my trial testimony to the effect that I had left the girl alive was also true.

Between the time I learned of Dr. Cassity's notes and the time I was able to obtain them, the New Jersey Supreme Court spoke on the subject. In an opinion dated July 7, 1964, in which the court discussed the manner in which the police had found the baseball bat, the court mentioned the results of the truth-serum test, stating:

> It is agreed that during the examination defendant referred to a baseball bat, but no one suggests he then admitted that he struck the deceased with it or revealed the disposition of the bat. On the contrary, it is agreed that defendant's story at the examination was pretty much the same as his testimony at the trial, wherein he denied that he struck the deceased at all.[9]

Everyone seemed to know more about the truth-serum examination than I did, and I must confess that I was a bit unhappy with assorted prosecutors and judges trying to tell me what I had or had not said. But finally I struck gold. Today, I have in my possession two sets of notes, one set made by Dr. Cassity, another made by Dr. Policastro, one of the other doctors attending the examination. The fact that there are two sets of notes is doubly important. Not only can one compare

[9] *State v. Smith,* 43 N.J. 67 (1964).

the notes to be certain that statements were correctly recorded, but in some cases one doctor recorded statements the other ignored, and vice versa.

The doctors' notes have never been made public, whole or in part. I present them here for the first time. In many instances, the doctors jotted down only fragments of my answers to questions. They are presented as they appear in the original. In other instances, I have deleted unfavorable references to persons not involved in the case, and statements not relevant to the issues. The reader must keep in mind that the notes were never intended to be a complete record of the examination. They are, therefore, exceedingly brief. Dr. Policastro's notes follow:

The following is a report of a neuropsychiatric examination of the patient in reference. He was examined in the Bergen County Jail, Hackensack, N.J., on Sunday, May 5, 1957. At that time patient was given an intravenous injection of Sodium Amytal, and while under the drug the following statements were made in the presence of [names missing]:

Smith: "Marihuana is too expensive. It costs a dollar a stick. I never smoked marihuana."

Dr. P[olicastro]: "How are you feeling now?"

Smith: "Good."

Dr. P.: "How long have you been here?"

Smith: "Two months."

Dr. P.: "Who was killed?"

Smith: "Julia [sic] Zielinski. I hate to see anyone die . . . She told me something. She said my wife was. . . . I slapped her and told her to get out of the car. She was coming up the road and it was Hommell and I thought it was her father. I got damn mad. Blood was puring [sic] down her face, neck, and her shoes were missing and her brown [sic] kerchief was missing. She had no shoes on. . . . She said: 'I heard your wife was . . . for. . . .' I told her: 'Get out of the car. . . .' She got out of the car and ran down the road. I heard a commotion. I came back . . . I was going to hit her father but I recognized Hommell. I don't know how she cut her head. . . . I argued with Hommell. He said: 'You rotten s.o.b. . . . she is mine!' I got in the car and went.

"She got in my car. She said: 'I love you.' Hommell grabbed her by the arm, pulled her to the ground. She was holding my legs and said take me home. I said Hommell will take [incomplete in the original].

"I know he killed her. I knew he killed her with the baseball bat. The bat was 15 to 20 feet [from] the entrance of the sandpit. I saw the baseball bat was broken in two.

"I saw her gloves on the ground."

Dr. P.: "How did you lose you [sic] shoe?"

Smith: "I smashed my ankle bowling and could not button my shoe. I threw bloody pants at the bridge. I know Hommell picked up the pants. He said he would take care of them and said if I said anything he would get after my wife and child. I did not wash the pants. . . . I washed the shirt and jacket. I asked him how she was. He said we are all [sic] in trouble."

The remainder of Dr. Policastro's notes concern my schooling, marital status, military record, and employment. There is no need to relate those details here.

Dr. Cassity's notes are more extensive, but far more fragmentary. In some instances, his handwriting is barely legible. Excerpts of his notes follow:

Amytol—Edgar Smith
Arrested.
Smiles—"almost went to sleep"—euphoric.
[Smith]: "Marihuana too expensive. Never smoked it.
[Smith]: "Baseball bat. Saw it was [incomplete in original] Got mad—grabbed bat."
Important? [Smith]: "Asked me to stop at sandpit—said she heard my wife was . . . with other man. Slapped her. Car passed and blew horn and stopped
(two minutes)
[Smith]: "She got out. Heard commotion—then she came back up road with Hommell—her head was bleeding—offered to take her to hospital. She got back in my car."

[Dr. Banay]: "Why didn't she go in other car?"

[Smith]: "Don't know. Hommell dragged her out of car."

[Dr. Policastro]: "Why not protect her?"

[Smith]: "I wanted to keep out of trouble."

Last he [Smith] saw of her.

[Smith]: "Met Hommell in town again 15 min. later. He told me not to say anything or 'we'd all [sic] be in trouble.'"

Blood? [Smith]: "Got it on pants when he [Hommell] dragged her out of car. [She] clung to [my] knees. Threw pants away. Didn't want to worry wife."

Bat? [Smith]: "Other fellow [Gilroy] had it in car. Grabbed it believing her father was after me for going with his daughter. . . . [S]aw Hommell and dropped bat by reflex.

"Hommell said I was rotten s.o.b. . . . She got in car and said: 'Take me home.' She said: 'I love you Eddie, take me home.' Hommell pulled her out of car."

Bat? [Smith]: "Went back second time to find books. Found her gloves, my shoe. [Bat] broken in two. [Saw] clean T-shirt. Shoe fell off when I got out of car.

"Hommell [said]: 'You're a no good s.o.b.' I told him about bloody pants—found one mile from car."

[Dr. Cassity]: "Why wash shirt and jacket?"

[Smith]: "Just that they were dirty."

Pants? [Smith]: "Told Hommell where pants were. Lady identified Hommell fishing for pants."

Finale? [Dr. Cassity]: "How did it happen?"

[Smith]: "Don't know who hit . . ." [Incomplete in original.]

Amytol Interview

Conducted May 5, 1957

S/ *John H. Cassity*

The most obvious question to follow these notes is whether their existence has been made known to the courts. The answer is that the results of truth-serum examinations are not admissible evidence as to the issue of guilt or innocence. The drug is well established as a standard, highly useful psychiatric tool, and few persons in the medical profession would challenge the four eminent specialists who conducted my examination. But the courts tend to trail along years behind science and technology.

Under special circumstances, courts have permitted the use of truth-serum examination results in an indirect fashion, but I know of no instance in which a court has permitted the introduction of truth-serum results as direct proof of guilt or innocence. That is an archaic attitude. How much more realistic it would be *to* put the results into evidence, allow both sides to present their experts, and then leave it to the jury to determine the issue of reliability.

The doctors' notes have not been a total loss, however. They have been put before the federal courts in connection with my latest appeal, to show that there is sufficient reason, and evidence, to believe that my statement to the police was not the candid, completely truthful, reliable, and voluntary statement of a conscience-stricken, guilty man—as the prosecutor would have the world believe.

Truth-serum examinations *are* susceptible, through skillful questioning, to manipulation for the purpose of bringing forth desired replies from the subject. It is for this reason, therefore, that I restate the fact that the examination was conducted by four eminent physicians, and that the prosecutor was fully and equally represented throughout the examination. Not only were the prosecution's representatives free to participate, but to insure the acceptability of the results, the drug was prepared and administered by the prosecutor's representatives.

Before leaving this subject, I should add that not once in the entire eleven-year history of my case has the prosecution challenged the procedure followed in administering the drug, the effectiveness of the drug in this specific case, or the reliability of the results obtained.

My appeal to the United States District Court, which followed Justice Brennan's Good Friday stay of execution, was in the form of a petition for a writ of habeas corpus, filed during July 1965. Mr. Buckley, meanwhile, had decided to write a magazine article, "The Approaching End of Edgar H. Smith," [1] in which he intended to solicit funds to pay my legal expenses. The appeal to the federal court was filed earlier than Mr. Buckley had expected; but rather than wait until the article was published and until the results of the solicitation of funds could be gauged, he went out on a limb and retained Mr. Lichtenstein to represent me, advancing the retainer from his own pocket.

The appeal was again before Judge Arthur S. Lane. He thought it over for a year, and in July 1966 dismissed the petition without a hearing on the merits.[2] Then, through a procedural maneuver, the judge sought to deny me access to the Court of Appeals. My attorney managed to settle the procedural problem by taking the matter to another judge, and on May 4, 1967, a three-judge panel of the United States Court of Appeals was convened to hear my appeal argued orally.

The appeal consisted of three major points:

1. That under the most recent Supreme Court decisions, it was impermissible for Detective DeLisle to question me after I had been indicted, and that his testimony to the effect that I had read over and acknowledged my statement was inadmissible.

2. That under the decisions of the United States Court of Appeals and the Supreme Court, it was a constitutional error to allow my jury to hear testimony regarding my statement before the statement was put in evidence, and for Judge O'Dea to tell the jury that he had found the statement to be voluntary.

3. That under the most recent Supreme Court decisions, I am entitled to have the courts reconsider the manner in which my statement to the police was obtained; I am entitled to have the courts consider all of the facts of my interrogation,

---

[1] *Esquire* (November 1965), p. 116.
[2] *United States ex rel Smith v. Howard Yeager, Warden, New Jersey State Prison at Trenton*   F. Supp.   (D.C.N.J. 1966).

not merely the facts contained in the trial record; and that such facts, when considered, will establish that my statement was the result of a coercive interrogation which failed to measure up to constitutional standards.

I do not wish to bore the reader with a lengthy exposition regarding the legal background and basis of the argument advanced to the court during the appeal—discussions of constitutional law tend to induce instant apathy in all but those who make that area of the law their business; but it might be useful to give the reader a general idea of the issues that were involved.

The key point in the appeal would seem to have been that concerning Detective DeLisle's attempt to cajole me into signing my statement. It will be recalled that Judge Ganey of the United States Court of Appeals, in his dissent from the denial of my first appeal to that court, had characterized DeLisle's action as "a shabby piece of police work which this court should not lend sanction to, or permit to go unchallenged." The judge went on to say "this subtle, coercive conduct" was corroboration that the statement had been obtained "from an overweary, distraught mind after hours of questioning."

Two facts should be kept in mind: 1) At the time Detective DeLisle questioned me in the back room of the county jail regarding the accuracy of my statement, thereby laying the foundation for the admission of the statement at my trial, I had already retained an attorney, Mr. Gaudielle, a fact known to both DeLisle and Prosecutor Calissi. 2) That three days prior to DeLisle's visit in jail, I was indicted by the grand jury. With these facts in mind, the legal basis for the key point of my appeal comes into sharp focus.

In May 1964, less than a year after Judge Ganey's perceptive dissent, the United States Supreme Court, by an 8–1 vote, confirmed his opinion when the court said:

Any secret interrogation of the defendant, from and after indictment, without the protection afforded by the presence of

counsel, contravenes the basic dictates of fairness in the conduct
of criminal causes and the fundamental rights of persons
charged with crime.[3]

Mr. Justice Stewart, who had written the court's opinion,
took the opportunity one month later in another case to explain
precisely what the court had meant in its May decision. "An
indictment," he explained, "marks the point at which a criminal investigation has ended and adversary proceedings have
commenced. It is at this point that the constitutional guarantees attach which pertain to a criminal trial. Among those
guarantees . . . is the guarantee of the assistance of counsel. . . ."[4]

It may be seen, therefore, that in addition to violating
his profession's ethical code—"A lawyer should not in any way
communicate . . . with a party represented by counsel . . .
but should deal only with his counsel"—the prosecutor's action
in sending his emissary, Detective DeLisle, to interrogate me
in the absence of my attorney, was a clear-cut constitutional
violation. Moreover, all the facts pertaining to this undisguised
constitutional violation were conclusively established on the
record by the prosecutor, so that there can be no argument as
to who did what, when, or where. It was the prosecutor who
put into the record the fact that I had been indicted on March
8; the prosecutor who established that DeLisle had questioned
me in the county jail on the eleventh; and the prosecutor who
established that the questioning had taken place outside the
presence, and without the knowledge or consent, of my attorney.

The second most important point in the appeal, as I judge
the situation, concerned the failure of Judge O'Dea to excuse
the jury from the courtroom while he heard testimony and
legal arguments as to the admissibility of my statement; and
his informing the jury of his legal judgment that the statement had been made voluntarily. The logic and evolution of

[3] *Massiah v. United States,* 377 U.S. 201 (1964); quoting *People v. Water-
man,* 9 N.Y. 2d 561 (1961).
[4] *Escobedo v. Illinois,* 378 U.S. 478 (1964).

the constitutional prohibition against both procedures is extremely complicated, and I would be putting the reader's patience and good will to a terrible test if I were to explain the genesis of the rules. Briefly, therefore, it boils down to this:

If the jury is permitted to remain in the courtroom and hear testimony and legal arguments pertaining to a statement by the defendant, and thereafter the judge rules that the statement may not be put in evidence, there is no mental eraser with which one can wipe from the minds of the jurors the testimony and arguments they have heard. Nor can the jurors be prevented from speculating as to what might be contained in the statement they know was made but that they are not permitted to read. Their speculations as to the contents could prove more damaging to the defendant than if the statement had been admitted into evidence. But if, on the other hand, the judge does admit the statement, and tells the jury that he has done so because he has found, as a matter of fact and law, that the defendant made the statement voluntarily, then it is too much to expect that the jurors will not be swayed by his opinion when the time comes for them to make their own assessment of the statement's credibility and voluntariness.

The foregoing is merely the gist of a complex legal issue —an issue on which even the federal courts disagree sharply— to show that the procedure followed in my case does not meet the exacting constitutional standards enunciated by the United States Supreme Court. The most significant error of Judge O'Dea was in permitting detectives to testify as to the statement's contents before it was put in evidence. The Supreme Court's rule is that "a jury is not to hear of a confession [or statement] unless and until the trial judge has determined that it was freely and voluntarily given." [5]

The third point raised in the appeal, that my statement was made involuntarily, was not so much a legal problem as it was one of a subjective interpretation of ten-year-old facts. The court was called upon to make what is known in sports as a "judgment call," meaning the issue is susceptible to varying

[5] *Sims v. Georgia,* 385 U.S. 538 (1966).

points of view, and the referee's decision, in this case the court's, is virtually beyond challenge. It is all a matter of opinion. Judge A. may study the facts of my interrogation and conclude that in their totality they form a clear picture of a coercive interrogative process, and that as a result my statement to the police was made involuntarily. Judge B., after reviewing the same set of facts, may agree that they portray something less than commendable police behavior, yet he may decide that they are not quite indicative of a clear-cut coercive interrogation. And both judges, with a minimum of effort, could find an enormous body of precedent to support their diametrically opposed judgments.

What then were my prospects for success with the appeal? That, after all, is what it is all about: one wins or loses; there are no tie scores. Experience teaches that predicting the outcome of an appeal in any court at any time is futile. There are precedents for practically everything, but the fact that no two cases are alike leaves the courts with the leeway to decide as they please, knowing that they will be able to cite a mile-long list of precedents tending to buttress their decision. And my case, aside from its merits, presents an especially difficult problem. Granted that my recitation of the facts is sufficient to warrant a reversal, and granted that the law is both abundant and obvious, the courts then must face the unassailable truth that a reversal of my conviction will be tantamount to an acquittal.

No case presents the appellate courts with a more difficult decision than does the criminal case in which many years have passed between conviction and appeal, and the difficulty of that decision increases in proportion to the seriousness of the offense and the severity of the punishment. In my case, for instance, however much the courts may strive to consider objectively the merits of my appeal, individually the judges are fallible human beings, each to a greater or lesser degree, but certainly to *some* degree, unable to ignore that 1) time is running out for Edgar Smith—if I fail to win I face execution; and 2) more than eleven years have passed since my conviction, and the changes wrought by time—key prosecution witnesses have died; other witnesses have moved away and may no longer be available; memories have dimmed; evidence has deteriorated; changes in legal rules, and the raising of constitutional standards, will render other evidence unusable—all combine to make it highly unlikely that I could be reconvicted if my present conviction were to be voided. It is clear, therefore, that my appeals present a moral dilemma which could very well be the determining factor should the courts find themselves sitting on the fence as far as the legal and factual issues are concerned. And this, I believe, is what happened in the United States Court of Appeals.

On January 2, 1968, the three-judge panel of the Court of Appeals announced its decision: for the second time in that court, I had lost by a 2–1 vote.[6] This time Judge Biggs dissented as a member of the regular panel. What was significant, however, was not that I had lost, nor even the split decision, but that the majority, in an opinion which defies both logic and judicial precedent—not to mention such "minor" points as the facts contained in the court's records of my case—had voted not to consider whether the appeal had factual or legal merit. The majority held, erroneously, that the merits had been fully considered and determined in the court's 1963 decision, from which Judge Ganey had so vigorously dissented.

To say that the majority statement is wrong is an understatement. The decision was so wrong, so contrary to fact and law, that one is led to conclude that the majority based its decision solely upon the desire to avoid taking a stand on the merits of my claims; it is too wrong to be simply an error in judgment. One does not wish to accuse the court of shirking its duty, of judicial buck-passing, yet one cannot avoid drawing conclusions when those conclusions are so blatantly obvious. Assuming, as one must, that judges of the United States Court of Appeals can read English, and further assuming that they are reasonably familiar with, at least, the highly publicized, most controversial decisions of the Supreme Court, then they

[6] *United States ex rel Smith v. Yeager, Warden,* F.2d (3 Cir., Jan. 2, 1968).

knew, and it will be shown that they knew, that the merits of my appeal could not have been settled by the 1963 court.

1. On the question of the constitutionality of my post-indictment interrogation by Detective DeLisle, when he sought to have me sign my statement to the police, the 1963 decision was utterly silent, as Judge Ganey pointed out in his dissent from that decision, when he characterized DeLisle's action as "a shabby piece of police work which this court should not lend sanction to, or permit to go unchallenged." But even if the 1963 court had settled the issue, that ruling would be irrelevant today, for as noted earlier, the Supreme Court changed the law in 1964, ruling that post-indictment interrogations are, as Judge Ganey had argued they should be, constitutionally impermissible.[7] Moreover, the Supreme Court has made its ruling retroactive, so that it does cover my case.[8] Hence, the majority in 1968 was doubly wrong: the 1963 court never considered the question, and the 1963 court could not have applied to my case a Supreme Court decision which did not exist in 1963.

2. The question of my trial jury having heard testimony regarding my statement to the police before the judge had determined its admissibility was not an issue before the court in 1963. Had it been, however, a 1963 decision on this issue would be irrelevant in 1968, for once again, as above, one finds that the Supreme Court ruling which applies to this issue was not made until 1964.[9] Thus, as above, the 1968 majority was doubly wrong.

3. On the third point, that I am entitled to a full hearing on the voluntariness of my statement to the police, and that I am entitled to have the court hear and consider all the facts, not merely those in the trial record, the 1968 majority decision is utterly uncomprehensible. It is conceded by both the court and the prosecutor that the 1963 court considered only the uncontradicted facts contained in the trial record; indeed, in 1963,

[7] *Massiah v. United States*, 377 U.S. 201 (1964).
[8] *Lyles v. Beto*, 379 U.S. 368 (1965); *Beatty v. United States*, 389 U.S. 45 (1967).
[9] *Jackson v. Denno*, 378 U.S. 368 (1964).

those were the only facts the court was authorized to consider. Yet even if the 1963 decision were correct on every point considered, I am still entitled to a reconsideration in 1968. The 1968 majority has no legal basis to claim "But we settled this issue in our 1963 decision," for the simple reason that in 1966, three years later, the Supreme Court said: "Prisoners are entitled to present evidence anew on this aspect of their confessions. . . ." [1]

The refusal of the majority to consider the merits of my appeal leaves no doubt in my mind that they came up against one of the difficult truths about my case, which is that if the merits of my appeal are considered, there is no way under the facts and law that an appeals court can avoid reversing my conviction. Faced with this unpleasant prospect, the majority closed its eyes and dismissed the appeal, ruling that the issues were settled by the 1963 decision, a ruling demonstrated here to be unfounded. Edgar Smith has become a problem for the judicial establishment, and an embarrassment.

Few people are able to grasp that my case, more than any other of its type, stands as proof of the flaws and breakdowns in our judicial system. It is not as if I were sitting here for eleven years throwing obscure technicalities at the courts in order to keep myself alive. The fact is that I have raised, particularly in the post-indictment interrogation issue, a problem of major constitutional dimensions. Yet in the eleven years since my trial, not a single court, state or federal, has ruled on the factual or legal merits of that issue. Am I not entitled to have some court, somewhere, sometime, say to me: "This issue is without merit, because . . ."? I believe I am, and until the courts finally realize that however tightly they shut their eyes, the problem my case presents will not disappear, they will find me on their doorstep awaiting a decision. I do not intend to give up—this year, next year, ten years from now, or ever.

In view of the split vote and the obviously incorrect ruling, my attorney, Stephen Lichtenstein, petitioned for a rehearing *en banc*. This meant asking the entire Court of Appeals, usually

[1] *Johnson v. New Jersey*, 384 U.S. 719 (1966).

seven judges, to reconsider the decision of the three-judge panel. That petition was filed on February 6, 1968, pointing out the errors in the majority decision, much as I have outlined them here, and at the same time asking some long-overdue questions:

> Edgar Smith has been incarcerated by the State of New Jersey for two months less than eleven years [Lichtenstein wrote in his petition], and in early June 1968 he will "celebrate" his eleventh year in the New Jersey Death House. Surely, the age of his case or the length of his incarceration cannot be the reason why this Court has turned away from the constitutional issues involved. Constitutional principles, without question the bastion of our criminal justice, are to be applied as readily to old as to younger cases. They do not dissipate their strength with each case, in relation to its age, as do certain of earth's elements. What, then, is it about Edgar Smith that repels the application of applicable constitutional principles? What causes this Court not even to discuss the serious [constitutional] questions raised by Smith's verbal, ex parte and post-indictment [interrogation]? What causes this Court to rely on a prior opinion that could not possibly have settled the *Massiah* issue? What causes this Court to refuse Smith permission to file a vital Affidavit concerning an alleged offer and refusal of a plenary hearing, and then deny his appeal on that very ground? What causes this Court to ignore uncontroverted allegations of police mistreatment and to rely on a prior opinion decided when the Court did not have those allegations before it?
>
> Edgar Smith has an absolute right to the advantages of applicable constitutional principles. If such principles are to be denied, Smith is at least entitled to know why.

Lichtenstein concluded the petition by saying:

> [Smith] is entitled to have a decision from this Court on the merits of the points raised on this appeal. What transpired during the first appeal is irrelevant. The standards have changed since that appeal. They have changed with regard to whether or not Smith is entitled to a plenary hearing. They have changed with regard to whether the hearing afforded Smith on the voluntary nature of his [statement] met constitutional require-

ments. They have changed with regard to the right of government officials to extract post-indictment statements from dependents who do not have the assistance of counsel. They have changed with regard to the significance of the failure of the police to advise a defendant of his constitutional right to remain silent, to have counsel, and notification that anything he says may be used against him. Smith is entitled to rulings based upon the new and broad concepts enunciated in these cases. He has not received such rulings.

My attorney's arguments, though well-constructed, legally sound, and forcefully to the point, failed to move the Court of Appeals. On March 15, 1968, the court announced that it would not reconsider its decision. As in all of my appeals to this court, however, the judges failed to reach a unanimous decision. Judge Abraham L. Freedman, in a lengthy dissenting opinion, took up where the previous dissenters had left off, agreeing with my contention that the 1963 ruling could not have resolved legal questions which did not come into being until 1964; but the majority, in a one-sentence opinion, ignored his arguments The majority said, in effect: "We decided all this in 1963," a ruling that has been shown to be incorrect. In the course of my two appeals and two petitions for rehearing in the United States Court of Appeals, incidentally, five separate dissents have been filed, three of them with lengthy written opinions.

The next step in my legal battle will be to ask the United States Supreme Court to review the decisions of the Court of Appeals. That petition will be filed about the same time this book is published, and the court's decision may be expected sometime in October. As always, one hopes and one waits.

The article Mr. Buckley wrote for *Esquire* brought in less than half the money required to finance my appeal then current. Many letters were received from all parts of the United States (a number of the letters containing marriage proposals!). Other messages were received from persons in Venezuela, Belgium,

England, France, and Spain. The most touching response to the article came from an elderly Negro woman in North Carolina. Unable to contribute money—she probably was as indigent as I—the woman knitted a beautiful sweater, sent it to my mother, and suggested that if necessary a few extra dollars could be raised by selling the sweater. Equally touching was a letter and a small check from a young Pakistani girl studying in the United States. She did not understand American law, she wrote, but experiences in her own country had taught her to recognize injustice. One man sent a check for a dollar, stipulating that his contribution be refunded on a pro rata basis if more funds than necessary were raised.

I was very much surprised and comforted to discover that there are so many people, all of whom have problems and worries of their own, who will take a few minutes out of their lives to express their concern for the plight of a complete stranger, and one convicted of a heinous crime. At a time when one hears and reads so much about public apathy, about people not wanting to "get involved," those who answered my call for help did much to restore my faith. But while letters and good wishes are always appreciated, the sad fact is that it takes cash on the line, and lots of it, to fight a legal battle. Hence this book, aside from providing the opportunity and the vehicle to tell my side of the story in its entirety for the first time, has become a practical financial necessity; it is the means whereby I can contribute in some small part to the financing of my appeals.

This would seem to be an appropriate time, while mentioning those who have aided my cause, to single out for special notice Mr. John Carley, a young Yale law student, whose part in my appeal has gone largely unnoticed.

Late in 1966, an article surprisingly favorable to my cause appeared in the *Bergen Record*.[2] The article, written by a staff reporter, was so obviously sympathetic to my case that the *Record*, a newspaper which regards Prosecutor Calissi as the original knight on a white charger, long overdue for canoni-

[2] *Bergen Record*, December 23, 1966, p. 1.

zation, promptly rushed into print with an editorial denouncing the effort to picture me as innocent, and citing as "proof" of my guilt many of the "facts" disproved by the prosecutor's own evidence introduced during my trial; for example, Smith's shoes, the editorial said, were "saturated" with blood of the victim's type.[3]

As a result of the article, however, and notwithstanding the editorial, John Carley wrote to offer his assistance in the preparation of the appeal. Certain legal points needed to be researched. He dug into the Yale Law Library and produced a series of lengthy memoranda which my attorney has characterized as "outstanding" in scope and appreciation of the issues involved. And young Mr. Carley did every bit of this work in his own free time—something law students have precious little of—and all without prospect of receiving one cent of compensation.

[3] Editorial, *Bergen Record,* December 29, 1966.

# CHAPTER TWENTY-THREE

IT IS THE PROSECUTOR'S THEORY OF THE crime that the following occurred: 1) That upon our arrival at the sandpit, Vickie and I held a conversation. 2) That I attempted to make love to her. 3) That she resisted my attempts. 4) That her sweater was pushed up and her bra was torn. 5) That she fought, got free, and fled from the automobile. 6) That I took a baseball bat from the back seat of the auto and pursued her. 7) That, approximately 350 feet down the road, I caught up with her and struck her down with the bat. 8) That for a reason obvious only to the prosecutor, I discarded the weapon. 9) That I dragged her back to the sandpit, up onto the dirt mound, crushed her skull, and dragged the body over the mound. 10) That I left the sandpit, stopped on Chapel Road to discard her pocketbook, then drove home. The evidence, unchallenged and uncontradicted, is that I arrived home at 8:57 p.m. The prosecutor has never questioned this time.

The theory is interesting; but if you stop to compare it with the evidence, and if you realize just what the prosecutor asks you to believe, you find a significant defect in the theory: it is filled with discrepancies.

There is, to begin with, the time element. From the trial testimony of Barbara Nixon, Myrna Zielinski, and Vickie's mother, and from the investigation report filed by the Mahwah police, in which reference is made to statement by Vickie's parents, and by Mrs. Nixon, it is clear that Vickie left the

Nixon home at approximately 8:40 p.m. This is the starting time for my calculations.

If one gives the prosecutor the benefit of the doubt, one may assume that I passed Vickie on the road within sixty to ninety seconds of the time she left the Nixon home. One might then be fair in assuming that within another minute I had gone down the road, stopped, turned around, driven back, and picked her up. This would have put her in the car at 8:42, or a few seconds later. This really gives the prosecutor the benefit of the doubt.

The drive to the sandpit has been clocked repeatedly at six to seven minutes. The reader will recall that my unchallenged testimony was that I had been forced to stop for a piece of earth-moving equipment being backed across the road, so the estimate of seven minutes to drive to the sandpit is a fair one, and puts me at the sandpit at 8:49.

To back out of the sandpit, drive down Chapel Road, stop to discard the pocketbook, as the prosecutor claims I did, and then to drive the one mile to my home, takes three, four minutes. Since I arrived home at 8:57, I must therefore have left the sandpit at 8:53 or 8:54.

Now one can readily see the incredibility of the prosecutor's theory. Between 8:49, the earliest time I could have arrived at the sandpit, and 8:53 or 8:54, the time I must have left the scene, is a time span of only four to five minutes; yet the prosecutor would have you believe that within this brief span of time it was physically possible for me to have done all of the things he claims I did: hold a conversation, attempt to make love, argue, struggle, get out the baseball bat, chase the girl more than the length of a football field, drag her body back an even greater distance, kill her, and then drag her body over the dirt mound. The reader can decide if this was possible.

Another claim by the prosecutor is that while in the car, and *before* the girl had suffered a single injury, I had torn her bra in an attempt to make love to her. So intent was he upon playing up the sex angle that he paid no attention to the fact that the bra was saturated with blood in the area between the cups. Yet these bloodstains tell an important story.

The girl was found with the bra around her waist. The waistbands of her jeans and her underpants were completely free of blood, and her abdomen was clean. The obvious question: If the bra was around her waist *before* she was injured, how did it *alone* become saturated with blood? If the saturation of the bra occurred while it was down around her waist, the tops of her jeans and panties, and the area of her stomach, could not possibly have been unbloodied.

The answer would seem to be that the bra was not torn until *after* she was injured, and this is borne out by photographs showing dried blood in the area between her breasts, corresponding exactly with the bloodstains between the cups of the bra. Also, the left shoulder strap of the bra reveals numerous bloodstains on the portion of the strap which goes over the shoulder. This confirms my claim that the left side of her head was injured when she returned to the sandpit with Hommell. The right shoulder strap is free of blood.

This prompts another question: If the girl was struck down, dragged back to the sandpit, then killed, how did the blood get between her breasts in sufficient quantity to saturate the bra? Lying on the ground, her head would have been lower than the chest area. Perhaps when she was dragged head first up the dirt mound? I shall show that she was dragged feet first.

From many hours of studying the testimony at my trial, and from careful analysis of both color and black-and-white photographs of the scene, the body, and the girl's clothing, I believe I have been able to reconstruct the events. I believe, too, that my reconstruction is far more logical than the prosecutor's, since every piece of evidence fits into mine.

It is clear that Vickie was injured and fully conscious for a significant period of time before she was killed. Three factors lead to this conclusion: 1) Her gloves were found to be grossly stained with blood, and strands of her own hair were found sticking to the palms. This establishes beyond question that she was wearing the gloves *after* having sustained an injury. 2)

Dr. Gilady found that her fingernails were "bitten very severely," a positive indication that *after* having been injured, and *after* having removed her bloodstained gloves, she remained conscious and in a state of fear or pain for some appreciable period of time, at least long enough to have bitten her nails "very severely." 3) The bra, as noted, must have been in place about her breasts when it became saturated with blood. This, again, is a positive indication that she had been standing *after* being injured, that she had been bleeding profusely, and that the blood had followed the natural body contours and had run down between her breasts. This, and only this, accounts for the presence of blood between her breasts but none lower on her body—the blood, when it reached the area between her breasts, was absorbed by the bra.

The girl's jacket is another article of evidence which tells a story. There is nothing to indicate that her jacket ever was off the body; yet on the inner lining of the jacket, in the area corresponding to the small of the back, there was found a large, circular, blood-saturated area, to which her own hair and fragments of bone were clinging. At some point, therefore, her head must have come in direct contact with that portion of the jacket, a circumstance for which the prosecutor's theory makes no allowance. I believe there is a logical explanation, but it must be explained within the context of all the other evidence. Alone, it makes no sense. Prosecutor Calissi failed to consider each item of evidence as part of a whole picture of what took place that night.

Vickie was injured. She was standing in the sandpit fully clothed, bleeding profusely from an injury to the left side of her head. The blood was flowing down the left side of her face and neck, and it followed the contour of her body down between her breasts. Her bra, which was still in place, absorbed the blood and prevented it from flowing down to her abdomen. At the same time, the left shoulder strap became bloodstained.

It is evident that the girl's sweater was in place at this time. Had it been tightly bunched above her breasts and under her arms, as it was when the body was found, it would have prevented the flowing of blood between her breasts, since it would have absorbed the blood.

Vickie, still wearing her gloves, put her hands to the wound, either to feel the wound or to staunch the flow of blood. Her gloves became bloodstained, and some of her hair, loosened by the injury, stuck to the palms. She removed the gloves, dropped them to the ground, and put her hands to the wound. This is the only logical reason why the photographs show her hands to have been bloodstained also.

I left the girl at the sandpit in the general condition just described. When I returned thirty minutes later, she was nowhere in sight, but the broken baseball bat, and what appeared to me to be a clean white cloth, were lying on the ground. If Dr. Gilady's estimate of the time of death is correct, and I believe it is, the girl was still alive when I returned. But where was she?

I believe that she had been struck down with the baseball bat and left lying near the dirt mound. The "scuffled area" found by the police, probably resulting from her struggle with her attacker, was near the base of the mound. When I returned to the scene, I did not go beyond the end of the dirt road, nor was I looking to see if the girl was there. I assumed she had been taken home. It is quite possible, therefore, that she was lying unconscious near the mound. Other persons argue that she was not there, that she was brought back later, but I have never seen a shred of evidence to support their argument.

The next question concerns the manner in which her clothing became disarranged. The torn bra made no sense to me until one day, in the summer of 1966, I was examining a photograph of the body. Then the answer came to me: The torn bra and the position in which the body was found are directly related. This is how I see it:

Vickie's murderer arrived at the sandpit several hours later, perhaps to see if she was dead, perhaps to retrieve the baseball bat and the white cloth I saw lying near the bat. No such cloth was ever found or alluded to by the police, but a clean white T-shirt is mentioned in Dr. Cassity's truth-serum notes.

The murderer, thinking she was dead, decided to drag the body over the dirt mound, to conceal it from anyone who might enter the sandpit. The girl's jeans were held in place by a two-inch-wide leather belt. The back of the belt is heavily scarred, and the shiny finish is scraped away. This indicates the girl was lying on her back when dragged up the mound. The absence of dirt and sand beneath the waistband of the jeans indicates that she was dragged feet first.

As Vickie was dragged up the dirt mound, her limp arms trailed back over her head, and her unsnapped jacket began to slide up her body. Soon her jacket had slipped so far up her body and arms that the inside lining was beneath her head. Thus the large bloodstain found *inside* the jacket. This is why she was found with the jacket off one arm and nearly off the other.

At the same time the jacket was sliding up the girl's body, her cardigan sweater also was sliding up her body so that by the time her body was dragged to the top of the mound, the sweater had worked its way up over her breasts and was bunched under her arms and chin. Also, the back of the sweater, which was in contact with the ground, was higher on the body than the front.

For some reason—perhaps she made a sound, or she began to regain consciousness—the murderer crushed her skull when he got her near the top of the mound. Photographs show her head was several feet below the crest of the mound at the time.

When Vickie's body was found, it was in a semi-kneeling position, the upper torso twisted, the right shoulder beneath. It was the position a person would be in if he lay on the ground on his back, brought his legs straight back over the head to touch the ground behind with the feet, and then relaxed and slumped to one side. What struck me as odd about the position of the body was the fact that the head was farther from the mound than the feet.

Since the girl had been dragged up one side of the mound feet first, her feet would have been farther from the base of the mound than her head if she had been dragged feet first down the other side. There is no doubt, therefore, that she had been pitched down the other side head first. Also, something occurred on top of the mound which resulted in the tearing of her bra. What happened up there?

Try to picture this situation: the body is dragged up the mound until the hips are on the top of the mound. The upper part of the body is lying down the slope. The girl weighed 120 pounds; the side of the mound was quite steep; and the ground consisted of soft, deep sand. It had been difficult for the murderer to drag the body under these conditions, but as he neared the top of the mound, the task became more difficult. The top of the mound was covered with grass and weeds, even more slippery than the loose sand. Then he realized that his task would be easier if he pulled the body into a sitting position, from which a push would send it tumbling down the other side.

The girl's jacket had slid up her arms and under her head, and the arms themselves hung down almost to the base of the mound. He had to grab something with which to pull the body into a sitting position, and the thing that first caught his eye was the bra, its whiteness revealed in the dark. He grabbed it in the most natural place, between the cups, his bloody hand staining the outside, and he pulled. The shoulder straps tore loose, and the bra was pulled down around the waist. Why?

If the body had been lying on a flat surface, such as a floor, the murderer standing over it, he could easily have pulled it into a sitting position; the strain would have been distributed along the wide, heavy backstrap of the bra. The distribution of the strain upon the bra was roughly equivalent to what it would have been if the victim had been standing, and if he had tried to pull her forward, toward him, by the bra. But the position in the sandpit was different.

Vickie's body was lying on the slope of the mound, slanting down and away from her murderer, who was atop the mound. In this position, he was not pulling at a right angle to the longitudinal axis of the body, as he would have if both he and Vickie had been standing. He was, rather, pulling the bra downward toward the girl's feet, putting the strain on the shoulder straps, not the backstrap. As the strain increased, therefore, the thin shoulder straps tore loose at the place where they were stitched to the cups. The sudden tearing caused the murderer to stumble backward, and as he did so, still gripping the bra, he pulled it down around her waist.

After releasing the bra and regaining his balance, he grabbed another handhold—perhaps the sweater bunched up under her chin, managed to get the body in a sitting position atop the mound, and pushed it forward. The body tumbled forward and came to rest in the peculiar position in which it was found the next morning.

I believe that anyone reading the foregoing reconstruction will find it far more logical and impressive than the fantasy concocted by the prosecutor. I could write another book simply to point out the holes in his theory, but I have time and space here to mention only a few others.

There is, for one, the highly unlikely claim that Vickie, her cardigan sweater pushed above her breasts, leaped from my automobile and ran more than the length of a football field without having had the sweater slide back down. This is patently implausible. Incidentally, why would anyone bother to push up a cardigan sweater which could much more easily have been unbuttoned, with or without a girl's cooperation?

There is the claim that I chased Vickie and struck her down *from behind* with a baseball bat. This overlooks the fact that her injury was to the left side of her head, whereas I am right-handed.

There is the claim that from the spot on Fardale Avenue, where Vickie allegedly was struck down, I threw the baseball bat a ground-level distance of about 134 feet, into the wooded area to the south. Has the reader ever seen a major league baseball player swing with all his might at a pitch, miss, lost his grip on the bat, and the bat fly out to the pitcher's mound? The distance from home plate to the pitcher's mound is 60.5

feet. Prosecutor Calissi claims I threw the bat thirteen feet more than *twice* that distance—a point corresponding to a spot six feet behind second base—and that I threw it that far through a thick stand of woods. Perhaps he would have us believe the trees parted like the Red Sea.

There is the claim that I *dragged* her body back to the sandpit, and that I did so without leaving a drop of blood, or even a mark upon the soft, sandy ground, over the entire 350-foot distance. That *is* amazing.

Add to these unsupportable claims the brief period of time I could have been with the girl, the fact that my shoes were practically free of blood, the fact that my clothing above the lower right leg was entirely free of blood, that my gloves and hands—as well as the steering wheel of Gilroy's automobile—were free of blood, that the tire marks on Fardale Avenue and on the dirt road and the footprints on the dirt mound all were unidentified, and that death seems to have occurred long after I had departed the scene, and the prosecutor's theory falls apart at the seams.

What about the time of death? All I can say is that Dr. Gilady's testimony seems to have been misunderstood completely. I shall try to explain.

The doctor performed his autopsy at 1 p.m. He found that the stage of rigor mortis apparent at that time was the stage usually reached after twelve hours, give or take an hour; and he stated that below-normal temperatures *hasten* both the onset and the progress of rigor mortis. It was here that the fundamental misunderstanding occurred.

The temperature the night Vickie was killed had dropped below freezing. Judge O'Dea mistakenly interpreted this to mean that any error in Dr. Gilady's testimony must have been to the long side, that is, increasing the number of hours between death and autopsy. Precisely the opposite is true.

If in normal weather it would have taken twelve hours for the girl's body to have reached the stage of rigor mortis found by Dr. Gilady, and if below normal temperatures *hasten* both the onset and progress of rigor mortis, then it follows that the colder it was the more quickly the twelve-hour stage would have been reached. In below-freezing temperatures, as the doctor pointed out, the twelve-hour-stage condition would have been reached in less than twelve hours. Hence his estimate of "twelve hours, or an hour or two less [less than twelve hours], because of the cold weather." To lengthen the time between death and autopsy, to move the time backward toward 9:30 p.m., the onset and progress of rigor mortis would have had to have been retarded, not hastened, and that would have required *above*-normal temperatures. Thus, the prosecutor's proof of below-freezing temperatures actually increased the probability that Vickie had died later, perhaps as late as 2 or 3 a.m., since the *twelve-hour stage* would have been reached "an hour or two *less*" than twelve hours.

The entire controversy could have been avoided if the prosecutor had demanded a complete autopsy rather than a slapdash job. No laboratory examinations of the girl's blood or vital organs were performed. The police knew exactly what and when she had last eaten, and an analysis of the stomach contents would have revealed the exact time the digestive processes were interrupted. This is the standard and most accurate method of establishing time of death. In this manner, taking standard data, time of death can be established within minutes. How superficial was the autopsy? Would you believe that the police did not even bother to request a blood test to establish the girl's blood type? At my trial, it was assumed that she had type O blood because this was the type on her clothing. Her blood type was never proved as a matter of fact.

Finally, there are the "mystery" photos, a number of photos placed in evidence by the prosecutor for the purpose of clarifying the testimony of his witnesses. I refer to them as "mystery" photos because they 1) dispute the testimony they were intended to clarify, 2) depict things the prosecutor would rather we did not notice, and 3) raise more questions than they answer. The mystery is why the prosecutor had put them in evidence. To illustrate, I have chosen two of the photos for discussion.

The first was placed in evidence to show the jury my pants lying in the wooded area on Oak Street, where they were found by the Ramsey police. The officers who found the pants identified the photo as one of a series taken at 7:45 a.m. by a county police officer summoned for that purpose. The officers also stated that the pants had been found at 6:20 a.m., after daybreak, and that they had been "clearly visible" from the roadway fifty feet away. I do not dispute the claim that these officers found the pants at 6:20 a.m., or that photographs were taken at 7:45 a.m., but I challenge the prosecution's representations that the photo in question is one of the 7:45 photos. My belief is that a mix-up in the prosecutor's office resulted in the wrong photo being brought into court. If I am correct, the photo constitutes falsified evidence. It is especially significant that of all the photos put in evidence by the prosecutor, only these photos were not identified by the photographer who made them; in fact, his name was not mentioned during the trial.

The photo in question shows the pants spread out on the ground, not rolled up or folded, in a sparsely wooded area, the ground covered by a thick carpet of dried leaves. The immediate area, which I estimate at ten feet in diameter, roughly circular, is intensely lit, the trees and leaves appearing a silvery white. Beyond this area, however, the ground and foliage darken progressively, until at a distance not exceeding 20 to 25 feet the background is pitch black, the trees no longer discernible. This is a classic example of flashbulb effect, and one immediately recognizes the photo as having been taken in near total darkness. A second photograph, showing three police officers, one of whom is holding the pants, and identified by two of them as being another of the same 7:45 a.m. series, presents a completely different scene: the entire area is brightly lit. One can see several hundred feet down the road, and the sky proves beyond question that this is a photo taken by daylight. The two photos are literally as different as night and day.

The questions which may be developed from an examination of these photos strike at the very integrity of the case against me. How could the pants have been photographed at night if they were not found until after daybreak? Were they returned to the area some night subsequent to their discovery, and spread out on the ground for photographic purposes? Was the photo taken *before* daybreak, and the pants left lying there for the Ramsey police to discover "officially" after daybreak? The officers did give contradictory testimony, one stating they had been "detailed" to search that specific area for the pants, the other stating that they had found the pants during a "routine patrol." I had not mentioned Oak Street to the police during my all-night interrogation, nor did they mention that street to me; it is clear, therefore, that if the pants were found during the night, the police were led to them by some other person.

The second of the "mystery" photos shows Vickie's body lying at the base of the dirt mound, and the police testimony was that the photo depicted the body "exactly" as found by Mr. Zielinski and Captain Wickham. I did not have the opportunity to examine this photo during my trial—my attorney did not allow me to see any photos during the trial—so it was not until several years later, when enlargements of the photos came into my possession, that I discovered what appears to be a newspaper sticking out from beneath the right side of the body. Clearly it is some printed matter, readily discernible as such, yet during the course of my trial there was a total lack of reference to such material found by the police. The prosecutor's witnesses described in great detail the appearance and location of the body, the clothing, the stones found in the area, the gloves, the kerchief, the tire tracks and footprints, and everything else that might in any way be related to the crime; but concerning the newspaper there was an absolute silence, and I find that inexplicable. A newspaper found beneath a body in a remote sandpit would seem to me, if I were a police officer, eye-catching and deserving of investigation.

Obviously the prosecutor and his witnesses had a specific and compelling reason for ignoring the existence of the newspaper. Some of the witnesses—I shall be charitable and say half of them—could have forgotten to mention it, and some of the others might not have known of it; but to deny that there is a clear pattern of official concealment, as evidenced by the silence of *every* witness, is akin to denying that Monday precedes Tuesday. Less certain is the reason for the official silence. Was it a local newspaper? What was its date? Was it examined for fingerprints, or for other identifying markings? What were the results of the examination, if any? Only the prosecutor can answer these questions, and he is not talking. For Prosecutor Calissi, the newspaper ceased to exist, as the tire tracks on the sandpit road, and the footprints on the dirt mound, have ceased to exist. Truly, the deeper one probes my case, the more he is drawn to the conclusion that the prosecutor ignored more evidence than he presented.

It seems that the more holes appear in the prosecutor's theory, however untenable I may prove his case to be, or how many questions I may raise, the question of who killed Vickie Zielinski may never be answered. As I stated in my prologue: it is perhaps too much to expect that this book can or will prove my innocence. I must be content to leave the reader with an abiding sense of doubt. Of course, I have an opinion, and a strong one at that, as to who killed the girl, and why she was killed, but I do not *know* as a matter of certainty and the libel laws are such that I cannot state my opinions. I know beyond a shadow of a doubt only that Vickie was alive when I left the sandpit. How she was killed is obvious. Why she was killed is something I can only guess at—a guess based upon my knowledge of Vickie, the personalities involved, and the environment within which the crime occurred.

Given thirty days of freedom in 1957, I do not doubt that I could have found the answers to all the questions: When? How? Why? Who? Today, it is probably too late. Most of the principals in the case are scattered. My wife has gone West with my daughter and her new husband. Hommell has returned, circuitously, as the reader soon shall see, to his former home in Florida. Mrs. Zielinski has divorced her husband, charging him with unspeakable conduct,[1] and her family has scattered.

---

[1] Court records reveal that Mrs. Zielinski charged that her husband had, among other things: "degraded and defamed" her in the presence of her children, called her "foul and obscene" names in their presence; "con-

Others have married and moved away. Some are dead. Still others have simply disappeared. Who killed Vickie Zielinski probably will never be known.

I have mentioned in the foregoing paragraph that Hommell has returned to Florida. The trip home, it appears, was not uneventful.

## HOMMELL ARRESTED IN FLORIDA
## STAR WITNESS AT TRIAL OF EDGAR SMITH
## FACING EXTRADITION ON BRUTALITY COUNT
### (Special to the News)

Vero Beach, Fla.—Donald R. Hommell, Jr., allegedly "the last person with whom Victoria Zielinski was seen prior to her murder in a Mahwah, N.J., sandpit on March 4, 1957," has been ordered extradited to Delaware to face charges of brutality at a juvenile home where he served as a guard. . . .

### ARRESTED FRIDAY

Hommell, who has resided in Ramsey, N.J., and here, was arrested Friday night on the brutality charges. . . .

The former Ramsey man made $2,000 bail. . . .

During an extradition hearing in the office of Gov. Ferris Bryant, Hommell said the American Civil Liberties Union took up cases of some 15 teen-aged inmates of Ferris Correctional School who said he beat them. He said the charges were kept alive for political reasons.

### KIDS DROP

The Delaware warrants accused Hommell of 19 counts of assault and assault and battery, listing punching and kicking the teen-agers and forcing them to stand with their arms out-

---

sorted" with other women in the family's presence; refused to become "in any way involved" with their only son; was "continually drunk" at home, attempted to "assault and batter" her in front of the family; was drunk and threatened to beat her after Vickie's funeral; put the family "in fear of our lives"; "committed sodomy with the family dog"; threatened to burn the house down with her in it; accused her of "whoring"; caused her to be "fearful of her life, safety, and health"; and threatened to "finish us all." *Zielinski v. Zielinski,* Amended complaint, Superior Court of New Jersey, Chancery Division, Bergen County, Docket No. M 3587-58R.

stretched until they dropped.

Hommell, who played baseball briefly at Ramsey High School before being dropped from the squad for reasons of discipline, said he worked in the maximum security section and was forced to defend himself from physical attack several times.

During the Smith-Zielinski case, Hommell was a key witness. He denied Smith's charges that he was the last person seen with Miss Zielinski.

The actual time of the murder of the Zielinski girl was never pinpointed.

Dr. Raphael Gilady, a county medical examiner, estimated the girl was dead about 12 hours, "give or take an hour" from the time of the autopsy. . . .

Bergen County Prosecutor Calissi, who lauded Hommell, whom he said he would be "proud to have for a son," said the killing could have been earlier than 11 p.m. but not exactly. . . .

Hommell's alibi for the evening of March 4, 1957, was that he was in Pelzer's Bar, Mahwah.

Years later Herb Pelzer, proprietor of the tavern, claimed Hommell never was in his tavern, but officials discounted the statement.

Hommell was arrested a year ago on a lottery charge. He was released after payment of a $1,000 fine.[2]

[2] *Morning News,* Paterson, N.J., June 6, 1964, pp. 1, 3.

# CHAPTER TWENTY-FOUR

THREE MEN HAVE DIED IN THE ELECTRIC
chair since I have been in the Death House, all three during a
five-month period in 1963. They were:

Ralph Hudson, forty-three years old, white, convicted of
stabbing his estranged wife to death during an argument before
dozens of witnesses in a restaurant where she worked as a waitress. The execution of Hudson, an alcoholic, drunk at the time of
the killing, stands as a clear-cut refutation of the claim that the
death penalty is reserved for the perpetrators of only the most
heinous, premeditated murders. He died February 26, 1963.
If he had had the money to retain a lawyer, or if he had been
intelligent enough to prepare an appeal for himself, there is
no doubt that Hudson would be alive today; and in light of
recent court decisions, he probably would have won a new trial.

Fred Sturdivant, twenty-eight years old, Negro, convicted
of killing his three-year-old stepdaughter during a sexual attack.
He died June 2, 1963, after five years in the Death House. Some
people believe Sturdivant was innocent of the crime. I do not.

Joseph Ernst, twenty-seven years old, convicted of shooting
to death a former girl friend. He was executed June 30, 1963,
after four years in the Death House. A devotee of Adolf Hitler,
Ernst was as mad as a hatter. He believed that reports of the
extermination of Jews were fabrications by Zionists. His final
act in this world was to delay his execution while he finished a
bowl of ice cream.

Executions in the State of New Jersey are carried out on
Tuesday nights at 10 p.m., but the preparations begin several

days before, when notifications, officially known as "invitations," are sent out to witnesses. At the same time, notice is sent to the executioner, who in the language of officialdom is called the "electrician"—a nice, sterile, make-believe title. The condemned man is notified six weeks in advance of the execution date.

By Monday, most of the arrangements have been completed, and the last visit with the family is permitted. The rules are not relaxed, however, and visitation with children, or with brothers and sisters, is denied if they are under sixteen years of age. There is absolutely no legal basis for this denial. The law governing the operation of the Death House states specifically that a condemned man may have visitation with "members of his family," but the prison authorities interpret the law to mean members of his family over sixteen years of age. The inhumanity of denying a man the comfort of seeing his children one last time before he dies makes no impression whatsoever on the prison authorities.

Tuesday is the day of final preparations. The man to be executed is taken out of his cell in the morning and given a shower, after which his head and right leg are shaved by the prison barber, so as to make better contact with the electrodes to be attached to his body. He is also given new clothing: shoes but no socks, undershorts, a gray denim shirt, and khaki trousers, the right leg of which is slit to the knee. He is then returned to his cell and left with his own thoughts until five o'clock. No visits are permitted that last day, another rule dreamed up by the prison authorities.

The last meal is served at 5 p.m., and here a few popular misconceptions must be cleared up. The last meal is not a sumptuous repast limited only by the imagination and tastes of the condemned man. For one thing, the meal is prepared in the prison kitchen by the prison cooks, and the result is that the meal comes out no better and no worse than the usual, everyday prison fare—bland, unseasoned, overcooked. That same meal is served to all the Death House inmates, not only to the condemned man.

If my memory serves me right, all three last meals served since I have been in the Death House consisted of cold, over-cooked, dried-out turkey, canned peas, greasy french fries, coffee, ice cream, and a large cake that on each occasion was thrown uneaten into the garbage. I would prefer to die hungry.

The officers detailed to escort the man to the execution chamber enter the Death House at 9:30 p.m. There are eight of them, mostly veterans of previous executions. Some of the escort officers are volunteers, as are nearly all the officers who crowd the execution chamber to assist the executioner, or simply to gape. One of the prison officers, since retired, used to speak with pride of not having missed a single execution in twenty years. Not content merely to witness the event, he kept a scrapbook of newspaper clippings describing the executions he had at-tended. A gift, no doubt, to be passed on to his grandchildren.

At exactly 10 p.m., the cell door is opened and the man is led to the execution chamber behind the green door. Some men stop at each cell on the way, to shake hands with those they are leaving behind. There is not much you can say to a man who will be dead in three minutes. That is how long it takes. The man walks into the room, sits down, the straps are tightened, and three minutes later the doctor pronounces him dead. No hysterics, no noise, no dimming of lights when the switch is thrown. That dimming-of-lights business is another popu-lar misconception fostered by a long line of Cagney movies. In real life—or is it real death?—the state is much more scientific. The electric chair draws current from a separate, outside power line, specially installed. So insulated is the process that anyone entering the Death House at the moment of an execution would never know it was happening.

But what does it all accomplish? That really is the essen-tial question. There are those who claim that the death penalty is a deterrent. That is a nice theory, and it probably is comfort-ing to those who might otherwise have qualms about their state engaging in the death business—the only way I can describe the custom of hiring one person to kill another. This is what the state does. It calls in this so-called electrician who, incidentally, lives in New York, and the state says to him: "Look, fella, we have a guy a jury says we have to kill, but we don't want any of our officials to get their hands dirty. We'll pay you $150 to come in and do the job for us, and we won't tell anyone who you are." So Mr. Anonymous comes to New Jersey late at night, does the job, grabs his pay, and skulks off back to New York to await the next call. That it is all done under the aegis of the law does not change the fact that one person was paid to kill another.

And what is accomplished? In 1963, after seven execution-less years, there were ten men in the New Jersey Death House. Since the three executions in 1963, the Death House population has grown to twenty-three. Is there a correlation? I have no idea, but it is obvious the executions did not deter the new-comers. One of the present inmates made a survey, asking the same questions of the last twelve men to be sentenced to death.

1. Who were Ralph Hudson, Fred Sturdivant, and Joe Ernst? What did they have in common?

2. When was the last execution in New Jersey?

Of the twelve, none could identify the men named in the first question; and only one of the twelve knew the year in which the last execution had been carried out, but he admitted that he had taken a guess.

I am not prepared to say what this proves, but it is certain that no penalty for crime, however severe, can serve as a deter-rent if the execution of the penalty is unknown to those it is intended to deter. Therein lies the problem: the state claims it kills people, or rather pays to have them killed, to deter others from killing; yet the state also goes to extraordinary lengths to keep its legal killing away from the view of those very persons intended to be deterred.

Examples: It is a crime in New Jersey to publish the date and time a specific execution is to take place. It is illegal to photograph an execution. It is illegal to have more than twelve carefully selected witnesses at an execution. And it is illegal, believe it or not, to have more than six representatives of the press at an execution. One is reminded of the words of Albert

Camus, who wrote: "We must either kill publicly, or admit we do not feel authorized to kill."

My own feelings, based upon eleven years in the Death House, and upon my close association with the thirty-six men who were sentenced to death during those eleven years, is that the so-called deterrent is a farce. It is a subject freely and frequently discussed among condemned men, and never have I heard one of them say he had stopped to think before his crime that he might be executed.

The root premise of the deterrent theory falls apart if you stop to consider a single truism: a person committing murder does not expect to be caught; and the more deliberate, premeditated the murder, the less the expectation of being caught. When that fact is accepted, as it must be, the fallacy becomes clear. No man fears, or is deterred by, a penalty he does not expect to pay.

Some people will argue, I am certain, that the fault in the deterrent theory is the failure to make the death penalty for murder prompt and certain upon conviction. Kill them as soon as they are convicted! That will teach the others a lesson! But again the fallacy arises. An absolute, hundred per cent guarantee that every man convicted of murder will be executed by the most horrible means, burning alive at the stake if you like, will not deter a man who is convinced he will not be caught. The only possible deterrent I can imagine would be certain execution coupled with certain apprehension. Guarantee both and it might make a potential murderer think twice. But it is impossible to guarantee both.

One of those who thinks capital punishment does more than simply kill people is New Jersey's self-proclaimed "liberal" governor, Richard Hughes. Says his excellency: "Show me that capital punishment does not deter potential murderers, and I will be the first to favor abolition." But scrape away the gloss and sanctimonious posturing and one finds that the governor, and those like him, are in fact demanding proof that the state should *not* kill, whereas they ought to be demanding proof that the state *should* kill. It is illogical and immoral; it suggests in no uncertain terms that the state is vested with a sovereign right to kill upon the supposition—proof of the validity of the supposition is neither required nor available—that killing serves a useful purpose, a legitimate end, and that this sovereign right to kill is to be freely exercised unless and until someone comes along to place in the governor's lap absolute proof that the supposition is invalid, and that the intended purpose is not realized. Should it not be just the opposite? Does not the absolute finality of death require that the act of killing be justified, rather than the act of letting live?

There is a curious double standard that comes to light whenever the state calls a public hearing on the question of capital punishment. The scenario never varies. The police are always represented by the head of this or that law-enforcement association, usually the Policemen's Benevolent Association. The testimony of this representative is predictable. Time and time again, as he tells it, the police have arrested men who have said: "I never carry a gun because I'm afraid of killing somebody and getting the chair for it." None of these deterred men are ever produced to confirm the testimony; no names, dates, or places are ever cited. The testimony is nodded over and accepted as if the witness had been citing Scripture.

Following the police representative come the experts: prison wardens who have never met a convicted murderer who had considered in advance the penalty for murder; [1] penologists who declare that capital punishment is a failure; and criminologists, sociologists, and psychologists, each with reams of statistical evidence and documented studies demonstrating the failure of the death penalty as a deterrent. Additional evidence is produced to show that a man with enough money to hire private counsel is rarely sentenced to death (it has happened only three or four times in New Jersey in the past twenty years); that it is rarer still for a man with private counsel to be executed (no one can remember when it last happened in New

---

[1] A few years ago, a newcomer to the Death House, who had moved to New Jersey from Georgia shortly before his arrest, told me: "Man, I didn't even know this . . . state had a death penalty."

Jersey); that few condemned men have had as much as a high-school education; and that Negroes, less than 10 per cent of the population in New Jersey, receive the majority of death sentences. In the past eleven years, the New Jersey Death House has never had a white majority. Currently, 66 per cent of the condemned in this state are Negro.

The testimony of the experts, and their documentation, is invariably dismissed as "interesting but inconclusive," nowhere near as reliable or impressive as the testimony of Police Chief Jones. And when the charade of public hearing has ended is usually when the governor will piously declare: "Show me that capital punishment is not a deterrent . . ." [2]

I do not claim to have the answers to the moral and legal questions inherent in the capital-punishment controversy. What is clear, however, is that unless the legislatures of the capital-punishment states do not soon come to grips with the problem, rather than burying it in semi-secret committees, where individual legislators do not have to stand up before the public and be counted "aye" or "nay," they are going to wake up some fine morning to find that the legislative function has been usurped by the courts. In Florida and California, the recent elections of right-wing governors favoring capital punishment—in Florida, the governor wants executions expedited; in California, the governor watched a baseball game while a young Negro named Aaron Mitchell watched the cyanide pellets drop—have resulted in federal court suits which have stayed all further executions pending the final determination of the issues. These suits, filed jointly by the Legal Defense Fund of the NAACP, and the American Civil Liberties Union, raise the most serious challenge ever to the entire system of jury selection in capital cases. Victory in either suit, objective observers agree, will for all practical purposes abolish capital punishment throughout the United States.

In New Jersey, in a case emanating from Bergen County,

[2] Since this chapter was written, Governor Hughes has warned the New Jersey legislature that he will veto any bill abolishing or limiting capital punishment. *The New York Times*, September 26, 1967, p. 50.

the State Supreme Court is preparing to hear arguments on the question of whether the court has the right to void a jury-imposed death sentence, substituting life imprisonment. This right is presently reserved to the governor through the constitutional provisions for the exercise of executive clemency. The seriousness and far-reaching implications of the court's decision to hear the question is evidenced by Prosecutor Calissi's intention to appear personally to argue for the state, an almost unheard-of event in a criminal appeal. Not once in the entire history of my case has he appeared in person to oppose one of my appeals.

The only real question yet to be answered is when and by whom the death penalty will be abolished, the legislatures or the courts. I do not adhere to the Communist theories of historical inevitabilities, but on the issue of capital punishment I am convinced that abolition is a foregone conclusion; and that those who seek to hold back the tide, to delay that which even they must know is inevitable, will only look that much more foolish for having done so. Their futile struggles of today are analogous to those of the Southern segregationists of a few years ago, and will prove as successful. Today's legal challenges may fail, as others have, but they will be followed by new and stronger challenges; and eventually the states that favor capital punishment will be a relic of the past.

One personal note to close this chapter. I have observed that a few newspapers have suggested that my own execution after so many years under an electric Sword of Damocles, as it were—I shall soon pass the record set by Caryl Chessman—might arouse the public against further legalized killings. I should like to state here and now, in response to the implied suggestions, that I am not a candidate for martyrdom; if nominated I shall not run, and if elected I shall decline to serve.

# CHAPTER TWENTY-FIVE

A NEW DEATH HOUSE WAS OPENED IN DE-
cember 1966. The old building, in which I had spent nine
and a half years under sentence of death, could not be enlarged;
and since all eighteen cells were occupied by the fall of 1966,
with no executions scheduled, new quarters had to be found.
The authorities, always hampered by limited funds, hit upon
the idea of erecting a wall across the interior of one of the
larger wings in the main section of the prison, thereby creating
two small wings. The wing finally selected for alteration had
been used for many years to house the prison's honor inmates.

When we moved to our new quarters on December 28, it
was necessary for us to walk a hundred yards or so across the
prison's inner courtyard. It was a memorable occasion for me:
the first time in nine and a half years that I had not had a roof
over my head and four walls closely surrounding me, and I was
temporarily blinded as I stepped through the door into the
sunlight. It was as if I were emerging from a dungeon, or
Plato's cave. Gradually, however, my eyes became accustomed
to the glare, and as I looked up and saw nothing above me but
the limitless expanse of cloudless winter sky, I was gripped by
a sudden feeling of insecurity, reminiscent of the initial seconds of my first parachute jump. For one fleeting moment I
yearned for the familiar surroundings of my old cell, just as
fourteen years earlier I had wanted to climb back into the
airplane from which I had jumped. Sunlight, sky, snow
remaining from a pre-Christmas storm: these things were completely foreign to me, as if I were seeing them for the first time.

The new Death House is no longer a Death House, or so the official fiction proclaims. Someone, probably a bright young bureaucrat with an Alice in Wonderland complex, came up with the notion that something—the image?—would be improved, and that someone—the inmates? the authorities?—would feel better if the term Death House were discarded and the designation "Three Wing" substituted. But to the inmates, none of whom are in here for stealing hubcaps, this name-changing is just another example of official gobbledygook, part of the state's let's-pretend-we-aren't-killing-people fiction. As Gertrude Stein might have put it: A Death House is a Death House is a Death House.

Our new quarters consist of twenty-seven cells on three tiers. It is a much brighter place, with fluorescent lighting and twenty floor-to-ceiling windows. The outer wall of the prison is only forty feet from the windows, four of which are directly opposite my cell on the second tier, and through them I can see both the sky and the Norway maples lining the street in front of the prison. Even the sun has ceased to be a stranger. The windows face east, so that as the sun rises above the wall each morning, my cell is filled with light. A far cry from the old building.

Between the Death House and the outer wall is a 40-by-200-foot recreation yard, formerly the exclusive playground of the honor inmates. Access to the area is through a door from the Death House. Each day an inmate-gardener from the prison's general population goes into the yard to tend the walks, mow the lawns, and care for the hundreds of flowers he has planted—zinnias, petunias, marigolds, pansies, lilies, snap-dragons, and begonias. At one end of the area is a small handball court, and alongside that is an inmate-constructed miniature golf course. Completing the scene are several concrete benches, and an always crowded birdbath.

The honor inmates are no longer permitted to use their private yard, for fear, one supposes, that they might approach too close to the Death House. Nor is the yard destined to be used by the inmates under death sentence. An effort would be made, we were most solemnly assured shortly after moving, to provide us with daily recreational periods. In this regard, the warden, Howard Yeager, has stated that "there is no reason why the condemned men should not be allowed out of their cells for exercise." [1] But the assurances proved empty.

The excuse for not permitting us to use the yard is that another officer (a guard) would have to be hired to maintain order among the inmates—a sensible precaution—and that the state officials refuse to allocate funds for this purpose. When it is suggested that one of the two officers always on duty in the Death House could handle the job, since there would be nothing for either officer to do inside if all of the inmates were outside, the authorities respond by shrugging their shoulders. This sort of logic tends to befuddle them. Hence, the recreation yard remains unused, and the Death House inmates remain in their cells twenty-four hours a day.

Life in the Death House—an oxymoronic phrase—is not as difficult as the uninitiated might imagine, but certainly, and unnecessarily, far more difficult than it should be, as the unused recreation yard indicates. One would assume, quite naturally, it seems to me, that the prison authorities would prefer to have the inmates keep themselves occupied in some relatively harmless fashion, but that is not the case. Unlike the situation in other parts of the prison, where hobby work of every sort is encouraged. Death House inmates are not permitted to engage in any of a number of harmless pastimes. Not even oil painting, a patently inoffensive method of passing the long hours of confinement, is permitted, though there are some indications that the idiocy of this restriction is becoming apparent to those in authority.

Model building, including the assembly of those premolded plastic models, another excellent time-killer, is strictly prohibited. Card playing is also taboo, and the game of checkers, because of the construction of the cells, is virtually impossible. Chess was popular for a while, each player in turn calling his move to the other, but the shouting back and forth

[1] *Sunday Press,* Asbury Park, N.J., July 16, 1967, p. 30.

soon got on the nerves of the other inmates, and it was discontinued.

A number of the inmates, of whom I am one, have felt the urge to write—as a creative outlet and to raise money to pay legal bills—but typewriters are not permitted in the Death House, though they are in every other part of the prison. The logic behind this restriction is difficult to grasp. We have been told that it is a security matter, that we might do something "inappropriate" with the metal components of the machine; but when it is pointed out that our cells abound in metal— there are enough readily detachable, high-grade spring steel parts in my bedspring to build two typewriters, the authorities mumble excuses about "security" and "policy." Because of the restriction on the use of a typewriter, every word of this book has been written, revised, and edited entirely by hand.

There is an interesting legal implication involved in the denial of the use of a typewriter, aside from all of the other considerations. At one point, while without an attorney, I had three days over a weekend to prepare and mail to the United States Supreme Court a supplemental petition regarding a petition for reconsideration of an appeal then before the Court. In addition to those copies required by the Court, a certified copy had to be served upon the prosecutor. With a typewriter, I could have prepared the petition and all the necessary carbon copies at one time, and all within a few hours. It was impossible to do so by hand, however; as the filing deadline passed, I had, both in effect and in fact, been denied the right of appeal.

Inmate-guard relations, and inmate morale, reached such a low ebb in February 1966 that the inmates went on a hunger strike, a fact not generally known outside the prison—officialdom at every level is loath to admit that things are ever anything but "normal." Tensions had been growing for many months, but the spark igniting the trouble was the decision by one of the guards to attempt to eliminate some of our privileges—and at the same time give himself more time to loaf.

One of the privileges was to have hot coffee available at all times, a not unreasonable compensation for the privileges—motion pictures (the latest), recreation yard, monthly food packages from home—that are accorded all prisoners except those in the Death House.

After several days, when it became apparent that the inmates were serious in their resolve not to eat until the issue was settled, and when news of the affair reached the officials in charge of state institutions, some of the withdrawn privileges were restored. Other compensatory privileges were promised, among them the assurance that we would be permitted to use the recreation yard. That promise, obviously, was a joke. The root causes of the trouble—boredom, restlessness, and deteriorating guard-inmate relationships—were left unsettled.

One of the things most resented by the men under sentence of death has been the recent practice of putting men in "the hole"—a dank, totally dark, indescribably filthy dungeon-like cell in another part of the prison. There, clad only in thin pajamas, the inmate is confined on a bread-and-water diet. There is no water for washing; he is not permitted a toothbrush; and in the wintertime, an open window turns the cell into a frozen-food locker.

During my first nine and a half years in the Death House, no inmate was put in "the hole." Arguments with officers were usually forgotten five minutes after they ended. Since moving to our new quarters, however, an argument with an officer is a sure-fire ticket to five days in "the hole," as a number of men have learned. And as in so many other things, a degree of discrimination against Death House inmates is apparent. Every inmate of this prison, when charged with an offense, has the right to appear before a court composed of three senior officials, who hear his side of the story before punishment can be imposed. Those under sentence of death, however, have no such right. Death House inmates charged with offenses are told simply: "You've got five days in the hole, beginning tomorrow." So arbitrary is the system that one inmate received five days in the hole for calling an officer a liar, while another inmate who attacked and injured an officer went unpunished.[2]

In all fairness, I must state that there are some excellent guards working in the Death House, men with whom the inmates get along well. There is no great secret to their success: when they come to work, they leave their personal problems at home; and if the inmates treat them decently, they do not go out of their way to make confinement more difficult for the inmates. It is a very simple formula. Some of the other guards should try it.

We do have some light moments in this abominable establishment, moments which often have been connected with the rather inept attempts of the prison psychiatrists to interview us. As they appear to most people, I think, psychiatrists appear to me to be but one step, two dried toads, a handful of powdered chicken bones, and sixteen hairs plucked from a bat's belly removed from being witch doctors—and quite ineffectual witch doctors at that.

I recall one occasion when a psychiatrist asked an inmate to draw a picture of a family. He would return to examine the drawing the next day, he said. That night, from a clothing advertisement in a newspaper, the inmate traced what must have been a Madison Avenue adman's dream of the ideal American family—mother, father, little girl, little boy—tall, slender, each exuding a vitamin-enriched health, and all with Pepsodent smiles revealing perfect, pearly white teeth. Only the family puppy was missing. The psychiatrist was beside himself with praise for the inmate's artistic abilities, and after studying the drawing, seemed convinced that he had found an incredibly well-adjusted human being. It was beautiful.

On another occasion, a psychiatrist-psychologist team arrived in the Death House to give an inmate a Rorschach test, the test in which the subject interprets so-called "ink blots." Unknown to these doctors, who had drawn their chairs up to

---

[2] Lest the reader think that I am crying sour grapes, I wish to say that I have never been involved in infractions of rules—a state of affairs subject to change after publication of this book.

the bars of the inmate's cell—they are not allowed to enter the cells—the escort officer standing behind them was signaling the inmate, telling him what to say. As each of the hand-painted, colored ink blots was flashed to the prisoner, he would study it for a moment, then turn his eyes upward and bite his lower lip in an attitude of deep thought, seemingly searching his mind for just the right description of the design on the card. In reality, he was watching for the guard's signal. Alas, to this day, the doctors do not know that they once spent an entire morning administering a Rorschach test to a prison guard. It would be interesting to know how he made out.

The wildest incident of all, however, and one I am always being asked to recount to new inmates, involved me. It began when a psychiatrist, a Ukrainian, who became terribly upset whenever anyone called him a Russian, came into the Death House several years ago and went around asking the inmates what they saw in various pictures he pulled from a paper shopping bag. All went well for him until he came to me.

The picture the doctor pulled from his bag depicted, as I recall it, a log cabin set in a snow-covered forest on the side of a mountain. Above the cabin, against an overcast sky, white smoke rising from the chimney had formed a cloud the shape of a ghost, or at least a child's Halloween version of a bedsheet ghost, complete with eye holes. It was pure fraud.

"Vot is dot?" the headshrinker asked.

"Vot is vot?" I asked, mimicking him.

"Dot," he said, pointing to the ghost figure. "Vot is dot?"

"Oh, *that*. That's a spook."

"Spook? Vot is spook?"

"*That's* a spook. It's a beauty, too."

"You mean is ghost?"

"No. I mean is spook."

"Explain. Vot is spook?"

"Gee, Doc, it's pretty hard to explain. If you were an American you'd know. You see, Doc, there are ghosts and there are spooks. I'm pretty square when it comes to ghosts, but I dig spooks pretty well. Man, I can spot one every time, and that there sure is a spook. Yes, sir, no doubt about it. No ghost could ever go up a chimney like that. Down maybe, but not up."

The poor doctor stared at me for a few seconds, then put his pictures back in his shopping bag and walked away mumbling to himself. I would love to have been in the office when he returned to tell his colleagues that what they had thought for years was a ghost was really a spook.

Incidentally, or perhaps not so incidentally, my Ukrainian friend was the last psychiatrist to interview me. Since that time, they have been avoiding me. I wonder why.

Given the restrictive policies cited in this chapter, the question arises: How *does* one pass the time in the Death House? For most inmates, the answer is reading and television, the latter having come to the Death House three years ago. I am not, myself, too much of a television fan, though I do make it a point to watch all three of the network news programs each night, and most of the news specials. Also, like other inmates, I regularly watch the talk shows: Johnny Carson, Joey Bishop, David Susskind, Merv Griffin, Alan Burke, and Joe Pyne—and, lately, William F. Buckley, Jr., on *Firing Line*. But the entertainment programs, generally, have an inane sameness that repels me.

Reading takes up most of my time. Having found myself unable to continue my formal education after exhausting my savings, I turned to reading as the next best form of self-education. I have developed a particular interest in politics and world affairs, and keeping abreast of them requires an enormous amount of reading. Fortunately, with twenty-three men in the Death House, many of whom subscribe to one or more newspapers and magazines, a great variety of these are available to me. My day begins with *The New York Times*, which I read from first page to last, including the financial section. In December 1966, just before our move to new quarters, I had the privilege of meeting Mr. Edwin Roth, the distinguished British newspaper columnist, who was being given a tour of the prison. He was in this country to attend the United Nations session called to deal with the Rhodesian problem, and our conversation naturally gravitated to that subject. Mr. Roth left the Death House slightly shaken by having met a man under death sentence who 1) understood the issues involved in the Rhodesian matter; 2) could quote the previous day's closing price of the pound sterling; and 3) could relate the latter to the former. He also left convinced, I think, that because I was sympathetic to the Rhodesian position, I must therefore be a confirmed racist, colonialist, fascist—or all three.

The *Times* is usually followed by the New York *Daily News,* the Philadelphia *Inquirer,* the *Bergen County Record;* and two Newark, New Jersey, newspapers—the *Evening News* and the *Star-Ledger.* In addition, I am a member of the Reader's World Press Club, which every second week supplies me with an English-language newspaper published in a foreign country. Through this service I receive such disparate publications as the London *Times,* the Manchester *Guardian,* the Jerusalem *Post,* the Baghdad *News,* the Beirut *Journal,* the Malay *Echo,* the Borneo *Bulletin,* the Saigon *Daily News,* the Calcutta *Statesman,* and the South China *Morning Mail.*

Then there are the magazines: *Time, Newsweek, National Review, New Republic, Atlantic Monthly, Commentary, Life, Look, Esquire, National Geographic* (I am a society member), and *Ebony.* I also read three Communist publications: the Russian *Moscow News* and *New Times;* and the Chinese *Peking Review.*

Finally, there are books. A sample of my reading over the past several months includes: Santo Mazzarino's *The End of the Ancient World;* Ortega y Gasset's *The Revolt of the Masses;* John King Fairbank's *The United States and China;* David Caute's *The Decline of the West;* Edgar Snow's *The Battle for Asia;* Senator Fulbright's *The Arrogance of Power;* Anthony Eden's *Foreign Affairs;* Karl Mannheim's *Ideology and Utopia;* and Herman Kahn's *On Thermonuclear War.*

I realize that the above may appear at first glance to be a tremendous amount of reading, but I do have twenty-four hours a day, seven days a week, week after week, month after month, with little else to do. Then, too, reading serves three distinct purposes: 1) It keeps me informed of, and in contact with, the world from which I have been banished—temporarily, I hope. 2) It helps me to pass the time, so that the long hours of confinement are more bearable. 3) The need to maintain a regular reading schedule, even while writing this book—if I fell behind I would never catch up—instills in me a discipline I have lacked in the past.

Still, I am often asked: Why bother reading all of that heavy stuff, rather than some pleasant light fiction, or just watch television? Why knock myself out when the odds against me are so formidable? My reply could be that I have found there is personal satisfaction to be gained in learning for the sake of learning, and that would be true. Or I could reply that the acquisition of knowledge, however esoteric, is never a waste of time, and that also would be true. But perhaps most compelling is the simple fact is that I read and study because I have wearied of being a half-educated lout in a world in which education is a parochial necessity. There is perhaps nothing more frightening to me than the prospect of finding myself stuck for the rest of my life in some dreary small town, working in some gas station or hardware store for sixty dollars a week. That would be going from one prison to another, from a cell to a cage, and I have had enough of prisons and cages.

**SO WE COME AT LAST TO THE END OF MY**
book, but by no means the end of my story. That goes on.
Today, more than eleven years after becoming a Death House
resident, I am doing precisely what I began doing the very
first day: waiting for a remote, faceless group of judges to
decide what may be my final appeal. And though I wait in a
larger, brighter Death House, now equipped with round-the-
clock television, time drags by as slowly as ever. As I write
these words, only one other man in the world, Sadamichi
Hirasawa, a seventy-five-year old Japanese, has been confined
under sentence of death longer than I. Hirasawa, who has been
facing the hangman's rope for twenty years, and I should be
delighted to surrender our records to the first volunteer.

There is little more I can say. I have told my story as best
I know how, leaving it to the reader to sift the facts, weigh
the claims and counterclaims, and ultimately to answer for
himself the questions posed at the beginning of this book: Did
justice triumph? Is Edgar Smith guilty? If at this point the
reader cannot respond with an emphatic "yes," then I shall
consider this book a success.

As for myself, I have paid a terrible price for my refusal
to give in to the system, for refusing to accept the neat, clean
compromise of pleading guilty to a lesser degree of murder.
I have lost my home, my wife and child, and more than eleven
years from the prime of my life, and I would be less than
candid if I did not admit that there have been moments when
I have wondered whether the enormity of the price has been
worth it. More than one night in recent years I have lain awake

in my solitary cell until daylight, filling my ashtray with countless half-smoked cigarettes, and asking myself questions which seem at this time to be unanswerable: What good has been accomplished by all this? Wouldn't it have been easier and better to have accepted the prosecutor's deal, serve seven or eight years, and be a free man today? Would anyone really care, or remember? Who, outside of family and friends, really gives a damn whether Edgar Smith is guilty or innocent? What is the limit a man can be made to pay for justice?

These questions, which creep into the mind and soul in the solitude of the night, could prove fatal if allowed to take root. When one is fighting for one's life, self-doubt can be as deadly as the electric chair. My defense against these doubts is my abiding confidence in the integrity of the judicial processes, and my resolution to go on fighting to achieve vindication for as long as it is legally and financially possible. It is anomalous, I know, that one who has received such cavalier treatment from the courts should hold the belief that his best hope for ultimate vindication lies with the courts, but so it must be.

Eleven years ago, when the bitter taste of my treatment at the hands of the police and prosecutor's detectives was fresh in my mouth, and when the words of Judge O'Dea's jury instructions still rang in my ears, the law, and the society represented by the law, were anathema to me. But the Edgar Smith of today is no longer the restless, immature boy of 1957. Infinitely more patient and tolerant of others, better educated, and with a greater insight into my own abilities and limitations, I have learned to face life as it is by learning first to face myself as I am.

I should like to believe that William F. Buckley was not being too extravagantly charitable when he wrote in his nationally syndicated column that "Edgar Smith went to the Death House not far removed from the wasteful class of humanity. . . . He emerges as . . . a most extraordinary man who may not succeed in triumphing over the chair, but has clearly triumphed over himself." [1]

[1] William F. Buckley, Jr.: *On the Right,* The Washington Star Syndicate, Inc., November 9, 1965 (release date).

Readers who may wish to correspond with the author are advised that prison regulations do not permit him to receive correspondence of any nature from unauthorized persons. Comments or inquiries may be addressed to the publisher.

EDGAR SMITH *was born on February 8, 1934, in Hasbrouck Heights, an upper-middle-class community in New Jersey about ten miles west of New York City. He was five when his parents separated, and he and his older brother were raised by their mother after the divorce in 1941. He had not quite completed his high-school education when he joined the United States Marine Corps in 1952, volunteering for parachute training. Most of his time in service for the next two and a half years was spent on regular flights throughout the Far East, carrying military and medical supplies, replacement troops, and wounded to and from places such as Honolulu, Itami in Japan, Johnston Island, Kwajalein, Guam, Okinawa, Formosa, Hong Kong, Midway, Manila, Korea, and what is now Vietnam. Discharged in November 1954 for a service-connected hearing loss, now permanent, in his left ear, Smith returned to his family home in Ramsey and tried his hand at various jobs. He was twenty-three years old, had a well-paying job as a machinist, and was living with his wife and infant daughter in a house trailer when he was arrested on suspicion of murder, tried, and convicted on circumstantial evidence. Since June 6, 1957, he has been kept in a solitary-confinement cell in the Death House of the New Jersey State Prison at Trenton.*

THE TEXT *of this book has been set in a type face named Bulmer. This distinguished letter is a replica of a type, long famous in the history of English printing, that was designed and cut by William Martin about 1790 for William Bulmer of the Shakespeare Press. In design, it is all but a modern face, with vertical stress, sharp differentiation between the thick and thin strokes, and nearly flat serifs. The decorative italic shows the influence of Baskerville, whose pupil Martin was.*

*Composed by Brown Bros., New York. Printed and bound by American Book-Stratford Press, New York. Typography and binding design by Golda Fishbein.*

hand-painted, multi-colored "ink blots" was flashed to the prisoner, he would study it for a moment, then turn his eyes upward and bite his lower lip in an attitude of deep thought, seemingly searching his mind for just the right description of the design on the card. In reality, he was watching for the guard's signal. Alas, to this day, the doctors do not know that they once ~~spent~~ had spent an entire morning ~~giving~~ (administering) a Rorschach test to a prison guard. One hopes he passed.

The wildest incident of all, however, and one I am always being exhorted to recount to new inmates, involved me. ~~It's~~ It began when a psychiatrist, a Ukranian, who became terribly upset whenever anyone called him a Russian, came into the Death House several years ago and went around asking the inmates what they saw in various pictures he ~~drew~~ pulled from a paper shopping bag. All went well for him until he came to me.

The picture the doctor pulled from his bag to show ~~the~~ me depicted a log cabin set in a snow-covered forest on the side of a mountain, as I recall. Above the cabin, against an overcast sky, white smoke rising from the chimney had formed a cloud in the shape of a ghost, or at least a child's Halloween version of a bedsheet ghost, complete with eyeholes. It was pure Freud.